MEDIA IN THE DIGITAL AGE

Media in the Digital Age

JOHN V. PAVLIK

 Columbia University Press   *New York*

Columbia University Press
Publishers Since 1893
New York   Chichester, West Sussex
Copyright © 2008 Columbia University Press
All rights reserved

Library of Congress Cataloging-in-Publication Data
Pavlik, John V. (John Vernon)
Media in the digital age / John V. Pavlik.
p. cm.
Includes bibliographical references and index.
ISBN 978-0-231-14208-3 (alk. paper) —
ISBN 978-0-231-14209-0 (pbk. : alk. paper) —
ISBN 978-0-231-51213-8 (electronic)
1. Digital media—Social aspects. 2. Mass media—Technological innovations.
3. Information society. 4. Information technology. I. Title.
HM851.P38 2008
302.23'1—dc22
2007041386
∞

Columbia University Press books are printed on permanent and durable
acid-free paper.
Printed in the United States of America
c 10 9 8 7 6 5 4
p 10 9 8 7 6 5 4 3 2

CONTENTS

LIST OF TABLES AND FIGURES

ACKNOWLEDGMENTS

I am grateful to all the people I interviewed for this book and the scholars and journalists whose work I have cited. Their comments, reporting, and observations were highly instructive and valuable to my analysis of digital media. I also owe special thanks to Everette E. Dennis, my longtime mentor, colleague, and friend, whose understanding of media and the technologies that influence them has proven invaluable to me in writing this book and in my overall study of the media. Most important, my sincerest thanks and love go to my family for their support and insights about media in the digital age. I dedicate this book to my daughters, Orianna and Tristan, and to my wife, Jackie.

FOREWORD
Everette E. Dennis

In the midst of the digitization of almost everything comes John V. Pavlik's welcome and truly comprehensive *Media in the Digital Age,* which has the virtues of exploratory enthusiasm blended with the insightfulness of sober analysis. Among the great hazards of writing about new media technologies and their impact is the likelihood that the work will be outdated well before it is published, but this book heads off that possibility by using contemporary and historical examples only as fixed moments in time, not necessarily as predictive statements about what will or might be. John Pavlik has been among our most ardent, reliable, and thoughtful navigators in explorations of the digital media world, from both a journalistic and a media industries perspective. Neither taken with exaggerated claims nor blind to the amazing possibilities of these new media, he has charted a course that maps the territory and then drills down in specific areas where deeper knowledge is needed.

Media in the Digital Age embraces and explains both hardware and software and their interrelated journey. Thus, it takes in digital delivery methods and the devices that offer access, but also considers audiences and their needs, digital producers, content providers, distribution, financing, the legal environment, as well as inventors and innovation. No book of which I am aware has such a scope, covering virtually all of the major topics necessary to get a handle on the digital age.

Pavlik comes to this task after nearly two decades of watching, working with, and navigating the digital world. He has led new media labs and ventures, headed two journalism programs, and fashioned innovative projects in a think tank. Along the way, he has written several books that have unraveled the complexity and confusion of digital media, while looking at its important applications and uses. He is always open-minded but at the same time critical.

This book is especially timely, coming as it does several years after the boom and bust of the first Internet revolution, sometimes called Web 1.0, and well into a phase that benefits from even more advanced technologies and human applications, which its promoters have dubbed Web 2.0. This is a time when the linear dimensions of early digital media have been surpassed by those who not only invite and demand user interface and interactivity, but also call upon all of us to be more improvisational in the process. The dreams and possibilities of the first Internet age have matured, and they benefit now from innovative handheld devices, creative content, and the whole shift in outcomes brought about by these so-called mash-ups. In a world where there is time shifting, shape shifting, power shifting, and other transformative experiences, knowing and understanding the digital landscape are essential.

This understanding is essential to users and producers (though who can tell the difference these days?), and it ought to deflect the exuberant and sometimes mindless enthusiasm of early dot-com entrepreneurs who were blissfully ignorant to both the business hazards and the benefits inherent in the new media world. This book, properly consulted, can head off ventures that look and sound like 1998 all over again. In other words, there is something to be learned from the first decade of the digital age, and this book sets a course to do just that.

In documenting the several sectors and frames that determine the shape of the digital age itself-although the long-term outcomes are still in play-John Pavlik not only answers questions of importance that help the reader-user go to the next level of understanding, but also poses questions that will elucidate a course to the future.

Although no one truly knows what the long-term effects of the digital age will be, whether it is the greatest thing since Guttenberg or simply an incremental step toward an even more revolutionary and transformative environment, those of us living in this brave new world need better means of understanding and coping with it. That's what this book offers with gusto, grace, and good judgment.

Having known John Pavlik since sometime in the previous century, I have marveled at his comfort level with digital innovation and change and with his ability to chart its course, understand its delay vectors, fathom its complexity, and explain all these things in lucid prose replete with human examples. His discussions and explanations are made with remarkable generosity toward others who have contributed and are contributing to the field, while establishing connections among them that enrich and illuminate our knowledge. Some commentators and scholars make this journey to understand the digital world in small segments, assuming that others will join that work with contiguous material and relationships, but John Pavlik makes no such assumption, realizing that a comprehensive treatment is vital to true understanding. That's what makes this book special: it is an outgrowth of his previous work, but it also harmonizes with other contributions to the field while breaking new ground at the same time. It has the benefit of context and clarity, and its readers are poised for a remarkable journey that will open channels of knowledge, provide background for them, and raise questions about what's next.

INTRODUCTION
New Technology and the Media: An Uneasy Alliance

Throughout history, technology and the media of public communication have traveled paths often intertwined. New technologies have often burst upon society, and media leaders have sometimes embraced them and sometimes kept them at arm's length, even when those technologies have presented clear opportunities to extend the reach, impact, and quality of the media. New technology has at times challenged media in subtle or explicit ways to change age-old practices and at other times presented threats to the viability of traditional media or media practices. On some occasions, technologies have raised serious ethical concerns. Media leaders have most often approached technological change cautiously, evaluating its costs and benefits. Yet, in some cases, visionary media leaders have adopted technology early on to dramatic and great advantage.

The advent of photography in the early nineteenth century was quickly seen as significant by Samuel F. B. Morse, most well known for his role in the invention of the electromagnetic telegraph.[1] Morse introduced American newspapers to the budding technology of photography after a visit to France in 1839, where he had seen the daguerreotype (an early form of photography invented by French artist and chemist Louis J. M. Daguerre and his collaborator Joseph Nicephore Niepce).[2] Upon his return to New York, he wrote this description of the daguerreotype: it is "one of the most beautiful discoveries of the age." His description was published in the *New York Observer* on April 20, 1839. Similarly, Walt Whitman, celebrated American poet and editor of the *Brooklyn Daily Eagle,* published in his newspaper on July 2, 1846, these poetic words of praise for the daguerreotype: "In whatever direction you turn your peering gaze, you see naught but human faces! There they stretch, from floor to ceiling-hundreds of them. Ah! what tales might those pictures tell if their mute lips had the power of speech! How romance then, would be infinitely outdone by fact."[3] Whitman's words seem to foreshadow the twentieth-century inventions of cinema with sound and television.

Newspapers across the country soon began publishing daguerreotype images, enriching the storytelling abilities of the newspaper medium. An early news photograph taken in 1853 using daguerreotype technology is available online at the U.S. Library of Congress Web site.[4] It depicts a boating tragedy on the Niagara River in New York (leading to the great falls on the U.S.-Canadian border) in which three men in a boat were overwhelmed by the river's strong current and crashed into a rock. As the Library of Congress notes, "The current carried two men immediately over the Falls to their deaths. The daguerreotype shows the third man, stranded on a log which had jammed between two rocks. He weathered the current for eighteen hours before succumbing to the river."

Newspapers later embraced the telegraph as well, despite its prohibitive cost. In fact, a group of New York newspaper publishers formed the Associated Press (AP) largely in order to make use of the expensive technology more economical.[5] A new form of newswriting emerged as well, now familiar to all in journalism as the inverted pyramid.[6] Due at least in part to the telegraph's cost and unreliability, the inverted pyramid encouraged reporters to put the most important facts first in case the telegraph failed during transmission.[7]

Guglielmo Marconi's invention of the wireless subsequently led to the advent of radio and thereby radio news reporting, which eventually laid the foundation for the most widely seen news medium in history, television.

Yet along the way media organizations have often not made the development of new technologies a central part of their business strategy, as noted by media management authority Robert Picard.[8] In fact, media organizations, in particular news organizations, have typically had very small budgets for research and development, often less than one percent of their overall operating budget. Many industries devote a considerably higher percentage of their operating budget to research.[9]

On a few notable occasions, U.S. media organizations have invested substantially in the development of new media technologies. Some media leaders invested significantly in the development of new forms of radio and television in the early days, and some have more recently invested significant amounts in the development of cable, high-definition, and digital television. In the mid-1990s, Time Warner invested millions of dollars in the ill-fated full-service network in Orlando, Florida, in an attempt to bring video on demand into the home. In Brazil, media giant O Globo annually funded the Center for New Media at Columbia University in the mid- to late 1990s in an attempt to harness new media applications in journalism. For several years in the 1990s, the Knight-Ridder newspaper company sponsored the Information Design Lab in Boulder, Colorado, supporting the innovative work of newspaper design expert Roger Fidler to develop the flat-panel newspaper. But media have more often than not shied away from investing significantly in new technologies and their development. Professor Picard notes that in 2006 not a single major U.S. media organization was a sponsor of the pioneering MIT Media Lab; it has taken Google, the Internet giant, and Bertelsmann AG, the German media giant, to lead the way (see the Media Lab sponsor list online).[10] Like cautious penguins, media executives most commonly prefer to let others test the waters first rather than risk diving in and becoming a quick meal for a killer whale.[11]

The rise of the Internet and World Wide Web is a case in point. These technologies have grown dramatically during the past decade or so. Citizens around the world have availed themselves of these technologies, thoroughly immersing themselves in everything from Web surfing to blogging to e-mail and instant messaging (IM). Yet, as noted in the 2006 edition of the Project for Excellence in Journalism's annual report tracking and analyzing the state of the American news media, U.S. newspapers and television network news divisions have only recently begun to make serious investments online to capture new readers and keep existing ones.[12] In its 2005 "state of the news media" report, the project noted that "creativity in new technology appeared to be coming mostly from non-news organizations like Google." Online revenues for news media are growing more rapidly than are print revenues (about 33 percent a year growth for online advertising revenues, versus 3 percent a year growth for print advertising revenues), but the former are still just a fraction of total advertising revenues for newspapers. One estimate suggests that online advertising revenues for news media will not overtake those of print until 2017.[13]

TECHNOLOGICAL OPPORTUNITIES

News media seeking an advantage in a shifting and sometimes shrinking news marketplace should look more closely at emerging new technologies as an opportunity to experiment and to build and keep new audiences. If they do not, other innovators will get there first, and the world of journalism and its role in society will continue to shrink.

Innovative news media can look to new technologies for potentially fruitful opportunities in four areas.

First, new technologies often present new and more efficient ways for journalists and other media professionals to do their work. Mobile and handheld technologies, for instance, are among the most significant technologies for journalists. Utilizing such technologies more widely in journalism would give newspapers the opportunity to keep reporters in the field gathering more news for longer periods. Newspapers should seriously consider providing such technologies to their reporters the same way that they now provide desktop computers and high-speed Internet access for communication and online research. Current handheld devices permit not just communication from the field, but also low-cost digital photography. Moreover, they can provide efficient access to navigational services such as Mapquest, permitting reporters to get helpful directions while in the field. Easy access to the global positioning system (GPS) can enable advances in reporting quality and precision and even help reporters to find their way to an unfamiliar location easily and quickly.

Second, new technologies can transform the nature of storytelling and media content in general in potentially positive and engaging ways, especially with younger audiences. For example, equipping reporters with mobile communications and news-gathering technologies can facilitate mobile blogging. Audiences around the world have already demonstrated their appetite for Weblogs (blogs)-online diary, text, and multimedia-and mobile blogging is among the next trends in Weblogs.

Similarly, newspapers and other news media can more easily produce news podcasts-audio or video programs distributed online-by equipping reporters with low-cost, handheld, digital audio-recording technology.

On a more advanced level, news media can look to experimental news storytelling forms such as the Situated Documentary that I and my colleague Steve Feiner, computer science professor at Columbia University, developed.[14] Utilizing wearable technologies, the Situated Documentary permits news consumers to visit sites of past news events (recent or distant past) and to relive those news events via immersive multimedia presentations embedded into the real world. My students have produced a series of situated documentaries about events that occurred on the Columbia University Morningside Heights campus.[15] The user can experience any of these past events told journalistically by walking the campus while wearing a computer with see-through head-worn display, high-speed wireless Internet access, GPS satellite navigation, and a head tracker to permit hands-free interactivity via gaze approximation-the wearer simply looks at an object for about a half-second to select it rather than pointing and clicking using a handheld mouse). The device is a rough approximation of a virtual time machine. With next-generation three-dimensional or stereoscopic videography now being tested in digital video laboratories, the possibilities will be taken to an entirely new level of realism. Creating content for presentation on this device is relatively simple. Content creators can design and edit multimedia content for mobile device display using location-aware features without relying on programmer assistance.[16] Similar systems are being tested in real-world museum applications, including at cultural and historical sites such as Pompeii, Italy.[17]

Third, new technologies have enormous implications for the management, structure, and culture of media organizations. For instance, by utilizing the technologies described earlier, a news organization can explore the possibilities of what I call the *virtual newsroom*. It is a newsroom without walls. It can be established in nearly any community using high-speed wireless Internet access and mobile media. Editors and reporters need not meet daily in a physical setting. Instead, reporters can stay where they should: in the field, gathering news, observing news events, interviewing sources, and otherwise keeping their finger on the pulse of the community or beat to which they are assigned. The virtual newsroom represents a potentially significant cost-saving improvement in news coverage.

Fourth, perhaps the most important opportunity presented by new technologies is the transformation of the relationships between news organizations and their many publics, in particular their audiences, sources, funders, regulators, and competitors. In many cases, these relationships are already being deeply transformed. The change is raising the question, "Who is a journalist?" With citizens blogging, podcasting, and otherwise publishing their own content, media of all types are seeing their marketplace fragment even further.

DIGITAL DILEMMAS

With these points, I do not mean to imply that new technology presents only positive possibilities for journalism, media, and society. In fact, many of the most significant effects of technology have been damaging or potentially so to journalism and media. Digital photography has led not just to the taking of less expensive news photos closer to deadline, but to the easier creation of doctored photos and manipulated news video that is visually authentic to even the most experienced eye. Online news has created an environment in which speed and currency often take precedence over accuracy, fact checking, and multiple sourcing. Media are increasingly struggling to maintain readers and viewers in an age of increasing audience fragmentation and channel proliferation driven by technological advance. Ethical concerns must be paramount in an age of lightning quick and powerful technological convergence. Otherwise, public trust in the news media will erode and whither. Without credibility, the news has little or no value, in either a democratic or a commercial sense. A remarkable case emerged in the fall of 2006 when the Fox network was planning to broadcast an interview with O. J. Simpson based on a new book he had written, *If I Did It*, in which he was to explain how he would have murdered his former wife had he murdered her. Simpson, a former professional football player turned movie star who in 1995 was acquitted of murdering his wife, Nicole Brown Simpson, was nevertheless convicted by many in the court of public opinion and in 1997 was found liable in a civil case. Fox and its parent company News

Corporation, headed by Rupert Murdoch, were accused of running the interview and sponsoring the publication of the book as pure exploitation of a sensational murder case and pursuing profit over ethics. Within a few days of the announcement of the interview, an ensuing firestorm of online and offline criticism forced Murdoch to pull the plug and cancel both the interview and the publication of the book, calling it an ill-conceived project.[18]

It is unclear whether the digital age will see more or fewer cases like the *If I Did It* situation coming to fruition or failure. Yet it is clear that the twenty-first century will witness a continuing and fundamental transformation of journalism and media in the digital age. This future promises to bring a highly fragmented and active media audience, intense media competition, and scarce advertising dollars. Through innovation, professional journalism and media can reassert their role as the information lifeline of democracy. The question is whether they and their leaders will embrace emerging technologies to help them do so. Or will decision makers simply follow others' lead, letting professional journalism and media fade into a limited and secondary role in a transnational and networked global society?

This book explores the many functions of journalism and the media in the digital age. As a central thesis, it posits that digital and networking technologies make possible better engagement of the public in a conversation about matters of public importance both at home and abroad. Whether the twenty-first century will see the fulfillment of this opportunity remains to be seen. Tensions exist on both sides of the media fence, potentially pulling media down the slippery slope of profit over principle. Nevertheless, citizens of all ages and status are in a unique position to shape, innovate, and enjoy media in the digital age.

1 / DIGITAL DELIVERY MEDIA

New media and digital convergence may often seem synonymous with the Internet and World Wide Web. Online newspapers, downloadable music and video, bloggers, and podcasts are among the most familiar examples of new, or digital, media. But in truth a wide host of technologies compose the full spectrum of media in the digital age. Among them are not only the Internet and the Web, but wireless and mobile media, digital television and satellite radio, digital cameras, digital music players, and other new or emerging technologies for mediated public communication. For the purposes of this book, I define *digital media* as the systems of public communication, the systems of content production and distribution, and the computer and networked-based technologies that support and shape them. The use of the term *public* is not meant to imply only the domain of public, or not-for-profit, media such as public television or the Corporation for Public Broadcasting, although they are within the purview of this book. Rather, the term includes all media that produce, deliver, and package content and communications for public rather than private discourse or consumption. As such, it includes all the traditional media of mass communication, including newspapers, magazines, books, radio, television, and the cinema, which are today undergoing a digital sea change. It also includes emerging new media accessed online and through other digital delivery media, many of which serve specialized audiences or communities and not a mass audience in the traditional sense.

Some interactive media lie in something of a gray area, such as IM, personal Web pages, and text messaging. These media are often meant as communications between or among individuals, yet they sometimes extend well beyond the interpersonal into the public arena and as such become part of mediated public communication, particularly when they convey content of a potentially much wider interest. Such was the case, for example, in 2006, when social-networking Web site YouTube featured video that sometimes quickly became part of a much bigger, public news story (e.g., cell phone video of University of California at Los Angeles campus police using a TASER to subdue a student for refusing to show his identification in a library November 14, 2006, was viewed on YouTube more than 100,000 times as of January 23, 2007, and has been incorporated into both local and national television newscasts).[1] These largely interpersonal digital media are also considered in this book, although only in the context in which they are relevant to mediated public communication.

The transformation of media in the digital age involves at least twelve dimensions, which I discuss in sequence in this book:

1. The medium of digital delivery;
2. The devices for accessing, displaying, watching, and listening to digital media;
3. The audience or users of digital media;
4. The producers of digital media;
5. Digital media content itself;
6. The distributors of media;
7. The financers, owners, and business of media;
8. The regulators and law of media;
9. The digital technologies of production (and encryption) that in many ways are fueling the explosive growth in media production and protection;
10. The inventors and innovators of the next generation of media;
11. The ethical framework surrounding or providing context for media; and
12. The next generation of media consumers, users, and creators—children.

I begin the examination of this transformation with a discussion of the medium of digital delivery for at least three reasons. First, the medium of delivery is a foundation for all other aspects of the media and their digital transformation. The qualities of the delivery medium influence what is possible in terms of how the audience interacts with the medium, the nature of emerging business models, and the regulatory frameworks that govern the media.

Second, the digitization of delivery media represents a fundamental shift from the analog system in which different media were delivered via different technologies, some having very little to do with the content or nature of the medium. For example, print media have been delivered in a variety of ways, including on the backs of trucks, in the shoulder bags of delivery boys and girls, and via the U.S. Postal Service. Television and radio have been delivered over the airways and via cable. In a digital environment, the content of all media types exists as a binary digit (bit) stream of ones and zeros. All media can be and are delivered through convergent digital delivery systems. Yet there are different digital delivery systems, some based on fiber optics, others by coaxial cable, and some by the airwaves, both terrestrial and extraterrestrial (i.e., satellite). Despite their common digital platform, these alternative systems have significant variations that influence and shape their capabilities and how they are managed.

Third, and perhaps most important, almost all aspects of media transformation in the digital age are dependent in large part on the delivery media. Ownership is often organized by delivery system. Access devices are designed at least in part for how they connect to different delivery media. Audiences and media users are organized and defined often in terms of the medium of delivery. Media regulation is typically defined by the delivery environment; even the Telecommunications Act of 1996, the most recent comprehensive federal legislation regarding the U.S. media system, is organized largely by delivery environment (e.g., different rules apply to different delivery media). Only production technologies are largely independent of the delivery system, although in many cases they are still somewhat influenced by it, at least in the short term (e.g., convergent newsrooms are increasingly emerging in the media system, yet the majority of media production is still organized and managed according to the delivery platform).

Nevertheless, it is important to note that technology does not determine the nature and future of media. People, policies, and politics are often of much greater influence in shaping media, whether digital or analog. Economics similarly has a profound impact on the nature of media. Technology makes possible many different media qualities and futures. This book is based on the notion that digital and networking technologies are enabling a transformation of media, one that is potentially but not necessarily a better system of public communication.

THE MEDIUM OF ONLINE DELIVERY

The digital transformation of the media parallels in many ways the ubiquitous deployment of broadband Internet access. Although most homes had dial-up access to the Internet in the 1990s, this slow-speed delivery meant that a very limited form of Internet access was possible. The first decade of the twenty-first century has seen widespread delivery of high-speed, or broadband, Internet access. The Federal Communications Commission (FCC) "generally defines broadband service as data transmission speeds exceeding 200 kilobits per second (Kbps), or 200,000 bits per second, in at least one direction: downstream (from the Internet to your computer) or upstream (from your computer to the Internet)."[2] Data transmission at this speed can deliver standard analog-quality (National Television System Committee [NTSC], the analog television standard in the United States) video on demand, although the network is subject to congestion and can affect the viewer's experience. Higher-speed services, such as 1.5 megabits per second (Mbps) can deliver digital-quality (Motion Picture Experts Group-2 [MPEG-2]) video on demand. Internet 2, the next generation of the Internet, promises even greater bandwidth availabilities. Higher-speed Internet service also means much faster connections to Web pages of all types, more rapid downloading of all file types, whether video or audio, music or digital books, software or other formats. Broadband access also means having an Internet connection that is always or almost always on and ready for use. Unlike a dial-up connection where nonuse usually results in a disconnection after a few minutes, a broadband connection normally stays on twenty-four hours a day, which means the user can go online and access a Web site or download content such as a photo or video at any time and without delay.

Always-on connections may be as significant a shift in Internet use as the higher speed has been. Research shows that with an always-on Internet connection, people go online frequently, but not always for long periods. They quickly check for an important e-mail. They use IM. They check the news headlines. They watch a music video. They download a favorite song. They may then move on to another task, and another household member may go online.

There are at least five different means of broadband delivery: (1) digital subscriber line (DSL), (2) cable modem, (3) terrestrial wireless (fixed and mobile), (4) satellite, and (5) broadband over power line (BPL). DSL uses primarily copper wire, but both it and cable modem utilize fiber optic cabling in their broadband networks. Cable television is the leading provider of broadband Internet services, followed by the telephone companies' DSL, direct-to-home broadcast satellite (DBS), fixed wireless services (including several technologies, such as Multichannel Multipoint Distribution Services and BPL. As of 2001, the total number of homes with broadband Internet access was 8.5 million. By year-end 2007, the total in the United States is expected to top 100 million and 400 million worldwide. Discussed in detail in chapter 8, the passage of the Telecommunications Act of 1996 has enabled heightened competition in the broadband services marketplace.

Although cable modem and DSL are the leading providers of broadband to U.S. homes (see chapter 3 for a discussion of Internet users for these delivery media), fixed wireless is increasingly important in the delivery of broadband to portable devices and therefore for video to mobile devices, such as cell phones. Broadband is increasingly popular because it can deliver a variety of enhanced services, including voice-over Internet Protocol (VoIP), high-speed music downloading, and video on demand.

Broadband wireless is also in the form of Bluetooth and Wi-Fi (wireless fidelity). Wi-Fi is the common vernacular for high-speed wireless Internet access. The technical standard is 802.11b. Both Bluetooth and Wi-Fi are local-area networking (LAN) technologies. They must connect to wide-area networking (WAN) technologies, such as DSL or other broadband services, in order to access the Internet. Wireless technologies targeting cell phones and other mobile devices are also available, such as General

Packet Radio Service (GPRS).[3] GPRS is sometimes referred to as 2.5G, a wireless technology falling between second- and third-generation mobile telephony. It provides moderate speed data transfer, or about 80 Kbps (a theoretical limit of about 171 Kbps is rarely if ever achieved). 3G technology has been rolled out commercially in some countries, such as Japan, and is rolling out slowly in the United States. An emerging wireless communication standard known as WiMAX has the potential to connect distributed Wi-Fi hot spots (places where Wi-Fi is available). It may also provide affordable broadband connections in rural areas where DSL and cable modems are not economically viable.

The online encyclopedia *Wikipedia* notes that "WiMAX is defined as Worldwide Interoperability for Microwave Access by the WiMAX Forum, formed in June 2001 to promote conformance and interoperability of the IEEE 802.16 standard, officially known as WirelessMAN."[4] It can deliver up to 70 Mbps and can deliver broadband services over a distance of seventy miles, although not at the full 70 Mpbs. This advance would be a boon to rural areas, developing nations, and any location where fiber optic connectivity might be difficult or prohibitively expensive, or even to urban areas as an alternative to cable modem or DSL service. Beyond these services is personal ultrabroadband technology—wireless broadband at more than one gigabyte per second (Gbps), many times faster than most broadband in 2006. Eli Noam, director of the Columbia Institute for Tele-Information, says personal ultrabroadband "will drive vast changes in mass media, consumer electronics, and ICT [information and communication technology]. In the home, numerous connected devices will form a 'cloud'—a next-generation home network that moves with the user."[5]

The growth of broadband has fueled or at least enabled a growing public appetite for online audio and video, both of which might be termed broadband "hogs," especially high-quality video. A growing concern about the distribution of online video is what it may do to the actual arteries of Internet traffic, the major Internet service providers, including the telephone and cable companies. An increasing chorus of these companies is warning that TV-quality and high-definition programming may choke the Internet. The bandwidth required to deliver such high-quality video is considerable. Although small, low-resolution video clips do not pose a problem, the increasing volume of high-quality video has carriers such as Verizon and AT&T contemplating charging content providers to guarantee delivery of large video files. Such an on-line toll poses other problems, of course, including potentially locking out smaller video providers.[6] As an alternative, cable TV giant Comcast is building an on-demand video service using Internet technologies.[7] This topic is discussed further in the context of "network neutrality" in chapter 8 on regulation.

With Internet access, video can be watched from wherever the viewer is, at home, office, or on the road—wherever there is Internet service, that is. With wireless broadband, viewing fall baseball playoff games via a laptop can be a completely mobile experience, whether one is sipping a latte at a Starbucks or catching lunch in New York City's Bryant Park or at any of the many thousands of other free or low-cost Wi-Fi hot spots around the country and the world. Wi-Fi has become so popular that even Zagat's offers a Wi-Fi destination guide. Internet consulting firm Frost & Sullivan estimates that as of 2006 there are at least 40,000 Wi-Fi hot spots around the United States, up from just 4,000 in 2002.[8] Frost & Sullivan expects the number to top 100,000 by the end of 2008. Among the emerging technologies is Internet Protocol television.

Thanks to my wife, who is a media and information technology professional, our home has a Wi-Fi network that allows members of the family to go anywhere in the home, patio, or yard and get high-speed Internet service on their computers, whether desktop or laptop or other handheld Wi-Fi-enabled device.

Consequently, my laptop and I are untethered and able to be anywhere in or around the home and still go online with broadband Internet access, so that I can watch all the games, do my work, and on a crisp October day sit comfortably by a roaring fire in a wood-burning stove and still be online.

Of course, I could watch the game on a television set and separately use my laptop. Research by media ethnographer John Carey of Fordham University shows that this phenomenon is not uncommon.[9] But this approach has several problems. First, my television set is not nearly as mobile as a laptop. Also, it may not have all the games that are available over the Internet. Further, my laptop is a private machine, whereas the television is shared with the entire family. Finally, the distinction between a computer and a television set is increasingly blurring. Both devices are performing the same functions more and more.

If Major League Baseball represented the totality of all the quality video available online, then there might be little to get excited about. But baseball is only the tip of the broadband video sports iceberg. By 2007, virtually all the major professional sports offer a wide range of online video services, ranging from live game coverage to compressed game video (where software is used to delete all the nongame action, so the game can be watched in much less than the time required on traditional television gamecasts) to highlights, sports shows, and much more. And sports represents only a very small portion of the broadband video universe, a topic I explore in detail in chapter 5.

DIGITAL TELEVISION

Although broadband Internet is a major component in the digital media delivery system, another significant part is the amalgam of digital technologies for delivering what is known as digital television, or DTV.

On one level, DTV is audio and video in computerized format, ones and zeros. The current worldwide broadcast DTV standard uses the MPEG-2 compression scheme. The first MPEG standard was for digital video and audio on computers and CD-ROMs and delivered over the Internet, and it led to the phenomenon known as Napster, which uses the audio component of MPEG-1—or Audio-Layer 3, abbreviated as MP3—to compress, store, and transmit music files.

MPEG-2 was established at Columbia University in 1993 for the all-digital transmission of broadcast-quality video and audio encoded at "bit rates" (the amount of computerized information transmitted per second) between 4 and 9 Mbps (MPEG-1 is coded at 1.5 Mbps). MPEG-2 is also efficient for transmitting higher bit rates and sample rates, such as high-definition television (HDTV). Because MPEG-1 is for computers, it is based on a scanning process known as "progressive," which is how computer monitors display video. MPEG-2 is for television and therefore also has to accommodate the different scanning process of a television display, which is called "interlaced." MPEG-2 also must accommodate the faster frame rate of broadcast-quality television, thirty frames per second.

In addition to broadband Internet, there are four main ways in which consumers see DTV today: (1) satellite, including DBS; (2) digital video/versatile disc (DVD); (3) digital cable; and (4) terrestrial broadcast.

COVERING THE GLOBE: THE IMPACT OF SATELLITES ON TELEVISION

When Sir Arthur C. Clarke in 1945 envisioned the "extraterrestrial relay," he set in motion titanic forces that would reshape the modern world.[10] His vision, which today we know as the communications satellite, not only has made global television possible, but continues to reshape that medium in profound ways.

Communications satellites are radio relay stations in space. The dishes for receiving satellite communications shrink as each generation of satellites gets increasingly powerful transmitters with smaller "footprints," or target areas, on the Earth.[11] Communications satellites carry press agency news feeds, digital radio with more than one hundred channels of CD-quality audio available nationwide (e.g., XM Radio or Sirius Satellite Radio) and global television including the Cable News Network (CNN) and the British Broadcasting Corporation (BBC), now digital in format.[12] Satellites also carry network television feeds on C-band or Ku-band satellites to affiliate stations across the nation and to cable head-ends (central control), making possible the WGN and WTBS superstations (i.e., local stations that have become national in distribution).[13]

Operation Iraqi Freedom was brought live to households in the United States and around the world from the remotest corners of Iraq via lightweight portable and digital satellite phones. In 2003, journalists used the digital Iridium, Globalstar, and Inmarsat satellite phones that weigh about 380 grams (about 13 ounces, or less than a pound) and work like a standard phone with compact and lightweight batteries providing nearly four hours of talk time and twenty hours of stand-by time. Consequently, the satellite phone became a standard tool for the so-called backpack journalist, providing extensive audio and video from Iraq. Just a dozen years earlier, when journalists first used satellite phones to cover war, the phones were analog, large, cumbersome, heavy (about twenty-five pounds), and difficult to set up, and they required a generator to maintain power.

For television news viewers, the new digital satellite phone meant more extensive, live, and up-to-the-minute reporting from conflict zones. What it did not mean was necessarily more independent or spontaneous reporting, although the latter did sometimes occur. In fact, in some instances the reporting was anything but independent and spontaneous as embedded reporters and their U.S.–based editors scheduled and promoted live reports from battleships, bunkers, and bomb sites where marines and other troops were often on hand to provide comments, observations, and greetings to the folks at home.

Because of the ubiquity and accessibility of satellite-delivered television, both the U.S. and Iraqi governments used the medium of television to promote their views of the war and their respective side's progress to the viewing public both at home and abroad. Regular press briefings from the United States and Iraq featuring government spokespersons, military officials, and other sources became a regular part of the daily coverage. Moreover, the Qatar-based satellite network Al-Jazeera emerged as a major force in international media coverage of the events in the region during the spring of 2003, sometimes offering video reports otherwise unseen in the United States or even prohibited by U.S. military censors (e.g., video of U.S. prisoners of war).[14]

Many news organizations, and not just the networks in the United States, relied on satellite phones in their coverage of the invasion of Iraq. Even reporters from small-size markets could afford the required technology, which includes not just the rental or purchase of the phone, satellite service, and satellite modem, but also a digital video camera and a portable computer such as an Apple G4 laptop for audio and video editing.

Journalists using the satellite system transmitted their live or recorded reports and spoke directly to their news desks back in the United States or elsewhere in the world without having to rely on the Iraqi telephone networks, which might become a military target. In some cases, such as at CBS News, reporters in the field were sent satellite images from their stateside news desks that they could use to better understand and plan their next assignment.

One commonly used satellite system is Iridium, a system of sixty-six low-Earth-orbiting satellites circling the globe at an altitude of 450 miles.[15] Of course, many other types of satellites orbit the Earth, many of which have important implications for television in the United States and around the world. Observation satellites typically orbit the Earth anywhere from 300 to 600 miles above the planet in asynchronous orbits, or orbital paths that move the satellites in continuously changing positions relative to the Earth.

These satellites often contain high-resolution cameras that can photograph the Earth or Earth-based objects as small as one meter in size. These remote-sensing satellite images are used in a variety of applications, including news reporting during military conflicts, natural disasters, and weather and environmental events. Satellite imagery was developed by the U.S. Department of Defense, and much of it became declassified and thus publicly and commercially available with the end of the Cold War.

GeoEye is one of the main commercial providers of satellite imagery used by news organizations.[16] These satellite images, says former CBS News producer and technologist Dan Dubno, give journalists and thereby the viewing public access to "denied areas."[17] Denied areas take many forms and occur for many reasons. A natural disaster such as an earthquake, volcano, or hurricane makes it impossible or extremely dangerous for anyone to enter the area. Remote-sensing satellites can give us important visual access to these areas during critical periods where lives may be saved by timely reporting. GeoEye, a remote-sensing company based in Dulles, Virginia, provided new IKONOS satellite imagery over an area in southwest Oregon in December 2006 to aid in the search for a missing man who left his family in a stranded car to find help. Authorities used the imagery as a search-management tool, and news media used it to help tell the story.

Wars or other military conflict also can result in areas being placed off limits to reporters. For example, the island of Diego Garcia in the Indian Ocean is a U.S. military outpost where no journalists are allowed. However, satellites can image the airbase located there with impunity from an orbital perch 423 miles in space. Remote-sensing satellite images

Figure 1.1 U.S. Navy EP-3 "Aries II" sits on a runway at Linshui Military Airfield, Hainan Island, South China Sea. GeoEye's IKONOS satellite collected this one-meter color image, 10:12 A.M., April 4, 2001, local time. IKONOS satellite imagery courtesy of GeoEye © 2007. All rights reserved.

can also be extremely helpful in understanding what may be happening on the ground during periods when the military has denied access to a location. Although the U.S. government has the power to interrupt commercial service in the name of national security or foreign-policy concerns, it has never done so. Such so-called shutter control was not implemented even during the invasion of Iraq in 2003.

One reason why restrictions were not imposed is that such an action might have triggered First Amendment questions. The government did, however, purchase all the imagery over Afghanistan and Pakistan during the invasion in October 2003. For a period of three months, no imagery of the area was made available. However, in January 2004, the Pentagon did not renew the contract with then Space Imaging (now GeoEye), and all of that imagery was made available for sale. Regardless of the means by which the images were not available—in this case through purchase

Figure 1.2 World Trade Center before and after September 11, 2001, shown using one-meter-resolution satellite image. IKONOS satellite imagery courtesy of GeoEye © 2007.

rather than through suppression—the result was virtually the same, notes Dubno. The government bought the exclusive rights to all the images, at least during the initial stages of the conflict, and no imagery was available for journalists.

Satellite images are essential to help make transparent to the public the events of the region. GeoEye owns and operates two high-resolution Earth-imaging satellites. Both satellites can see objects on the ground as small as one meter in size (see fig. 1.1). GeoEye senior executive Mark Brender, formerly an ABC network news producer who covered national-security affairs, has always been a strong proponent of "open skies" and "global transparency" policies. He was an early advocate of commercializing spy satellite technology. Imagery from high-resolution imaging satellites can provide very contextual "before and after" pictures of events unfolding on the ground (see fig. 1.2). "Before imagery" comes from the archives, and the "after imagery" is collected as soon as a satellite is programmed to image an event and then passes overhead. Seeing the region from space can dramatically improve public understanding of the environmental impact of things such as oil well fires, but without necessarily putting anyone's life at risk or compromising U.S. military tactics. In the long run, promoting the use of the satellite imagery in the news helps both journalism and public understanding of important matters such as the conflict in Iraq or even global warming.

Satellites have other far-reaching implications for television and media in general. A class of satellites orbiting the Earth roughly 6,000 to 12,000 miles above ground in asynchronous orbital paths is used for navigation and location. The U.S. Department of Defense created the GPS using these satellites. GPS technology is used for a wide range of applications, such as locating a ship at sea, an airplane, an automobile, or a person carrying a GPS receiver.

The media, including television, increasingly use GPS technology to help provide locational information for reporters, photographs, and video. Reporters traveling to remote areas such as the desert of Iraq often travel with a GPS receiver to help them keep track of their location. Moreover, GPS technology can now be used to embed a time, date, and location stamp—a digital watermark—onto still images or video. A GPS stamp can be vital in providing copyright protection for news images and video as well as for authenticating photos and video. Picture an exclusive photo or video of an alleged Iraqi cache of possible chemical weapons, and consider the value of a GPS stamp in authenticating the exact location, time, and place of the photo or video.

The case of the March 2003 front-page publication in the *Los Angeles Times* of a photograph that was altered in violation of *Times* policy points to the need for such authentication. According to the *Times,* the published photo of a British soldier directing Iraqi civilians to take cover from Iraqi fire was actually two photos.[18] Photographer Brian Walski, who in 2001 won the Photographer of the Year award from the California Press Photographers Association, used his computer to merge the two photos into one. He apparently thought the merged, or composite, photo was better than either of the two actual photos. He was fired for his wrong-doing, but reportedly explained it this way: "When I saw it, I probably just said, no one is going to know. I don't know. I've tweaked pictures before—taken out a phone pole. It's not a common practice, but you can do it. I can't speak for anyone else, but I imagine they've done it here and there. This was going overboard—taking pictures and putting them together. I think it's just that I wanted a better image. Then when I did it, I didn't even think about it."[19] Digital technology makes discerning such a fake news photo very difficult. Walski's composite photo was discovered only when a reader noticed the same person twice in the image, which started a chain of events that led editors at the *Los Angeles Times* to question the photo's authenticity. When confronted with the evidence, Walski admitted he had merged two similar photos to create one more dramatic image, even though he knew this procedure violated the *Times* policy.[20] Had the *Times* required its photographers to use a GPS stamp on all photos, the doctored photo would have been much more difficult to produce because it would be very difficult to insert a false GPS stamp (though not impossible for a computer hacker).

Although this case is from a print publication, the same problem can occur in television, and a digital watermark containing a GPS stamp can similarly help ensure the veracity of news video feeds and protect the copyright, or intellectual property rights, of those feeds.

DIRECT BROADCAST SATELLITE

Weather satellites, widely used in televised and online weather reporting, travel in geostationary orbits (fixed position relative to the Earth) 22,223 miles above ground. Making national media headlines in the spring of 2003 along with the war in Iraq was one particular geostationary satellite technology orbiting at this 22,223-mile altitude: DBS. Since the mid-1990s, DBS has become a major provider of DTV service in the United States and around the world. In the United States, the two leading providers of DBS service are DirecTV and the DISH Network, both all digital in format with extensive programming offerings through the efficiency of digital compression, as well as interactive and on-demand capabilities.[21]

DBS television services are increasingly popular. They utilize a fixed 18-inch-diameter antenna attached to the home to receive the television transmission from a geostationary (fixed position relative to the Earth) satellite. Stanley S. Hubbard founded United States Satellite Broadcasting in 1981, and successful DBS satellites were launched over the next decade. There were 320,000 paying DBS subscribers in the United States by 1994, and the number has grown steadily since then. The total number of subscribers to DBS services in the United States is now more than 27 million, making it a principal means by which U.S. households receive DTV and digital audio.

As of June 2006, DirecTV, the leading U.S. DBS provider, had 15.4 million subscribers.[22] Based in El Segundo, California, DirecTV transmits digital satellite television and audio (XM Radio) to homes in North America, South America, and other parts of the world. Owned by the DirecTV Group, it is a subsidiary of Rupert Murdoch's News Corporation's Fox Entertainment Group. Rupert Murdoch, whose global News Corporation is among the most far-reaching media empires, long sought DirecTV.[23] In April 2003, the board of General Motors, which had owned Hughes's DirecTV, accepted Murdoch's multibillion dollar purchase offer. DirecTV complements Murdoch's international DBS holdings, including British Sky Broadcasting (B-Sky-B) in Europe and his Fox television holdings in the United States.

Most of the programming on DirecTV is national networks, comparable to what is seen on cable television. DirecTV offers programming in high-definition format; additional interactive services; and some local channels, including CBS, ABC, NBC, Fox, PBS, CW, MyNetworkTV, *i*, and some independent stations. In the larger markets, locals channels are carried on the main satellite, but in smaller markets they are carried via another satellite where high-definition and most Spanish-language programming is located. This means the viewer must install a slightly larger oval dish capable of receiving signals from both DirecTV satellites simultaneously. One of the most distinctive programming packages available exclusively on DirecTV is NFL Sunday Ticket, a premium football sports package that allows DirecTV viewers to watch all NFL games each Sunday during the NFL season, typically September to December.

Competing with DirecTV is EchoStar's DISH Network, based in Englewood, Colorado, with 12 million paying subscribers.[24] Launched in 1996, DISH delivers a programming package similar to DirecTV's. Its on-screen interactive, or electronic program guide (EPG), enables viewers to navigate through the hundreds of channels of available digital programming.

To minimize piracy of their transmissions, which had been a significant problem in the early days of satellite television, DirecTV and the DISH Network deliver their programming in encrypted form using a smart card installed in each home receiver. At the January 2007 Consumer Electronics Show in Las Vegas, Nevada, DirecTV introduced the first light-weight, compact mobile satellite television receiver, the Sat-Go. Packed in a hard plastic case and weighing roughly twenty-five pounds, the portable receiver sells for about $1,000.[25] The Sat-Go was invented by Rick Rosner, a television pioneer who has also created and produced television shows such as *CHiPs* and *The New Hollywood Squares*.[26] The Sat-Go permits subscribers to DirecTV to tune in to satellite television anywhere they can receive a signal without the need for a rooftop or otherwise hard-wired dish antenna. Potential users of the Sat-Go include the Federal Emergency Management Agency.

News, entertainment, and sports programming are thriving national and global commodities thanks in large part to the technological capabilities and economic efficiencies of satellites. The immediacy, scope, and coverage of television news, especially during times of crisis, has benefited directly from the miniaturization, ubiquity, and cost effectiveness of satellite communications. What remains to be seen is whether those responsible for the use of satellites in television will employ this marvelous global technology to create better television or merely a more profitable one.

DIGITAL VIDEO/VERSATILE DISC

Since its development in the early 1990s, the DVD has emerged as an important medium for delivering digital-format movies to the home. From Disney to Warner Bros., the major Hollywood movie studios now release for sale or rental new, older, and classic titles on DVD. Many titles include never-before-seen footage and other materials, providing not only better visual and sound quality than videotape, but also additional content, such as outtakes, director commentary, deleted scenes, interviews with leading actors, and the like. Whereas video home system (VHS) resolution is 210 horizontal lines, laser disc has 425 lines and DVD 540 lines of resolution. The viewer also has more control over the viewing experience, choosing among various screen formats, such as wide-screen (cinematic) or conventional full-screen TV viewing. Viewers typically also can choose the language in which they listen to a movie on a DVD, usually English, French, or Spanish. DVDs offer high-quality sound, with a higher sampling rate than audio CDs, as well as Dolby Surround Sound, with six audio channels. DVD discs look just like the 4.75-inch-diameter audio CDs.

More than 20,000 movie titles are available on DVD, and more than 20 million DVD discs are sold annually, with total sales topping one billion each year in the United States. *Titanic* on DVD sold more than one million units in the year following its release.[27] Consumers have purchased more than 50 million DVD players, whose price has fallen below $100 and which are often integrated with other devices. Minivans and other automobiles are now equipped with DVD players to reduce the stress of long-distance family travel.

DIGITAL CABLE TV

Advanced cable television systems are rapidly converting to digital. As of June 2006, almost two-thirds (59.1 percent), or 65,500,000, of the 110,900,000 U.S. television households subscribed to basic cable television.[28] Approximately half of these cable subscribers, or 32,898,000, are served by digital cable television.

However, as John Carey notes, "Cable systems are about two years behind schedule in the roll-out of digital cable systems. They are definitely headed in that direction, but it will take a little time to get there."[29] In digital format, cable providers can offer not only more channels via compression, but also interactive services, ranging from e-mail to Internet service to interactive program guides to video games. In any case, these digital cable systems require the installation of a set-top box because the vast majority of viewers do not have DTV sets (which would be required to decode the digital signal). These set-top boxes, which are essentially computer processors attached to a television set, also require the installation of computer software programs. But the set-top box is paid for and installed by the cable company, and the charge to the cable consumer for the television service may be relatively modest, at least in terms of the monthly bill. Moreover, the EPG for cable TV is superior (in 2006) to the guide for satellite TV. Time Warner's digital cable system's EPG has a variety of user-friendly features, including a resizable video window that can be shrunk to half size to allow the viewer to watch one program while searching through the hundreds of other channels. One potentially user-friendly option typically not available on some cable television EPGs is rearranging the channels of programming by viewer preference, although viewers can sort programming by theme, title, and channel number.

Wink is a popular set-top program available for digital cable systems (and other DTV systems). Based in Alameda, California, Wink gives viewers limited access to interactive programs and advertising. When a red italic *i* is superimposed on the screen, Wink viewers push a button on their remote controls to see an overlay of text and graphics. This overlay enables viewers to access more information or order products. Wink is software installed by the cable operator or satellite provider. It is what might be called "store and sweep" technology. It allows the viewer to interact only with the set-top box, not with others and not with the program. The viewer's response is stored in the box, and the next day the box is swept for data. Wink is being installed in more than 14 million digital cable homes, including subscribers to Time Warner Cable, Charter Communications, Cox Communications, AT&T, Comcast Cable, Insight Communications, RCN Cable, and Adelphia, and it is free to the subscriber. Cable operators get a portion of a transaction fee from Wink each time a viewer makes a purchase via the system. It is expected that by the end of 2007 more than three-quarters of the nation's more than 60 million cable customers will have access to digital cable and related interactive services such as Wink.

Digital cable television also offers viewers an increasingly impressive array of not only more than two hundred channels of local and network programming, premium movie channels, and special event programming (e.g., live sporting events), but also on-demand movies and other programming. Much of what is available on demand is a premium (i.e., available for a fee), but some is available for free, including selected documentaries and other programs.

Digital cable television also has the potential to offer a range of other services to the consumer, including telephone and broadband Internet services. At the same time, telephone companies are now entering the broadband communications fray and offering DTV and other services via their fiber-copper hybrid switched networks. Although the regulatory hurdles are still being cleared, a growing number of markets enjoy unprecedented competition in the form of both cable and telephone companies' offering competing television, telephone, and broadband Internet services.

TERRESTRIAL BROADCAST DTV

Consider this question: What percentage of U.S. households receive terrestrial TV, analog or digital, on their primary television set via an over-the-air antenna? Seventy-five percent? Fifty percent? Twenty-five percent? Each of these numbers is too high. Although as recently as the mid-1970s terrestrial broadcast TV dominated the viewing landscape, in 2007 the scene has changed drastically, when just 20 percent of U.S. households (around 60 million viewers) receive over-the-air terrestrial TV signals on their primary TV set. The other 80 percent are connected to cable, satellite, or something else, meaning that some 240 million viewers watch television programs via cable or satellite.[30] That is not to say they do not see the programming carried on terrestrial stations; they in fact see many programs produced and carried by terrestrial television stations and by the networks to which most stations are affiliated. Federally mandated must-carry rules ensure that these stations are available on cable (see chapter 8 for details on must-carry rules). But the signal carrying these programs is not delivered to the primary set in the vast majority of U.S. households via terrestrial transmission.

Against this backdrop, consider the following facts regarding the conversion to terrestrial DTV, which will require households to acquire a new antenna to receive the terrestrial DTV signals as well as either new DTV sets or digital conversion boxes to watch the digital signal on analog TV sets.

Now being implemented in the United States and much of the world is a new generation of television that is digital in format. The Advanced Television Systems Committee (ATSC) has since its inception in 1982 been developing a new standard for DTV in the United States. This standard has also been adopted in Canada, Mexico, Taiwan, and South

Korea, and is under consideration elsewhere. The ATSC digital standard replaces the NTSC analog system that has been in place in the United States since the 1940s and largely unchanged since the introduction of color in the 1950s. The new digital standard offers a number of technical advantages over the previous analog standard. It supports wide-screen 16:9 (the ratio of the screen width to height) images that are the same in aspect ratio as motion pictures seen in movie theaters. The resolution of the images can also be greatly increased, up to 1920 × 1080 pixels, which is at least six times the resolution of the analog standard. ATSC can accommodate various image qualities, ranging from standard definition to high definition.

Using current compression technologies and the available bandwidth for terrestrial transmission, up to six virtual channels can be broadcast on a single TV station's allocated 6 megahertz (MHz) digital channel, a process called *multiplexing.* Broadcasters might use one channel for general, free TV (as required by the FCC) and the remainder (current MPEG-2 compression would allow roughly six channels of conventional NTSC-quality television to be multicast over the assigned digital spectrum) to transmit niche programming, such as twenty-four-hour local news, as has been suggested by Mark Thalhimer, former director of the News of the Future Project of the Radio and Television News Directors Foundation.[31] Ed Quinn, president of McGraw-Hill Broadcasting and general manager of KGTV in San Diego, reports that his station has successfully produced a twenty-four-hour local cable news channel, and he can see successfully transmitting this same content via one of the company's digital channels.[32] Quinn adds that his San Diego station has also streamed digital video news via the station's Web site, as a complement to its on-air transmissions. In the case of a shooting at Santana High School, the station drew 450,000 visitors to its Web site, mostly to view on-demand streaming video news reports on the shooting. Broadcasting veteran Jim Topping warns, however, "Despite the heady talk of multiple channels for stations to market and re-purpose programming, there has been little effective use. There is no business model to speak of that promises a return on the additional channels of DTV. And, no one has yet proposed how to effectively promote or market 5–6 additional channels."[33]

Yet it is very likely that digitization will lead to even more programming specialization and audience fragmentation. In Great Britain, for example, the BBC has already launched BBC America, a twenty-four-hour digital video channel offering U.S. viewers programming from the United Kingdom, including live half-hour newscasts. The channel is available on both digital cable and satellite systems, and it targets upscale audiences.

The new digital standard also offers higher-quality audio using "Dolby Digital AC-3 format to provide 5.1-channel surround sound." The AC-3 format includes six channels of sound, with five channels for right front, center, left front, right rear, and left rear, and one channel for the subwoofer, a loudspeaker dedicated to the bass audio range. Dolby Digital also supports monophonic and stereophonic sound. The digital ATSC television standard also supports various datacasting services. *Datacasting* is a form of broadcasting data over wide areas using the same radio waves used to transmit DTV. It can include the delivery of Internet content, EPGs, interactive games, and new video formats, such as 360-degree video.[34] DTV is "transmitted on radio frequencies that are similar to standard analog television, with the primary difference being the use of multiplex transmitters to allow reception of multiple channels on a single frequency range (such as a UHF or VHF channel)."[35]

The first commercial television station to broadcast a DTV signal was WRAL, a CBS affiliate in Raleigh, North Carolina, which sent an experimental HDTV transmission on July 23, 1996. It had a very limited audience; it was shown using the only HDTV display set available in the market at the time, a test Panasonic 46-inch HDTV set at a local Circuit City store.[36]

HDTV sets started becoming commercially available in the United States in 1998, and HDTV broadcasts increased by the end of that year. Among the first HDTV broadcasts was the launch of the space shuttle *Discovery*. Analog NTSC transmissions are scheduled to end in the United States on February 17, 2009. As of October 3, 2006, the number of commercial and educational television stations in the United States that broadcast digitally, with a simultaneous transmission of an analog signal, was 1,122. Other DTV stations are on the air periodically under experimental or special temporary authorities.

DTV conversion can cost from $2 million to as much as $20 million per station for high-definition capability, a tough pill for smaller stations to swallow, especially in markets where annual profits are less than a million dollars and often one-quarter of that. "Even amortized liberally," says Jim Topping, long-time ABC television executive and the former general manager of KGO-TV in San Francisco who shepherded the station into the digital age, "that is a cost that will be monstrous unless their corporate ownership is well funded and willing to invest long term." Topping notes the fear that small ownership groups may as a result disappear in the near future. "DTV may be the financial straw that breaks the business camel's back," he explains, "forcing station sales to larger groups with deep pockets."[37]

One small-market station has found a way around the high DTV price tag, however. In Kingsport, Tennessee, DMA 93, WKPT, obtained a digital signal on air for just $125,000. George DeVault, president of Holston Valley Broadcasting Corporation and owner of the station, decided to forego HDTV initially and bought and installed a digital system to put a standard-definition television signal on air. "We have not decided to forego HDTV forever," DeVault explains. "We just decided to go first with standard definition multicasting. Our network (ABC) has an average of one movie every couple of weeks in HDTV and only one regular series *(NYPD Blue)* in HDTV right now. If we were a CBS affiliate I'd be hard-pressed not to transmit HDTV from the start."[38] The station's DTV system has four basic components: (1) a digital video encoder/multiplexer for two standard-definition television streams at a cost of $64,000; (2) a 500-watt DTV transmitter at $54,000 (this is the transmitter power output wattage, which translates into the effective radiated power [ERP]; the station will be increasing power from 5,400 watts ERP to 200,000 watts ERP later); (3) a 200-foot transmission line and various peripherals at $2,000, installation not included; and (4) a transmitting antenna at $3,600.

According to Ed Quinn, the only DTV station on air in Denver by late 2006 was KDVR, the Fox affiliate. Quinn says the lack of DTV in Denver is not for lack of trying. All the stations there have transmission towers on nearby Look-Out Mountain. Written before there was such a thing as DTV, the original covenants call for no modification of those towers. A consortium of broadcasters in Denver proposed tearing down their analog towers and replacing them with a single, digital tower, "a candelabra of digital transmitters," Quinn explains. "But, over the years, people have built up homes all around the edge of the mountain and now many oppose making any changes on the mountain top. Politicians have waffled." As a result, there is only one digital signal in Denver. "This is the 18th [largest] market in the U.S. Moreover, it's costing us a fortune. We've already spent a million dollars in legal and consulting fees."[39]

Public-television stations are also converting to DTV. Of the Public Broadcasting Service's (PBS) 271 member stations, 200 were broadcasting digital signals by October 3, 2006, covering 90 percent of U.S. households.[40] Digital stations serve all the top-ten markets. PBS distributed its first high-definition programming to member stations in 1998 and in January 1999 began feeding two digital services for use by its digital stations. One is a high-definition channel, and the second is a four-channel multicast, offering a cross-section of programming, including a twenty-four-hour children's channel and PBSU, a how-to channel. PBS has continued its development and distribution of enhanced broadcasts as well.

For those stations that have installed DTV, it is expensive to broadcast both a digital and an analog signal. Most would presumably prefer to broadcast only one signal. Topping adds, "Electric power for DTV transmitters is usually above $100,000 additional annual expense—putting aside what's happening in California—for every station large or small."[41] DTV sets have also caught on slowly with consumers as well, mainly because the typical DTV set costs $1,000 or more.

Jack Goodman, general counsel of the National Association of Broadcasters, called on regulators to require TV set manufacturers to install a DTV tuner in all sets sold in the United States, much as the outgoing analog sets must have a VHF/UHF tuner and a V-chip (a microprocessor that allows parental control of what is viewed on a TV set).[42] The cost to include a DTV tuner is minimal, roughly $25–50 a set. With 25 million sets sold annually in the United States, this is the fastest way to move toward the FCC's goal of getting 85 percent of U.S. households DTV enabled by 2009. In 2002, the FCC mandated that by 2007 all television sets sold in the country must have a DTV tuner.[43] Fordham University's John Carey reports, "Nearly three in four people who have purchased a DTV set have not purchased a receiver to pick up HDTV signals. They are using their DTV sets to watch DVDs."[44] Congress is considering a coupon program to subsidize the purchase of home digital converters when millions of users' existing analog TV receivers will go dark without analog broadcast signals in 2009.

CONCLUSION: FROM COUCH POTATO TO MASHED POTATO

Terrestrial broadcast DTV can be simply the same as regular TV, but digital. DTV can also be interactive, and it has sharper pictures and better sound. A variety of companies and commercial research centers are working on interactive television, such as Joost, WatchPoint Media, RespondTV, Liberate, PowerTV, OpenTV, and WowTV, some of which have already rolled out DTV terrestrial broadcasting services in Europe.[45] On the academic side, the MIT Media Lab and others are working on interactive DTV services as well. Viewers can currently see (or participate with) interactive TV in the form of "Enhanced TV," which is broadcast most often by ABC, although the first nationally broadcast enhanced DTV program was Ken Burns's Frank Lloyd Wright documentary aired by PBS in 1998. ABC's Enhanced TV synchronizes customized interactive content over the Web during many of its programs, from *Who Wants to Be a Millionaire,* where each week more than 125,000 Americans tried to answer Meredith Vieira's questions before the contestant did, to *Monday Night Football,* which offers an interactive play-along synchronized game as well as live statistics and facts about the players and teams. ABC has initially focused on the "two-screen" platform whereby viewers have an Internet-connected computer in the same room as their television. More than 40 million homes in 2007 are capable of such TV-Internet convergence, which is closer to a critical mass than the 2007 set-top box installation numbers. Viewers can also access other types of single-screen Enhanced TV programming, typically via Microsoft's MSN TV 2, which marries the Internet and television on the TV screen. Consumers pay about $200 for the MSN TV box and $10 (broadband) to $22 (dial-up) a month for the service. However, few television programmers are offering advanced interactive TV content because it is still early in the game, and many homes lack digital, always connected set-top boxes. This may be the reason why the retail interactive set-top box business has stalled. Once the cable and satellite distributors install advanced interactive DTV boxes in all their subscribers' homes, the interactive DTV programming offerings will take off.

There are many implications of and questions regarding interactive DTV for those in the television industry. For example, how will interactive DTV affect the existing system of ratings? When every viewer can interact with a program and rate not just the show but every scene change, how will audience measurement occur? Will networks and stations want to record viewers' channel-surfing habits? Will viewers experience a privacy backlash?

Jonathan Leess, former senior vice president of ABC's Enhanced TV and Disney/ABC, and now president/CEO of DoubleVision Media, Inc., offers the following observation about the future of interactive television. "The imminent marriage of 'two-way, always-connected' technologies and the passive television experience is going to have a profound effect on every facet of this industry."[46]

Will programmers prefer to multicast or to program HDTV or to use some combination? CBS is the first network to broadcast its entire prime-time schedule in HDTV. A portion of the PBS schedule is also available in high definition. Jack Goodman of the National Association of Broadcasters says that commercial broadcasters are now transmitting about 1,000 hours of HDTV programming annually. Due to the low installed-based number of high-definition sets (i.e., number of households with HDTV receivers), however, few viewers can see the programs in HDTV.

One area where digital conversion may have a more direct return to stations, Topping explains, is in "master control" systems, which include staff reduction, cleaner operations, and the ability to operate multiple station sites from a single control point. Digital conversion for news departments has been hit or miss. Most stations in the top seventy-five markets have access to digital editing, used mostly for production, promotion, and special series. "But only larger markets," Topping observes, "have been brave enough to face the changing technical specifications for field cameras, mixed formats inside the department, or the need to dub material from digital to analog and back."[47] And, as noted, DTV can also be watermarked to provide better protection of intellectual property rights and copyright.

In the end, will the public interest be better served by DTV? New technology holds that promise. Will the realities of the television business lead DTV toward a vast but interactive wasteland that Newton Minow once lamented in the analog days of the medium?[48] Post-Internet economics pose that peril.

2 / DEVICES TO ACCESS DIGITAL MEDIA

The term *digital convergence* refers to the coming together of all media types in a computer-based form, typically including wired or wireless connectivity to the Internet or a LAN. Nowhere is digital convergence more apparent than in the devices used to access, display, consume, experience, interact with, and create digital content. Since the 1990s, a wide range of digital devices have emerged to give consumers and content creators alike increasingly powerful, portable, and productive tools for experiencing or producing media in the digital age. At the same time, although convergence is apparent, there are still many diverse types of digital media devices, some of which are highly specialized in their functionality. This chapter examines the digital devices for accessing and interacting with digital media content, including both those highly converged as well as those highly specialized. Chapter 9 examines the digital technologies involved in the production of media content.

TYPES OF DIGITAL DEVICES

Although computers are often thought of as among the most modern of technologies, computational devices have been around for many centuries. As early as the first century B.C., the ancient Greeks invented perhaps the first computer, an astronomical calculator known as the Antikythera Mechanism.[1] In 2006, researchers exploring off the coast of Greece found gears and other parts of the Antikythera in a sunken Roman ship.[2] Yet it was not until the age of the digital computer, in which data are processed in binary form as 1s and 0s, that widespread media applications became possible.[3] Analog computers processed data in physical measures or quantities along a continuum and had limited capability to process or display media content such as audio and video.[4] Invented in the late 1930s and early 1940s, electronic digital computers were used by the media as early as 1952 for reporting election results.[5] In the 1960s, the development of precision journalism, or the application of scientific methods to journalism, was based largely on the use of digital computers to process large sets of data.[6] These early media utilized punch cards to input data and printouts to see the results. Computer displays were monochrome cathode ray tubes (CRT) and were limited to the display of text and simple graphics. The limited processing power of early computers and CRT technology prevented them from having any significant use in the display of media content such as photographs and motion pictures or in the projection of sound. Rapid and significant advances in the digital computer and related technologies since then have transformed media, including access and display devices. In the 1970s and 1980s, as teletext (one-way text and graphics transmission) and videotext (two-way text and graphics) trials developed, computer displays were used to present text and simple graphics.[7] Now, in the first decade of the twenty-first century, computer-based devices for accessing and displaying media content have become widely available and used in the United States and around the world. Digital devices in 2007 can display or present virtually all forms of media content, whether audio, video, text, graphics, or photos.

Digital media access and display devices come in at least two basic forms: fixed location and mobile. Each of these forms includes several alternatives. Fixed-location devices are primarily desktop personal computers; television sets; displays that are either digital or analog and connected to a digital set-top box enabling access to digital data, whether cable or satellite television or the Internet; as well as various peripheral devices such as DVD players, digital video recorders (DVRs), and video game consoles. Desktop computers typically provide a wide range of media access capabilities through a combination of various hardware (e.g., central processing unit, mouse, keyboard, flat-panel display, and speakers), software applications, and high-speed Internet delivery. Among these access capabilities are: browsing the Web, particularly for media content of all types, such as online news and entertainment, photos, graphics, and animations; searching for, downloading, sharing, viewing, and listening to audio and video; playing video games (both online and off); and accessing blogs and podcasts.

DTV DISPLAYS: THE VANISHING PICTURE TUBE

Familiar to most American homes is the fixed-location media device known as the television set. Since the 1950s, most U.S. homes have had at least one television set and often two or more. Not only are television sets or displays growing in screen size, quality, cost, and ubiquity, but the form they take is undergoing a digital transformation. Fewer and fewer households watch television on a set with a CRT, a device that was for six decades a mainstay of the television set industry and the American home. Fewer and fewer CRT devices, the central component of the analog TV set, are being manufactured and sold. The CRT was also used as the primary display device for personal computers until the advent of flat-panel screens. Now, the cube-shaped heavy picture tube is fading from the marketplace. "After the holidays, the days of picture-tube TV's are gone," said Geoff Shavey, the TV buyer for discount warehouse chain Costco, in late 2006. "One year from now, we will not sell picture-tube TV's."[8]

Costco had already reduced its picture-tube products to three models in 2006, down from ten in 2005. Like most other retailers, Costco is selling greater numbers of wide-screen plasma and liquid-crystal display (LCD) flat-panel TVs as well as projection video systems. Although more expensive than traditional TV sets, these digital display devices take up less cubic space (a 40-inch CRT analog set can weigh several hundred pounds and have a footprint in excess of 9 square feet), can be hung on a wall or from the ceiling, and offer superior picture quality and better audio. Flat panels also generally emit less electromagnetic radiation than CRTs, thereby reducing a possible health concern, although certain high-frequency emissions persist.[9] Prices for plasma and LCD sets are dropping. A 42-inch plasma TV set can cost less than $2,000, and the 32-inch flat-panel sets are only slightly more expensive than CRT alternatives, or about $700. Fueling the transition to digital sets is the federal government mandate that all TV sets include a built-in digital tuner to receive over-the-air digital broadcasts as well as other components for parental controls.

Like many other set manufacturers, Panasonic is leaving the picture-tube business. As recently as 2005, Panasonic sold only thirty picture-tube models in the United States. By 2006, its only offering was a 20-inch analog set. In 2007, it has offered none. Picture-tube TVs were 78 percent of the market in 2004, but just 54 percent in 2006, reports the Consumer Electronics Association.[10] Sales of CRT sets have gone flat, so to speak. In contrast, flat-panel TV set sales increased from 12 percent of all TVs sold in 2005 to 37 percent in 2006. Front- and rear-projection TVs represented 9 percent of sales in 2006, and the sale of plasma screen sets is also growing. It is worth noting that the new devices also have a new shape: rectangular. This more cinematic display coincides with the rise of HDTV, which features not just better picture quality and sound, but a wider aspect ratio (ratio of screen width to height), 16:9 versus 4:3 in the old analog CRT days. At the same time, more programs are being produced in the cinematic wide-screen frame. One significant advantage offered by CRT sets, however, is durability. Some CRT sets have lasted for decades, but it remains to be seen whether the new digital displays will last nearly as long.

Motivating much of the conversion to the newer digital displays is the enhanced visual and sound quality of HDTV, which displays 1,080 lines of detail in contrast to the 480 lines on a standard set. This means an HDTV set has a considerably sharper picture. Some set manufacturers also make a low-end high-definition model with 720 lines. Not all flat-panel sets are high definition, at least not at the 1,080 line level. Those that operate at the 720-line resolution automatically downgrade a full high-definition signal to the lower level. The same is true of rear projection and other types of DTVs. These sets are called enhanced-definition television, which is better than standard television, but not improved enough to be considered HDTV. The HDTV sets are more expensive, up to $6,500 or more in 2006. They also come with a label of either *i* (interlaced scanned video) or *p* (progressive scanned). Interlaced scanning means every other line is displayed, and a moment later the other lines are added to the image. This is how analog sets work, and it allows the picture to be displayed quickly but somewhat fuzzily, sometimes showing jagged edges when there is fast motion on the screen, such as in sports coverage. Progressive scan is a newer digital technology and is how computer displays work, as well as many DTV sets, including flat-panel displays. It draws each line separately and virtually instantly because of fast computer-processing chips. Thus, a 1080*p* set has a clearer picture than a 1080*i* set and has no jagged edges when there is on-screen motion, so of course high-definition *p* sets cost more.

There are also two types of high-definition DVD players: HD DVD and Blu-ray DVD. Both offer substantially higher resolution than conventional DVDs, which have 650 lines of resolution, although it is not clear whether viewers will see enough of a difference to warrant the cost differential. HD DVD players are entering the marketplace slowly, largely because of the high price, but also because of the lack of a common standard. An HD DVD player costs about $500 and a Blu-ray player about $1,000. A DVD made for the HD DVD will not play on the Blu-ray player and vice versa. Consequently, only about 1.5 million homes in the United States have high-definition DVD players. As of 2006, there were about one hundred HD DVD and fifty Blu-ray DVD titles in the marketplace. Both systems incorporate Advanced Access Content System copy controls to limit illegal copying of DVDs or music files. Blu-ray has a storage capacity of 50 GB for dual-layer discs, whereas HD DVD has an upper limit of 30 GB on a dual-layer disc. This difference enables the Blu-ray system to play back DVDs encoded at a higher level of resolution or of a longer length, but it is not yet clear whether viewers will discern a difference. As of 2006, it was also not known how many titles will top out beyond the 30 GB capacity. A sampling of movies on DVD gives an idea of general storage requirements: *The Last Samurai* (27.3 GB), Mel Brooks's *Blazing Saddles* (25.4 GB), *The Phantom of the Opera* (24.8 GB), *The Bourne Identity* (22.7 GB), and *The Fugitive* (18.2 GB). Time Warner is hoping that consumers will be more inclined to buy high-definition DVDs and players if the studios release movies encoded in both the Blu-Ray and HD DVD formats. At the Consumer Electronics Show in Las Vegas in January 2007, Warner Bros., a division of Time Warner, announced its new dual-format high-definition disc, dubbed the Total HD disc.[11] Some high-definition DVD players also offer the option to record video. Blu-ray vendors offer disc burners for desktop computers and mobile burners for notebooks.[12]

Regarding the high-definition DVD technology, it is important to emphasize that it is an unsettled technology. Because the HD DVD and

Blu-ray DVD are still competing for marketplace dominance, there is no universal standard yet. Either of the competing platforms may ultimately go the way of Betamax, which lost out in the 1970s to VHS-format videotape, an inferior (i.e., lower-resolution) television video recording and playback technology that gained an advantage in the marketplace and wound up becoming the standard. It is not yet clear whether HD DVD or Blu-ray is superior technologically, but consumers have shown a reluctance to buy either device because both are expensive and there is no guarantee which will last or dominate the market. In January 2007, South Korea's LG Entertainment announced its plan to introduce a dual-format high-definition DVD player.[13] At the same time, Time Warner announced that it would manufacture DVDs that contained both formats. However, each strategy will increase costs and may not resolve consumers' confusion.

VIDEO GAME CONSOLES

Transforming the fixed-location media device marketplace is a new generation of video game player consoles, including the Sony Playstation 3 (PS3), Microsoft Xbox 360, and Nintendo Wii. The PS3 combines both powerful video game technology and DVD Blu-ray technology, and the Xbox 360 includes HD DVD technology. One of the biggest drawbacks of these devices is the cost, about $500 each. "The PlayStation 3 will look very inexpensive [compared] to the Blu-ray (DVD) player," said Van Baker, an analyst at research firm Gartner. But it is still an expensive device. "You're paying 100 bucks for the privilege of having a Blu-ray player [built in]. It is a very aggressively priced movie player."[14] Video game consoles require a television or computer display to play the game as well as speakers for audio playback. By combining the Blu-ray DVD technology with the PS3 and the HD DVD technology with the Xbox 360, Sony and Microsoft are betting on the consumer's finding value in the combined functionality of the single device. These game players also include high-speed Internet connectivity to enable online game playing and downloading of software and movies. Nintendo's Wii has a unique feature in which the device that the user operates to play the games is a wireless handheld remote control embedded with a miniature, micron-size infrared sensor.[15] Through this image sensor, the Wii lets the user play a variety of physical games such as swinging a virtual baseball bat or firing a virtual weapon.

PERSONAL DIGITAL VIDEO RECORDERS

TV programming may sometimes start out analog, but a personal DVR, such as TiVo (a name created incorporating "TV" and the letters *i* for interactive and *o* for *vox*), can convert and record it digitally, giving the viewer greatly expanded control over the time and content of the viewing experience. Because DVRs were initially sold as an alternative to videocassette recorders, the market for them grew slowly at first, when the technology required the purchase of an expensive and separate box. The adoption of the DVR has paralleled the growth of digital cable and satellite TV, though; both services have begun to offer consumers a low-cost option to introduce a DVR device and service into the home. In these cases, the television signal is delivered in digital form to the home, where it is processed digitally by the DVR, and then can be displayed on either a DTV set or an analog one.[16]

John Carey, Fordham University professor and authority on telecommunications and interactive technologies, says DVRs have been slow to take off owing in part to "early high prices and in part to consumers not understanding what the technology can do."[17] Yet, Carey adds, "those who do have these devices report that they love them." DVRs can perform a number of functions, including automatically record programs without requiring a complex set up by the user. A typical DVR can record up to about thirty-five hours of high-definition programming or two hundred hours of standard-definition programming, but this capacity is purely a function of storage, and as storage prices fall, capacity will increase in future generations of DVR technology. DVRs also permit the viewer to pause live television, get instant replays of a program (e.g., during a game or a Super Bowl half-time show), access interactive program guides and other interactive features, and output recorded programs to portable media such as DVD or VHS tape. Some DVR systems notably include a popular "fast forward" feature that enables viewers to avoid watching commercials. The viewer navigates all these various features via a sophisticated wireless infrared remote control that permits not only channel surfing and volume control, but also program recording, playback, and other video management and interactivity such as home shopping.

DVRs cost about $300 to $800 for the set-top box. This cost is often covered by cable or satellite providers who subsidize the initial cost in order to obtain a monthly subscription fee. Monthly fees range from about $10 to $20. TiVo charges a monthly fee of $10 per month or $200 for a lifetime subscription. TiVo set-top boxes and video recorders are manufactured by a number of companies, including Sony and Phillips. As of January 2001, TiVo's subscriber base was 154,000, but by 2005 the number had topped 3 million.[18] With the integration of DVR boxes and service with DTV delivery such as cable or satellite, the adoption of DVRs in U.S. households is growing, according to "On-Demand TV 2006: A Nationwide Study on VoD [video on demand] and DVRs," a study by the Leichtman Research Group.[19] A study released by Mediamark Research reports DVR users are more affluent and consume more media.[20] These studies show that 12 percent of, or 18 million, U.S. households had a DVR as of 2006, a fourfold increase since 2004. DVR households record on average about eleven programs a week, a 23 percent rise from 2005.[21] It is expected by 2009 that more than 47 million U.S. households will have a DVR.[22] Adoption of DVR technology has grown rapidly internationally as well. A January 2007 report from B-Sky-B indicates that its subscribers had purchased more than 2 million DVRs.[23] With at least 20 million DVR users worldwide in 2006, the number is expected to reach 250 million by 2011.[24] Apple's DVR-type device, the AppleTV, combines DVR functionality with a wireless network capability to transmit multimedia such as movies, songs, and photos to other digital devices (television sets or computers) within the network range. AppleTV was selling for $299 in 2007.[25]

MOBILE ACCESS DEVICES

Mobile access, display, or playback media devices include at least three types of digital appliances: portable computers, digital cell phones, and specialized mobile digital devices. Portable computers come in laptop,

Figure 2.1 Lenovo ThinkPad X60 Tablet PC has a touch-sensitive screen that rotates. Photo used with permission of Lenovo.

notebook, tablet, and even pocket-size forms. Laptops are portable but slightly larger than notebooks, and they often have more functionality, such as a built-in DVD player. Notebooks are optimized for efficiency and lightweight portability. They are usually somewhat cheaper than laptops. Tablet computers are all-screen devices (sometimes with small keypads on the side) or hybrid laptop/tablets, such as the Lenovo X60 ThinkPad Tablet (see fig. 2.1), which has a keyboard as well as a 12-inch screen that flips around to fold flat.[26] Some tablets are lightweight, but others, such as the X60, can weigh four pounds or more. The screens on tablet computers are touch sensitive and are designed for rugged outdoor use. Some laptops, notebooks, and tablet computers are capable of playing video and of running a variety of media applications, and they may be used for media production such as video or audio editing. Increasingly, they have built-in broadband wireless capability, such as Wi-Fi. Although some laptops and notebooks are as cheap as $500, most run more than $1,000. Tablets typically start at about $1,500, but can run more than $4,000.

Even smaller are pocket-size computers. One notable example is the Oqo Model 2, a pocket-size computer with a slide-out keyboard and running the Windows Vista operating system.[27] Weighing less than a pound, the Oqo Model 2 measures 5.6 by 3.3 by 1.0 inches, has a 60 GB hard drive and a 5-inch display. It has many of the features of other mobile computers, including a Wi-Fi Internet connection, and sells for $1,499.[28] For size reasons, it does not have a DVD drive.

The high price of notebooks, laptops, and tablet computers has put them out of the range of many consumers, especially the economically disadvantaged. The problem has been especially acute in many developing nations. In response, MIT Media Lab founder Nicholas Negroponte and media research scientist Walter Bender have developed a fully functional $150 laptop computer for the developing world. The innovative laptop has a variety of features that make it possible to produce it for far less than the standard price. Among the adaptations is a low-power approach. The normal laptop requires about 45 watts of electricity and a powerful, heavy, and expensive battery that needs electricity to recharge. The $150 laptop runs on just 2 watts and gets its power from a hand crank. One minute of cranking gives the laptop ten minutes of use. Power is saved in an unconventional LCD display just 7.5 inches in size and illuminated with either backlighting or in low-power monochrome form (i.e., black and white). As a fortunate by-product, the display is easily visible in natural-lighting situations where the display of many conventional laptops is difficult to see because of glare and the bright illumination of sunlight. The $150 laptop has no hard drive. Rather, it relies completely on flash memory (solid-state computer memory), which is cheap, powerful, and uses little power. Moreover, flash memory means there are no mechanical or moving parts in the laptop, thereby saving even more money and power.[29] The use of flash memory has grown dramatically in the early years of the twenty-first century. In 2006, devices with flash memory amounted to 68 percent of all sales, according to the NPD Group, a research firm; flash memory was little used a decade earlier. Primary producers of flash memory are SanDisk, Creative, Samsung, and iRiver. Flash memory is significant in portable devices not only because it does not require any moving parts, but also because it can increase the speed of data recall compared to standard hard drives or CD-ROM drives. It also improves product durability and reduces cost and battery power needed.

The $150 laptop has a Wi-Fi connection and automatically builds a peer-to-peer mesh wireless network with other $150 laptops in the vicinity. The laptop also features a child-friendly intuitive design requiring little in the way of specialized training to use. A sealed rubber keyboard helps prevent against spillage problems. It runs on a slimmed-down version of the open-source Linux operating system.[30] This new laptop does not run the Windows operating system, and perhaps for this or other reasons Microsoft's founder Bill Gates has been critical of it.[31] Undeterred, Negroponte and his partners have won agreements from leaders of a variety of nations to purchase the laptop, including Argentina, Brazil, Libya, Nigeria, and Thailand. The goal is to have one laptop per child in those countries.[32]

Digital cell or mobile phones come in two basic forms. Most common are those designed primarily for voice communication but with limited additional media functionality. In addition are the so-called smart phones (some versions running Windows software are called a *pocket PC*), which feature not only voice communications, but also a wide range of other media capabilities, including Internet access. Cell phones designed mainly for voice communications but with limited media services typically include text messaging, picture taking, and image viewing. Wireless network access is relatively slow via services such as GPRS and is relatively expensive. Newer devices have added increasing capabilities, including downloading and playing MP3 music files, taking pictures, shooting video, and downloading and viewing video files. As such, these mobile phones represent a transitional form to the smart phone. One thing these devices typically lack is a full QWERTY keyboard (QWERTY refers to the upper-left top row of alphabetic keys on a keyboard). Instead, they have a standard twelve-key telephone keypad, with limited alphanumeric key entry.[33] The QWERTY keyboard was designed in the 1860s by Milwaukee newspaper editor Christopher L. Sholes, who also invented the first modern typewriter and used the QWERTY keyboard in his invention.[34] Sholes designed the QWERTY keyboard as an alternative to the then standard alphabetic keyboard, which often resulted in stuck keys during high-speed typing. The QWERTY design slowed down typing by spacing often-used keys far apart and thereby avoiding the stuck-key problem. Once established as the standard for all typing interfaces, including the computer, the QWERTY keyboard has itself stuck in the marketplace, despite the fact that its purpose is no longer relevant in that there are no mechanical or moving parts to get stuck while typing on a computer, cell phone, or other digital device. Nevertheless, absent reliable voice command or other methods for inputting complex information or instructions to computers, a keyboard of some sort is an essential tool for digital media devices.

Smart phones are convergent digital media devices that provide voice capability and a wide range of other media capabilities, for both consuming and producing media content. They also have full QWERTY keyboards, although the keyboards are usually small and require thumb typing. Smart phones are usually larger, thicker, and heavier than limited-function digital cell phones. Among the media applications available on most smart phones are playing MP3 files, recording audio, taking photographs, shooting and watching video, surfing the Web, sending and receiving e-mail, playing video games, and accessing the Internet via high-speed wireless connectivity. Broadband Internet access is sometimes provided via Wi-Fi or Bluetooth technology, although other options are also available.

As a veteran Treo user, I have extensive personal experience with a multifunction smart-phone device. Early Treo models ran exclusively the efficient and reliable Palm operating system. More recent Treo models also run Windows CE, a limited Windows operating system for mobile devices. In addition, the Treo has a camera and various other functions such as a Web browser and organizer; and users can install various functions such as an electronic book (eBook) reader. In early 2007, the Treo 750 was introduced as the first Treo offering Wi-Fi service. Previous models included only Bluetooth, a limited broadband wireless LAN technology that facilitated communication with other Bluetooth devices located within a few feet of each other. Bluetooth is not a primary means of high-speed wireless Internet access, but Wi-Fi provides this capability. Wi-Fi access also often costs little or is free to the user. It permits broadband wireless communications within about 200 feet of the base station. Bluetooth is typically limited to about 30 feet, although some services can reach up to about 330 feet.[35]

As an experiment for this book, I purchased on a two-week trial basis a T-Mobile mobile digital appliance (MDA) in August 2006. The T-Mobile MDA runs as its operating system Microsoft Windows CE. Equipped with various advanced features, it includes a high-resolution camera; Real Player for multimedia, including MP3s and video; IM capability; e-mail via GPRS; and (in comparison to the Treo) broadband wireless via both Bluetooth and Wi-Fi. Two weeks was long enough to evaluate the T-Mobile MDA fairly. Its advanced features, especially the Wi-Fi Internet access, are intriguing and promising. Unfortunately, compared to the Palm operating system, which boots up instantly, the Windows CE system is slow, clunky, and unstable, requiring at least five to ten seconds and sometimes much more time to start up. With a handheld device, this amount of time seems like an eternity and is simply far too slow. Also, the keyword search feature is slow. Synchronizing requires Outlook, which has both pros and cons. On the plus side, it means easy coordination with desktop e-mail, if one uses Outlook for e-mail. On the minus side, because I had been using the Treo device with the Palm system for several years, I had assembled a large and valuable database of contacts and a full datebook. Converting it was technically possible onto the MDA via Outlook, but after many hours and several days of work, only part of the address book and portions of the calendar had ported over, and large portions failed to synchronize. Synchronization was often slow and unreliable; the device would sometimes freeze and at other times would synchronize quickly. Whether it would synchronize was also uncertain. On both the T-Mobile MDA and the Treo, one can install and utilize eReader software, which is available for both Windows and Palm and is a smoothly operating piece of software. It allows users to access and display eBooks and other documents on their hand-helds. For me, this is a valuable tool. Available exclusively on hand-helds running Windows, Powerpoint is a nice application as well. Unfortunately, the T-Mobile MDA does not permit the user to project from the device onto a screen or to edit or create a Powerpoint file. Powerpoint is available only for viewing on the MDA, which is of limited utility. Certain devices can be attached to the MDA to permit the projection of a Powerpoint file from the MDA, but this approach defeats the purpose of utilizing a compact hand-held. Otherwise, one may as well use a compact laptop or notebook computer. Also worth considering are the Motorola Q, the Blackberry Pearl 8100, and the Cingular 8125 Pocket PC smart phones. All these devices include a full QWERTY keypad, e-mail and Web access, megapixel digital camera, media player, and mobile phone. Both the

Motorola Q and Cingular 8125 Pocket PC run Windows CE, whereas the Blackberry Pearl 8100 runs the Blackberry operating system. The Cingular device includes Wi-Fi, but suffers from some of the same flaws as the T-Mobile MDA.

Associated with these hand-helds are a variety of peripheral devices, including mini portable storage devices offering increasingly massive memory at low cost. The Treo, the T-Mobile MDA, and other similar smart phones incorporate expandable storage or memory slots in the form of mini standard flash memory storage disks (less than an inch in size and wafer thin) with up to 2 GBs of storage for as little as $69 in 2006. Costs for storage have been steadily dropping over the past fifty years, and there is no indication the trend will slow or stop in the coming years. Among the particularly useful portable storage devices for mobile media are Universal Service Buss (USB) sticks, which can plug into just about any standard digital device and can store one or more GBs of data for less than $100. USB sticks with 128 MBs of storage capability—enough to store thirty songs, ten or more digital books, one hundred photos, or ten minutes of digital video—are given away at trade shows. The Poynter Institute for Media Studies, for example, gave them away as promotional gifts to educators who attended the 2006 annual convention of the Association for Education in Journalism and Mass Communication and who signed up for Poynter's online journalism school, News University, funded by the Knight Foundation.[36] I gave my "bracelet USB stick" to my neighbor, a single parent raising four teenagers and in need of enhanced digital storage capabilities. Like most portable or desktop computers, Negroponte's $150 laptop features multiple USB ports that are useful for connecting USB sticks or many other USB-compatible devices (e.g., printers, cameras).

Specialized digital mobile devices are also increasingly common. They most often come in the form of an MP3 player for listening to music or other audio content, although increasingly these mobile MP3 players also feature video playback and viewing options via a small 2- or 3-inch LCD screen. Introduced into the marketplace in 2001, Apple's iPod dominated the market with a 70–80 percent market share in 2006.[37] However, MP3 players were available long before the introduction of the iPod. I still have and use a very reliable Kazoo MP3 player from RCA, four of which I bought for less than $100 each in 2000 for my family prior to our trip to

Singapore, where I was headed to be the inaugural Shaw Distinguished Visiting Professor of Media Technology at Nanyang Technological University. Weighing only a few ounces and fitting easily into the palm of one's hand, the Kazoo runs on two rechargeable AAA batteries and accepts an expandable memory card. Its only real flaw is that the software interface required to install music (MusicMatch) is no longer supported by RCA or anyone else. Competing with the iPod in 2007 are a variety of alternative MP3 players, many of them also capable of displaying video and performing other functions, as well as offering greatly expanded memory or music/video storage capability. Devices such as Microsoft's Zune pack 30 GBs of storage. The Zune also permits Zune-to-Zune music file sharing. Both the Zune and the iPod are on the pricey end of the MP3 spectrum, at about $250 or higher. Another interesting option is the Sansa player MP3 device. It offers only 8 GB of storage, but can play music or video with a nice 1.8-inch thin film transistor color screen in a sturdy package and for a lower price than some of the alternatives, at about $100. The audio and video run using the Windows Media Player 10. This means it can run any format file off subscription services such as Rhapsody or Napster. The device is not designed to play songs downloaded from iTunes, but with a little code added to a Mac, the iTunes file names can be modified so the Sansa will play the files.[38] A related audio device is the XM2Go portable satellite radio listening and recording device. Offered by XM Radio, the XM2Go permits users to access their satellite radio service from anywhere in North America, whether in their car, on foot or a bike, at home or office, with or without Internet access. Yet because the device is an MP3 recording and playback device, listeners have the option to record songs, create playlists, and listen to the music of their own choice rather than those of a central programmer.

Many of these specialized devices, including the iPod, are rapidly converging with cellular technology.[39] In June 2007, Apple introduced its new iPhone, a thin (11.6 millimeters) light-weight hybrid device that is both an iPod as well as a mobile phone, with a price tag of about $500.[40] It features a two-megapixel digital camera and other applications. The future will likely see more convergent handheld communication and media devices.

One of the interesting devices in the specialized category is the eBook reader. Early generations of eBook devices were of limited audience interest for several reasons: they were expensive, performed a single function, and were relatively large and heavy. Few consumers could justify spending several hundred dollars for a portable device on which to read an eBook when a paper form would be cheaper, lighter, and less damaged by accidental dropping. The latest eBook device introduced in late 2006 by Sony employs innovative electronic ink made by E Ink of Cambridge, Massachusetts.[41] The technology mimics the quality of regular paper. It is not backlit as are typical screens and requires a light source in the room to see the page of text, graphics, or images. At the same time, because it does not involve a backlit screen, it uses far less battery power. Complementing the eBook, the Sony Connect online bookstore carries about 10,000 books from six publishers, including HarperCollins of News Corporation and Simon & Schuster of CBS.[42] The Sony eBook, or Portable Reader, sells for about $350. Whether consumers will find the price tag acceptable for a single-function handheld device remains to be seen. Convergent eBook devices may have greater marketplace potential.

Portable video game players are also included in this category of specialized devices. Nintendo, Sony, and Microsoft are the leading providers of these players. However, none of the new generation of game players, such as the Nintendo Wii, Sony PS3, or Microsoft Xbox 360, includes portable versions, at least as of 2007.

DEVICES FOR VIEWING DIGITAL VIDEO

Viewing video distributed online requires a computer or a handheld device such as a video-enabled cell phone or some other digital video playback device and access to the Internet, typically broadband or high-speed access, either wireless or landline. Video providers are increasingly producing original video designed specifically for either online viewing or viewing on a small-screen mobile device. The screen size mandates special design considerations such as the use of only relatively large text on the screen for easy reading; usually reduced amounts of text; still images that require less bandwidth; and different types of shot selection, framing, and editing of pictures. For example, long shots with small objects are almost useless when displayed on a small screen because the viewer is unable to discern what they are. Close-ups are particularly important, and limited camera movements are required because excessive or rapid panning, zooming, and other camera movements may result in pixelation when delivered online, especially via wireless delivery media.

The online video explosion is about more than just television. In fact, it forces a reconsideration of just what constitutes television. Listening to satellite radio on May 3, 2006, I heard a decades-old but still funny comedy routine by Bill Cosby about what he called the inherent stupidity of watching golf on television. What made it especially amusing to me, an avid golfer who likes watching golf on television, was Cosby's reference to the plethora of television channels available at the time: a whopping seven. Today, with satellite and cable television systems, most U.S. homes have access to hundreds of channels of scheduled, premium, and on-demand video programming delivered to their "television set." Through broadband Internet access, oftentimes through the same digital network delivering television programming, these same homes can have access to potentially millions of "channels," if that is the right word for it, of video programming, whether scheduled or on demand, free or for purchase, delivered to their computer or another digital device such as a personal digital appliance or cell phone. In terms of video volume, the online video/television offers millions of hours of viewing, and this amount is growing dramatically each day. The biggest challenge for many users or audience members is finding the video they want or might enjoy watching.

Watching video on any digital device requires a software player. These players are usually available for free, although sometimes there are fee-based advanced players with more features or capable of playing video at a higher quality of resolution, frame rate, and size, or capable of offering additional premium content. Video software players sometimes come preinstalled on digital devices or computers, but downloading, installing, and upgrading may be needed or recommended. Upgrades add features for the viewer, but they also can include hidden tools that allow distributors to better track viewing or to restrict viewing based on copyright restrictions. In September 2005, the BBC provided some 5,000 of its viewers with a computer program called the interactive media player, which allowed them to download most of the BBC's television programs for up to seven days. Among the programs available for online viewing were the long-running soap opera *EastEnders*, nightly newscasts, and major sporting events.[43]

Cell phones typically require additional technology (hardware and software) to view video programs downloaded from the Internet. One such device is the Slingbox, which attaches to a high-speed Internet access device such as a home computer and then uses wireless technology to deliver the video content to a cell phone.[44] Consumer electronics giant Sharp reports that it will soon introduce an LCD-screen TV for the Japanese market that enables viewers to watch HDTV, use a remote control to access the Internet, and store TV shows on an internal hard drive (or DVR).[45]

DIGITAL AUDIO

Audio playback has also been transformed by digital technology. Not only are portable devices equipped with powerful playback technology, but home entertainment systems feature advanced digital sound systems that were once the exclusive province of movie theaters. Surround-sound systems featuring Dolby Digital high-definition sound or Digital Theatre Systems audio technology are common to new DVD or HDTV systems, and with powerful subwoofers they pack an impressive audio experience into the home theater. Price is still a significant factor because these systems can run up from $150.

One of the problems inherent in all digital devices is that because they are computer based, they periodically need to be rebooted. From time to time, their internal processors get clogged up with various programming snafus, and even the best-designed devices will slow down or stop working altogether. The only way to get them to run effectively again is to give them a hard reset or restart by powering them down and then up again after a thirty-second or so delay. Some devices will automatically do this when they detect a problem. At other times, the user must do the restart, which may even require an additional digital signal from a cable or other system provider, much to the viewer's annoyance because he or she may have to wait minutes or sometimes hours and may miss a scheduled program or recording. Powering down a device incorrectly or unplugging a device incorrectly can cause internal computer problems, such as erasing the memory or worse, which can of course cause much consternation for the user. The reboot problem is one new to the digital age and did not plague analog devices.

NEXT-GENERATION TECHNOLOGIES

Future directions in digital display technologies will likely reflect at least three trends. First, display technologies are on a trajectory of increasing miniaturization. As a consequence of Moore's Law, which says that the number of transistors on a computer chip doubles every eighteen months, leading to faster more powerful computing technology in less space, display technologies are getting lighter, cheaper, and less intrusive.[46] Wireless Bluetooth ear pieces for voice communications are already increasingly prevalent. In addition, the relative portion of users who are finding wearable media technologies acceptable is growing, and as more media applications emerge for wearables, usage will increase. In 2007, most wearable devices involve audio media for listening to music or voice communications. Wearable visual displays are growing in effectiveness and utility and will likely emerge as a next-generation technology. Possible harmful health consequences of long-term use of wearable electronic devices, including cell phones, is a subject of some concern and research.[47] I examine this topic in further detail in chapter 12, on children and digital media.

Second, the intuitiveness of the devices' design is continuing to improve, especially for human users without advanced training. The devices seem more natural to use, and a wider spectrum of users thus find them more palatable. Their adoption will thus continue to grow toward 100 percent penetration of the marketplace.

Finally, and not unrelated to the previous two trends, more and more devices are capable of multiple functions. Single-function access and display devices are gradually fading in the marketplace as users find that multifunction devices mean less to carry yet expanded capabilities.

BATTERIES

Power is a necessary part of all devices for accessing media. Although in some cases power is available through a wall outlet, mobile devices rely on batteries, and batteries have historically been a significant complication and constraint in all devices' design and utility. In short, batteries have had a variety of problems. Although they generally will not pose a danger to the user of mobile media devices because of their low amperage, several computer manufacturers were forced to announce product recalls in 2006 (e.g., Dell's recall of 4.1 million laptop batteries in 2006) because a widely used Sony battery was found prone to overheating and catching fire. In addition to this hazard, batteries have been limited by their short life (generally less than ten hours of continuous use without recharging), weight, and size. After several years of use, most batteries will no longer hold a charge and must be replaced. Battery disposal is also an environmental problem, and recycling of batteries (and of computers in general) has been slow to develop. Because of their ubiquitous demand, portable rechargeable batteries constituted a $6.2 billion market in 2006, a market that will likely continue to grow in the decade ahead and beyond. Companies such as Sony, Sanyo, Matsushita, and Samsung will produce more than one billion batteries in 2007.

One of the difficulties in making batteries that are more powerful in smaller packages is that those batteries become more volatile and potentially unstable, thus the spate of notebook battery fires in 2006. The chemical composition of lithium-ion batteries is the trigger for fire: carbon, oxygen, and a flammable fluid. "The battery is made of a thin layer of lithium cobalt oxide, which serves as the cathode, and a strip of graphite, the anode," note Damon Darlin and Barnaby J. Feder. "These are separated by a porous insulator and surrounded by fluid, a lithium salt electrolyte that happens to be highly flammable."[48] Lithium ions on a charged battery move from the cathode to the anode to provide the energy as the battery is used. While charged, the cathode is highly unstable without most of its ions. Should a spark happen, the temperature of the cathode can top 275 degrees, hot enough to cause the cathode to release oxygen. "A fire starts, and as heat builds," Darlin and Feder explain, "the battery begins what scientists call a 'thermal runaway.' In the case of the Sony-made batteries recalled by Dell, a microscopic metal particle that contaminated the electrolyte during manufacturing caused the spark."

To avoid flammability, researchers are working on developing batteries that do not contain carbon, oxygen, and fuel, but such power sources are likely years away from the marketplace. An alternative is the development of miniaturized versions of the fuel cells being created for cars. Fuel cells involve hydrogen rather than oxygen. Such microcells hold great potential for laptops, cell phones, and other portable devices because they can retain up to ten times the power of batteries of similar size.

Nanotechnology, which involves technology manufacturing on a molecular scale, may also help in the development of miniature batteries. "Designer" molecules may serve as catalysts for fuel cells. Intel and IBM have announced a remedy that works from the other side of the problem—battery consumption. They have created a chip that consumes much less power than previous generations of chip sets.

CONCLUSION

Devices for accessing or displaying digital content are undergoing dramatic change. They are becoming more intuitive in design, lightweight, unobtrusive, portable, less expensive, increasingly powerful, and multifunctional. Virtually all types of media content are available through these digital devices, whether text, images, motion pictures, sound, or any combination of these modalities.

One of the problems in this arena is the continually changing technology and lack of uniform standards. Consumers who want to access media using devices with the latest tools face an expensive proposition, not to mention potentially rapidly obsolete devices. Moreover, many devices are customized for particular content distributed by proprietary commercial services. For example, a device optimized for music downloaded from iTunes may not play MP3 files downloaded from Napster, and vice a versa, at least not without hacking the software code, a challenge potentially worthy of Robert Langdon of *Da Vinci Code* fame. This topic of *digital rights management,* as it is known, is examined in chapter 8 on regulation of and law for media in the digital age.

3 / AUDIENCES OR USERS OF DIGITAL MEDIA

"Audience" is an evolving concept. In the days of terrestrial broadcast television and radio, and even in the early days of cable, television viewers and radio listeners were typically called the *audience*. This term was also sometimes used to describe those who read the newspaper or consumed any of the other mass media, such as magazines, books, and movies. *Audience* suggests a passive receiver of mediated messages. Something of a marketing term, it reflects the idea that the media are delivering audiences to advertisers. It is increasingly becoming antiquated, however. In today's digital, online age, video is not just something people watch. Newspapers are no longer something people just read (if they ever did, among coupon clippers or letter-to-the-editor writers). When people go online to a newspaper Web site for the latest news, they often post comments on the paper's discussion board and navigate the paper's multimedia and search tools. They are no longer passive couch potatoes, at least not much of the time.

More appropriate terms for many consumers of media are *user* and *producer*. The video user is becoming far more active or interactive. Video is downloaded, accessed on demand, stored or saved for later viewing, fast-forwarded through, searched, sorted, edited, redistributed, uploaded, clicked on or otherwise manipulated in video games, and subject to a host of rapidly evolving interactive features. Only occasionally is it just watched. Users are often highly mobile and watch short video segments, sometimes serialized and viewed on demand, and sometimes for a fee. Users equipped with video-capable cell phones or other MDAs shoot their own videos and transmit them to friends or family. Although the practice has been slow to develop in the United States, users in many other parts of the world where advanced digital cellular networks are already in place engage in high-quality video phone calls from one mobile device to another. I tested one such system while visiting Stockholm, Sweden, in November 2005 and found the video more than satisfactory in terms of resolution, frame rate, and audio quality.

As discussed in chapter 1 on delivery media, users of digital media can access and interact with media content in a variety of ways. Numbers of users or audience members are aggregated, or counted, according to the three digital media forms they use: television viewers; listeners to radio, also increasingly digital in form; and Internet users. For each of these three main forms, there are user subcategories worth noting, such as broadband Internet users, terrestrial versus satellite radio listeners, and cable versus telephone versus satellite versus over-the-air television viewers.

This discussion begins with an examination of overall Internet usage, primarily in the United States, but with some international discussion for comparison purposes, as well as a look at broadband, or high-speed, Internet usage, which is rapidly becoming the norm. Then the chapter looks at users of digital television and radio, as well as of other media types. Finally, much of the chapter is devoted to the convergence and interactive transformation of the media user from passive to active, to the problem of the digital divide, and to the potential social and political ramifications of the evolving media system, such as social fragmentation and the evolution of the public sphere in the digital age.

INTERNET USERS

Overall Internet usage in the United States has stabilized during the past few years, reaching 74 percent in February 2006. With a U.S. population in excess of 300 million, this means there are at least 225 million Internet users in the country, combining usage at home, work, and school.[1] Estimates from Nielsen/NetRatings released on March 14, 2006, show the number of U.S. households with a broadband Internet connection increased 28 percent in just twelve months, rising from 74.3 million in February 2005 to 95.5 million in February 2006. With roughly two persons per broadband household, this means that the majority of those in the United States who go online do so via a broadband connection.

Table 3.1 Broadband Internet Delivery in the United States
(MILLIONS OF HOMES)

Year	Cable Modem	Digital Subscriber Line	Satellite	Fixed Wireless	Power Line	TOTAL
2001	5.5	2.5	0.3	0.2	—	8.5
2002	7.9	4.4	0.5	0.4	—	13.2
2006	26.9	21.3	1.5	0.5	0.1	50.3

The broadband structure of the U.S. Internet user base has been grow-ing steadily, jumping at least 10 percent annually. Home broadband pen-etration was 33 percent in February 2003, 45 percent in February 2004, 55 percent in February 2005, and 68 percent in February 2006.

Table 3.1 outlines the growth of broadband services to the home in the United States since 2001.[2] Note that the number of homes is in mil-lions; the number of Internet users, including broadband, is of course higher because households on average have more than one person. International patterns of broadband growth are similar to those in the United States, especially in information societies, including Europe and parts of Asia, such as South Korea, Taiwan, and Japan. Some portions of the world lag behind, especially less-developed economic regions, in-cluding much of Africa, Latin America, and the Middle East. In these regions, the digital divide is significant.

Although access technology has become increasingly ubiquitous, digi-tal devices to go online are often expensive and sometimes rapidly obso-lete. The cost and need for replacement or frequent upgrade have helped generate a digital divide between those with the means or resources to acquire and utilize these devices and those without the means or the ed-ucation. Access problems are especially acute between the urban middle and upper classes, on the one hand, and low-income inner-city groups, on the other, as well as between suburban and rural areas. Low-income inner-city groups, often of minority racial or ethnic backgrounds, and rural communities suffer from less access to devices and to the band-width for high-speed Internet service. A 2006 Pew survey of people eigh-teen years and older in the United States showed that the disparity in Internet access between whites and blacks narrowed only somewhat in the previous decade.[3] In 1998, 42 percent of white American adults said they used the Internet, compared to just 23 percent of African American adults (a gap of 19 percentage points). By February 2006, 74 percent of white adults said they go online, compared to 61 percent of African Americans (a gap of 13 percentage points). In contrast, 80 percent of English-speaking Hispanic Americans say they go online.[4] The survey did not examine non-English-speaking Hispanic Americans, but it is suspected that Internet usage is significantly lower among this group.

Taken as a whole, the gap in access to digital technologies tends to expand further the economic disparities that already exist between higher and lower socioeconomic groups. Ironically, rather than enable the gap to narrow, these potentially democratizing technologies can result in just the opposite impact. Social mobility and equality can also be adversely affected, as those with less access to digital media devices may be at a disadvantage educationally. This technologically enabled inequality is even more severe beyond the geographic and political boundaries of the United States and of other Western and advanced information technology societies. In much of Africa, especially sub-Saharan Africa; much of South Asia and the Pacific; portions of the Caribbean, especially countries such as Haiti, the Dominican Republic, and Cuba; as well much of Central and South America, the digital device divide is significant and worsening rather than improving. One country in particular has suffered from limited access to the Internet: North Korea, increasingly isolated politically, economically, and socially from much of the world and in economic decline, has almost no Internet access (see chapter 8).

USERS OF OTHER DIGITAL MEDIA

Many media now in digital format are delivered via the Internet and World Wide Web. They include online newspapers and magazines, books delivered electronically, and other traditional media (e.g., online music and video). The user base of these online, digital media is large and growing rapidly. What is lagging far behind in many cases is an effective business model to support online digital media. Chapter 7 examines this topic in detail. In addition, video games, which are now fully digital, have a large and rapidly growing audience, including not just for specialized game player consoles, but also on multipurpose handheld mobile devices, such as mobile phones.

Table 3.2 Digital Media Users in the United States 2006 (MILLIONS)

Year	Digital Cable TV Subscribers	DBS Subscribers	Video Game Players	Satellite Radio Subscribers	Online News Consumers	Online Video Users
2006	33	27	145	12	164	107

Table 3.2 provides a summary of the audience or user patterns for other media in digital format.[5] As the table shows, DTV has a substantial audience. The subscriber base for digital cable is 33 million. The average cable TV household has two or more persons, making the digital cable TV audience, or interactive user base, at least 66 million persons, assuming each person in the household at least occasionally views some television.

DTV's audience is actually substantially higher than the numbers for digital cable TV alone would suggest. Another 27 million households subscribe to DBS, and with an average household size of at least two persons, the viewing audience for satellite DTV is more than 54 million persons (very few homes subscribe to both cable and satellite, so it is reasonably safe to add these numbers for an accurate net total). Add to that total the growing number of subscribers to DTV service via digital telephony (a relatively small number as of late 2006, but poised to grow rapidly as more local communities and their public-utility commissions permit telephone companies to deliver television service), and the overall viewership of digital television comes to at least 120 million persons, perhaps closer to 150 million, or roughly half of the total U.S. population. A growing portion of Americans go online to watch television programming. One in ten Americans watches broadcast television programs online, according to the *Conference Board Consumer Internet Barometer Study* released on October 25, 2006.[6] This national survey of 10,000 households across the United States shows that news is the most popular form of online programming viewed and that people watch TV online because of personal convenience and the absence of commercials. Yet few indicate they would be willing to pay for online television programs.

Viewing Video Online Around the World

The trend toward watching television programming online is not unique to the United States. A November 2006 survey by the BBC shows a similar pattern of increased viewing of television online in the United Kingdom.[7] Young persons are especially likely to watch video online or on mobile devices. More than 28 percent of those age sixteen to twenty-four in the United Kingdom watch video online or on mobile devices more than once each week. Roughly 10 percent of those age twenty-five to forty-four are regular viewers of online video. But just 4 percent of those older than forty-five watch video online regularly. Yet three-quarters of all U.K. Internet video users say they watch more online video in 2006 than they did in 2005. Of some concern for traditional television distributors, one in five people who watch online or mobile video at least once a week report watching much less conventional television as a result. Approximately one-quarter (23 percent) say they watch slightly less TV as a result of watching online video.

Many homes are also equipped with DVD players and other devices for viewing digital video, or what might be termed DTV, and many others view digital video via broadband Internet. Although these homes are no doubt duplicative with other DTV venues (i.e., they have multiple DTV devices in their homes, and they can use other DTV venues outside their homes), the total number of persons in the United States who viewed at least some digital video, or what might be called DTV, was likely at least 200 million as of 2006. Few homes are currently equipped to view DTV programming delivered via terrestrial broadcast television, but the number will likely grow in coming years, which will add to the overall DTV viewership.

Digital radio has a sizeable audience that is growing rapidly.[8] Some 12 million persons subscribe to digital satellite radio. Many subscribers are part of households with more than one member, which likely increases the listenership significantly. This number is further expanded because satellite radio services are also available to subscribers for online listening. We can also add the more than 28 million persons who listen to other digital radio services online, such as online radio stations. Arbitron/Edison Media Research reports that since 2005, the weekly Internet radio audience has increased 50 percent in the United States to roughly 28 million persons.[9] As of May 2006, 12 percent of Americans older than the age of twelve listened to Internet radio each week, a 50 percent increase since May 2005, when just 8 percent listened to Internet radio each week. For persons age eighteen to thirty-four, nearly one in five (16 percent) listened to online radio during the past week.[10]

XM Radio had just less than 8 million subscribers at the end of 2006, and Sirius Satellite Radio had just more than 6 million.[11] They announced plans to merge by the end of 2007. In addition, most terrestrial radio stations are now broadcasting digitally, and many millions of consumers have digital radio receivers, particularly in their cars. Satellite and online radio may be expanding the audio listenership pie. Analog radio has become largely an automobile market, but with Internet, satellite, and cable delivering audio or radio programming, the home market and the mobile audio market outside the home show signs of growing. Where this leaves traditional, over-the-air radio is unclear. The conversion of analog stations to digital terrestrial transmission opens new possibilities of delivering a new form of radio potentially more attractive to an increasingly demanding and sophisticated radio audience.

Combining the reach of the various digital delivery platforms, the total listenership for digital radio is likely in excess of 50 million in the United States. However, the terms *listenership* and *radio* may be somewhat obsolete or in need of a radical overhaul. Although digital services continue many of the traditions that define radio in its predominantly analog days, digital radio is really much more than just centrally programmed audio content. Listeners are highly involved and engaged interactively with many digital audio or radio services. They click on links for additional text or multimedia content that complements the audio. They click to indicate their listening preferences and tastes. They click to record a song or artist. They create their own station or playlist. They view text or graphic displays on screens that tell the name of the song or artist.

At the same time, listening to radio, at least in its traditional form, is declining or, at best, stagnant, especially for young people, historically one of the stronger audiences for the medium. Data from Edison Media Research show that since 1996, listenership for radio has dropped 20 percent among teenagers in the United States, a rather precipitous decline. In 1996, youths from ages twelve to seventeen listened to radio (then almost exclusively analog) an average of about 15.75 hours per week. By 2006, average weekly listenership in this age group had dropped to 12.75 hours per week. This decline is due largely to the rise of digital, on-demand interactive media such as MP3 players, IM, blogs, social-networking Web sites, cell phones, and the like, explains Larry Rosin, president of Edison Media Research.[12] This dramatic decline in the radio audience brings to mind a conversation between me and my now twelve-year-old daughter a few years earlier when on a family road trip. She said, "Daddy, I don't like this song. Can you play my favorite one instead?" I responded, "Sorry, sweetheart. This is radio. You can't just play any song you like whenever you want it. It's not like on the Internet or your MP3 player." To which she stated, "I don't like radio."

Video games have become a major part of the digital media mix, with an estimated 145 million Americans routinely playing them. As of 2007, they are virtually all digital,[13] a dramatic increase since the invention of the first video game in 1971, when Arcade-game manufacturer Nutting Associates produced the first *Computer Space* machine, which was packaged with a 13-inch black-and-white analog television set.[14] Perhaps surprisingly to some, the overwhelming majority of video game players are not children. In fact, the average age of a gamer in the United States is thirty-three, and 25 percent of the players are fifty or older. The majority of gamers are male (71 percent). But there are really two types of gamers: casual and serious. Nearly three-quarters (71 percent) of all casual gamers are forty years old or older, and even more of the total (76 percent) is female.[15] Casual gamers play games that have simple graphics and less complex rules, similar to the classic Pong, and do not usually require a significant time commitment, and they can play them on cell phones. Serious gamers focus more on sophisticated and intensive games such as the online game *World of Warcraft,* which make up a significant portion of the $30 billion worldwide video game industry.

Video games have developed into a full-fledged virtual sport, with major competitive events around the globe, many of them extensively covered by media and many watched online by large and growing audiences. The world's top gamer is a twenty-something known as Fata1ty because of all the killing he does in online games, and whose real name is Johnathan Wendel.[16] Fata1ty has won more than $300,000 in six years of video game tournament playing. The tournaments are now typically broadcast live online to audiences in excess of 100,000. Compare that number to the viewership of the top-rated program on CNBC, a leading financial journalism cable channel. In 2006, the top-rated show was *Mad*

Money, featuring Jim Cramer, former journalist and wealthy Wall Street trader, drawing an audience of 350,000. Does an audience of 100,000 qualify as mass media? Maybe not. But many shows on cable and satellite draw audiences of about that size.

One of the more unusual but revealing video games is called *Second Life.*[17] It is a three-dimensional online virtual reality populated by 1,814,140 persons from around the world as of December 4, 2006. It is targeted at adults, and an alternative version, *Teen Second Life,* is aimed at a thirteen- to seventeen-year-old audience.[18] Community standards are clearly laid out for both environments, and participants are expected to follow the rules for appropriate behavior and can have their accounts terminated for inappropriate behavior. It is an online virtual-reality game created by the Linden Company, based in San Francisco. In *Second Life,* which opened to the public in 2003, each participant creates an avatar, a three-dimensional representative of himself or herself, and then enters the virtual world. Fairly realistic in appearance, *Second Life* gives the user a highly involving experience in virtual or computer-based reality. Users communicate primarily via text messages, but can also send and receive audio and video files, including streaming video. Some users have also incorporated Internet telephone services, such as Skype (discussed more fully in chapter 4), into their *Second Life* interactions. I joined *Second Life* as "Quentin Yap" in 2006. Because I was new to online virtual realities populated by other people, my first experience was somewhat unsettling. Only moments into the virtual reality I encountered more than half a dozen people—or, rather, avatars operated by real people. More than 12,000 people were simultaneously logged into *Second Life* at the same time, and more than 600,000 players, including me, had logged on during the previous six months. *Second Life* features many intriguing dimensions, including an economy based on Linden Dollars, which as of December 2006 could be redeemed for actual U.S. dollars at a conversion rate of three hundred to one. The U.S. Internal Revenue Service is reportedly looking into how to tax such transactions, although critics contend such a plan would be a mistake.[19] *Second Life* includes real estate, journalists who report on the virtual reality, and a college with actual classes. The visualizations of scenes in the virtual reality are complex and detailed, and they are continually evolving as members can either select from predesigned appearances

Figure 3.1 Mint Powers empowers her creator in *Second Life*. Image used with permission from Deirdre Scott, DesignPolice.

or design their own. Basic membership is free, but a premium level of membership gives users access to advanced capabilities and experiences. One intriguing *Second Life* character is Mint Powers, an animated black superhero created in December 2002 during the beta phase of the game by Deirdre Scott, technologist, visual arts curator, and founder of DesignPolice. Mint lives in the Green Region of *Second Life* and is CEO of her own company (see fig. 3.1). *Second Life* has captured considerable media attention for some of its more unusual features. ABC's *Good Morning America,* the BBC, and the *New York Times* have profiled it. One of the more intriguing aspects of *Second Life* is that it features a campus of the New Media Consortium, which sometimes provides mixed-reality experiences[20] One such mixed reality was a MacArthur Foundation press conference hosted on the New Media Consortium campus, where the launching of a major funding initiative to support research on new technologies was announced. *Second Life* also offers a highly developed digital library on its "Information Island." Real-world librarians have taken considerable interest in this online library initiative.[21]

Online communities can also generate political agendas that reach beyond the realm of the virtual. One example is the Active Citizen Project.[22] In this virtual community, people make platforms for their real-world communities and design media messages to convince other participants in the virtual community to vote for their platforms. Then the participants vote and take these platforms to elected real-world leaders as a mandate.[23] In 2006, votes were taken to determine what problems in major urban areas such as New York and Philadelphia were of the greatest concern to the citizenry. Top problems identified were crime (chosen by 1,350 persons), the economy (420), education (291), and discrimination (159). The basic right that people say they are missing the most is freedom of speech (chosen by 872).

A NIGHT (AND DAY) AT THE OPERA: WHEN OLD MEDIA MEET NEW

Tuesday, August 22, 2006, started out with a plan: to get the kids up at 7:00 A.M., be on the road by 7:30, and arrive at the Delacorte Theater in Central Park, New York City, by 8:30 to get tickets for a free performance of the Public Theater. Up until 8:30, the plan worked almost perfectly. The trip to Manhattan was uneventful, with little traffic, even crossing the George Washington Bridge. We drove to West Eighty-First Street and Central Park West in under an hour and unloaded the minivan for a stroll into the park on a warm summer day. But at the theater, a small, newly posted sign threw a monkey wrench into the otherwise best-laid plans. That night's performance of Bertolt Brecht's *Mother Courage and Her Children,* starring Meryl Streep and Kevin Kline, was canceled due to a neighboring free performance of the Metropolitan Opera in the park's Great Lawn.

Initially disappointed but undaunted, we looked around and spoke to a few other frustrated (at least momentarily) would-be theater goers. The options quickly became clear: either leave the park and return Thursday for the next free performance of *Mother Courage* but arrive closer to 6:00 A.M. to get tickets because of all the potential pent-up demand or walk over to the Great Lawn, stake a spot with a blanket and chairs, and wait for the free opera at 8:00 P.M. With a laptop and mobile personal digital assistant (PDA) in hand, the family was able to make a decision easily.

I would sit with the stuff, log onto the recently installed Central Park free Wi-Fi network, keep working on my book, do e-mail, and read the *New York Times* online. The other family members would visit a nearby museum. Having arrived relatively early before the formation of the eventual 50,000-person crowd (as noted that day by Peter Gelb, general manager of the Metropolitan Opera), we got a prime location directly in front of the stage about 50 meters from the performers. While waiting throughout the day from this almost front-row seat, I could watch the latest video postings on the crisis in the Middle East, read reviews of the opening night performance of *Mother Courage* from just the previous evening, and decide whether a 6:00 A.M. return visit would be worth it on Thursday. Not only that, but I could enjoy the rehearsal of the full orchestra and vocalists that precedes the opera's opening-night live evening performance. I even made it onto a Korean television digital newscast when a crew captured audience reactions during the rehearsal. Once the rehearsal concluded, I could listen to music on my MP3 player or digital radio built into my PDA, also a phone and camera, which would come in handy for recording the day's activities and perhaps posting them to my blog. My family would rejoin me during the afternoon, providing food and bathroom breaks. The kids could watch a DVD of the just-released *Pirates of the Caribbean.*

The day featured glorious sunshine and a gentle breeze on a mid-August day. Power would be no problem with a spare laptop battery and a solar battery charger. So much for late-summer dog day afternoons in New York. Later, we could enjoy an online reprise of the live performance. Mr. Gelb announced that Met concerts would now be available via the Internet and satellite radio.[24] Viva *La Traviata* in the digital age of media.

Media in the digital age have become ubiquitous, interactive, mobile and portable, wireless, on demand, modality rich, and instantaneous. Some of these qualities are certainly also characteristic of analog media. Printed newspapers, magazines, books, and transistor radios are portable; television is modality rich. But many of these qualities are unique to the digital age and are heightened intensely or combined in a technological milieu known as digital convergence. Not all the features of digital-age media are improvements, at least from the audience perspective. Cost is perhaps the biggest setback. These media are not cheap. Content is often cheap or even free to the audience in the digital age, but it is also some-times quite expensive and increasingly so. It is never really free. In the age of analog media, the real product being sold by media organizations was the audience. The audience was being aggregated by content dis-tributed free or at low cost for the purpose of delivering an accumulated audience to advertisers seeking to mass-market a product at a relatively low cost per thousand pairs of eyes or ears. Although some media con-tent was sold at a low cost to audiences, such as a fifty-cent newspaper, most of the cost of producing, printing, and delivering the paper was covered by advertising. The low newsstand price was in effect subsidized by the advertising. The role of the audience in the media cost equation is evolving significantly in the digital age. Although audiences are obtain-ing more control over their media, they are also shouldering more of the cost burden. Consider the migration of the NFL's *Monday Night Football* in 2006 from ABC, where it had been broadcast free since its inception as analog TV more than thirty years earlier, to cable's ESPN, also a Disney property, but now digital and no longer free to the viewer. Moreover, the technology to access digital-age media is not cheap. The Media Lab's $150 laptop is an exception; most media devices are not affordable to all in the digital age. This means an expanding digital divide and potential gap between media rich and poor, a social fragmentation and eventual erosion of the information glue that serves to hold democracy together.

Technology exerts a sometimes subtle but profound influence on the political and social fabric, as outlined by Neil Postman in *Technopoly: The Surrender of Culture to Technology* (1993).[25] With a growing gap between the media rich and the media poor in the digital age, these subtle and sometimes not-so-subtle effects will likely be more negative than posi-tive for society and the political process. Groups such as the economi-cally disadvantaged and rural will likely be increasingly excluded from important economic opportunities afforded by digital, networked media as well as online discourse and debate about matters of public impor-tance. As Pierre Levy notes, cyberspace has important implications for how we learn and communicate, and groups with poor or no online access will be excluded from these opportunities[26] Some barriers will be physical, others psychological. Social theorist Jean Baudrillard contends that media, particularly in the digital age, are for many people replacing reality with an artificial copy world.[27] In this hyperreality, as he calls it, people seek simulated stimuli and little more. They have only reality by proxy. For instance, a person viewing dramatic video depictions of violent behavior may psychologically move into a world where the reality of violence is replaced by the perceived reality of violence. These media portrayals are oftentimes highly unrealistic, although visually compelling, and show little of the long-term and emotional consequences of violence. This problem is exacerbated in the digital age where online and immersive media make living in a media hyperreality even more intense, plausible, and ubiquitous.

TAKING CONTROL

While writing this chapter, I noticed my thirteen-year-old daughter Tristan sitting in front of a computer. I asked her what she was doing, and she replied, "Watching the news." Taking a closer look, I saw that she was watching a video produced by the *New York Times* and available on the nytimes.com home page. "What's the story about?" I inquired. "It's about a candidate for mayor of Newark," she replied. The video was seamlessly playing in nearly full-screen mode, with high-quality audio, and with what a professional might call broadcast-quality production values. A quick perusal of the nytimes.com site reveals a selection of well-done video reports on a variety of topics, ranging from breaking news to technology reports. If my experience with my daughter is any indication, the video news habits of the elusive next-generation "audience" are undergoing a dramatic transformation. Data from a number of other sources confirm this sea change—which some might call more of a tsunami.

According to comScore/Media Metrix estimates, more than half (56 percent) of the U.S. online audience has viewed streaming videos in the past year. Consumers viewed 3.7 billion video streams in March 2006 and about one hundred minutes of video content per viewer per month, compared to an average of eighty-five minutes in October 2005.[28] Video viewing on cell phones is expected to rise in the coming years as the number of video-enabled cell phones rises from 3 million in the United States in 2006 to an estimated 15 million by 2009.[29]

I surveyed my students at Rutgers University to explore the younger generation's views on and experience with online and mobile video.

Although this sampling was admittedly nonscientific, the comments from selected students offer a somewhat pixelated window into the world of new media from a user perspective. The results suggest that although some users embrace mobile and online video, they do so with certain expectations and concerns about the quality of the experience as it compares to more traditional media, digital or analog.

Student One: I watched an animated short that a friend "gifted" to me via iTunes. It was OK, but I enjoyed it much more when I hooked my iPod to my multimedia dock and watched the same video on my TV. Even in its compressed format, the picture was pretty good, and it sounded better on my speakers than it did coming from my earbuds.

Student Two: I think movie shorts and music videos or short newscasts would be fine on a hand-held device. Apple just came out with an iPod capable of handling feature-length movies. Even with the longer battery life and brighter screen, it's the screen size that's the real issue. I'm a bit of a movie buff, and my preferred format is to watch a movie in letterbox on my TV with surround sound. You just wouldn't get the same experience watching a movie on your iPod. On the other hand, by carrying a dock [device to connect two devices] with you, you're not tied to whatever movies happen to be on offer at your hotel when traveling. I could see the value in toting along a few movies or downloading my favorite newscasts and watching them while overseas (on the hotel TV). Then again, I also have a portable DVD player and a laptop capable of playing movies and music, and both have larger screens than my iPod. I guess if it came down to taking just one device, I would take my laptop and call it a day.

Student Three: I watched some video clips on a Siemens PDA, which has a big screen and a good resolution. The image was good, even the subtitles were OK; [it's] just that one has to pay special attention and to watch the display more closely. However, the only inconvenience was that the movies, video clips imported from the computer, have to be transformed to a different bit rate.

Regardless of my students' views, the audience for mobile media is expected to grow dramatically in the decade ahead. The number of video phones in United States went from one million in 2005 to 20 million in 2007. It is expected to top 250 million worldwide by 2010.[30]

THE NEW AUDIENCE RELATIONSHIP

One of the biggest news stories of 2006 almost wasn't. And if it had not been for the World Wide Web, it might never have been. In late September, ABC News broke a story about the inappropriate sexually explicit e-mails that Representative Mark Foley (R-Florida) had sent to congressional pages. The story resonated through the media, and within hours of its broadcast Foley unexpectedly announced his resignation from Congress. The ripples of the story and the scandal it produced spread through Washington, D.C., and throughout the Republican Party in the weeks leading up to the midterm elections in November of that year. Many pundits suggest that this story and the resulting political fallout associated with it not only led to Foley's resignation, but also contributed directly to the loss of several contested congressional seats previously held by Republicans and the surprising return to a Democrat-controlled Congress.

This story and perhaps the political turmoil that followed in its wake might not have occurred, however, without the existence of the World Wide Web and the empowered, voting public that have arisen along with it since the early 1990s.

National Public Radio's (NPR) *All Things Considered* reported on October 6, 2006, that although several major media outlets had seen the troubling e-mails sent by Foley to his pages, none felt the story was strong enough to go public, at least on the air or in a daily newspaper.[31] Holding some of the e-mails as early as 2005, editorial staff at the *Miami Herald*, the *St. Petersburg (Florida) Times*, and Fox News felt they lacked enough information to report the Foley story. They checked the accuracy of the e-mails. They contacted Foley's office. They talked with the parents of the pages involved. ABC News's Brian Ross decided to post information about the e-mails on ABCNews.com on Thursday, September 28, 2006. Within hours, individuals who identified themselves as former Foley pages sent Ross much more explicit IMs in which Foley appeared to be asking the pages about sex. The next day ABC News producer Maddy

Sauer called Foley's office and read some of the explicit messages seeking confirmation or denial of their authenticity. According to Ross, Kirk Fordham, Foley's former chief of staff, called ABC back twenty minutes later and said, "The congressman is going to resign, and we want to make a deal with you." The deal was that Foley would admit the messages were authentic and that he would talk exclusively with Ross, but that Ross would not publish the messages. Ross rejected that deal and posted the messages online, so the story went forward.[32]

Just as convergence has exerted dramatic impact on the reporter-source relationship, it is also changing the relationship between journalists and their audiences. Again, the most basic example arises from the advent of e-mail. In days past, reporters would typically write or produce their reports, and only the most unusual stories would generate more than a letter or two or phone call (typically from a source misquoted) from the audience.

With the rise of e-mail, most reporters who have published their e-mail addresses typically now get deluged with messages from their readers, viewers, or listeners. The Middleberg-Ross survey shows that many reporters now consider responding to readers via e-mail as part of their job, with more than half doing so at least occasionally.[33]

The best reporters cull through their e-mails and find occasional nuggets of gold, including well-written comments from highly informed experts. Some reporters also spend time on list-serves (electronic mailing lists), discussion boards, and other online forums where persons interested in particular subjects often meet to talk. Reporters sometimes find story ideas or potential sources in these forums and often engage readers who want to talk about a story recently reported by the journalist. The Middleberg-Ross survey shows that by 2001 a majority of journalists were using the Internet to develop story ideas, compared with just 30 percent in 1998.

Online dialogs can inform both reader and reporter and can help build a healthier relationship between the two. This interaction is a significant and dramatic change from previous centuries' practice of journalism wherein the typical reporter rarely engaged the audience in a meaningful conversation. With newspaper readership eroding steadily in the United States, especially among younger audiences who have grown up living in the world of interactive media, this fundamental shift in the nature of journalism may be the lynchpin to survival in the twenty-first century, at least for print journalism. The evolution from a one-way to a two-way dialog can strengthen the role of journalism as sense maker in society. Many online newspapers and news sites openly seek interaction by inviting readers' comments on columns, news reports, and blogs. In 2006, readers were invited to provide their comments at news sites on everything from the midterm elections to the execution of former Iraqi leader Saddam Hussein. And readers are regularly invited to comment on breaking news items reported in the blog called *On Deadline* published at USAToday.com. Not all the news items are of great political or social importance, but they are often topics that generate reader interest. A case in point is an item published on December 26, 2006, about a woman in Japan who was sentenced to twenty months in prison for playing loud music, much to the annoyance of her neighbors. Comments from readers included: "Is this for real? Prison time for loud music? So is the neighbor's legs broken, she can't walk over and ask that the music be turned down? Seems a bit extreme to me" (posted by Dave in Las Vegas, December 26, 2006, 9:41:02 A.M.); and "20 months for playing music too loud, should have put noodles in her ears" (posted by xygen nguyent, December 26, 2006, 9:37:46 A.M.).

In outlining a general systems theory of human communication, psychologist and psychiatrist James G. Miller argues that communication is one of two necessary life functions that cut across all living things.[34] In his theory, communication is the metabolism of information and operates to facilitate adaptation to a changing environment. It operates from a cellular level all the way up to a societal level, where journalism and the media perform this function. Digital, online media perform this function in the most rapid, interactive form yet invented.

MIT professor Pablo J. Boczkowski explains in his book *Digitizing the News* (2005): "News in the online environment is what those contributing to its production make of it." It is moving "from being mostly journalist-centered, communicated as a monologue, and primarily local, to also being increasingly audience-centered, part of multiple conversations and micro-local."[35]

Nevertheless, journalists need to exercise caution when delving into the world of e-mail, chat rooms, and other online activity. The Middleberg-Ross survey reveals that many journalists doubt the credibility of many online sources, and rightly so. They rate only trade association Web sites as "more credible" than "not credible," and they say that the most questionable content is found on message boards and in chat rooms.

News veteran and technology expert Daniel Dubno adds:

> With the advent of Google, everyone can broadcast information and everyone can research information across the intellectual universe. The problem is, as it's always been, determining the bona fides of the data and the merits of the information conveyed.
>
> What is truly exciting (though still more promise than reality) is the likelihood of seeing enhancements to search engines like Google that will provide measurements of "credibility" or ranking of "value." Google's "PageRank" features now provide a rough measurement of how well re-garded (or at least how widely referenced) an information provider is or is viewed during a Google search. As technologies to evaluate searches are enhanced I have reason to anticipate an array of "authentication tools" will emerge to help journalists and others make informed decisions on the merit of information posted on the Web."[36]

Web sites featuring strong search engines as well as extensive media content are attracting growing numbers of visitors. Although Microsoft is still the most visited of all Web sites with 501.7 million visitors as of November 2006, Google and Yahoo! are closing in rapidly. Google's sites drew 475.7 million in November 2006, up 9.1 percent from the previous year, and visitors to Yahoo! sites grew to 475.3 million, up 5.2 percent from the previous year.[37] In contrast, Microsoft's total number of visitors increased just 3.3 percent from the previous year.

Reporters must always bear in mind their main function: to report. They cannot afford to get sidetracked into tangential conversations with readers or sources—or worse, to start worrying about the consequences of a story to the extent that they experience reporting paralysis. A jour-nalist maintains a fine balance between telling the public what it needs to know, even when the truth may cause hurt or pain, and being respon-sible and ethical in reporting and respecting personal privacy.

In some ways, a more intriguing development is the growth of the Weblog, or *blog:* "a series of updated posts on a Web page in the form of a diary or journal, often including commentary on, and hypertext links to, other Web sites. Posts are in chronological order and can contain anything from simple text, to music, images and even streamed video."[38] Blogs created by newspapers are increasingly popular. Nielsen/NetRatings reports that U.S. newspaper blogs drew 3.8 million unique visitors in December 2006, an increase of 210 percent since December 2005.[39] This number represents more than 10 percent of the total volume of unique visitors (29.9 million) to newspaper Web sites in general in December 2006. Newspaper Web site traffic had grown about 10 percent since December 2005.

Although some blogs are created by journalists writing outside the confines of their news organization, many are produced by audience members. The Pew study on the Internet and the public in 2006 reported that more than "48 million Americans—mostly those with high-speed Internet access at home—have posted content to the Internet," much of which is in the form of personal blogs.[40]

Because blogs are not subject to the same journalistic standards of objectivity, accuracy, and detachment of traditional news organizations, they are often much more passionate and some might say honest in expressing the emotional aspects of the truth, such as in the case of the abuse of Iraqi prisoners or the aftermath of the 2004 Asian tsunami. At least in part because of this characteristic and the belief that blogs may include information traditional news media may edit out, blogs have grown enormously popular, sometimes rivaling traditional news sites in terms of unique visitors. Jody Raynsford reports that Robert L. Belichick, a healthcare worker from Chicago, is a reader of blogs because they have "information that will never see the light of day in the print or TV media realm. . . . [N]ot one major media outlet in the U.S. reported that the U.S. excised over 8,000 pages from the Iraq declaration since it contained information about the U.S. companies that supplied all of the biological and chemical 'weapons' to [Saddam]."[41]

Blogs also blur the boundary between who is a source, who is an audience member, and who is a journalist. In some cases, the blog creator may be all three. Bloggers may see an item reported in a traditional news outlet, gather their own information, and post a response on their blog. Journalists themselves have noted this phenomenon. On May 26, 2004, for example, journalist J. D. Lasica wrote about when "consumers are creators."[42] He quoted from Jan Schaffer, executive director of J-Lab, the Institute for Interactive Journalism, who on April 18, 2004, spoke at the Broadcast Educators Association convention in Las Vegas, Nevada, called "Convergent Audiences: When Consumers Are Creators."[43] The typical nonjournalist blogger, though, is like Nancy Watzman, who uses her blog *Muckrakingmom* to report and comment on a variety of topics of potential interest to mothers, but who pays special attention to where motherhood and politics intersect.[44] In her November 29, 2006, posting "Mother's Milk and Politics," she commented on the participation of women in politics. "The good news is that women are breaking through in greater numbers in politics than ever before, with a record number of women set to take their oaths of office for the 110th Congress come January, as I wrote about here. The bad news: women will nevertheless be woefully underrepresented, comprising just 16 percent of the new Congress. And women were the source of just 27 percent of the past election's larger campaign contributions, according to new analysis from the Center for Responsive Politics (CRP)." Money, she adds, is the "mother's milk" of U.S. politics.

Convergence, according to Watzman, "puts the focus not on the consumer, our audiences, but on the supplier, the news organizations. It becomes an exercise in Us vs. Them." She notes, "I think we are focusing on the wrong 'C' word. Rather than focus on convergence, we should be focusing on connections and how new digital tools can help us build all kinds of innovative, new connections with our audiences. The potential of new media is not simply more noise but more meaningful interaction and hopefully more meaningful learning." Audience expectations are also evolving. News via the Internet comes on demand and instantaneously. In a broadband environment, the news is modality rich and highly interactive. Audiences are increasingly accustomed to and increasingly demanding news that is customized to their interests.

CONCLUSION: THE COMING AGE OF INTERACTION

Convergence is reshaping the landscape of journalism and the news media in a variety of ways. Newsroom structures, journalistic practices, and news content are evolving. Perhaps most important, the fundamental relationships between and among journalists, their sources, and their audiences are undergoing a technological transformation. This sea change has far-reaching implications for the nature and function of journalism in modern society.

Reporters are increasingly supplementing and sometimes supplanting face-to-face news gathering with Internet-based reporting. Web searching, e-mail, and list-serves are increasing staples in the reporting food chain. Although most reporters still rely on personal interviews and observations, they also often use the Internet for material when meeting deadlines, working on weekends, or doing follow-up work, including fact checking. Moreover, with economic shortfalls afflicting many news organizations, increased productivity is a pressure felt acutely in a growing proportion of newsrooms, a pressure that sometimes translates into journalistic shortcuts.

Technological advances present new opportunities to improve news gathering by enabling journalists on deadline or on a budget to cast their net more widely to include nontraditional sources and experts located in faraway places.

Technology is also reshaping the relationship between journalists and their audiences, producing a more interactive form of journalism. In the traditional world of media, interactivity between producer and audience is almost nonexistent, limited for the most part to a few letters to the editor. In the Internet age, many journalists are in almost daily e-mail contact with at least some audience members, or users.

This interactivity promises to help increase understanding between journalists, their audiences, and their sources, bringing the potential for improved accuracy in news reporting. Achieving this potential will take more than technology alone. News organizations and the journalists who staff them need to make a conscious effort to employ effectively and ethically the digital tools available today and soon available on tomorrow's technological horizon. By engaging sources and audiences in a daily dialog, whether online or off, they can improve the quality of their reporting and reestablish themselves as central to the democratic process in the United States and around the world.

One of the most significant questions for media in the digital age is whether what philosopher Jürgen Habermas calls the *public sphere* will take root in the interactive and online arena.[45] Habermas defines the public sphere as "a network for communicating information and points of view," gradually transforming into public opinion.[46] Early indicators suggest that the answer is a tentative yes. The so-called blogosphere, discussion groups, and other forms of interactive communities have increasingly emerged online as environments where a wide swath of issues, concerns, and cultures are debated, discussed, and dissected critically. These virtual communities sometimes generate more heat than light or insight, but they also oftentimes grapple intelligently and thoughtfully on the issues of the day. On occasion, they generate energy and influence that reach into the real world of media and politics and shape the events and decisions of the day. Some of the biggest question marks regarding the public sphere in a digital environment have to do with accessibility, inclusiveness, and the protection of privacy—principles that Habermas describes as essential to an effective public sphere. In a networked environment such as the Internet, the digital divide often prevents or limits for financial reasons any inclusiveness and accessibility across social and economic classes, and privacy is sometimes at significant risk. I discuss these issues more fully in chapter 8.

4 / PRODUCERS OF DIGITAL MEDIA

Whether text, audio, or video, media of all types in the digital age come from an exploding array of sources, or *producers of content*. In the analog world of newspapers and other print media such as books and magazines, a relatively small number of increasingly large publishing companies came to control the means of print publication. With a handful of national newspapers, most papers have been largely local media, once privately owned but increasingly publicly owned as part of national newspaper groups or chains. Magazines have long been largely specialized in terms of audience and content and distributed most often regionally or nationally. Books have been the province of mostly national or international publishers.

With the advent of the World Wide Web as a medium of public communication in the 1990s, there has been an exponential increase in the diversity of sources of media production, especially those dealing with text and graphics. In everything from personal Web sites to blogs, a vast array of individuals and organizations across the nation and around the world produce huge volumes of often largely unfiltered content. Sometimes drawing an audience as small as one, producers of this content are not as concerned about audience as they are about simple self-expression. An interesting example is *Chasing Windmills,* an independent Minneapolis-based blog where its filmmaker founders have posted provocative and artistic two-minute daily episodic videos since 2005.[1]

Of course, most traditional publishers, whether of newspapers, magazines, or books, have adapted their own print products for online distribution and consumption. In some cases, the adaptation has been minimal, simply putting the same content online that had been exclusively in print. In other cases, the content has been significantly modified and enhanced with original content. A detailed discussion of content strategies in the digital environment is given in chapter 5.

Audio content has seen a similar pattern of growth in the diversity of producers, though somewhat delayed and on a smaller scale. The sharing of audio files in the MP3 format has been robust, but the production of original audio content has developed slowly with online streaming of audio files in the 1990s. Independent audio production has taken off only since the advent of podcasting in 2000.[2] Like other traditional analog media, radio and other forms of audio content (e.g., audio books) had been the domain of mainly a small number of large, centralized, corporate and nonprofit media organizations. Digital technologies have enabled literally millions of persons and organizations to produce their own audio content and post it online, whether as podcasts on personal Web sites or on central online distributors, such as iTunes or elsewhere. Of course, traditional broadcasters have also developed extensive audio content in the form of podcasts. In addition, other digital vehicles, such as communication satellites, have provided distribution platforms for other audio media production.

In the traditional world of analog television, video programming was originally produced by a select group of production companies and distributed by a limited and finite number of broadcasters who tightly controlled what made it on air. Cable television has reflected somewhat more diversity of producers, at least at the national level, with programming in 2006 coming from roughly two hundred national programming networks, such as Arts & Entertainment (A&E), Home Box Office (HBO), and the Weather Channel. Yet many of these networks are owned or controlled by common parent companies. Nevertheless, cable also includes some opportunities for local diversity of production, with mandatory public-access channels. Public access represents a relative drop in the overall bucket of the total amount of television programming, however.

Since the introduction and development of digital technologies, video production and distribution have grown dramatically. At the same time, the diversity of sources of video has grown wide and varied, from high-end professional producers to mom and pop producers, son and daughter producers, and just about everyone else. Much of this expanded video production does not find its way onto national programming networks, over-the-air broadcast television, cable, or telephone-based television networks. Rather, most of it appears on alternative distribution media, such as YouTube and elsewhere.

RANGE OF QUALITY

Much of the diverse content produced by widely ranging sources is of very limited quality or interest. Some online video, for instance, is produced by young, independent videographers looking for an alternative vehicle to reach an audience. Digital video is sometimes produced by average citizens who may have home movies or audio they want to share with friends and family or who may simply have exhibitionist tendencies, so much of this video is not worth watching by outsiders. In a growing number of cases, professional news organizations are openly seeking photographs, audio, and video captured by lay citizens using their cell phone cameras or other digital devices. In recognition that millions of citizens have these news-gathering devices and can easily and quickly e-mail the image, audio, or video file to a news editor, global news services such as Reuters and Yahoo! have established formal programs to encourage citizens to submit their mobile news material. Starting December 5, 2006, photos and videos submitted by lay citizens have been placed throughout Reuters.com and *Yahoo! News*.[3] Reuters also began distributing some of the submissions in 2007 print, online, and broadcast media outlets that subscribe to its news service. It plans to develop a service devoted to lay citizen–submitted photographs and video because it views lay citizens as a potential stringer base of millions. Many news organizations have used digital photographs taken by amateurs to supplement their own coverage of major events such as the London subway bombing and the Asian tsunami. Yahoo's news division has used digital images first posted on Flickr, the company's photo-sharing site. Camera phone videos are increasingly providing supplemental news coverage. The 2006 racist rant by Michael Richards, the actor who played Kramer on *Seinfeld*, was recorded on a cell phone and then posted on TMZ, the celebrity news site. Video of the December 30, 2006, execution of former Iraqi leader Saddam Hussein was captured on a cell phone or other mobile device

Figure 4.1 Fan films boldly go digitally where none has gone before. Photo used with permission of HiddenFrontier.

and distributed on the Internet and from cell phone to cell phone.[4] The grainy video eventually made its way to traditional news media as well, where, for example, part of it was aired on *NBC Nightly News with Brian Williams* during a report on the evening of January 1, 2007.[5]

So-called fan films are among the most interesting examples of video produced by nontraditional video creators. Although fans have long made their own versions of popular motion pictures or television shows, distributing them on the Web is a new and significant phenomenon. Moreover, digital technology has allowed fans to take these films to entirely new production heights and levels of distribution. *Star Trek* episodes made by fans are perhaps the most notable for their production values (see fig. 4.1). Some feature high production values and include amateur actors and producers who contribute their time, energy, and resources not for profit, but just for fun or perhaps to get noticed. Paramount Pictures, which owns the copyright for *Star Trek,* has not challenged these digital fan films legally because the fans have not made them for profit. Although some are amateurish and not worth watching, some are almost indistinguishable from the real thing—except for the fact that none of the actors is a recognizable star.[6] Some of the notable examples of Web sites featuring fan versions of *Star Trek* include Newvoyages.com, usshathaway.com, ussintrepid.org.uk, starshipfarragut.com, startrekexeter.com, and hiddenfrontier.com.

Many short fan films, or videos, are also being made. Users of social-networking sites such as YouTube are creating videos to accompany their favorite songs and posting the homemade music videos online.

In some cases, nontraditional providers can bring diversity to the television mix. One example is *Barrio 305,* an independently produced online video magazine about Latino culture. Much of the coverage has focused on the rise of urban Latino youth in South Beach, Miami, Florida. It is produced in English and Spanish, and though its production values are not quite at the level of much commercial television, it is still a useful alternative voice.

In other cases, online video is of somewhat less value, at least as independent journalism. A case in point is an online video produced by the American Institute of Certified Public Accountants.[7] The video podcast titled *Pillars of Success* profiles the story of four African American CPAs, whose numbers still total less than one percent of all CPAs. The subject matter may be worth consideration, but this production is obviously promotional and of limited general utility.

Political candidates are increasingly turning to the Web to make important campaign speeches and otherwise communicate directly with the public without the filter of traditional news media gatekeepers. On January 20, 2007, Senator Hillary Clinton announced her entrance into the 2008 U.S. presidential campaign via a video Webcast.[8] She also fielded questions from viewers submitted via the Web during a subsequent live Webcast, an interactive capability heightened in the online arena. News media captured video from Clinton's Webcast and featured it in their own video newscasts that day.

NO COMPREHENSIVE GUIDE TO ONLINE VIDEO

If there is a one problem facing consumers of online video, it is the task of sorting through all the video trash for the occasional video nugget of interest or quality. There is no comprehensive and current programming guide for online television and video. *Real Networks' Real Guide* offers a useful guide to online audio and video programming, but it is incomplete. What is needed is a comprehensive and continuously updated Web portal and search engine for online TV and video that encompasses all online video formats from MEPG-1 to MEPG-4, Audio Video Interleave, Quicktime, RealPlayer, Windows Media Player, and the various other video formats online as well as all the various digital video–distribution platforms. The current situation essentially requires users to know all the locations of online TV and video and regularly visit them for updates. Many producers employ syndication technology known as really simple syndication (RSS), which uses the extensible markup language (XML)—which is an advanced version of hypertext markup language (HTML), the basic building block code of the World Wide Web—to notify subscribers automatically of newly released or updated content, whether new video, audio, text, graphics, or photographs.

TRADITIONAL PROVIDERS

A considerable amount of video comes from established, familiar, and traditional sources such as news and entertainment companies, television networks and stations, public television, sports teams and leagues, arts organizations, and the government. One significant change in video news production from just a few years ago is that many news providers who once specialized in print, major newspapers such as the *New York Times* and the *Washington Post,* as well as news agencies such as Reuters and the AP , now produce extensive video for online and other distribution[9] The AP makes its news video available through member newspaper Web sites, such as that of the *New York Daily News,* which on May 25, 2006, published a text story and AP video report about the power outage that shut down the northeast corridor of New Jersey Transit's commuter train line to and from New York City.[10]

An excellent example of quality journalism being produced originally for an online audience comes in the form of a video report titled "A Shifting Bolivia," produced for the *New York Times* on the Web by reporter Juan Forero.[11] Forero reported from Bolivia on Evo Morales, who in January 2005 assumed the office of president of Bolivia. Morales is an Aymara Indian and former coca grower who is decriminalizing the growing of coca, "a staple of the indigenous culture and the prime ingredient in cocaine," and making other fundamental changes to his country's struggling economy, but with significant social and political implications.[12] The thirteen-minute multipart Web-exclusive video report features an interesting combination of video and stills, in English but also with Spanish actualities (audio sound bites from sources interviewed) either subtitled or dubbed in English.

Washingtonpost.com also produces quality original online video journalism, such as its October 4, 2005, report "Fueling Azerbaijan's Future."[13] The ten-minute documentary-style report provides a detailed examination of the former Soviet republic's economic development through its oil resources.

CONVERGENT CONTENT PROVIDERS

An interesting case in media production is the Belo Corporation, owners of some two dozen news media properties around the country, including television stations, interactive media, and the *Dallas Morning News,* well known for its quality local and regional journalism. Belo has now developed a converged news operation where video is often produced and distributed alongside traditional newspaper reporting.[14] On May 19, 2006, I conducted telephone interviews with two Belo executives, David Duitch and John Granatino. David Duitch, Belo's vice president, Capital Bureau, has responsibility for managing both the print and the broadcast operations of the bureau.[15] He has been behind the Washington bureau's drive to produce videos for the *Dallas Morning News* Web site. Among the best examples of online video journalism at Belo comes from the *Dallas Morning News* Washington Bureau, where veteran newspaper reporter Jim Landers has distinguished himself in the new media age by shooting and editing his own video to accompany his newspaper reporting. Landers specializes in international reporting on how developments around the globe impact communities in north Texas. He has mastered a new form of storytelling and has produced quality video reports on a variety of stories, including economic problems in the West Bank and oil concerns in Saudi Arabia.[16]

Belo's John Granatino, vice president of news and operations for Belo Interactive, noted that increasing numbers of the Belo audience are broadband enabled. "Roughly 80 percent of our online audience has broadband Internet access," he explained to me. The audience, he added, expects broadband content, especially video. "Fortunately, we have it at our TV stations. We also create original video reporting. It's a 'must do,' not a 'should do.'"[17]

The audience has grown considerably for Belo's online video journalism. "We're seeing a doubling, tripling, of video streams over the past year. We're now doing 2 million video streams a month across twenty sites around the country," Granatino stated. The video segments tend to be short, but in some cases video blog (or *vlog*) reports can actually be longer than a video report on television. "Our reporters often give behind-the-scenes looks, and this might take a bit longer," he noted. Video advertising is also growing, especially for national Web sites, but even for regional ones, helping support such original online video reporting.

Among a growing number of news organizations with video reporting capabilities is the *St. Petersburg (Florida) Times,* once exclusively a newspaper organization. "We [now] think of ourselves more as a journalism company than a newspaper company," explains Kevin McGeever, city editor for tampabay.com, the portal site where sptimes.com resides. "A year ago we weren't even thinking about video," he noted. Now the company produces it regularly. "Some stories lend themselves better to video or are well told in moving images rather than in words or words alone," McGeever added. "We're working to change the culture of the newsroom, and video is not something journalists at newspapers always think of."[18] Stories for which the *St. Petersburg Times* has produced original video include the 2006 immigration marches and the 2005 hurricane preparation. Particularly interesting is a special report on the petting of the manatee, an endangered species living in the waters of the Tampa region and increasingly approached and harassed by snorkelers in violation of federal law.[19] The site obtained unique footage showing snorkelers approaching the manatee and coming in illegal and harmful physical contact with the large marine mammals. This legacy newsroom is thus embracing a culture change. Tampabay.com is the "first edition" now, and "we will publish at the height of interest. . . . Yet," McGeever added, "it's nice if the video has an evergreen quality and audience interest can last more than a few days."

Another example of quality online video reporting being produced by a local journalism organization comes by way of the *San Francisco Chronicle*. A four-minute original *San Francisco Chronicle* online video report titled "Ski Jump Spectacle on Filmore Street" went online on September 30, 2005, at www.sfgate.com. It featured a dramatic look at both the creation of a ski jump in the waning days of summer on a steep San Francisco street and the actual ski jump competition.

A notable development regarding even these recognized quality sources of video is the sheer volume of video being made available online, either live or on demand. Most of these sources have found that the cost of quality video production has fallen dramatically or that they can leverage their resources by making the video available online after it has had its premier on conventional television. Once a video has aired, it is often made available for on-demand viewing online, either for a fee (ranging from modest amounts of about one dollar to substantially greater amounts) or for free.

NEW ONLINE PRODUCERS

In some cases, major Web portals such as Yahoo! are producing significant amounts of original content for the Web, including journalism. One exemplar is Kevin Sites, a veteran war correspondent who has covered global war and disaster for several national networks and now is producing original video news reports on various conflict zones around the world for Yahoo.[20] His "Africa in the Hot Zone" involved in-depth, on-location reporting from Mogadishu, Somalia, and elsewhere.

INTERNATIONAL PERSPECTIVES

With the rise of digital media, international producers of video and other media content have developed new opportunities to participate in the global flow of information and media programming. This development is vital because for most of the analog age of media the flow of information and media programming have been dominated by the United States and other advanced information societies. As Jesús Martín Barbero and others have articulated, communication and information are basic agents of social change and development. As such, it is essential that all countries and regions are able to participate fully in the global media and communication system.[21] Nestor García-Canclini has noted that digital technology is reshaping the cultural industry, the collection of companies and institutions that create, distribute, and control media content.[22] It is critical that participants from all parts of the world and from all social and racial groups have access to these technologies of production in order to contribute to the growth of cultural creativity. As Theodor Adorno and Max Horkheimer of the Frankfurt school of critical media studies have explained, this process of cultural production is fundamental to the creation of social and political meaning and power.[23]

Understanding the impact of technology on this process is critical to evaluating the potential of digital media to help reengage disenfranchised groups in the political process both domestically and internationally.

FAKE NEWS: ONE MAN'S EXPERIENCE ON *THE DAILY SHOW WITH JON STEWART*

Not all the news or newslike content produced in the digital age is meant to be taken seriously.[24] And sometimes when it is, it should not be. The sudden and dramatic increase in the number of distribution channels for media content, including video, has created something of a programming vacuum, and because the media abhor a vacuum, producers have raced to create new and entertaining forms of content to fill the void. Among the more popular of program producers is Jon Stewart, the wry comedian whose specialty is fake news, a genre that has captured the eyeballs of an expanding generation of would-be television viewers of real news.

In the spring of 2005, I became something of an accidental celebrity on the Rutgers campus: I was interviewed for Comedy Central's *The Daily Show with Jon Stewart*. Since being on the show, I have even had students ask for my autograph and have seen attendance at my occasional public lectures swell significantly. Students have interviewed me for campus publications and television about what it is like to be on *The Daily Show*.

How did I, the chair of a department of journalism and media studies, come to be on this popular show specializing in "fake news"? What was it like being on a show that, according to research, 21 percent of Americans eighteen to twenty-nine years of age say is a primary source of their news?[25] By way of comparison, only a slightly higher percentage of this age group, 23 percent, report that the major television evening news programs serve as a primary source of their news.

Well, it is a long story, but here are the highlights.

As a department chair at Rutgers, the state university of New Jersey, I have seen significant funding cuts to the departmental budget in recent years. These cuts have made the job of teaching nearly six hundred undergraduate majors increasingly difficult, sometimes forcing us to cut key programs and classes, but also to seek innovative alternative funding opportunities and resources.

One unique opportunity developed in the fall of 2004 when the campus daily student newspaper agreed to sponsor the hiring of an instructor for the department's advanced reporting course, which had been off the class schedule the previous semester because of state funding cuts. In exchange for its support (several thousand dollars per semester), the paper would be permitted to enroll a half-dozen of its reporting staff in the class, even though they were not majors in the department and might not have met all the prerequisites. Instead, the instructor of the course, an award-winning journalist with more than twenty years of daily newspaper-reporting experience and a veteran teacher in the department, would review each student's qualifications and decide on a case-by-case basis whether each should be admitted into the course.

As department chair, I was pleased to able to make this novel arrangement because the class would otherwise not have been offered. Nevertheless, from the outset, I made clear to the editorial leadership of the student paper that this arrangement was experimental and might not be something that the department or the paper would want to repeat. I indicated that a thorough review would be made of the course at its conclusion to determine whether the unique funding and teaching arrangement would be repeated. Moreover, there might be significant changes in how the course would be structured and taught to ensure the highest-quality education for the students enrolled. An important part of the chair's job is not just to find ways to offer the full curriculum in an increasingly financially challenging time, but to make sure that the curriculum is of the highest possible quality and meets its educational goals.

At the conclusion of the course, it was clear that the class was a success, as it had been when previously offered. Ten of the eighteen stories produced by students in the course were published in the student newspaper, most running on page 1 and online. None of the stories published was challenged for accuracy. One of the stories, a series on tuition hikes, won a third-place award in the investigative and enterprise reporting category in the New Jersey Press Association's Better College Newspaper contest.

Yet the course had its problems. Some students were not properly identifying themselves when conducting interviews. I knew this first-hand because one student interviewed me for a story, and although she identified herself as a reporter for the student newspaper, she never mentioned that she was also doing the story as part of a class assignment. Some students were also relying extensively on e-mail to conduct their interviews. I was also aware of this practice because a student in the class attempted to interview me this way. Although e-mail has its place in modern news gathering, it does not and should not replace face-to-face interviewing or even audio interviews conducted over the telephone. E-mail can be effectively used when following up with a source or when other attempts to conduct in-person or phone interviews fail (perhaps a source is out of the country) and a deadline is fast approaching. On the one hand, nuance and other important aspects of an interview can be lost by using only e-mail. On the other hand, follow-up e-mail responses from sources can guarantee accurate quotes, the value of which cannot be underestimated.

Overall, the biggest problem with the course was that some students were settling into a comfort zone of rarely or never leaving the campus when on assignment, doing many of their interviews via e-mail. The advanced investigative course is the department's highest-level undergraduate reporting class, so these students might not take another reporting course before graduating. In this course, as in many other reporting courses, students usually cover campus stories, but I wanted to make sure that the students in this class were challenged to get beyond the comfort of the campus.

After the conclusion of the semester, I reviewed the course with the instructor and discussed changes that needed to be made to improve the course if offered in the future, including getting the students to identify themselves fully, not to overrely on e-mail to do their interviews, and to go off campus for at least some of their reporting. This last change, I felt, was among the most important because it would ensure that the students would not graduate without ever having conducted at least one in-depth investigation off campus. The experience of investigating off campus would be vital to them in pursuing their professional careers as journalists. Beginning reporters need to know where city hall is. They need to know how government works. They need to know how to pursue a story beyond the ivy-covered walls of a 240-year-old campus.

As exciting as this story of academic innovation might have been, it never would have captured the attention of the producers of *The Daily Show* without a bit of additional drama. The drama came in the form of a student who for the course did two investigations dealing with the use, or lack of use, of student evaluations in various academic departments and by faculty, the first of which was published in the student paper. The student interviewed me for this story.

The student's second investigation, a critical examination of the athletics program at the university, was rejected by the student paper as being too opinionated. The paper's editors asked her to make certain changes, in particular to add balance by expanding the sources used, but she declined. The editors also offered to publish the article on the op/ed page, but she again declined.

It was then that my role in the story started to pick up. An online education news source caught wind of the campus developments and decided to run a story suggesting a link between the student paper's rejection of the athletics story and my separate and unrelated decision to focus future offerings of the advanced reporting course off campus.[26] It was alleged that the university was censoring its students, banning them from reporting critically about the campus, particularly the athletics program. This was untrue. The student paper is independently run, and I had no contact with the paper or its editors since the beginning of the semester. Further, the student paper had recently run other articles critical of the athletics program.

After the story ran online, the state's press picked up its scent. Within days, reporters from a half-dozen of the state's newspapers called me for an interview. They wanted to know why the university was censoring its students. I explained that there was no censorship, but many of the reporters had already made up their minds and only wanted to get a good quote.

Because the campus is located just a few miles from New York City, producers of *The Daily Show* caught wind of the swirling controversy and decided it was rich fodder for a humor piece that would appeal to college-age students, a prime component of the show's audience. Moreover, with distribution on both cable and the Internet, the story would have great "legs," so to speak. An assistant producer called my office and asked for an interview for the show. My policy is to accept media interview requests, so I said yes.

Over the next two weeks, producers and assistant producers from the show called me several times, conducting additional "preinterviews." The lead producer on the show explained how he in fact was an experienced journalist. He had studied journalism as an undergraduate at New York University and had even been editor of its student daily newspaper. Then, after graduation, he had spent several years as an assistant producer for CBS News at the network level. He never said anything funny or anything to imply he was planning a comedy bit, although his intent was obvious given the nature of the show. He went out of his way to impress me with his journalistic credentials and used various techniques and terminology common to television news. He talked about the "preinterview," "the "interview," and the "correspondent" who would interview me. After scheduling and rescheduling the interview a couple of times, he finally settled on a date in March when the "news team," as he called them, could come to campus and conduct the interview. The date was coincidentally during campus spring break, so I explained that there would not be many students around, but the producer said that would not be a problem.

At 4:30 P.M., the "news team" arrived, with one producer, the "correspondent" (Ed Helms), a camera operator, and a sound/lighting operator.

As the technicians began to set up, the producer and I chatted. He reiterated his news credentials and then posed a few friendly softball questions about the story to help create a relaxed atmosphere.

Meanwhile, the "correspondent" laid low. He paced in the hallway outside my office. Helms seemed to be actively avoiding any interaction before the interview and, like a character actor, to be trying to get into his part. On *The Daily Show* Web site, Helms's official biography explains that his background is in stand-up comedy. "For years Ed worked in the comedy trenches as a stand-up comedian, eventually earning regular spots at NYC's top comedy clubs and an appearance on the Fall 2002 season of Comedy Central's *Premium Blend*."[27] He has no apparent background in journalism. After about twenty minutes, the setup was complete, and the interview began. I was seated in my office, and Helms sat opposite with the single camera shooting over his shoulder. From this point on, it quickly became obvious that this was fake news, not real news. Just before the first question, the producer handed me a release and asked for a signature. He said that without this signed release they could not proceed. It was a standard release used in entertainment programs.

Then, unlike in a typical news interview, in this interview the correspondent clearly had no idea what he should ask. Instead, the producer handed him a list of questions—or, rather, a list of numbered questions, from 1 to approximately 30. The producer had a copy, and he sat just outside of the camera's field of view. Helms would say, "Now what should I ask?" and the producer would respond with a series of numbers, such as "7, 9, and 14." Helms would then ask question 7, and I would answer. After the same process for questions 9 and 14, Helms said, "I don't know where to go from here. What should I ask?" The producer, who was the "journalistic" brains of the operation, would then identify another three or so questions by number only, obviously in order to keep me from knowing what Helms was going to ask—in other words, to keep me in the dark as long as possible so that they would get a spontaneous answer with as little forethought as possible, perhaps with me laughing, pausing, or clearing my throat in a way that could later be edited to make me look silly, sinister, or stupid.

After roughly three hours of the "interview," the crew then set up again, pointing the camera at the correspondent. He then reasked the questions, this time for the camera and the microphone. The wording of the questions now did not correspond precisely to the wording used during the interview (e.g., "Do you expect me to believe that?" versus "Do you *really* expect me to believe that?"). They were also sometimes asked in different sequence (e.g., 7, 9, 14 versus 14, 9, 7). He sometimes asked the same question in three or four different ways, trying different inflection and tone. The producer would coach him, telling him to ask it this way or that way (e.g., "accent *really*" and "accent *that*"). It was clear they were making sure that they would have the best possible phrasing to edit for greatest comedic effect back at the studio. In some cases, entirely new questions were asked. Some were cleverly orchestrated and prepared sight gags, some slapstick. At one point, the producer pulled out his cell phone and made a call. A moment later Helms's cell phone rang, and he answered it while being filmed. Of course, it was the producer calling him, but Helms pretended it was someone else. As he extended his arm and hand, apparently attempting to give his cell phone to me, he said, "It's for you," but then quickly, "No, wait, it's your student . . . don't answer it." He pulled back the phone, stood up, ran to the office door, opened it, and tossed out the phone, the camera operator trying to catch it on videotape all the while. Later, Helms retrieved his phone, unharmed. Once he said, "I think I know what the problem is," then pulled out a Hertz rental car map of the tristate area (*The Daily Show* apparently rents from Hertz), and he said Rutgers should use a map like this one to explain to its students where they should do their reporting. He pulled out a black marker and blotted out New Brunswick and said, "Just tell your students to stay away from this area. Everything else is fair game."

In the end, the three-minute *Daily Show* report contained a number of interesting segments. One featured Helms leading a Rutgers student into the "athletics" department, explaining to her that he would show her how to do investigative journalism. He walked up to the receptionist and said, "I'm here to interview the athletics director." When the receptionist said, "I'm sorry, he's in a meeting," Helms simply responded, "Oh, OK," and turned around and left with the student in tow. This skit was, of course, meant as ironic humor, a commentary on the pathetic state of investigative journalism in the real world of television news. But what made the segment truly funny to those in the know was the fact that the supposed athletics department office Helms visited was not actually the athletics department. It was a fake athletics department, apparently an office at a Viacom property in Manhattan, Viacom being the parent company that owns both Comedy Central (of which the *Daily Show* is a part) and CBS. Another ironic although not necessarily funny twist was the fact that the crew that visited the campus forgot to follow one of the basic rules of television news, one that even beginning television news-reporting students know to follow: shoot some background video (B-roll). The *Daily Show* crew neglected to shoot any campus B-roll that they could use to establish the location as Rutgers. Consequently, two-days before the segment was scheduled to air, they called the chair's office with a frantic request: Could Rutgers messenger them some B-roll of the campus? They would pay for the messenger. Rutgers broadcast instructor Steve Miller got them some campus B-roll shot digitally by a broadcasting student. When the piece aired, the B-roll was a key part of the segment, but it was used without any on-screen credit being given to the Rutgers student who shot it.

At one point, the segment was available for on-demand viewing on *The Daily Show* Web site video archive.[28]

A SEA CHANGE IN JOURNALISM: CONVERGENCE, JOURNALISTS, THEIR AUDIENCES, AND THEIR SOURCES

In reporting on the day's events, journalists rely on two key relationships: with their news sources and with their audiences. These relationships are most fundamental for at least three reasons. First, without reliable sources, a journalist cannot get the facts needed to prepare the story. Second, without an audience, there is no point in telling the story. Third, and most important, maintaining integrity in these relationships is basic to establishing and maintaining credibility, or believability, the only real value a journalist has. When the integrity of the reporter-source-audience relationship is violated, not only does the individual journalist suffer, but the credibility of the entire news organization or even institution is damaged. Consider the 2003 case of former *New York Times* reporter Jayson Blair, who, as the *Times* itself admits, "fabricated comments, concocted scenes and lifted material from other newspapers and wire services."[29]

Not only was Blair forced to resign his post at the *Times,* but the paper's top editors had to relinquish their posts over the credibility crisis.

Convergence, defined in terms of the integration of media forms in a digital environment and fostered by both technological and economic forces, is exerting profound influence on these relationships, in both subtle and not-so-subtle fashion.

THE CONFLICTED REPORTER-SOURCE RELATIONSHIP

Journalists have most often had a conflicted relationship with their sources and their audiences. At times, they have nurtured close relationships with their sources, often cultivating them over a period of years while on a "beat." Covering everything from city hall to the White House, the environment, health, science, and technology, all reporters develop reliable, expert sources whom they can call upon when needed for a breaking story, an investigative report, or a feature. Yet they cannot afford to get too close to these sources. Although they want their sources' trust so that the sources will reveal sometimes uncomfortable and even dangerous truths (e.g., consider "Deep Throat," the famous anonymous inside source who was key to *Washington Post* reporters Bob Woodward and Carl Bernstein's investigation of the 1972 Watergate break-in), they do not want to compromise their journalistic independence or be co-opted.[30] Reporters covering the police beat sometimes go so far as to ride in patrol cars with cops. They cultivate police sources to get a truthful picture of what really happens on the street. Yet they do not want to start becoming a cop's buddy or risk losing the critical, skeptical edge necessary to effective journalism. Reporters who get too close to a source can sometimes fail to ask the tough question that needs to be asked and answered to inform the public fully.

Convergence is gradually transforming the reporter-source relationship. For one thing, it has introduced more technology into the equation. Prior to the advent of personal computers, e-mail, the Internet, and the World Wide Web, reporters usually communicated with their sources in two ways. First and primarily, they talked with them face to face. They went to sources and interviewed them. They went to locations of breaking news and talked to witnesses, officials on site, and those affected or involved. Since the rise of the telephone as a widely adopted technology in the first half of the twentieth century, reporters have also used the phone in talking with sources. The phone was especially helpful in setting up interviews, finding sources, and interviewing sources who were not available locally or when the reporter was on deadline and did not have the time to meet someone face to face. The face-to-face interview always had the advantage over the telephone interview. When talking to someone face to face, reporters could be sure they were talking to the person they thought they were talking to. They could also use nonverbal cues to guess when someone might be lying or when a question deserved a follow-up. Even on the phone, a reporter might sense from the tone of a source's voice that a follow-up question was in order.

Reporters rarely resorted to postal mail, faxes, or telegrams to communicate with a source because these methods were generally inadequate and usually too slow for a reporter on deadline (deadlines almost always preclude the mail). Sources often deluged reporters with written communication, including press releases, but most reporters generally disregarded or discounted this type of communication as public relations.

The rise of computer-mediated communication has begun to erode face-to-face and even telephone interviews, however. Although most quality journalists still prefer face-to-face interviews, the fact is that, in many cases, sources may be tough to reach or pin down, and when on deadline, reporters may take whatever means they can get to reach a source—and that means may often be e-mail. This is especially true when follow-up information is needed or when a reporter is fact-checking a story. Expert sources, especially those in science, medicine, or higher education, may have a strong preference for e-mail communications and may specifically request that a source contact them via e-mail, particularly if they want a timely response. For the business news wires, reporters sometimes rarely leave their desks, doing almost all their investigating either via the phone, e-mail, or other Internet-based communication.

E-mail communication can provide certain improvements to the reporter-source relationship. For example, local reporters—especially those on a tight budget typical to small- or medium-size newspaper, television, radio, or cable news markets or online news sites—can greatly expand the diversity of their source pool by using e-mail as well as other online sources, such as list-serves, news groups, and Web sites. Through e-mail, a local reporter can reach an international expert in health research for a story on an important medical breakthrough when a face-to-face or even telephone interview might be impossible (e.g., because of scheduling, time zone differences, or travel/time constraints).

Research shows that reporters are making increasingly extensive use of e-mail, the Web, and other online sources for information. In a national survey of journalists, public-relations executive Don Middleberg and former Columbia journalism professor Steve Ross found that journalists' use of the Internet and e-mail has grown dramatically since 1998.[31] Of roughly four hundred magazine and newspaper editors surveyed in 2001, more than three-quarters said they use the Internet on a daily basis compared with just 48 percent in 1998, spending five hours on average online at home and nine hours online at work each week.

E-mail also makes it more practical and efficient to fact-check stories, especially those dealing with complex technical issues, including health, science, technology, and business stories. In the past, the reporter might first conduct a face-to-face interview and then fact-check through a phone call. But doing fact-checking over the phone necessarily limits what can be done on deadline; it also reduces the chances of detecting an error because the source will not actually see what is written and may not catch and thus not be able to correct an error heard in a phone call from a harried reporter. But via e-mail the source can see exactly what the reporter has written and respond in writing when he or she identifies an error. Such precise communication can prevent serious mistakes from occurring, and its value cannot be overstated. Faxes can be used, but they have far less utility in today's modern high-speed e-mail environment. Of course, reporters need to be careful when and to whom they show portions of their stories. If it is a critical investigative report, a source may not only strenuously object to publication of material that contains criticism, but may take legal or other action to subvert that publication (e.g., a source may publish material on an alternative Web site contradicting the reporter's story, even before the reporter's story has been published). Reporters also do not want to tip their hands to potential competitors for a scoop.

Journalists can find a variety of important new tools in the digital environment. Among the more potentially useful is Internet telephony, which gives low-cost and sometimes free access to voice communications both domestically and internationally. Consider the case of Skype,[32] which is available for free use to anyone in the world who visits the Skype Web site, downloads and installs the software, and registers with Skype. It requires a computer with Internet access and pretty good bandwidth, as well as a microphone and speakers, preferably a headset to prevent feedback or echoing during the voice communication. Calls anywhere in the United States or the world are free from one Skype user to another. Moreover, for a journalist on assignment, Skype offers some utilitarian features in tracking down potential sources. For example, Michael Shafer, a political science professor at Rutgers University, runs an institute involved in studying human rights issues around the country and the world, about which it publishes reports online and off. In a 2006 project, Shafer's team needed to talk with Iraqi citizens following the country's first post–Saddam Hussein democratic elections. They wanted to find out how Iraqis learned about the candidates. Operating on a limited budget, Shafer's team used Skype to find and interview their sources. Skype allows users to search for other Skype users in a variety of ways. Searching by name is simplest, but other options proved especially useful to Shafer's team. They sorted by country (Iraq), language spoken, age of the Skype user, and gender, thus quickly obtaining a list of potential interviewees who might provide something of a cross-section of Iraqi citizens, albeit citizens of relatively high socioeconomic status. Shafer's team used Skype to place the calls at no cost. Needless to say, the Iraqis interviewed were quite surprised to be called in this fashion for such a project, but they were generally happy to talk and provided valuable insights into how Iraqis learned about the candidates. Reporters anywhere in the world can use these same features to find and talk with sources all the around the world at no cost. If they want to talk with people who are not Skype users, a modest fee applies, but of course in this case the Skype search features are not available, although other Internet search tools are.

Technology has also given reporters greatly expanded access to entire classes of source material previously rarely seen, if ever. For example, remote-sensing satellite imagery is now a routine part of reporting on a variety of stories, ranging from environmental reporting to military conflict. Satellite imagery can provide vital access to denied areas, help-ing the public understand critically important stories in a timely fashion. Dan Dubno, former producer and technologist at CBS News, explains:

> The success of getting satellite imagery into the hands of journalists in a breathtaking timely manner is the first part of what I see as the major transition to astonishingly accurate graphical displays. By that I mean imagery coupled with geographic information that's updated on a nearly instantaneous basis. Basically, we've now seen satellite imagery delivered in an extremely timely fashion so people in newsrooms are getting imag-ery within hours or, at worst, days of when they request it. This imagery is being merged with other data that are significant for more insightful news stories, including GIS [geographical information systems], crime statistics, census data, economic data, weather and disaster-related information. None of this would be particularly useful without base imagery to clearly show the viewers what's going on.
>
> We've transitioned from simply getting imagery to now integrating imagery with real-time data or data with other significant news value. A year ago I doubt if anyone in newsrooms could tell you what a [digital el-evation model] was or even what GIS is. Now every significant news entity is exploring how to integrate geographical data into its news graphics."[33]

Dubno, an expert in newsroom technology applications, notes on his Web site that "[b]roadcasters are using these [satellite] pictures to reveal 'denied areas' of the Earth: taking viewers to places where governments or nature otherwise bar access. In recent days, North Korean and Iranian nuclear sites have been made public."[34]

These same opportunities are beginning to transform journalist-source relationships at newspapers, including those in medium- or small-size markets, although the impact is still in its beginning stages. Herb Jackson, a veteran journalist at the *Bergen County Record* (New Jersey) and inaugural North Jersey Media Group journalist-in-residence fellow at Rutgers University, is an expert in the applications of GIS and other data to reporting. He observes,

> At a regional daily like mine, its use will continue to be uncommon, but will grow to be a more common tool in reporting the news as editors

see what major dailies like the *New York Times* and lately even the (New Jersey) *Star-Ledger* can do when databases are combined with maps and aerial photography to tell stories. New Jersey seems to be on the leading edge of this curve, with many base maps available for free download and satellite photos available on CD or DVD at a nominal cost.

Using GIS allows you to take data and present it in a graphical format that can really grab readers. You can run a chart that says taxes went up this much in 50 or 500 different towns, but if you color code each town, with the biggest increases in red and the smallest in green, everyone's looking at the map to see if their town is red or green. I don't know if they have the same reaction to a column of percentages.[35]

CONCLUSION

Convergence also poses serious challenges to journalists' independence in covering military conflict, crime, and even conflict situations on the domestic front. In these cases, it is not just a technological matter, but also one of ownership or economics. With news organizations increasingly part of behemoth, multinational public corporations composed of media properties of many types (e.g., print, broadcast, cable, online, satellite), there is increasing pressure on reporters covering military conflicts to accept Pentagon press rules that mandate or virtually require the embedding of reporters with the military. As was evident in the 2003 invasion of Iraq, reporters embedded with the U.S. military were frequently less likely to report critically on the U.S. military than they would had they not been embedded. Although some reporters were able to maintain their independence and critical edge, the result of embedding was sometimes a blurring of lines between independent journalist and government representative. Robert Jensen, a journalism professor at the University of Texas at Austin and author of *Writing Dissent: Taking Radical Ideas from the Margins to the Mainstream* (2001), made the following observations in the *Boston Globe* column "Embedded Media Give Up Independence," on April 7, 2003:

> CBS News's Jim Axelrod, embedded with the Third Infantry, discussed an intelligence briefing he sat in on and said, "We've been given orders."

Realizing the implications of what he said, he revised himself: "Soldiers have been given orders." On that same day, NBC anchor Tom Brokaw began reporting on "how successful we were" in a battle before correcting himself: how successful "the United States was." The anchors were similarly American-centric as they had more somber news to report, including Marines engaged in heavy fighting in southern Iraq and a British jet shot down by a Patriot missile, killing two airmen.[36]

This loss of independence was only natural and to be expected because reporters who spent days or even weeks living side by side with military personnel found themselves relying on the soldiers for their personal safety and probably found it difficult to be critical of those same personnel. In losing their detachment, many reporters also lost the critical ability to perform the watchdog role of the fourth estate, or fourth branch of government. Instead, the press (referring generally to all media types) in some cases became more of a lapdog. The reporting in early 2004 by CBS News's *60 Minutes 2* and by Pulitzer Prize–winning nonembedded investigative reporter Seymour Hersh on the U.S. military's abuse of Iraqi prisoners at the notorious Abu Ghraib prison underscores the need for an independent press corps during times of military conflict.[37]

This chapter outlines four forms of content in a digital media environment. Each form is examined in terms of its relative strengths and weaknesses, advantages and disadvantages. Case studies are analyzed in the context of these forms, with particular attention paid to content forms designed specifically to exploit the capabilities of new digital and networked media.

CONTENT RULES

Content is a core component of all media, regardless of their form. With the rise of digital, or computer-based, technologies, media content is undergoing dramatic changes. A summary of the four fundamental content forms is outlined as a typology in table 5.1. This typology is based on the intersection of two dimensions of media content in the digital media age: first is the degree of originality of the content, with most content being either repurposed for media and digital delivery systems or created as original or new content. Some content is a hybrid of repurposed and original content. The second dimension is the extent to which the content is designed to utilize the unique qualities of digital media, in particular interactivity (including user-created content), multimedia, and nonlinearity of presentation or storytelling, although there are other aspects of digital media design as well (e.g., video for small screen or mobile devices; video created using computational cameras, such as 360-degree video; and haptic/tactile media, such as the three-dimensional fax or home printer). Most content from established media companies

Table 5.1 Typology of Content Forms for Digital Media

	Repurposed Content	Original Content
Traditional Media Design	Form I	Form III
Digital Media Design	Form II	Form IV

tends to follow a traditional media design—where storytelling or presentation of content goes primarily one way from the organization to the audience, is noninteractive and linear (with a fixed beginning, middle, and end), and is limited in the range of media modalities employed. Digital content is increasingly utilizing a new media design, although much of this content is produced by the public user of digital media in addition to by nontraditional media organizations.

Dividing these two dimensions into two forms—repurposed or original and traditional media design, on the one hand, and design unique to digital media, on the other—presents a two-by-two typology with four content forms.

As table 5.1 shows, these four content forms are:

I. Repurposed content utilizing a traditional media design or model,
II. Repurposed content featuring a design unique to a digital media or online environment,
III. Original content based on a traditional media design or model, and
IV. Original content featuring a design unique to a digital media or online environment.

FORM I: REPURPOSED CONTENT

Each content form presents certain opportunities and costs for media. Form I is the least expensive and least risky in at least the short term for established media organizations. It entails content previously developed, tested, and proven to have an audience. Whether text, audio, or video, analog or digital, this content is relatively straightforward to produce and package for digital distribution. The biggest obstacle to repurposing content is obtaining the rights to distribute this content digitally or to protect it against illegal copying. Rights costs often depend on the media type or format, with text being the least expensive, audio (especially music) being somewhat more expensive, and video being the most expensive, depending on the original production values employed. Costs might range from tens or hundreds of U.S. dollars for a story in a daily newspaper distributed online to much more for other media. Consider the case of the highly acclaimed civil rights documentary *Eyes on the Prize*. Originally aired on television during the medium's analog days in 1988, the award-winning series did not air between 1993 and 2005, nor had it been released on VHS or DVD or any other format, analog or digital. The main reason: rights and permissions. Featuring material from more than eighty footage sources, ninety-five still archives, and one hundred songs, clearance rights for the material gradually expired. It took the producers years to raise $915,000 for research, rights clearance, and postproduction costs, explains Sandra Forman, Blackside attorney and director of the "Eyes on the Prize" Renewal Project. After a thirteen-year hiatus, the series aired again in the fall of 2006 on a television system now largely digital in format.[1]

Adapting form I content for digital distribution may entail as little as formatting it for digital media (e.g., CD or DVD, or online via the Internet or World Wide Web). This process is relatively simple and inexpensive. For a text document (e.g., a newspaper story), Web distribution might entail creating a fixed-form version parallel to the analog version of the document, which would involve creating a portable document format (PDF) version. Depending on features encoded into the PDF, the document will look like the analog version, whether printed on paper or displayed on a screen. It may or may not be copy enabled and keyword searchable, depending on the rights holder's or distributor's concerns about copyright protection or other factors.

In general, content in digital or online form is often no different than that available through conventional delivery systems. For example, many television stations and network news operations produce the same type of television news reports that they have long produced for analog, over-the-air television or cable distribution, but they instead deliver it via the Internet and other digital delivery media such as digital cable, digital satellite, and digital terrestrial broadcasting (television or radio). In the transition from one form to another, subtle and unanticipated changes may sometimes occur, as was the case in the 1970s when the introduction of videotape in television news was linked to new patterns of story editing and shot selection. Media producers may be unaware of the changes, as was demonstrated in research conducted by newsroom pioneer and technologist Adam Clayton Powell III (see chapter 10 for more on Powell).[2]

DTV often consists of the same shows, programs, movies, and the like, but they are simply made available online or via other digital delivery media and viewed on computers, DTV sets, TV sets with a digital adapter, and digital handheld devices (e.g., a digital mobile phone or PDA). This approach allows valuable access to archival video material that might otherwise be difficult to find—for example, the collection of video interviews conducted since 1956 by Richard D. Heffner, long-time host of the public-television program *The Open Mind,* the longest-running interview program on television. Historian and university professor of communication and public policy at Rutgers University, Heffner continues to conduct these important interviews, and the program is still on the air. An increasingly complete archive of the program is now available online, with video, transcripts, and more.[3] A visit to the site on May 12, 2006, offered access to Heffner's classic interview with the late civil rights leader Malcolm X, conducted June 12, 1963.

Copyright protection is a key issue for all four content forms and is examined in more depth in chapter 9.

FORM II: REPURPOSED CONTENT MODIFIED FOR THE DIGITAL DOMAIN

In many cases, content repackaged for the Web or other digital distribution forms may include additional interactive features. As such, it represents form II content, or content that is repurposed but adapted to features unique to the online or digital media environment. Among the most common adaptation is the insertion of links or hyperlinks in the form of Web addresses.[4] A link is often a useful modification that can add value to a previously published piece of analog content by enabling readers or viewers to see the content in a broader context, such as historical precedent or related background material. Many readers have come to expect such links, and providing them can help keep them satisfied at relatively little cost. Yet many media organizations fail to provide links in repurposed content (or even in original content) placed online out of fear that readers or other audiences or users will never to return to the original content once they have clicked on a link. This thinking often assumes that one's content has so little value that audiences or users, once departed, will not be inclined to return. It is worth noting that images or video can also be encoded with clickable links, or hot spots, to related online content; links are not limited to text-format content. An example of such interactive video that I produced with an embedded link is available online.[5]

In 2006, Time Warner began an experiment in interactive television with more than 160,000 of its cable subscribers to test a system that allows them not only full DVR capabilities to select what they watch and when, but also an indication of what those programs look like on screen. Viewers can select video clips on the latest headlines or market news. They can click on an icon and get selected in-depth weather reports. Such interactivity has been under development in fits and starts since at least 1977, when Warner Cable rolled out its pioneering interactive cable TV service QUBE in Columbus, Ohio.[6]

Movies delivered on DVD often incorporate additional interactive or on-demand features, such as scene selection, director commentary, deleted scenes, games, and music videos.

Many television program producers and distributors are increasingly looking to distribute their content online, either for streaming or downloading to desktop or laptop computers; to handheld devices, including mobile phones, iPods, and PDAs; and to handheld computer/communication devices, such as the Treo (which runs the Palm operating system; a variety of devices running various other operating systems are also available). On April 10, 2006, Disney, based in Burbank, California, announced that its television network, ABC, would be making several of its most popular television shows available in May and June for free download to various platforms, including episodes of *Desperate Housewives, Lost, Commander in Chief,* and the entire 2005–2006 season of *Alias.* Viewers would be able to download the episodes the day after they air initially on television.[7] As with many other television show providers, video programming is being made available to extend audience reach, but the content itself is not being modified other than for easier downloading (e.g., possibly in compressed format) or for different display (on small screens) or perhaps without commercials.

In some cases, video content providers are making additional video available live or in real time. CNN.com, for example, announced in early

2006 a new premium online video news service streaming live news coverage from multiple news sources.[8]

For young Internet and television viewers, a popular online video destination is Yahoo! Music.[9] Formerly known as Launch, the site streamed more than one billion music videos from January to November 2003, more than quadrupling the number of videos streamed from the previous year.[10] Headquartered in Sunnyvale, California, Yahoo! is among the largest of Internet portals, with more than 400 million unique visitors a month and nearly $2 billion in net income for 2006. Among Yahoo's specialties are music videos on demand, although other video, audio, and interactive services are also available.[11] As of July 2006, Yahoo! Music offered a database of more than one million songs.

"As teens and young adults increasingly turn to the Internet as their medium of choice, we feel there's great potential for them to turn to Yahoo Music for the music video content that they would normally get on television," said David Goldberg, vice president and general manager of Yahoo! Music. "We are dedicated to giving music fans a great user experience on Yahoo Music and will continue to provide them with access to the videos they want, when they want them."[12]

Yahoo! Music also offers viewers a chance to see music video premieres, such as the more than forty videos on the site in 2003. It had the exclusive online debut of Britney Spears's video *Me Against the Music*, featuring Madonna, in fall 2003. Spears's video was viewed more than 2 million times in the first five days after its Web premiere.

Among the most promising examples of form II content is another music Web site, Pandora.[13] This site offers registered users free access to more than 10,000 songs that have been analyzed by a musical team and sorted and classified by a wide range of musical qualities, including rhythm, melody, harmony, lyrics, and more. Users create their own "radio station" by selecting an artist or a song, and Pandora automatically generates a playlist based on assembling songs and artists with musical qualities like those of the originally selected artist or song. Users can create up to one hundred stations. While listening, they can continue to refine their station by indicating which songs and artists they especially like or dislike. At any time, a listener can stop or pause the station, and then later resume playing that song. Under the site's licensing arrangement, listeners can skip six songs an hour should they choose to do so. They can look at all previous songs played and purchase them or get more information about them, but they cannot look ahead to see what is coming up. The advertising-supported or advertising-free subscription-based business model is discussed in chapter 7. Users can log onto the site from any Internet-connected device and access their stations. Pandora's creators, the Music Genome Project, started working on the system in 2000 and continue to expand the music database under the leadership of founder Tim Westergren, a veteran musician and music executive. Independent bands can send the Music Genome Project a CD of their music, and if the company's reviewers like it, they may add the songs to the Pandora database. One area of music not currently included in Pandora is classical.

FORM III: ORIGINAL CONTENT ADHERING TO TRADITIONAL DESIGN

Content form III involves the creation, distribution, and protection of original content, whether text or multimedia (i.e., audio or video), but adhering to a traditional media design or presentation model of this content. This form is generally digital text produced for online newspapers, magazines, and books, as well as digital audio, images, and video for either online or other digital distribution, such as digital cable, satellite, DVD or CD, and HDTV.

This content adheres to traditional standards of production and may be relatively expensive to produce (especially for video), but not innovative in design. Free or low-cost distribution of such content was often the norm during much of the twentieth century.

Original digital content is oftentimes produced by nontraditional media organizations or producers. With the falling price of digital production technologies and the ability to distribute content, including video online or via other distribution channels, this form of original content has become increasingly common in the digital age. For example, various arts, educational, and cultural institutions produce extensive streaming video of live programs offered by those institutions. Illustrative is the May 15, 2006, video Webcast of a live seminar on the popular television series *Boston Legal,* hosted by the Museum of Television and Radio in New York. The seminar featured live commentary from the program's cast and creators, including stars William Shatner and Candice Bergen as well as creator and executive producer David E. Kelley.[14]

Established media organizations are increasingly producing original content designed at least minimally for digital distribution. In many cases, original digital video production is designed specifically for online distribution, but not extensively utilizing new media capabilities. One appropriate illustration of such original video production customized for the online environment is Viacom's mtvU, the original broadband Web site produced by MTV for college and university students. Among the best video reports yet produced by mtvU is *Translating Genocide: Three Students Journey to Sudan,* a twenty-minute original online video produced in documentary style by three U.S. college students who traveled to Africa. Premiered online on April 7, 2005, the video featured an on-location examination of the genocide in Darfur, supplemented by original photographs and limited interactive features.[15]

Media organizations are also testing the online video waters of various television formats. Among them is the *Late Night Fox Show,* an online network talk show that on February 25, 2005, featured *American Idol* contestant Jon Peter Lewis.[16]

Some accommodations to digital delivery systems are often made for form III content. This slightly adapted content is transitional between forms III and IV. Among these accommodations are certain metadata (i.e., data about the content), including content descriptors. For video, program descriptions are provided, enabling interactive programming guides and DVRs such as TiVo, or offering viewers more background information about the program they are watching or might watch. Secondary audio programming (SAP) is also often provided, as it is routinely for premium television channels such as HBO, Showtime, and Cinemax. SAP enables these programmers to deliver their video simultaneously in English and another language, typically Spanish in the United States and thus permits audiences to select the language in which they would like to hear the program in (e.g., movies are often dubbed in a second language, and there is no additional cost to delivering SAP on digital cable or other digital media). Interestingly, HBO airs its programming simultaneously on two different channels, one in English and the other in Spanish on HBOL (L for "Latin"), even though the vast majority of channel subscribers (via either digital cable or satellite, which is completely digital) have access to SAP and can watch the English-language primary HBO channel in Spanish simply by selecting SAP. HBOL does include some programming produced originally in Spanish, such as the original series *Boxeo de oro* as well as some Spanish films, which can be run with English SAP.

HDTV presents an interesting example of form III content. Although much HDTV programming follows the same narrative structure of traditional television, the higher resolution, more vivid colors, wider aspect ratio, and improved audio can make the HDTV experience more compelling. At the same time, the higher resolution of the images can bring both advantages and disadvantages. Imagery of nature, landscapes, and other subjects can be more realistic and detailed, but imagery of people can bring such clarity that minor skin imperfections become more visible. For many actors and television journalists, this characteristic can require more careful attention to makeup. In the adult movie industry, which is generally embracing the HDTV format, it can mean not only more attention to makeup, but even cosmetic surgery for actors and actresses.[17] The adult movie business in 2006 produced 7,000 titles on DVD, generating $3.6 billion in sales in the United States.

Another television feature available digitally is closed-captioning, although this feature is also available via analog distribution by delivering the closed-captioning in the vertical blanking interval.

Digital content can also be watermarked to help protect copyright and prevent unwanted copying and distribution[18] I discuss this topic further in chapter 9.

NBC Weather Plus illustrates the current nature of network television experimentation with the digital form. It offers something of a hybrid of repurposed and original programming reformatted for a digital display. The television screen is divided into three parts. The largest portion of the screen is a video image, sometimes a weather-related video news report produced for network television and sometimes a conventional weather forecast with a weatherperson superimposed over a weather map of the region being discussed. This portion is virtually identical to the weather forecast on the evening news. The conventional forecast is periodically replaced by a slide-show presentation of a static weather map with locations, temperatures, and other weather-related information displayed, as on the Weather Channel, occasionally with dynamic satellite weather imagery superimposed, and accompanied by an elevator-music soundtrack. The bottom of the screen is a banner showing summaries of various local-area forecasts (high and low temperatures, likelihood of precipitation, etc.). The left-hand part of the screen displays a close-up of one of the local forecasts and a banner advertisement from a channel sponsor. NBC Weather Plus is aired twenty-four hours a day on digital cable or digital terrestrial television, which because of compression can accommodate multiple channels of television programming, known as *digital multiplexing.*

G4 television, a cable and satellite television channel and Web site, demonstrates the potential to combine television programming and Web content in the digital age.[19] One of the more popular shows on the channel is the original *Star Trek* series, but on G4 it is called *Star Trek 2.0.* It encourages viewers to play along with the show via the G4 Web site; they can interact with plot developments in the show, comment on their favorite characters' actions, such as Mr. Spock's use of the Vulcan mind meld, and play the "Spock" Market, potentially amassing a fortune in Federation Credits and thereby rule the universe. User Web comments and actions are displayed live during the airing of the show.

A notable hybrid of forms III and IV is illustrated by a movie produced and distributed via Disney. Called *High School Musical,* this Disney movie exploits the increasingly common home use of DVRs, especially by young viewers. *High School Musical* features several scenes where characters demonstrate dance steps to home viewers. When the program was aired, young viewers were thus encouraged to dance along. I observed my then eleven-year-old daughter and her friends watch the movie and then dance along with the characters-instructors. The dance steps were far too complicated for me to hope to replicate with my two left feet, but for my daughter and her friends, who deftly invoked the instant replay and slow-motion features of their DVR, it was a source of immense dancing pleasure to practice and eventually master the complex maneuvers based on a choreographed adaptation of a basketball game put to contemporary hip-hop music. The girls quickly internalized the moves and put on quite a show of their own. Moreover, they demonstrated that in the digital age, the notion of a TV-land couch potato may quickly become a thing of the past.

FORM IV: ORIGINAL CONTENT DESIGNED FOR THE DIGITAL DOMAIN

Form IV represents the possible future of media. Here, original content features designs and capabilities unique to a digital, interactive media system. Among the types of content seen, heard, and otherwise experienced in this category are blogs; podcasts; 360-degree or spherical images and video; interactive content; and all media types, including original hypermedia, video with hot spots (i.e., embedded links or other media objects, such as high-resolution images), immersive media (e.g., virtual or augmented reality, including the Situated Documentary developed by me and my colleague Steve Feiner, discussed more fully later in the chapter), three-dimensional graphics or objects, navigable or zoomable images and video, and three-dimensional sonic or acoustical environments.[20] This content can be presented on or accessed either by fixed digital devices (or by analog devices connected to a digital box or adapter, such as is often the case with analog television sets connected to digital cable or satellite systems) or by portable, wireless media and may be formatted particularly for handheld or wearable devices with either small or immersive (e.g., head-worn) displays with audio headsets and other features (see figs. 5.1, 5.2, and 5.3).

Blogs, Podcasts, and Other New Media

Form IV content can be developed by professional media organizations and is increasingly being done so. An interesting example is a bilingual (English/Spanish) multimedia report on the *New York Times* Web site. Published January 14, 2007, the text of the report on the rise of Pentecostal Christianity in New York and around the world is primarily in English, but it is supplemented online with photos, video, and audio in the voices of some of the sources interviewed, many of whom were Spanish speaking.[21] English subtitles are available on screen, translating the Spanish audio. Yet in many cases form IV content is being developed by citizens without any formal media training or connection to a media organization. Bloggers, podcasters, and Web site developers who have a story to tell are the bread and butter of form IV. As of October 2006,

Figure 5.1 Columbia University Mobile Journalist Workstation research prototype. © 2002 Computer Graphics and User Lab, Columbia University.

in fact, more than 57 million blogs had been created, many by average citizens without a professional media background or connection.[22]

Some blogs are produced professionally, but with limited budgets. Many of the best blogs are produced by journalists in addition to the regular reporting they do for a parent newspaper or other news organization. David Carr, who covers primarily business stories for the *New York Times,* also writes a blog on the Academy Awards race. His blog, he says, is like "a large yellow Labrador: friendly, fun, not all that bright, but constantly demanding your attention."[23] One popular video blog (or *vlog*) produced on a shoestring budget is *Rocketboom,*[24] a three-minute daily vlog covering current events and affairs in New York City. Its stories range widely, from major news to unusual Internet culture, with an emphasis on international arts, technology, and the drama of the

Figure 5.2 An augmented-reality view of Low Library on the Columbia University campus. This view of Low Library shows a set of virtual flags that represent portions of multimedia Situated Documentaries. This image was captured from NTSC video shot through one eye of a Sony LDI-D100B 800 x 600 resolution, color, stereo, see-through, head-worn display. © 1999 Tobias Hoellerer, Steve Feiner, and John Pavlik, Computer Graphics and User Interfaces Lab, Columbia University. Thanks to Steve Feiner for providing these images.

blogosphere. The site features a complete and searchable archive of its video reports and is distributed using RSS technology.

Many media organizations depend in large part on content contributions from lay persons, typically without pay. Slashdot, Digg, OhMyNews, Wikimedia (e.g., Wikinews, *Wikipedia*), and many other online operations invite persons from around the world to create, submit, and edit content for online presentation. Even News Corporation relies on mostly teenagers for the "content" available on its immensely popular MySpace social Web site, with an estimated 55 million registered users as of April 2006.[25] Social-networking sites are growing at a tremendous rate and feature extensive user-contributed content of many forms, from text to pictures to movies. As popular as they are, these sites have some serious downsides. For example, because of MySpace's popularity among the

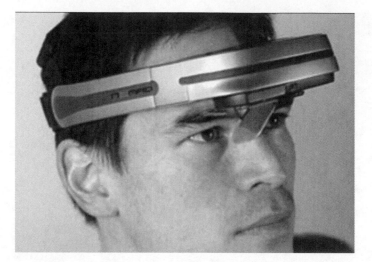

Figure 5.3 Nomad augmented-reality headware. Photo used with permission of Nomad.

young, who often use it to post personal information they hope to share with their friends, it is also frequented by pedophiles and other predators. Some scholars also point out that, in a certain sense, such commercial use of free user-provided content is a form of nonpaid exploitation of users who may be drawn to the allure of media fame.[26]

A serious concern arising from the citizen journalism emerging online is the credibility, reliability, accuracy, and trustworthiness of such content produced by individuals who may have no training in journalism ethics or professional standards and who do not always operate within a system that can provide professional editorial guidance. In fact, numerous cases have emerged where significant errors occurred in citizen-produced online content.

Blogs do not always feature original reporting. They usually feature more commentary than fresh information, as tended to be the case during coverage of the 2006 midterm elections in the United States. A November 2006 report by the Project for Excellence in Journalism, which is affiliated with the Pew Research Center, concluded that television Web sites did perhaps the best job of covering the election as it unfolded, but that blogs fared the most poorly. The study tracked thirty-two different outlets, including television news, Web sites, cable and network television, newspaper, magazine, blogs, and aggregators such as Google and Yahoo. The Web sites delivered results quickly, permitted users to delve deeply into exit poll results, and displayed interactive maps offering results from hundreds of races. "Most news organizations are still finding their way in this new multimedia environment," said the report, compiled by Tom Rosenstiel, director of the project. "The exit poll may be more important today, not less," Rosenstiel added, "since users are probing that information directly, functioning as their own editors going state by state, looking for demographic information, late deciders and more."[27] MSNBC.com was particularly easy to navigate with its range of searchable features such as election results, videos, and discussion boards. Newspaper Web sites tended to be slow in reporting results, and blogs tended to provide little original reporting.

Wikipedia

On *Wikipedia,* the English-language free encyclopedia consisting largely of contributions from nonpaid lay citizens, a highly publicized error occurred in May 2005 when contributor Brian Chase anonymously posted a hoax *Wikipedia* entry about John Seigenthaler Sr., former assistant to Attorney General Robert F. Kennedy. The hoax entry implied that Seigenthaler may have played a role in the assassinations of President John F. Kennedy and his brother Robert. It stated, "John Seigenthaler, Sr. was the assistant to Attorney General Robert Kennedy in the early 1960's. For a brief time, he was thought to have been directly involved in the Kennedy assassinations of both John, and his brother, Bobby. Nothing was ever proven."[28]

The erroneous and possibly libelous entry was soon discovered, and, because any user can log onto Wikipedia.org and modify most entries, the hoax entry was replaced with Seigenthaler's official biography by veteran journalist Eric Newton, then of the John S. and James L. Knight Foundation and formerly of the Freedom Forum. *Wikipedia* contains more than 1.2 million entries, most of which are produced by approximately 1,000 regular users, many of whom are site administrators. On any given day, roughly one hundred to two hundred entries may be protected from public editing, primarily due to frequent vandalism or disagreements about what should be written. Some entries, such as those for George W. Bush, Islam, and Adolf Hitler are "semiprotected," or available for editing by people who have been registered at the site for at least four days. *Wikipedia* is funded largely by user contributions of $50 to $100.[29] In October 2005, Seigenthaler contacted Wikipedia.org founder Jimmy Wales, and "Wales took the unusual step of having the false information hidden from the public in Wikipedia version logs. As a result, the unredacted versions of the article could be viewed only by Wikipedia administrators."[30] Chase later admitted to the false posting and apologized to Seigenthaler, who accepted his apology. The affair drew considerable attention to *Wikipedia,* challenging the legitimacy of the site as a source of reliable information.

Then the journal *Nature* commissioned a study to compare the accuracy of *Wikipedia* with the professionally produced online *Encyclopedia Britannica.* Published in December 2005, the *Nature* study found that *Wikipedia* and *Britannica* are about as accurate in science entries, which suggests, the journal wrote, "that such high-profile examples (like the Seigenthaler and Curry situations) are the exception rather than the rule."[31] Adam Curry, a developer of podcasting, had been involved in an erroneous report on podcasting on *Wikipedia,* which was subsequently corrected. Perhaps most important, the *Wikipedia* case points out the self-correcting nature of citizen-produced digital media. Whereas traditional media organizations feature professional training and editing as a primary means of minimizing error, citizen-produced digital media feature collective knowledge and widespread public review as principal mechanisms to minimize and correct error. Although studies to date are minimal, initial research suggests that both approaches can produce quality results. Nonpaid citizen-produced digital content is of course considerably less expensive to create.

The Situated Documentary

An exemplar of form IV content, with many of its advantages and disadvantages, is illustrated by the Situated Documentary, a new form of documentary developed by me and my colleague Steve Feiner, a professor of computer science and the director of the Computer Graphics and User Interfaces Laboratory at Columbia University, along with our students.[32]

Through an interdisciplinary collaboration over the past decade, this research team has applied the technology of mobile augmented reality systems to journalism. The adaptation is called the Mobile Journalist Workstation (MJW) and enables a reporter to capture audio and video, including 360-degree video from any location, or to display multimedia presentations embedded virtually into the real world surrounding him or her, thereby telling a story in an immersive, three-dimensional format. The reporter is thus able to attend or relive previous news events as a virtual participant in the past, either recent or distant. The MJW system as a form of mobile augmented reality brings together a diverse array of convergent, digital technologies, including camera, microphone, see-through head-worn display, head-orientation tracker, high-speed wireless Internet access, wearable computer, handheld computer and display, GPS, and battery pack. The head-orientation tracker enables gaze-approximation, hands-free computer interactivity (i.e., it doesn't require the use of a mouse): the user simply looks at an object in the field of view for at least a half-second and thereby selects it, much as a user with a desktop computer would use a mouse to place a cursor over an object and click on it to select it. In the field, gaze-approximation interactivity is particularly useful in permitting hands-free computing applications.

Using this array of technologies, our students have created a series of prototypes that we call Situated Documentaries because they are located, or situated, where the events occurred, and users can visit these locations to experience the news stories in their original context. They are an example of what some call *location-based media*. Situated Documentaries can also be experienced in a virtual sense from a remote location by overlaying the story content onto a virtual background and providing online user access.

Situated Documentaries produced to date cover such topics as the 1968 Columbia University student strike or revolt; the tunnel system that honeycombs beneath the university's Morningside Heights campus on the Upper West Side of Manhattan; the story of Colonel Edwin Armstrong, the Columbia engineering professor who invented FM radio and later committed suicide; the early research of physicist Enrico Fermi, who began building a nuclear pile in the basement of a Columbia building and enlisted the help of players from the football team to transport radioactive materials via the tunnels; and the prehistory of the campus when in the mid–nineteenth century it was home to the Bloomingdale Asylum for the Insane, with one of the buildings still standing on the campus near West 116th Street. Samples of these Situated Documentaries may be seen online.[33]

The Situated Documentary is a revealing example of form IV content because it simultaneously illustrates the dramatic possibilities of content designed specifically for a digital media environment and demonstrates the slow diffusion of such innovative experimentation by established media companies. To date, only a few commercial experiments have been conducted with this array of technologies, one at *Clarin,* the largest Spanish-language newspaper in South America (Buenos Aires, Argentina), and another in Europe, primarily at museums interested in the technology as a way to provide multimedia tours of cultural or historical sites outside the physical confines of museum facilities (e.g., the story of the historic eruption of Mt. Vesuvius and its impact on Pompeii, Italy).[34]

A number of nonmedia commercial enterprises are developing mobile augmented reality content applications for the marketplace. Among the leaders is Nokia, which is testing a system on its 6680 mobile phone. Using software called Mobile Augmented Reality Applications, the Nokia system allows users to identify objects viewed on the screen of a camera phone.[35] The prototype Nokia phone also includes a GPS, an accelerometer, and a compass. Through the combination of technologies and software, the modified 6680 can identify restaurants, hotels, and landmarks, and give links and related information about these objects on the phone's screen. The San Francisco–based company Geovector is conducting a similar mobile augmented reality project in Japan as well. Its system does not provide as extensive on-screen annotation, but it does offer location-based content to the user via a mobile phone.

Further Experiments in Digital Content

Other digital media experimentation is under way at the Integrated Media Systems Center (IMSC) at the University of Southern California. Directed by media pioneer and veteran news executive Adam Clayton Powell III, the IMSC is engaged in creating the next generation of journalism technologies, including innovative online video applications. Through a partnership with MacNeil-Lehrer Productions, the IMSC is exploring immersive, interactive, three-dimensional audio and video formats and tools for recording, producing, and transmitting digital news and information, including via the Internet.[36]

Media companies are slow to implement form IV content for a number of reasons, including the unproven nature and audience appeal of such unusual content as well as its potentially high production cost. Yet some major media companies are experimenting with original content produced for portable digital media devices. News Corporation's Fox Television has commissioned a cell phone serial drama *24: Conspiracy,* dubbed a *mobisode* (i.e., a mobile episode). Director Eric Young was hired to produce 24 one-minute mobile episodes for a spin-off of the hit television series *24*. He was reportedly most vexed by the problem of displaying bullet holes, which are not uncommon on the violent drama series. Mr. Young learned that making video for a pocket-size screen is quite different from producing for a 27-inch television set. His solution was to make the bullet holes extra large and use twice as much blood to make the bullet holes and wounds easily visible on a cell phone screen.[37]

Well known for its music videos, MTV is also developing original video programming for cell phones. Its first domestic cell phone production is a series of three-minute documentary-style video reports on the world of hip-hop. Starring Sway Calloway, *Sway's Hip-Hop Owner's Manual* debuted in 2006.[38]

Another example of a provider of video produced exclusively for mobile devices is NBC Mobile, which is producing original news and feature material specifically and exclusively for hand-helds such as cell phones.[39] For example, the mobile video reports on *Wine Tasting with Ed Deitch* have examined topics such as new electric wine bottle openers and new vintners. NBC Mobile also produces a vlog for cell phones, such as the three-minute report on the Iraqi elections on December 16, 2005, or *Entertainment Buzz,* a series of two- to three-minute segments on movies, celebrities, and popular entertainment.

A number of news organizations are producing original live news coverage of breaking events delivered via the Web, including either to the desktop or to hand-helds. Among them is WDEL television, which has debuted a live online video news program covering Delaware's top stories of the day. Similarly, WCBS2.com/KCAL provided live Web-exclusive video coverage of Hurricane Katrina on August 31, 2005, including on-location and in-studio video. This station's going live online was a hallmark.

Not all the experimentation is by familiar news organizations. Gotv network, based in Sherman Oaks, California, is making video reports for MDAs, with a stated objective of tailoring video news for viewing on 2--by-2-inch screens.[40] A four-minute Gotv report on December 12, 2005, provided breaking news coverage of Golden Globe nominations in Los Angeles, combining still imagery with video close-ups of host and producer Athenia Veliz-Dunn.

The emergence of original video programming for MDAs has not gone unnoticed by the national organizations that recognize and award excellence in the media. The National Academy of Television Arts and Sciences, for instance, announced in November 2005 a new category for the Emmy Awards that would recognize outstanding original programming for computers, cell phones, and other handheld devices, including the video iPod.[41] Peter O. Price, the president of the academy, said that seventy-four entries were received from newspapers, magazines, and movie studios, the greatest number ever in any category. "In this digital world, everyone is capable of launching video programming," said Mr. Price.[42]

Titanic director James Cameron is continuing to experiment with digital technologies to develop new forms of motion picture storytelling. With $200 million in funding from 20th Century Fox, Cameron is at work on a hybrid motion picture that blends live actors with digital characters that are expected to be as lifelike and authentic in appearance as their live counterparts and that will populate a photorealistic virtual world on screen.[43] The science fiction epic *Avatar* is scheduled for theatrical release in 2009 and will be displayed in three-dimensional format, which will require theaters to update their projection technology to accommodate the requirements of the digital movie.[44] The movie will be shot using a high-definition three-dimensional camera developed over a period of six years by Cameron and special-effects expert Vince Pace.[45] *Avatar* will utilize motion-capture technology to create the computer-generated creatures in the movie: a live actor's movements and interactions are recorded and then synthetic images are overlaid to create the computer-generated creatures or characters. Similar technology has been used effectively in movies such as Peter Jackson's 2005 remake of *King Kong*. Weta, the New Zealand–based firm that produced the special effects for Jackson's *Lord of the Rings* trilogy, will produce the special effects for *Avatar*. Contemporary video games also use motion-capture technology.[46]

CONVERGING MULTIPLE FORMS

In the shape of competitors XM and Sirius, satellite radio in many ways represents the potential of combining content forms I, II, III, and perhaps even IV, thereby offering a media product of unique value.[47] Satellite radio provides on a subscription basis hundreds of channels of audio programming largely free of commercials, much of it repurposed, but some of it original. Whether repurposed or original, the programming is adapted to the digital media environment. In general, the radio receiver for satellite radio is digital and has a screen to display text and graphics, as well as speakers for audio playback. The text accompanying the audio typically includes information about the channel, the program, and the song being played (name of the song and artist, or title of the show for which the song was created). In addition, the text contains information about sports, finance, and other customizable topics. In these ways, digital radio (satellite or terrestrial) can be substantially more than analog radio.

Most satellite radio channels are music, including contemporary hits, popular music grouped by decades going back to the 1940s, American standards, Broadway music, jazz, Latin jazz, classics, hip-hop, world music, Spanish-language music, and much more. Audio programming also includes a diverse array of other options, including old-time radio programs (e.g., *The Shadow*), comedy, news, talk (e.g., Sirius offers Howard Stern; XM, Oprah), and extensive sports programming (e.g., XM offers the entire slate of Major League Baseball games, and Sirius offers the entire slate of National Football League games). Much of the satellite programming is also available to subscribers via the Internet.

That said, satellite radio is largely devoid of one very important form of content long a strength of radio: local news. As of April 2006, XM began to offer traffic and weather reports and news programming from Bob Edwards, formerly of public radio, but little in the way of local journalism. Sirius offers more news programming, including local traffic, weather, U.S. news from Fox, financial news from CNBC, NPR programs, and international news. Neither of the competing satellite services is in a position to offer extensive local radio, which would require a substantial commitment of bandwidth and other resources, especially to produce quality original local journalism. Even with advanced digital compression, providing thousands, hundreds, or even dozens of local news channels would rapidly consume a substantial portion of available bandwidth and be expensive to produce. Both competitors do provide fairly extensive local or regional traffic and weather reports, with much of it utilizing computerized, or automated, speech-synthesis audiocasts.

A notable exemplar of content that is transitional between forms II and IV (repurposed content and original content designed for digital media, respectively) is *mash-up media,* or content created by merging together data or information published by others and thereby presented in a new form, with new possible understanding or meaning. The innovation in experimental news and information presentation provided by a Web site known as ChicagoCrime is illustrative.[48] ChicagoCrime is a freely searchable database of crime in Chicago, the third-largest city in the United States, with a population of roughly 3 million. ChicagoCrime is a convergence of data published by others, but put into a new form that is both easily accessible and visual. The data being merged, or mashed up, are from the crime data reported by the Chicago Police Department, the Citizen Information Collection for Augmented Mapping (a system developed by the Chicago Police Department for use by its police officers), and mapping and satellite data provided by Google.[49]

By mashing up these data, ChicagoCrime provides users a highly detailed, interactive, and useful look at where crimes have been reported in Chicago. Users can browse the data in a variety of ways: by crime form, including arson, homicide, assault, and gambling; by street all the way down to the block level, with which they can map nearby crimes; by date with hour-by-hour lists of all crime reports; by police district or beat; by ZIP or postal code; by ward; by type of location, including automated bank teller machines, Chicago Transit Authority train, gas station, or bowling alley; by city map, where users can sort crimes by various criteria (e.g., person, property, society) and view them on one map; or by route, where users can draw a line on the map of Chicago and see crimes along that route. Users draw the route simply by clicking on two or more points on the map displayed on screen, and the Web site automatically connects the dots. Then crime reported anywhere on that route will be displayed. This information might be useful if a person or family walks or plans to walk, drive, or take the bus along a particular route, to and from school, work, or house of worship. Crime data available go back to November 2005 and will be stored indefinitely on the site. Having grown up just outside Chicago, I would have found this particular Web site of immense value on a recent trip to the Windy City (so dubbed because of strong winds off Lake Michigan, one of America's five Great Lakes). As a test of the system, I selected a route I traveled to dinner on my recent visit and was somewhat shocked but not entirely surprised by the density of the color-coded virtual pins in my mapped route, identifying dozens of crimes of many types (e.g., criminal possession of a weapon, battery, domestic battery, theft, burglary, narcotics possession).

In Park Slope, Brooklyn, a similar mash-up, location-based medium has been developed by the writer Steven Johnson.[50] Through his Web site, Johnson collects and presents various information, from a museum review to a parent's opinion of a neighborhood school to a police report, all mashed-up via Google Earth and Yahoo! Maps.[51] Users can enter ZIP codes or neighborhood names and find news and other information about those neighborhoods.

Mash-up media such as ChicagoCrime or Outside.in may not exactly be storytelling. They are more like what one might call an on-demand, interactive, and customizable information graphic, but they are visually the sort of news or information graphics often seen in newspapers or other news media, and they represent what U.S. news media like to call "news you can use." What is more useful to citizens than being able to find out precisely and immediately how dangerous their communities are? Unfortunately for the news media, this service is not being provided by one of their own. It is another example of someone else outside the news community delivering innovation in news and information. Providing community news was once the almost exclusive domain of local newspapers. Unless newspapers find a way to capture and utilize the capabilities afforded by digital media, their exclusivity may be a thing of the past. The *New York Times* has applied the technique of mash-up media to its travel section to create an interactive map that combines dozens of its travel features on spending thirty-six hours in different communities around North America.[52] Google Earth offers news media opportunities to develop more creative and visual forms of mash-up news media. Network television news operations such as *ABC World News with Charles Gibson* by 2007 made extensive use of Google Earth to provide three-dimensional virtual fly-ins to remote locations of news stories around the globe.

In 2006, ChicagoCrime added an item that might be considered closer to storytelling: the police blotter. It provides in text form the reported stories behind the crimes, courtesy of the *Chicago Journal* newspaper. Here is an example from 2006:

> April 19
> 10:20 P.M.
> Robbery
> 1100 block N. Western Ave. Restaurant
> An armed robbery occurred at Subway, 1129 N. Western, at 10:20 P.M. April 19, according to police reports. A man wearing a black hooded sweat shirt and a mask walked in the door, up to the counter, pulled out a blue steel handgun, and made his threat: "Give me all your money, I'm not playing around." After getting an unreported amount of cash, the man took off on foot. Police have not yet made any arrests.

Another example of repurposed or mashed-up media in transition between forms II and IV is Google News, which is news culled automatically, categorized, and presented on the World Wide Web through computer algorithms.[53] The economics of the Google News aggregator is driven by the high efficiency of computerization of knowledge processing. Millions of Internet users already rely on the site for news on a regular basis, with many of them having registered with the site and customized it to reflect their personal news interests and appetites. One of the features available is the automatic tracking of news on particular subjects of personal interest or based on a keyword, such as the name of a person, organization, or thing. Categories with news automatically sorted, presented, and updated frequently (the currency of a news story is always indicated in the number of minutes since online publication) include the world, the United States, business, science/technology, sports, entertainment, health, and "most popular" (subjects viewed by the largest number of people). News is culled from 4,500 sources from around the United States and the world. For October 2005, Nielsen//NetRatings reported that Google News had 7.1 million unique visitors that month.[54] This number indicates that the site is far less popular than other news aggregator sites, with Yahoo! News enjoying 25.4 million unique visitors and America Online (AOL) News attracting 15.1 million unique visitors in that same month.

An interesting variation on the idea of mash-up media is provided by the natural-language processing group at Columbia University's Department of Computer Science.[55] In this case, the data are even more mashed up than by Google News and by computer, and move farther into form IV content. Professor Kathleen McKeown's research group has applied a branch of artificial intelligence (AI) known as natural-language processing to develop the Columbia Newsblaster, an AI system that mashes up published news reports from dozens (and potentially even hundreds or thousands) of news sources available online and synthesizes them into easily read news digests.[56] As reported on the Newsblaster Web site, the "system automatically collects, clusters, categorizes, and summarizes news from several sites on the Web (CNN, Reuters, Fox News, etc.) on a daily basis, and it provides a user-friendly interface to browse the results. Articles on the same story from various sources are presented together and summarized using state-of-the-art techniques. The Newsblaster system has already caught the attention of the press and public. A recent analysis indicates that Newsblaster receives tens of thousands of hits a day, and news agencies that have written articles about Newsblaster include the *New York Times, USA Today*, and Slashdot."[57]

Based on a synthesis of material culled from eleven articles published by news sources around the world on April 11, 2006, here is what Newsblaster reported about the possibility of war in Iran. Some might say Newsblaster passes the Turing Test (computer pioneer Alan Turing's famed test of AI: Can a person tell if he or she is talking to or interacting with a person or a computer?).

WASHINGTON—A magazine news story suggesting the President George W Bush administration will go to war to stop Iran from developing a nuclear bomb is long on hype and short on facts, a senior administration official said Sunday. The New Yorker's Seymour Hersh claims in his report that the Bush administration is increasing clandestine activities inside Iran to create regime change and to plan a major air attack. WASHINGTON (Reuters)—The Bush administration insisted on Sunday its priority was to seek a diplomatic solution to the dispute over Iran's nuclear ambitions, amid reports of stepped-up planning for possible US air strikes.

On this same day, typical of any day, Newsblaster generated its stories based on published news stories from more than two dozen sources around the world, including the BBC and the *Washington Post*.[58]

For those interested in the potential of mash-up media, a useful resource online is the "programmable Web."[59] This Web site provides an easy, step-by-step approach to making mash-up media as well as dozens of other popular mash-ups and other mash-up resources.

CONCLUSION

This chapter has examined four content forms for digital media: form I, content repurposed for digital media but based on a traditional media design; form II, original content developed for a digital media environment but still based on a traditional media design; form III, content repurposed for digital media but adapted somewhat to fit a digital media design; and form IV, original content designed specifically for a digital media environment. Content forms I, II, and III are the most commonly produced by established media companies and organizations. Form IV content is produced mostly by individuals or small, entrepreneurial organizations, with traditional media tending only to experiment with it in a tentative fashion. Despite this small range of producers, form IV content offers the greatest potential to engage the next generation of media user, which has grown up with and is accustomed to an interactive media system and for whom creating and consuming content are equally familiar. Moreover, appetites for a more interactive and customizable journalism are emerging in which traditional news media face a somewhat dubious future, with audiences for traditional news media forms dwindling.

Further research is needed to assess the extent to which these content forms are being developed internationally and in which of them innovation is occurring.[60] Such research has particular relevance to established media organizations' seeking a new opportunity in the digital age. As Lorenzo Vilches has written, digitalization is changing the structure of media content and organization.[61] Understanding this transformation will be fundamental to developing effective new forms of media content in the digital age. Everette E. Dennis, Distinguished Felix E. Larkin Professor of Communication and Media Management at Fordham University, once observed, "Broadcasters are storytellers, newspapers are fact-gatherers and organizers of information and news magazines are kind of a hybrid of both."[62] In the digital age, one might argue, all media should explore a hybrid approach that blends all three traditional roles plus interactivity in the media model for the twenty-first century.

6 / DISTRIBUTORS OF DIGITAL MEDIA

Since the dawn of modern mass communication, those who have controlled the means of media distribution have wielded enormous power. Distributors of media have often exerted significant influence over public opinion, reaped huge financial gain, and often held the ear or eye of elected officials and other leaders, whether local or national or international.

In many cases, the distributors and producers of media have been one and the same. The producers of media content have sometimes controlled the means of distribution, but under U.S. antitrust regulations they have been forced to divest these convergent interests. When the vertical integration smacked of monopoly or even oligarchy, Hollywood's movie studios were forced to sell their movie theater interests. In the case of television, however, the major networks have traditionally relied on affiliated local television stations to distribute their programs. The growth of cable and more recently of satellite television has provided the networks with additional options for delivery. But as these systems have converted to digital format and the number of channels has exploded, important changes have occurred in the television-distribution system. The size of the audience for the individual network, channel, or program has shrunk. Competition for audience has grown dramatically. Despite rising prices for commercial time, relative advertising resources for individual shows have been reduced. Moreover, the growth of broadband Internet has introduced yet another means of distributing television programming. The Internet, digital cable, and satellite also offer on-demand program distribution. Movie theaters are converting to digital motion picture distribution and display. At the same time, the traditional distribution systems, digital though they may increasingly be, are still tightly controlled and impose substantial barriers to those seeking to distribute their content. A case in point played out in dramatic fashion in 2006 when the National Football League, itself a major industry player with annual revenues of more than $32 billion, launched its NFL Network but struggled to get the valuable video on cable franchises around the country.[1] As of December 2006, the NFL Network is available in just 40 million of 110 million U.S. households with television, which resulted in significant frustration for many football fans. When the Green Bay Packers played on a Thursday night in December against its archrival the Minnesota Vikings, cable franchises such as Charter Communications did not carry the NFL Network, thus preventing many fans throughout much of the Packers' home state of Wisconsin from seeing a game that in years past they would have been able to watch on over-the-air television. Charter declined to carry the new network ostensibly because it did not wish to impose any additional fees on its viewers—reportedly seventy cents a month.[2] The NFL Network is carried on satellite television, however, so all subscribers to this digital distribution system were able to watch the game.

TRANSFORMING THE SYSTEM

The entire media system is in a state of flux. In many ways, there is far less control over the means of distribution of television, or video, programming and other forms of content. According to nineteenth-century philosopher, political economist, and socialist revolutionary Karl Marx, this lack of control represents a potentially fundamental shift in society. Marx contended that in every society and every epoch there is a ruling elite, and the ideas of the ruling elite are the ideas that dominate the society. The elite include government leaders, media owners, and others who own and control the means of production. These elite need social and economic stability to maintain their position of power and wealth. To an extent, Marx's model applied most clearly during the analog age of television, radio, newspapers, and other mass media, which were dependent on expensive and limited means of production and distribution. In Marx's view, media and other social and political systems are disinclined to challenge prevailing ideology. In fact, they tend to support and propagate the basic ideology of a society through what Antonio Gramsci calls hegemonic culture, or the process through which the values of the bourgeoisie become the accepted values of all.[3] This media-driven hegemony leads to the empowerment of certain cultural beliefs and values at the expense or exclusion of others. Dominant ideas or views can become even more dominant and entrenched, making social or political change more difficult.

Although news media in a democracy such as the United States do question government, big business, and other aspects of society, they do not often challenge the basic ideology of capitalism and democracy. This absence of critique was obvious during the Cold War era, when the Soviet Union was typically portrayed in the media as the enemy of the United States. And such a model has been extended to the modern era, with states such as North Korea and Iran characterized as rogue or terrorist states in opposition to the United States. The ideology of democracy and capitalism is accepted and reinforced to provide the economic engine to support the media. Ownership and control of material production is the key to the dissemination of this ideology. The question in the early twenty-first century is whether Marx's views still apply in the digital age. The answer is: possibly. Digital technologies put far greater control over the means of production and distribution in the hands of the individual rather than in the grasp of corporations. There is less hegemonic ideology and greater diversity of voices and ideas in this transitional digital media system. This diversity is demonstrated, for example, in the rap "50 Shots," inspired by the November 2006 slaying of an unarmed black man in Brooklyn, New York, by an undercover police squad, invoking memories of the similar slaying of African immigrant Amadou Diallo in the Bronx in 1999. In the 2006 case, when aspiring baseball player Sean Bell and some friends were leaving a strip club in Brooklyn that the police had been staking out as a suspected prostitution operation, they were involved in an accident with an unmarked police car, and the police opened fire, launching a fusillade of fifty bullets, several of them striking and killing Bell early on the morning of his wedding. In a city torn by racial tensions, accusations of excessive force by the police quickly ensued, and the hip-hop emcee Papoose compiled an angry, obscenity-laced rap titled "50 Shots." Unable to obtain air time on conventional analog radio

Figure 6.1 Video of former Iraqi leader Saddam Hussein's execution on December 30, 2006, recorded using a cell phone. Photo posted on YouTube.com.

stations, Papoose posted his uncensored rap online.[4] The rap has also received airtime on satellite radio.

Yet emerging new voices on the Internet are sometimes acquired or appropriated by commercial interests. Such is the case with a great many Internet applications, such as the early file-sharing services. Napster is perhaps the most recognized example. It provided many early Internet users with unparalleled ability to share files of all types, whether music or video. But, after extensive legal challenges, Napster closed shop and then reemerged as a mainstream commercial operation designed to deliver online music for a profit. The example of YouTube's distribution of the Saddam Hussein execution video is also relevant here.

Although the number of companies that control distribution of media, including television, through traditional channels has shrunk, the fact is that traditional channels are less important in the overall system of media distribution. The Internet and other digital distribution systems are delivering an increasing portion of the overall volume of media content. Among the new competitors are the various telephone companies. These telecommunications firms, also facing a flux in their own markets, range from giants such as Verizon ($72 billion in 2005 sales) to smaller wireless companies such as Cingular ($34 billion in 2005 sales).[5] Only a few years ago these companies would not have been considered distributors of media programs or content, but with the rise of digital broadband they are now increasingly important players in the distribution of media. Whether with regard to MP3 music files, video to mobile phones, or television to the home via a phone line, telephone companies are vying to control the distribution of media content. And giant Internet companies have entered the media-distribution business in a major way. Among the leaders are Google and Yahoo, each company valued in the billions of dollars (Google had a market value of $132 billion as of October 2006) and both controlling digital content distribution via the broadband environment.[6] Verizon has also launched FiOS TV, a digital television network delivered to consumers via a fiber optic broadband network. It is marketed as a direct competitor to cable and satellite television. Verizon is not producing new programming or funding the production of new programming, but instead is packaging and delivering programming with an emphasis on diversity. FiOS TV also offers features available exclusively in a digital environment, such as on-demand programming of current movies, children's shows, sports programs, and high-definition channels. Offerings include international premium channels such as RAI (Italian), TV5 (French), ART (Arabic), and TV Japan; domestic premium channels such as HBO and Cinemax; and basic channels such as ESPN, Discovery, and TNT. FiOS TV includes a DVR and is partnering with independents who produce or have enough content to fill a channel (such as the fifty ethnic video channels). Once completed, the fiber optic network will have cost Verizon $20 billion. As of 2006, the network passed (i.e., the fiber is installed near these homes, allowing connectivity) 20 percent, or 6 million, of the 30 million Verizon customers. Verizon is adding 10 percent a year to its fiber network.[7]

Consequently, because of the challenges posed in these early stages of digital content distribution, traditional media companies are having to adapt and employ a variety of strategies to distribute their content. Few have found clear answers defined in successful business terms.

Many producers of video and other forms of content are making this content available online through their own Web sites. For example, CBS News makes its video and text news reports available online, as do the other networks, such as ABC News video on demand and CNN video.[8] Particularly popular at the networks and their affiliates is supplementing stories reported on evening newscasts with additional Web video related to those stories. On NBC Nightly News with Brian Williams on May

12, 2006, for example, Broadway celebrity Maria Friedman, star of the Broadway Show *The Woman in White,* was interviewed about her battle with breast cancer. The interview on the evening news was brief, but Williams also invited viewers to visit the NBC Web site for additional video.[9] Video is also supplemented on Web sites by additional text reporting, graphics, photos, and links to related material. News media are moreover inclined to make their video available through online video aggregators. MSN video, for instance, provides an extensive combination of video from a variety of sources.[10]

Another increasingly popular video aggregator is Google Video.[11] Based in Mountain View, California, Google groups its video into a variety of presorted categories, including the top one hundred (most-viewed videos). In May, high on this list was the complete video from the annual White House Correspondents Association dinner, featuring a roast of President George W. Bush in 2006.[12] This year's dinner drew extensive news media coverage, particularly of a Bush impersonator who wore a facial prosthetic to complete his impersonation. Little attention was given to the politically incorrect satire of Stephen Colbert, who was the officially featured comedian of the night, but his lampooning of the president is available in its entirety on demand on Google Video. Next on the list is Google Picks, which Google describes as "a small section on Google Video that highlights videos that have been selected by Googlers as suggestions for cool videos that users might want to watch. Think about it like the 'Staff Picks' section at a video store. Selection criteria may include, among others, the following: uniqueness of content, user value, newness to index, seasonality, and quality of video." Then, there are random videos, animation, comedy, commercials, educational videos, movies, music videos, news, sports, and TV shows.

Google News offers another form of news content aggregation and distribution.[13] News from 4,500 news sources (according to Google) from around the world and online are sorted and presented in nine or more categories, including top stories, the world, the United States, business, science/technology, sports, entertainment, health, and "most popular." Users can also customize the page or subscribe to an RSS feed that automatically sends news updates.

Google Video and search engines such as Yahoo! permit users to search for video, which is generally limited to keyword searching of the title or text descriptions of the video. Experimental tools are emerging that permit searching based on video content itself, such as a face seen, a type of action occurring, or colors and shapes shown.

Nielsen/NetRatings reported that Google Video drew 7.3 million unique visitors in April 2006, making it the fourth-largest online video provider at the time.[14] Number one was YouTube, based in San Mateo, California, which attracted 12.5 million unique U.S. visitors that month.[15] YouTube invites individual users to upload their own personal videos for sharing with other interested persons. It limits most videos to no more than five minutes in length, and many are short clips, from a few seconds to a minute or two. In some cases, entire movies are uploaded, but in short segments. The videos are sometimes professionally produced and oftentimes feature humor, such as Weird Al Yankovich's video for the song "White & Nerdy," a parody of Chamillionaire's hip-hop hit "Ridin' (Dirty)."[16] YouTube is as much a social-networking site as a video provider, and the former function may in large part be what is drawing the large number of unique visitors to the site. In September 2006, YouTube Inc. solidified its position as the leading video-sharing site when it signed a deal with Warner Music Group to air its music videos and share advertising revenue. Numbers two and three on the online video list with more than 10 and 7 million unique visitors, respectively, in April 2006 were Microsoft's MSN and News Corporation's MySpace, which is also largely a social-networking site. Then, in October 2006, Google announced that it had reached an agreement with YouTube to acquire the video-sharing site for $1.65 billion. This move established Google as a leading distributor of video in the digital age by giving it a total of nearly 20 million unique visitors to its two major video sites (i.e., Google Video and YouTube).

YouTube's popularity underscores one of the dramatic changes in the nature and function of media in the digital age. In an increasingly common scenario, online media are influencing the agenda of more established media. In a prime example, YouTube featured in August 2006 a video of Senator George Allen, the Virginia Republican, calling a college student of Indian descent *macaca,* a racial slur.[17] The video had been viewed 326,894 times as of December 22, 2006.[18] Allen called the student *macaca* apparently without fully understanding the meaning of the term and used it because the student, S. R. Sidarth, a volunteer for Allen's opponent, was in attendance as an observer shooting video of Allen's campaign event. The YouTube video quickly shot to the top of the site's most-viewed list, subsequently moving from the Web to a story on the front page of the *Washington Post* and on to cable and network television news shows.[19] This case was not an isolated one. In October 2006, when the midterm elections were beginning to heat up, a controversial political advertisement aired on television featuring actor Michael J. Fox lobbying on behalf of a Missouri Democrat who favored embryonic stem cell research. The spot contained video of Fox, who suffers from Parkinson's disease, rocking back and forth, the symptoms of the disease apparent. Conservative talk show radio host Rush Limbaugh immediately accused Fox of not taking his medicine just to make the disease's symptoms more apparent. Then, when Limbaugh was informed that it was in fact the medicine that caused the rocking motion, he retracted that statement and apologized, but then added further criticism of Fox for exploiting his illness for political gain. Viewers outside Missouri could see snippets of the controversial ad during stories on the evening news about the controversy, or they could do what many journalists did—go to YouTube.com, search for "Michael J. Fox," and immediately pull up copies of the ad in its entirety. Viewers could see both the ad and other related material. In fact, many journalists not only obtained copies of the ad through YouTube, but found related video material of other celebrities who had lobbied on behalf of stem cell research or other issues and then incorporated clips from those videos into their reports, thus contextualizing the Fox controversy.

Many bloggers and podcasters are also including video on their Web sites.[20] A number of Web sites, including mefeedia, podcastvideos, and vlogdir, serve as aggregators or directories of the thousands of video on blogs and podcasts.[21] Although much of this video is of dubious quality and of narrow or personal interest, some of it occasionally has had newsworthy and social value. When the tsunami hit Banda Ache, Indonesia, in 2004, much of the most viewed video of the destructive impact of the tsunami was provided via personal vlogs.[22] Extensive video of the anti–World Trade Organization protests in Seattle in April 1999 were also posted on vlogs. In one case, the posting resulted in the arrest of a vlogger who would not reveal his sources to a federal prosecutor. I examine this topic in chapter 8 on media regulation and law.

The Starbucks Corporation, which was among the first companies to install wireless Internet access at its stores, is experimenting with Wi-Fi-delivered entertainment video. Among the video programming available is free film footage of blues artists such as Muddy Waters and blues documentaries produced by Martin Scorsese. Various other sources of online video are also available, including downloadable and streaming video on demand of full-length feature films from Movielink and CinemaNow. The downloadable video files are DVD quality and take about thirty seconds to ten minutes to start watching, although downloading the entire movie may take thirty to ninety minutes, depending on the Internet connection speed. More than 1,000 current releases and older films are available for prices of about $3 to $5 a movie.[23] Interestingly, although the movie is downloaded via the Internet, the viewer can store the video in a variety of formats and can watch it on a television set or computer screen, depending on his or her preferences. The viewer can also save the movie on a laptop for later viewing at another location.

As the courts gradually resolve the issue of copyright in the digital domain, many movie providers will likely begin to take advantage of using the Internet as a means of cheaply and directly delivering to consumers worldwide secure video on demand, pay-per-view content, and movie rental services. Since at least 2005, Miramax has been distributing online a portion of its movie library, offering more than two hundred movies for purchase or rental to anyone with a computer and fast Internet connection. For $3.95, I purchased and downloaded in about twenty minutes via a high-speed Internet connection a digital copy of *Quantum Project,* which I watched on my computer and enjoyed a full-length, full-screen display very similar in sight and sound to the display of the same movie at home on an analog television from a VHS-tape copy.

Lionsgate has similarly been offering its movies online for purchase or rental, with more than 150 movies available for free. Sony Pictures Digital Entertainment Inc. is set to launch its online movie-distribution service Moviefly, as is Disney, which is also planning to release its own set-top box. Online movie distribution is poised to grow as concerns about security and online piracy are resolved. In early 2007, Sonic Solutions introduced Qflix, a new digital software lock that consumers can use to burn DVDs of movies downloaded. Prior to this new security software, consumers had been blocked from burning downloaded movies to DVD because no available software conformed to the studios' agreed-upon content-scrambling system.[24]

Sports are also increasingly popular as broadband Internet DTV fare. On April, 13, 2001, the National Basketball Association offered the first live video and audio Webcast of a game, the Dallas Mavericks against the Sacramento Kings.[25] The Webcast transmitted at near-broadcast quality, with about thirty frames per second (the actual frame rate was affected by factors such as network congestion, etc.) and CD-quality sound. Transmitted using the "streaming" media player from RealNetworks (a streaming media player plays video or audio in near real-time without requiring the audience member to download the file, which might be very large and may require a long delay), this free Webcast had 120,000 visits from Internet users in eighty-seven countries. It is not clear whether future gamecasts will be offered for free or a fee. Major League Baseball has started charging users to tune in to real-time or archived Webcasts of video and audio of its games and has lured more than one million fans to pay substantial fees for the feeds ($4.95 for the World Series video package; other rates for monthly or season packages).[26] MLB.com video is generating a multi-million-dollar annual revenue stream for the sports league. Live audio of the games is distributed to XM Radio subscribers.

A premier provider of a wide range of types of video online is RealNetworks, which through its RealPlayer offers quality video online, including from ABC News, CNN, Fox Sports, iFilm (independent films), and the Weather Channel.[27] The latest RealPlayer (version 10 as of 2007) offers near-DVD quality video over broadband Internet connections, wireline, or wireless. The full SuperPass Real Video service costs $14.99 a month, but a reduced video-programming package is available for free (a lower-quality software package is also part of the free option). The Seattle-based RealNetworks has had its software downloaded by 300 million users to stream audio, video, and other multimedia content.[28]

Aggregators of motion pictures are also drawing a growing amount of online viewers. CinemaNow and Movielink are among the premier movie aggregators. CinemaNow provides movies from Sony, MGM, and Lionsgate, with current features such as *Fun with Dick and Jane* and scores of older movies in a wide range of categories.[29] Movielink provides movies from five studios, including Metro-Goldwyn-Mayer Studios, Paramount Pictures, Sony Pictures Entertainment, Universal Studios, and

Warner Bros. Studios.[30] Current features include movies such as *Brokeback Mountain* and *Memories of a Geisha,* as well as a large collection of older movies. Prices for both services range from a few dollars to rent an older movie to $20 or more to rent or buy a current release, with viewing restrictions in effect. Viewers have various payment options, including per minute viewing for certain types of video content (e.g., mature). Warner Bros. says it will make hundreds of its films and shows available by late 2007 for paid download through the broadband video file-sharing site BitTorrent.[31] Peer-to-peer file-sharing networks are especially popular for downloading television programs. Sites such as Limewire, well known for sharing of music files, are also heavily trafficked by users downloading popular television programs, from *Buffy the Vampire Slayer* to *The Gilmore Girls,* much of which is available at no cost. It is not always clear as to the legality of the downloads, although copyright rules are ostensibly in effect.[32] A wide variety of sites also offer legal downloads of television programs for a fee.[33] Viewers join these sites, pay a fee, and then download any of thousands of television programs and view them on the computer or a television set connected to an Internet access device.

Another increasingly popular video aggregator online is Apple's iTunes music store, which made its name selling copyright-protected music files for download to iPods or other MP3 devices.[34] With the video iPod (and other video capable devices) on the market, selling videos for downloading was a logical next step. Among the options available for the online consumer are buying at a discount an entire season of a TV show such as *Desperate Housewives* and downloading any of more than 3,000 music videos or hundreds of television shows and watching them commercial free at $1.99 an episode. Programs are provided from a diverse array of television networks, including ABC, NBC, MTV, ESPN, Sci Fi Channel, Comedy Central, Disney, Nickelodeon, and Showtime. Fox Entertainment provides downloadable episodes of *24* and *Prison Break* via iTunes. Viewers can also create iPod-compatible versions of their home movies using iTunes and can buy and send music videos and TV shows as gifts to anyone with an e-mail address. They can organize their videos into playlists and limit children's access to videos. Viewers can also access reviews and ratings of shows from other viewers.

One question that arises for network affiliates in this age of TV show downloading is: Will the role of the affiliate be undercut or reinvented?

If viewers can easily download a show after it has aired, will they be less inclined to tune into a rerun on a network affiliate? The answer seems obvious.

Stimulating the growth of video-distribution online is digital video start-up Brightcove, whose technology enables anyone who produces video to distribute it easily and inexpensively for viewing or downloading from various Web sites. The *Wall Street Journal* reports that groups as diverse as a Yoruba language and culture center in Nigeria, a news site in the Slovak Republic, and a political blog called Wizbang in the United States are distributing their videos via the Web using Brightcove technology.[35] Brightcove is not the only provider of Internet video technology spurring the wave of diverse online producers, however. Others, such as XOS Technologies, are making it possible for universities large and small to let their alumni and others tune in online to collegiate sports from anywhere in the world.[36]

Gradually entering the media-distribution fray are the organizations once known as the phone companies. Just as the digitization of cable television has enabled cable TV firms to enter the telephone or voice-communication business, telephone companies can use their digital network infrastructure to deliver media services, including cable TV and broadband Internet services. For the consumer, this increased competition is an opportunity to see potentially improved customer service and possibly lower prices. It remains to be seen whether this opportunity truly emerges.

Verizon Wireless has entered the music-distribution business by permitting subscribers to download songs over the air. Subscribers were initially required to pay a flat monthly fee for the service, but in July 2006 Verizon introduced a download fee option of $1.99 per song. This altered arrangement may be a reflection of increased competition from other digital music distributors such as iTunes, which are based on a per song download model. Given the typical Verizon Wireless phone plan, downloading a song would likely cost an additional few cents if it required two minutes of network airtime.

Network television operations are also exploring new strategies for delivering their content. Most of the major television networks have already begun distributing at least some of their most popular programs online. As of the fall of 2006, viewers with Internet access can go to

ABC television's video-programming Web site and watch shows such as *Grey's Anatomy, Six Degrees,* and *Ugly Betty* online, free, and on demand twenty-four hours after the shows premier on television.[37] Flash Media Player is required to view the video, but it installs quickly and easily on most personal computers. For best viewing, broadband Internet access is needed, at least 500 Kbps. The Flash Player automatically tells the viewer if there is sufficient bandwidth. Lower bandwidth will not noticeably affect the audio quality, but the video may lose resolution, look somewhat grainy or pixelated at times, perhaps drop a frame or two occasionally, and even stop if the connection is particularly slow. The programs come with limited commercial interruptions. As a test in October 2006, I watched episodes of *Grey's Anatomy* and *Ugly Betty* online via a wireless broadband connection, and both played seamlessly. The programs had three brief commercial interruptions, and a commercial logo was displayed above the video window, indicating the name of the program's corporate sponsor. In today's commercial-skipping age, these embedded commercial messages may be an effective option for programmers and corporate sponsors alike if they want to be sure to reach an audience. It is worth noting that when the programs are watched online via broadband, the video quality is quite high, appearing to be near DVD quality, although the screen size is limited to nine inches. The audio quality is also high. The video offers some interactive supplemental features, including pause and fast-forward features, information about the episode, and its run time. It is interesting to note that with the majority of the commercials stripped away, an hour-long television program can be viewed in around forty-three minutes online—one way to pick up a few minutes in the course of an otherwise overscheduled day. The implications of online video distribution for program scheduling are also potentially profound. Moreover, if the programs are available online on demand, the need for a cable television subscription or for a DVR becomes somewhat dubious. Viewers may soon be able to assemble their own à la carte video programming on their computers. Major League Baseball permits viewing of its games online to paying subscribers. Video news services are available online. Entertainment programming and movies are available online on demand. A full slate of video programming available on demand online may be available sooner rather than later.

Time Warner's AOL Television is an aggregator and distributor of an extensive collection of vintage television shows, all of which are available for free viewing by online users.[38] System requirements are a personal computer running the Windows XP or Vista operating system, Windows Media Player 10 (or the most recent version), and a broadband Internet connection. Thus equipped, viewers have at their fingertips on demand hundreds of episodes of some seventy classic shows, ranging from *Adventures of Superman* to *Gilligan's Island* to *Wonderwoman*. Notably, Vista includes the Windows Media Center, which provides a variety of multimedia functions, including "store photos," "audio and video," as well as "play and record television shows." It also accepts digital cable television, so a set-top box or separate DVR is unnecessary.[39]

One might ask, What is left for the cable television program distributors? As the marketplace for video has fragmented in the digital age, NBC Universal has launched a new company to distribute video programming to Internet sites, including its own and others. The National Broadband Company (NBBC) will include programming from NBC's television network and local stations and from other companies. Audiences typically will be able to download or stream the video program at no cost. They will be required to view commercial messages inserted before each video segment. Revenue will be shared among the program's creator, the Web site owner, and NBBC.

Motivating NBC was the emergence of some of its own programming on the Internet. In early 2006, "Lazy Sunday," a segment from NBC's long-running comedy program *Saturday Night Live,* popped up online. Viewers had recorded the bit and uploaded it to YouTube, to their own blogs, or onto pages on MySpace. The online demand for the segment was apparent and convinced the executives at NBC that the genie was already out of the bottle.

NBBC is a joint enterprise between NBC Universal (owned by General Electric) and NBC's affiliate stations. The affiliates own about one-third of the company, and they expect the online syndication market to generate new outlets for the news and entertainment programs they produce. It is an effort to compete with online video aggregators. "If we really want to compete with big aggregators like Yahoo and Google, we need our video in as many places as possible," said Randy Falco, former president of NBC Universal Television Group and current chairman and CEO of AOL Limited Liability Company.[40]

Distribution of video programming is also moving to mobile devices. In 2007, Sony, one of the world's largest producers and distributors of motion picture entertainment, digitized its five hundred largest-grossing movies for online distribution and viewing on mobile devices. Although not originally created for mobile devices, these movies will find a potentially large audience on the more than 50 million cell phones, portable media centers, and the Sony PS2 and PS3 game console devices now in use in the United States. Sony hopes that hits such as *Spider-Man* and *Hitch* will find a new audience on the mobile platform. In some ways, it is following the example set by Apple in the distribution of music online and now of video programming and movies. At the same time, the motion picture industry is concerned that putting movies online will spur file swapping and pirating of movies, as has been the case in the music industry. This topic is discussed in chapter 8 on regulation.

Video and music are not the only media forms finding new distribution channels in the digital age. Primarily text-based analog media are also widely distributed in digital form, especially online. Newspapers have since the 1980s made an increasing portion of their content available online.[41]

Satellite radio companies, including both XM and Sirius, have become important aggregators, packers, and distributors of media content in the digital age. One of the more interesting dimensions of this process is the distribution of the so-called back catalog of media content. For example, well-known folk singer and activist Pete Seeger has found a ready and growing audience on satellite radio. The XM folk channel frequently features songs by Seeger and his 1950s group the Weavers, such as "Goodnight, Irene" (written by Leadbelly), which topped the pop charts for thirteen weeks in 1950, as well as the original songs "Where Have All the Flowers Gone," "Kisses Sweeter than Wine," "Wimoweh" (a.k.a. "The Lion Sleeps Tonight"), and "If I Had a Hammer."

One day in the fall of 2006 I was driving to work and listening to a satellite radio channel when I heard a comedy bit from 1979 by Gilda Radner, the late comedian who made national fame starring in NBC's long-running *Saturday Night Live* show. A character Radner created, Roseanne Roseannadanna, entertained and grossed out graduates of the class of 1979 Columbia Graduate School of Journalism in her commencement address. Having been a professor in the school from 1995 to 2002, I had never heard Radner's commencement address, but found it very entertaining in 2006. As Radner cautioned, "Remember, it's always something. If it's not one thing, it's another." Truly words to live by in the digital age.

DIGITAL CINEMA

Motion pictures have since their invention been distributed on celluloid film. This practice is finally changing in the digital age. It was technically impossible until recently to obtain in digital format the image quality of projected film. In May 2002, filmmaker George Lucas catapulted digital cinema forward with the blockbuster sequel *Star Wars, Episode II: The Attack of the Clones,* the first major live-action motion picture shot entirely on digital video. This movie demonstrated that digital could deliver imagery that had as high a quality as celluloid film. Yet the distribution of digital cinema was still in low gear at the time. Most theaters showed the movie on 35-millimeter film transfers, although a few displayed it on digital movie projectors that displayed at either 2,000 or 4,000 pixel resolution, comparable to celluloid film and even better than HDTV and with no graininess. Digital pictures are free of dust and scratches; their audio continues to feature digital surround sound; and there are no acoustical dropouts often experienced at reel changes because digital movies have no reels. Since Lucas's pioneering effort, a growing number of filmmakers are shooting digitally, including Steven Soderbergh and Robert Rodriguez, and more theaters are playing these movies digitally. Digital distribution of movies is also accelerating. *Wikipedia* reports that "[t]he major Hollywood studios agreed to a (digital) standard in mid 2005, and it is expected to become widespread during the following three-to-five years."[42] Hollywood executives have long had their fingers on the pulse of new technologies, in particular technologies for production and distribution of motion pictures.[43] There are several ways digital movies can be distributed—via satellite or the Internet or a fixed-medium device such as a DVD. A single movie stored digitally creates a multigigabyte file, typically about 20–30 GB or more.

By delivering digital movies over the Internet, the cost of motion picture distribution is dramatically decreased. There is no longer the need to produce potentially thousands of copies of movies on celluloid film and ship them across the country and internationally. A single celluloid print can cost $1,200, and a global distribution requiring 4,000 celluloid prints of a movie can cost $5 million. As *Wikipedia* notes, "In contrast, at the maximum 250 megabit-per-second maximum data rate defined by DCI for digital cinema, a typical feature-length movie could fit comfortably on an off-the-shelf 300GB hard drive (about one hundred dollars), which could even be returned to the distributor for reuse after a movie's run. With several hundred movies distributed every year, industry savings could potentially reach $1 billion or more." Costs can be even further reduced by satellite or Internet delivery.[44]

One of the biggest concerns about shipping movies digitally is the potential for piracy. This threat can be minimized using strong encryption technology. Digital display of movies can also reduce the likelihood of illegal copying in the movie theater via camcorders if a digital watermark is inserted on the movie, making it more difficult to copy cleanly. Digital movies can also be encoded with other data that can guarantee the correct synchronizing of soundtrack and subtitles as well as the display of subtitles for the hearing impaired. Other metadata inserted in the movie can provide automated light dimming and drawing of curtains in the theater. A digital movie can also link back to a central database to monitor the number of times a movie is displayed, which facilitates and reduces the cost of accounting.

DIGITAL BOOK DISTRIBUTORS

Electronic books are also being distributed online. Among the leading distributors are the eReader commercial site and the not-for-profit Project Gutenberg.[45] These digital bookstores provide a collection of instantly available full-text works that dwarfs even the largest brick-and-mortar booksellers. Project Gutenberg offers limitless copies of more than 19,000 book titles from the public domain as well as a few copyrighted works for which the copyright holders have granted permission for free online distribution. A division of Motricity, eReader offers more than 17,000 book titles, mostly copyrighted books available for purchase and download.[46] Many of the roughly thirty eBook distributors also offer other downloadable digital products, such as audio books. And authors can upload their own books to these sites for distribution, an option not generally available in the traditional book-distribution business. In total, as of November 2006, about one million books were available online in digital form worldwide for download.[47] An estimated 1,692,964 eBooks were reported sold in 2005, a 60 percent increase from 2003, according to a survey commissioned by the International Digital Publishing Forum. Eighteen eBook publishers contributed to the 2005 report, including DigitalPulp Publishing; Elib AB; Ellora's Cave Publishers; E-Reads; Fictionwise, Inc.; Hard Shell Word Factory; Harlequin Enterprises Ltd.; HarperCollins; Houghton Mifflin Company; John Wiley & Sons, Inc.; McGraw-Hill; Pearson Education; Random House; RosettaBooks; Simon & Schuster; Stonehouse Press; Time Warner Book Group; and Zondervan.[48] Adding to the number of copyrighted books sold is the more than 2 million public-domain eBooks downloaded from sites such as Project Gutenberg, bringing the total number of eBooks downloaded in 2005 to nearly 4 million. Yet compared to the number of conventional books sold in 2005, some 2 billion, eBook distribution is still insignificant statistically speaking.[49] Sales of conventional printed books did decline, however, by 44 million units from 2003 to 2004. It remains to be seen whether the public appetite for books in electronic form will grow as it has for online news and entertainment as well as other forms of digital media. As improved and less-expensive eBook reader devices enter the marketplace, book-reading habits may evolve as habits for other digital media have.

CONCLUSION

Distributors of digital media are growing rapidly in virtually all segments. Whether movies, television, radio, text-based media such as newspapers or magazines, or even long-form text narratives such as books, the distribution of media content in digital form is swelling rapidly and in many cases overwhelming traditional distribution channels. The only significant exception at this point is book distribution. Although eBooks are nearly ubiquitously available online, the public appetite for them has grown only slowly. Only a few million eBooks are downloaded each year by a small number of persons. Yet it is not surprising that the oldest of all public-communication media and the form with the longest-held habits of consumption and distribution would be slowest to change. Moreover, the display or access devices for eBooks are still not fully comparable to or advantageous in comparison with print forms. As a result, eBooks are still something of a niche product. As habits and preferences evolve and display technologies improve, eBook distribution may accelerate. Digital cinema distribution is also growing somewhat more slowly than the distribution systems for most other digital media, but it is poised for rapid growth.

Distribution in digital form offers product sellers many advantages over the physical distribution of analog media products. Increased speed, improved control and monitoring, cost reduction, and greater efficiency (i.e., there is no waste—no overshipping or returns in digital distribution) are four of the greatest advantages of digital distribution. For these reasons alone, distributors of media are aggressively pushing digital distribution.

Leading digital media distributors are in some cases the same as analog media distributors. In many cases, however, new companies or not-for-profit organizations have emerged as leading if not dominant players. Google is perhaps the foremost distributor and aggregator of digital media, including not just news and information, but also audio and video. Google is also deeply involved in the scanning of books with an eye toward the creation of the world's biggest digital library and perhaps biggest book-distribution system. Apple's iTunes has emerged as a major distributor not only of digital music, but also of movies and other forms of multimedia. Together, these new and evolving digital media distributors are rewriting the media delivery landscape and helping the consumer move ever closer to a system of fully on-demand media.

7 / FINANCERS AND OWNERS OF DIGITAL MEDIA

Funding and ownership of U.S. media of public communication have evolved continuously since at least the eighteenth century. Most media have been commercial in nature, but have changed in ownership structure from largely family-owned, independent media to more publicly traded, chain or group-owned media conglomerates often national or international in scope. Offering greater economies of scale, these large media organizations bring a different set of values and principles to the media enterprise, sometimes subsuming media operations and interests within much larger multi-industry corporations (e.g., NBC is owned by General Electric). When the media, including newspapers and broadcasters, were family owned, there was generally less pressure to make a profit, although many did generate huge profits. The focus was more often on serving in the public interest, and media were generally seen as a public trust. One of the reasons family-owned media could operate in this fashion was that there was relatively little competition, and barriers to entry were high, in contrast to today's saturated media environment. Many urban communities did have competing English-language daily newspapers, but the host of alternative news and entertainment sources from satellites to the Internet to ethnic and immigrant media either did not exist or were much less a factor. Broadcasters received the use of the airwaves from the government at no cost and were in a position to reap huge financial rewards.

Nevertheless, even family-owned media required at least some level of profit to sustain publication or broadcast. Under the modern system of largely publicly traded, conglomerate media ownership, the pressure to generate profits is greatly increased. Consequently, many decisions are made less on the basis of creating a quality media product and more on generating short-term profit or shareholder value. This approach sometimes means layoffs. Time Inc. laid off 600 employees in 2006 and another 289 in early 2007, largely in response to dwindling advertising revenue and heightened competition from the Internet.[1] The 2007 cuts represent about 5 percent of Time Inc.'s 3,300 editorial employees worldwide. The editorial positions cut were primarily at the company's print magazines, such as *People*. Time Inc. executives report they made the cuts in order to allocate more resources to the Web.[2] People.com set its own record for Web traffic in a twenty-four-hour period, with 39.6 million page views following the Golden Globe awards on January 15, 2007. The prior record for People.com was 28.3 million page views following Tom Cruise's November wedding. Time Inc. is keeping all of its so-called laptop correspondents, who work in Los Angeles but report online and by phone to editors in New York. The company still generates an annual profit margin of 18 percent.

The *Philadelphia Inquirer* in 2007 laid off seventy-one newsroom employees (17 percent of its staff), and seventeen of the journalists who were laid off, almost one-quarter of the total, were minorities, thereby reducing the diversity of the newsroom.[3] For newspapers, newsroom staffing cuts can mean relying on more wire-service copy. It sometimes means less investigative reporting. In television, it can mean more reality-based shows, which cost less to produce. For local TV news, it can mean more crime reporting and adherence to the adage "If it bleeds, it leads." It can also mean making greater investment in new media as well as organizing and managing more efficient media operations that can compete with international media companies. The good comes with the bad. One thing that has not changed substantially for the better is diversity of media and media ownership in the digital age. Mainstream media have tended to be owned and controlled by powerful, wealthy white men. There have been exceptions to this rule, such as Katherine Graham of the *Washington Post* Company and John H. Johnson, the late founder of Johnson Publishing, publisher of such leading magazines as *Ebony* and *Jet* and the world's largest African American–owned and operated publishing company.[4] And some major media companies do have minorities and women in positions of senior leadership, such as Robert Parsons, CEO of Time Warner, and Pamela Graham Thomas, chairman of CNBC, the NBC cable news channel.

Media in the digital age have become something of a commodity, a product that is viewed oftentimes purely or largely in business terms, much as clothing, food, and energy are. In the days of analog media, when a far greater portion of media were private, family enterprises, newspapers and network news divisions were typically viewed as special—enshrined in the First Amendment and serving in the public interest. As such, news and other media were held to a higher standard but not always expected to turn a profit, though they usually did. In the twenty-first-century marketplace, media are increasingly seen as little different from other big businesses. Typifying this view of media as commodity are the observations from Hani A. Durzy, a spokesman for eBay, the major online auction site where just about anything can be bought and sold, including media properties. Durzy says of eBay, "Media buys are a commodity. . . . They (buyers and sellers) felt that there's [sic] some efficiencies that could be wrung out of the existing system."[5]

Complicating the picture in 2006 was the development of private equity firms buying major publicly owned media companies. The November acquisition of Clear Channel Communications by equity firms Thomas H. Lee Partners and Bain Capital Partners for $26.7 billion is the biggest buy so far.[6] Potentially of concern is whether such equity firms will continue to view media as a public trust or merely as an investment designed to spin off cash. The situation also raises possible issues regarding federal media ownership rules as well (see chapter 8). Thomas H. Lee Partners is part of an equity group that bought Spanish-language broadcasting company Univisión for $12 billion, and both Bain and Lee are part of an equity group that bought the radio broadcaster Susquehanna Pfaltzgraff for $1.2 billion.

Complementing the commercial media sector is a smaller number of media that are publicly funded, largely through government support, corporate and foundation grants, and gifts from private citizens who compose at least a portion of the audience. Outside the United States, publicly supported media, especially on the broadcast side, are much more extensive. In the case of the BBC, funding comes largely through a license fee on every household that has a television set in the United Kingdom. In both the United States and the United Kingdom, the public broadcasters are designed to operate independently of governmental or political influence, although this separation is not always easy to maintain.

As society moves steadily into the digital age, the financial and ownership structure of media is continuing to evolve. The ultimate form or forms of media financing and ownership may be quite different than they have been, although it is likely that some combination of commercial and nonprofit or public media will continue. Driving much of this transformation is the Internet, which has spawned significant opportunities to develop global, or what media expert Montague Kern calls *transnational,* media companies.[7] These companies' operations transcend international boundaries, delivering content and interactivity via the Internet to communities defined more by areas of interest, language, and culture than by geographic or political boundary.

Much online media content is available at no cost to the consumer. Some of this content is produced by individuals or organizations not particularly concerned with the cost of production or distribution because they are private citizens producing the material for their own interests. Or some of the producers of the online content may be groups with a public-relations, public-affairs, or publicity agenda.

FOUR BUSINESS MODELS FOR DIGITAL MEDIA

Much of the most popular online content, including online video with the highest production value or news focus, is produced by established or emerging news or media companies seeking to make a profit or to at least to offset their video production and distribution costs. In these cases, at least four main business models are taking shape in the digital media space.

Robert Picard describes media business models as an architecture encompassing "the resources of production and distribution technologies, content creation or acquisition, and recovery of costs for creating, assembling, and presenting content."[8] As such, the business models for media in the digital age are based in part on the business models that prevailed during the analog age. Given the new and evolving qualities of the digital media system, however, the business models are similarly evolving to exploit or satisfy the requirements of a transformed media system. Louisa Ha and Richard Ganahl note the distinction between business *models* and business *strategies.*[9] Models are modes of practice, whereas strategies are means to attain the business goal. M. S. Ming and B. P. White have outlined four digital media business models based on sources of revenues: advertising, e-commerce or transactional, subscription, and bundled or partnership.[10]

Advertising-Supported Digital Media

An example of a popular online video service free to the user but supported by advertising is Yahoo! Music.[11] At this site, users can access thousands of free music videos on demand, but before the music video starts, the user has to watch a thirty-second commercial, typically one of the same commercials produced for television. Users have a variety of options at Yahoo! Music, including registering and customizing the site, searching for a particular music video, or watching top one hundred videos, including Shakira's number-one ranked "Hips Don't Lie." Users can view one video without registering and logging in, but after viewing one video, they must log in, which requires registration (i.e., providing a user name, password, and e-mail address). Internet music providers, including online radio services such as Pandora, face a major financial hurdle in paying the royalties being potentially imposed on them in federal legislation pending in 2007. These fees may force such online music providers out of business.

Partly as a consequence of the growth of on-demand video and other digital video services, brick-and-mortar video stores that rent and sell videos are in rapid decline, with growing numbers going out of business.[12] Ironically, many of these small "mom and pop" video stores came into being in the 1970s and 1980s as a by-product of a previous new media development, the introduction of the home videocassette.

ROO, a commercial online video broadcast network, announced in May 2006 the introduction of an online video upfront buying system for advertisers trying to reach online audiences via Web video. It delivers more than 40 million video impressions each month via more than 130 Web sites, permitting the targeting of audiences by lifestyle or demographics and delivering spot advertising.[13] Some of the Web sites included in the ROO network are Verizon Broadband Beat, Excite, iWon, News.com.au in Australia, thirty-six local U.S. television station Web sites, and Music.com.

Yahoo! Music is a good illustration of the advertising-supported business model in a new media environment. The site provides more than 7,000 music videos ranging from hip-hop to pop to jazz on demand and for free, each video generally preceded by a thirty-second commercial message. It is essentially the same business model that MTV has employed successfully for more than twenty years on television, but now the videos are on demand and online. The viewer is not forced to watch the videos as scheduled by a network. There is instant gratification—or at least near instant, because there is a short commercial shown before the music video. Today's on-demand media generation gets exactly what it wants, and the business model works. The video is great, my thirteen-year-old daughter says.

"Do you like Yahoo! Music?" I ask.

"I love it," Tristan responds.

"How's the quality of the video?" I follow up.

"It's excellent," she answers. "Except when you go full screen; then it gets a little blurry." Whether the music video is worth watching or listening to is another matter.

An important question for those in the traditional television business is: How does television adapt to a changing video environment where the viewer is in much greater control of the viewing experience? How does television maintain its audience? And what is the shape of the business model in a highly competitive digital video universe? Viewers increasingly do not care whether they watch their favorite video on television or on a computer. They want quality content presented in high resolution, with a high frame rate, and with excellent quality sound. Perhaps just as important, they want their video on demand and will pay for it only when it is packaged uniquely. Online video will not likely replace watching television, but it will erode the already shrinking television audience, especially among young viewers.

A growing number of newspapers recognize that online developments are transforming the media business. In response, a consortium of 176 daily newspapers in the United States signed a deal with Yahoo! in November 2006 to share content and classified advertising.[14] Newspapers have traditionally relied on classified advertising as a major source of revenue. As mostly local media, newspapers in the analog age were a relatively effective means for persons who were selling or buying goods and services to find each other. In the age of digital media, especially the Internet, printed newspapers are an almost antiquated means of delivering classified advertising. As a result, online classified advertising sites such as Craigslist have grown dramatically, taking away much newspaper revenue in the process.[15] Online classifieds are far more efficient in connecting sellers and buyers of goods and services. Online auction sites have also drained away much advertising revenue from newspapers. Online auction sites have the large advantage of facilitating connections between buyers and sellers and of setting optimal market prices for goods and services.

Some online operations employ multiple or combined business models. Such is the case with hip-hop mogul Chuck D's rapstation.com. As the founder of pioneering rap group Public Enemy, Chuck D is a leader not only in the music industry, but in new media as well. His hip-hop portal features an online rap television station as well as a radio station, both of which offer free programming supported by advertising revenue. His site also provides downloadable MP3s for a fee and employs other revenue-generating strategies to supplement an advertising-based model. Chuck D encourages entrepreneurs and artists to use the tools of digital production and to do it all themselves. Because the margins for the music business are tight in the digital age, he admonishes the aspiring would-be media mogul: "The money you make is the money you save."[16]

Online advertising also enables a wide variety of tools to maximize advertising efficiency and targeting. Google has been in the forefront of developing these tools. Buying advertising on Google begins with the advertiser's signing up at adwords.google.com. Then the advertiser selects the keywords that will trigger its advertising messages and links during user searching and e-mail communication. A Wisconsin deli owner may wish to be found with "Milwaukee deli" and "Milwaukee lunch." After registering, the advertiser is requested to provide search terms, and Google will offer variations such as "Racine restaurants" or "Racine sandwiches." The advertiser then sets a budget (say $1.00 a day) to pay for the search terms. Google sells the keywords auction style. The more an advertiser pays, the higher the advertisement will appear when a user searches on Google. For a "Milwaukee deli" advertisement, six cents to ten cents per click might produce ad position four to six. Getting a more prominent position would require a higher bid, perhaps $2.00 per click.

Online media, or media with an online presence, are eligible to participate in Google's AdSense program as well,[17] which places on the media Web site interactive advertisements from companies and organizations who buy ads from Google. When a user clicks on any of those ads, Google automatically provides a payment back to the media organization based on that click. As such, Google's AdSense program offers a no-cost vehicle for any media organization, large or small, to generate revenue without committing any resources to the effort other than providing space on their Web site to host the ads. Google does stipulate certain rules and conditions for participating in the program, such as agreeing not to publish pornographic content. An example of a media organization that participates in the Google AdSense program is the *Online Journalism Review*.[18]

Total expenditures on online advertising have been growing dramatically and in 2006 totaled more than $16 billion in the United States. Although this amount is still not as large as the amount spent for advertising in traditional media, the volume gap is shrinking rapidly. Advertising sales in traditional media totaled $150 billion in 2005 in the United States, reports Robert J. Coen, chief forecaster for Universal McCann, part of the Interpublic Group. Internet advertising revenues have grown significantly since at least 2000. Coen forecasts a 15 percent growth in Internet advertising in 2007.[19] "The trend that will continue to affect the media universe in 2007 is the ongoing shift in advertising dollars from traditional media into nontraditional media, most notably the Internet," Fitch Ratings states in its forecasting report. The report adds that television, radio, and newspapers will "experience slow growth and ongoing audience declines . . . and ad spending continues to follow consumer patterns."[20] The Newspaper Association of America has predicted that spending for advertisements on the Web sites of newspapers in 2007 will rise 22 percent from spending in 2006. In contrast, advertising spending in the print versions of those newspapers in 2007 will rise just 1.2 percent from spending in 2006.[21]

Online advertising is increasing even more rapidly in some international markets, such as Great Britain and China (e.g., tencent.com). In Great Britain, online advertising expenditures are growing at roughly a 40 percent annual rate and totaled 14 percent of overall ad spending in 2006, according to media buying agencies. That is reportedly the highest level in the world. It is more than twice the percentage in the United States.[22]

Consequently, Google and other media firms are spending billions of U.S. dollars acquiring online advertising firms, such as DoubleClick (acquired in 2007 by Google for $3.1 billion) and aQuantive (acquired the same year by Microsoft for $6 billion).[23]

One of the thorny problems facing online advertisers is measuring the audience. A common indicator is called the *click through,* when a user clicks on an ad and is sent to the advertiser's Web site. It is a key step in getting the consumer to the site where he or she can buy a product. Advertisers usually pay based on the expected or actual click-through rates obtained. In principle, it is a powerful idea because it reflects consumer intentions to buy. It is a measure significantly closer to an actual purchase than is possible in traditional analog media advertising, where consumer action cannot be directly assessed (in contrast, DTV interactive advertising, for example, enables the assessment of consumer behavior). In analog media, only eyeballs or ears exposed to an advertisement or commercial can be measured. The problem with click throughs, however, is that they can be manipulated. Software agents, or even human agents, can click on online ads in order to inflate the click-through rate artificially. This is known as *click fraud.* Google and other online advertisers require their advertising partners to sign agreements indicating they will not engage in click fraud. Nevertheless, the problem persists, and some online marketing research firms are developing more advanced tools that may measure actual purchase behaviors associated with online advertisements.

Further complicating the matter is the increasingly interactive nature of advertising in the digital age. A growing number of marketers are developing interactive advertising campaigns to draw consumers into more involving, intimate relationships with their products and thus potentially to leverage the social-networking aspect of the Internet. For example, some marketers are exploiting the opportunity presented by consumers equipped with cell phone cameras. Millions of consumers visiting popular tourist destinations such as New York City's Times Square are using their digital cameras to snap photos or shoot videos not only of people and places, but of the larger-than-life outdoor advertisements ubiquitous in Times Square. Consumers share these images with their friends and family and post them to social-networking sites such as YouTube, where thousands or even millions of other consumers can see these commercial messages. Video of professional racing's Nascar's 2006 display of race cars was viewed on YouTube more than 2,000 times by early December of that year.[24] Dozens of bloggers wrote about the Nascar display and posted photos on the Flickr Web site.[25] Visitors to Times Square shot video of magician David Blaine performing there and posted them to YouTube, where they were seen more than 19,000 times.[26] Measuring audience exposure to this potentially effective marketing is a complex challenge requiring a sophisticated system of tracking.[27] Coincidentally, outdoor advertising in Times Square and elsewhere is undergoing its own digital transformation as billboards themselves are rapidly being converted to digital format. In early 2007, the Outdoor Advertising Association of America estimates that approximately 400 billboards are digital in the United States and that the number is expected to reach 90,000, or one-quarter of all outdoor signs, by 2017.[28] Advertisers can make three to four times as much revenue off a digital sign. The total marketplace for outdoor advertising is estimated at $6.7 billion in 2007. Digital signs also enable a variety of new capabilities, such as the display of full-motion video, animated graphics, and instant updating. Some billboards can even "talk" to individual viewers. These digital signs read radio signals received from passing cars whose drivers have previously filled surveys, and then they display messages customized to those drivers.[29]

Digital distribution of music and other media content is transforming the entire media business. R&B singer Akon's 2006 CD *Konvicted* opened to hot sales. Nearly 300,000 copies sold in the first week, pushing the CD to the number two position on the Billboard chart.[30] iTunes also sold nearly 250,000 copies that week. Akon was born Aliaune Thiam in Senegal before moving to New Jersey with his family, including his father, jazz musician Mor Thiam. His hit single "Smack That" sold 69,000 downloads in its first week of release,[31] and his songs were also topping the chart of a new system tracking the sales of ring tones. *Konvicted* produced 269,000 ring-tone sales. The Warner Music Group reports that total recorded music sales for 2006 increased industrywide almost 3 percent, to $3 billion. Its digital revenues in 2006 grew 96 percent, or $104 million, some 12 percent of total revenues.[32] The growth from digital revenues such as ring-tone sales and iTunes more than offset a drop from traditional CD sales for the industry and for the Warner Music Group in particular.[33]

Further adding to the interactive marketing and sales mix in the digital age are online video games being spun off from other media properties, such as television shows or movies. One example is the 2007 video game spin-off of HBO's *The Sopranos,* a long-running series about organized crime in the northeastern United States. Players use their digital cameras to shoot photographs of advertisements for the show and trade them in for virtual tokens. The A&E network, which is running the contest in concert with its airing of the program on television, rewards players with bonus points if they obtain photos that tie into various aspects of the show, such as places and people. The photos are scanned via optical-recognition technology to process automatically the potentially millions of submissions. In the end, the winner of the interactive video contest will win a suitcase stuffed with $100,000.[34]

MDAs such as cell phones are also emerging as advertising media. In December 2006, Verizon announced it would begin accepting advertising messages delivered to subscribers' cell phones. Such advertisements might take a variety of forms, including images, audio, and video.[35]

Sponsored Digital Media

Corporately sponsored media production has also emerged as a significant force in the online arena. Among the leading sponsors is German car manufacturer BMW, which established BMW Films to produce a series of award-winning films that were made available for online distribution at no cost to viewers.[36] At a cost of an estimated $9 million, *The Hire* series consists of short movies (five or six minutes) about a risk-taking professional driver driving a BMW.[37] The movies star major Hollywood actors such as Madonna and Mickey Rourke, and they are directed by a series of well-known directors, such as Guy Ritchie *(Snatch),* Ang Lee *(Crouching Tiger, Hidden Dragon),* John Frankenheimer *(Ronin),* and Wong Kar-Wai *(Happy Together).* BMW worked with its advertising agency, Fallon Worldwide, to oversee the production. *The Hire* action films are no longer available for viewing online, but a new series of six comic *Hire* films is in production.[38] The entire series is essentially a commercial message for its sponsor, BMW, with its product placed visibly on screen almost continuously for the viewer.

A wide variety of firms are increasingly turning to this model of sponsored media that emphasizes product placement. Companies such as Burger King, Office Max, and Anheuser-Busch have developed plans to produce their own programs distributed in a number of ways. All are exploiting the opportunities of new media to deliver programs to audiences increasingly able to avoid traditional advertising messages. Burger King is making a feature-length movie with digital technology and starring the "King" character of its mainstream marketing campaign. Office Max produced a program on the ABC Family channel. Anheuser-Busch is developing its own online TV network online, called BudTV.[39]

Something of a hybrid between advertising and sponsored media content is the promotional technique of product placement, or *stealth advertising,* when for a fee or some other economic arrangement a product or its name or some other facsimile is inserted into a television or radio program, a movie, a book, the editorial content of a Web site, or some other media content without identifying the promotional item to the audience as a piece of commercially sponsored content (as in the Burger King movie and BMW films mentioned previously).

Product placements are nothing new to the media. In fact, in a feature film produced in 1896 by the Lumiere brothers (the inventors of the motion picture), an associate's product, Lever's Sunlight Soap (Lever is now Unilever), can be seen, having been intentionally inserted as a product promotion.[40] Since then, many movies, books, newscasts, and other media programming have featured product placements—all meant to serve as promotional vehicles. With the rise of digital technologies and the increasing level of control the audience possesses to avoid advertising, such as using a remote control or a DVR to zap or skip commercials, product placements are becoming increasingly common in media content. One of the most familiar product placements in today's media programming is the phrase, "I Googled 'em." Such product placements are increasingly common, and digital technology is making them even more ubiquitous. Commercial messages can be embedded virtually in programming, Web sites, and other digital media content, and they can even be customized to the individual audience member, thus maximizing the potential commercial impact. Product placements are thought to be highly effective. Perhaps the most well-known example is the placement of Reese's Pieces in the 1982 Hollywood blockbuster *ET: The Extra-Terrestrial*.[41] It has been reported that sales of Reese's Pieces shot up 65 percent within two weeks of the theatrical release of the film. Fees for such product placements can be substantial. Hershey Foods, whose products include Reese's Pieces, agreed to promote *ET* with $1 million worth of advertising. Danny Thompson, president of Creative Entertainment Services, reports that Exxon paid $300,000 for its name to appear in *Days of Thunder;*[42] Pampers paid $50,000 to be featured in *Three Men and a Baby;* and Cuervo Gold spent $150,000 for placement in *Tequila Sunrise*. Moreover, no medium is immune. Although an egregious ethical violation (more on this in chapter 11), even newspaper and magazine editorial content can and does sometimes contain paid-for product placements. According to the *Christian Science Monitor,* revenue from product placements in "magazine editorial copy—the stories and photographs—is expected to rise 17.5 percent to $160.9 million this year [2005], and in newspapers by 16.9 percent to $65 million, says a report from PQ Media in Stamford, Conn., released in July."[43]

Premium On-Demand Media

Premium on-demand media refer to those media programs that consumers can purchase and access immediately, or on demand, whenever and usually from wherever they wish as long as they have an online or networked connection. Such premium media are widely available and make up an increasing portion of the total media pie. Premium media—or media channels or programs that require a fee from the audience—have existed in one form or another for many decades. Theatrical movies can be considered premium media, as can many books, magazines, and even newspapers, although many have been widely available for no cost to the audience through libraries. Networks such as HBO and Showtime are well-known premium television channels. What distinguishes today's premium media is that in the digital, networked environment they are available on demand. Consumers can get instant media gratification, for a price. Whether a downloadable song, an on-demand movie, or a premium Web site, all media content is increasingly available in the form of on-demand content for a fee.

Prices for on-demand premium media range from about a dollar for previously aired television shows and songs to high-priced ($20 or more) anime features and new Hollywood motion picture releases. Among the most financially successful online video franchises to date is Major League Baseball's Web site MLB.com, which provides live near-broadcast-quality streaming video of all its games for a single-season fee or a monthly fee as well as on-demand archived games. Only non-local games are available on it, though, in order to avoid competition with local TV game broadcasts and attendance at the games themselves. Millions of viewers have already signed up for MLB.com, making it a financially lucrative arrangement for professional baseball. An estimated 800,000 subscribers are paying $79.95 annually for the video available on the site, bringing in annual revenues of roughly $70 million.[44] Other sports have brought in millions of online viewers for network video streams, including more than 5 million to CBS Corp.'s Web site to watch the National College Athletic Association's tournament college basketball games for free. Charging for such sports programming may be in the offing.

In October 2006, NBC Universal forecast expectations of approximately one billion U.S. dollars in annual revenues from digitally delivered media by 2009.[45] This amount is up from $300 million in digital media revenues in 2006. At the same time, the multimedia giant announced job cuts amounting to 5 percent of its total workforce. The cuts will save the company $750 million by 2008. The company's total profits in 2006 were $2.1 billion.

Not all premium digital media are on demand. Among the most successful premium services are DVD rentals and sales. In the case of Netflix, DVD rentals are ordered by subscribers online but delivered via the mail. With 6.3 million subscribers and about $1 billion in revenue for 2006, Netflix made up some 12 percent of the $8.4 billion annual DVD rental business.[46] In January 2007, it began delivering digital movies online on demand via a video-streaming service free to Netflix subscribers.[47] Streaming movies rather than making them available via downloading lets the video begin playing almost immediately on a television set or a computer and prevents unwanted storing and copying of the movies.

The Cost of Creating Content

Although digital production technologies and online file-sharing and social-networking sites make it possible to produce content of all types for little or no cost, producing quality content still requires time and other resources, such as talent and experience, which oftentimes translate directly into financial cost. A freelance reporter might be paid fifty cents or a dollar a word for a story published in a daily newspaper in the United States, but this is just the marginal cost and does not take into account the full cost of the production and distribution of the newspaper that will contain the story, including the cost of editing the story, libel insurance, printing the paper, delivery via truck to the newsstand or home reader, and even online distribution. For an episode of a nationally distributed television program, costs can easily run to hundreds of thousands or even a million U.S. dollars or more. In 2000, the popular television show *Law & Order* cost $2.2 million an episode to produce.[48] A music video or popular song might cost tens or even hundreds of thousands of dollars to produce, and the cost to produce a feature-length Hollywood motion picture might easily run into the tens or hundreds of millions of dollars.[49]

An increasing number of digital media providers are developing the option of online payments made electronically via PayPal or other online payment systems.[50] One experimental not-for-profit online video documentary developed a PayPal option that allows viewers to make direct donations online to support the production as well as a scholarship program for students at a historically black college studying digital media production.[51] Using an online payment system has a number of advantages over the use of a credit card, including better security for the transactions and thus greatly reduced potential for fraud or identity theft. A small-budget digital media initiative might use online micropayments to subsidize the production of serialized content. For instance, a production might obtain online payments of about one dollar from each of 10,000 visitors to a site for each of ten installments. Over the course of a year, this approach could provide majority funding for a limited-budget production. Moreover, if additional funding mechanisms are utilized, such as Google AdSense, a micropayment approach would be particularly effective.

Some content providers make selected content available for free, either as a promotion or to extend program reach. Many newspapers, for example, make much of their content available for free on the Web. Yet many are gradually increasing the pay portions of their sites. The *New York Times,* for example, introduced Times Select in 2006, a premium portion of its site giving only paying subscribers access to editorials, op-eds, columnists, and other content such as the online news archive. In the television realm, many video programs are available online only if a fee is paid, perhaps $1.99 an episode. These developments, in combination with the rising popularity of DVRs and digital cable services that let viewers view programs at anytime, are leading to the decline of a former staple of broadcast television: scheduled programming. Today, on-demand programming is increasingly the norm. With the exceptions of news, first-run programs or movies, and live event coverage, on-demand viewing is increasingly the way viewers of all ages watch their television. Not only that, but they watch or listen wherever they want, on both handheld and portable digital devices, as well as via wireless networks (e.g., Wi-Fi, Bluetooth).

One popular type of video content online is adult, sexually explicit material. It is widely available, increasingly of high production value or at least transmitted online or downloaded at high resolution and frame rate, and has a large audience willing to pay for the content, particularly on demand. File-sharing networks such as KaZaa, known especially for the distribution of MP3 music files, are also popular havens for the sharing of pornographic video files, sometimes in violation of copyright agreements.

Sites that offer mature content online, such as CinemaNow, have introduced an interesting feature possible only in an interactive, on-demand environment such as the Internet. Viewers are able to see a complete minute-by-minute scene list, select a scene to watch, and be billed for only the minutes viewed.

In some ways, just as adult video drove the general consumer acceptance of videocassettes in the 1980s, online pornography is facilitating the development of online video early in the twenty-first century. One study reported in November 2003 that among men ages eighteen to thirty-four, 19 million (almost two-thirds of the 32 million U.S. males in that age group, 27 million of whom go online) had visited an adult site in the past month and had viewed online adult video materials.[52] This is substantially higher viewership than among females in that age group. "Since 18–34 year-old [sic] men aren't engaging with TV broadcast networks to the same degree as females, it's not unexpected that this trend would hold true online," said Peter Daboll, president of comScore Media Metrix, which developed the report. "Advertisers and networks alike would be well-advised to reconnect with these consumers through the many online brands to which they are still attracted." Moreover, he added, "The fact that more than 75 percent of 18–34 year-old [sic] men in the U.S. are using the Internet seems to take at least some of the mystery out of the decline in TV viewing among this prized demographic." These men are spending an average of thirty-two hours a month online.

ALTERNATIVE FINANCIAL MODELS

Some digital media seem to subscribe to the view "we lose a little on each sale, but we make it up on volume." In the case of *Rocketboom,* a popular vlog, its creators rely on very inexpensive production technologies and a patchwork of possible funding mechanisms to stay afloat. The *Rocketboom* Web site explains: "We differ from a regular TV program in many important ways. Instead of costing millions of dollars to produce, *Rocketboom* is created with a consumer-level video camera, a laptop, two lights and a map with no additional overhead or costs."[53] Also, *Rocketboom* is distributed online, all around the world, and on demand and thus has a larger potential audience than any TV broadcast. "However, we spend $0 on promotion, relying entirely on word-of-mouth, and close to $0 on distribution because bandwidth costs and space are so inexpensive. While TV programs have traditionally been uni-directional, *Rocketboom* engages its international audience in a wide range of topical discussions." *Rocketboom* cofounder Andrew Baron explains the vlog's funding approach: "The most obvious form of revenue, especially on a large scale, is through motion advertising. Also, Apple obviously created the pay-per video industry. Content creators can also enjoy revenue from licensing to various distribution platforms. It's really a global economy for all content. Subscription for extra content and high quality files is another route. We are working on all of these options simultaneously while building up our own network of Web sites."[54]

THE END OF RELATIVE CONSTANCY

With the growth of the Internet and other digital media, the economics of media content has started to change dramatically. For much of the twentieth century, a media consumption model known as *relative constancy* prevailed in the United States and much of the developed world.[55] In this model, the average consumer paid a relatively constant portion of her or his disposable income for media, roughly 3 percent. Over the past decade or so, however, with the explosion of digital media, the portion of disposable income spent on media has increased by one-third to one-half, or to roughly 4 percent of disposable income. This change is due largely to pay cable and premium television channels, as well as to digital satellite television and radio, downloadable music, and the rising unit or subscription cost (relative to inflation) of many newspapers, theater movies, music, and books. Until the 1980s, roughly 70 percent of U.S. households, for instance, had their primary television set tuned via a set-top or housetop antenna to free over-the-air television transmission. During the past two to three decades, however, this portion of homes receiving over-the-air television stations directly via home antennas has dropped off precipitously. Instead, by the mid-1990s, less than 20 percent of U.S. homes were receiving over-the-air television transmissions on their primary television set, as noted in chapter 1.[56] Although most homes still regularly view programming provided by terrestrial broadcast television stations, they receive the stations' transmissions via their cable or satellite television provider, which is a pay service.

Potentially reversing this decline in over-the-air broadcasting viewership is the emergence of digital multiplexing. With the launch of digital transmission, broadcasters can opt to transmit either a single HDTV signal or, with compression, between six (standard-definition quality) and twenty (VHS-quality) channels. This opportunity is unprecedented for local television stations to compete with cable and satellite and even the Internet. The full conversion to digital transmission is scheduled for 2009, when analog transmissions will cease. Local stations can be affiliated with more than one network simultaneously. They can program different content on different channels. Some broadcasters such as the Tribune Company are already experimenting with multicasting, featuring channels dedicated to weather, traffic, or other local programming. Tribune has made a deal with a music programmer for another channel. Stations may lease out a channel for subscription TV but must pay a penalty under federal rules. All viewers need is a cheap rabbit ears antenna to receive such multicast channels free. University of Southern California communications professor Michael Epstein reports that in a market such as Los Angeles, where there are thirty-six UHF and VHF stations, the mathematics of digital multiplexing are compelling. If each of the thirty-six stations starts delivering six channels, the market will have 216 channels of over-the-air TV, all potentially for free. A growing number of Epstein's students are canceling their cable subscriptions, buying a pair of rabbit ears, and, with an $80 digital TV signal converter, watching lots of channels of free TV on their cheap and reliable analog set. In New York, NBC Universal and Clear Channel Outdoor have already announced plans to utilize the potential of digital multiplexing to launch a new television network aimed directly at and exclusively for New York City's medallion taxis and their passengers. Taxis equipped with digital flat-panel displays and affiliated with Clear Channel Taxi Media will give their riders access to NBC television programming such as news, entertainment, and traffic. NY10, New York's Taxi Entertainment Network to be launched in 2007, will also permit riders to pay their fares by credit or debit card and access GPS data and flight schedules.[57]

The rise of pay media is fueling growth in the digital divide, both in terms of access to digital devices and the Internet as well as to pay media of all types. As pay media grow in dominance, it will become increasingly difficult for the economically disadvantaged both in the United States and in the world to access media of all types, including news and entertainment. These groups are most likely to be the urban and rural poor. The problem will be exacerbated by the growing relative portion of disposable income required to access the Internet and other pay media. Moreover, not only will accessing content be more difficult and expensive for the poor, but participating in online communities will become more problematic. As these online communities increasingly play a prominent role in public discourse and decision making, economically disadvantaged groups may see their relative influence in society decrease even more. In the age of analog media, local newspapers were relatively inexpensive, and terrestrial broadcast television and radio were free and provided extensive news coverage. As the digital age develops and a growing proportion of these media are increasingly expensive, the poor will be disenfranchised even further from media. Without equitable media access throughout all social strata, democracy will suffer as fewer and fewer of the poor will have ready access to news and information. Moreover, as lifelong learning via pay media becomes a growing part of twenty-first-century life, the poor may fall even farther behind educationally and economically. The knowledge gap between media rich and media poor identified in research by sociologists Philip Tichenor, George Donohue, and Clarice Olien is likely to widen much more in a pay digital media system.[58] It will be necessary for government or industry groups to set policy and take steps to augment free or low-cost media options to sustain an effective media system for persons in all social and economic strata.

FILE SHARING AND MICROPAYMENTS

The shift in video-program-viewing patterns has been accompanied by a similar shift in music and other audio programming usage. Music file-sharing and downloading sites, including iTunes, Napster, and Limewire, have already transformed the music-distribution business. Combined with megagigabyte handheld storage and playback devices available for around $300 or less, consumers have extensive playlists available at their fingertips. One of the advantages offered by online services such as iTunes is that parents can choose to buy (or to allow their children to buy) either "explicit" or "clean" versions of songs available for download. Clean versions have eliminated cursing, explicit sexual references, and the like in the lyrics. Children may be disappointed but may ultimately find the lyrics more creative.

SATELLITE RADIO

Internet-based radio stations and satellite radio are also dramatically altering listener patterns, in terms of both their listening habits and their expenditures. Radio has historically been a widely available free medium, supported by commercials or government tax dollars, corporate and foundation gifts, and listener donations (in the case of public radio). Satellite radio is rapidly changing this historical fact of radio life.

Satellite radio providers Sirius and XM are expected to have a combined subscribership of more than 12 million in the United States by the end of 2006.[59] This is a relatively small portion of the total radio listenership, though; Arbitron's annual *Radio Today* report indicates that 94 percent of people age twelve or older (more than 200 million in the United States) listen to radio each week.[60] The 12 million satellite radio subscribers paying about $12 a month represent only a portion of the total actual listenership of satellite radio. Many subscribers live in households with two or more occupants, and most or all of them are thus also part of the satellite radio listenership, thus doubling, tripling, or even quadrupling the total weekly listenership for satellite radio, which is a much more significant percentage of total radio listenership than subscribers alone. Moreover, the portion of the audience willing to pay for radio is likely to be the cream of the marketing crop, so to speak: a higher-income, more highly educated audience willing and able to pay not to be exposed to commercially sponsored radio. This audience is particularly likely to be the traditional audience of public radio. Consequently, public radio, which has of late increasingly been incorporating on-air commercial sponsorship messages, may see its over-the-air audience shift to satellite radio. This change likely explains why NPR has teamed up with Sirius to make NPR programming available via satellite. Some public-radio programming is also available on XM.

One of the problems for traditional radio and media in general is that newer digital media are skimming away that part of the audience that has more economic market power, income, and education. Satellite radio is an excellent example. It naturally draws people at the high end of the economic scale. It is relatively expensive as far as radio listening goes. Terrestrial broadcast radio has always been free, or virtually such, at least in the United States. Radio receivers can be purchased for a few dollars, and every car comes with a radio as standard equipment. In contrast, satellite radio not only requires the purchase of a receiver that might cost hundreds of dollars, but the monthly service is about $10 or more. Only the relatively well-to-do are likely to subscribe, which leaves terrestrial broadcast radio, including commercial and public radio, with an audience largely at the lower economic end of the scale. Marketers may find this audience increasingly unattractive and may be less willing to pay top dollar to reach it. Fewer and fewer advertisers may find commercial radio a desirable advertising medium, which in turn means that fewer resources will return to terrestrial radio, whether analog or digital, thus further eroding the quality and listenership of local radio. What adaptations local radio introduces, particularly by way of content strategies, remains to be seen.

At the same time, terrestrial radio is also converting to digital transmission. As stations convert to a digital format and listeners begin to use digital receivers, new radio possibilities emerge. Digital radio can utilize compression to transmit up to a half-dozen audio channels where only one was possible previously. High-definition radio, where interference can be virtually eliminated, allows AM radio to achieve the audio quality of traditional, static-free FM radio. FM radio can be improved to the audio quality of CD or DVD digital sound. Supplemental text messages can be associated with audio transmissions. Channels can be automatically retuned as cars travel from one transmission region to another.

To date, both Sirius and XM are losing more money than they are taking in, but the future may see more black than red ink, particularly if the firms merge at some point down the road.[61] Some people in the terrestrial radio industry see the future of satellite radio as limited largely to being a niche broadcaster.[62]

One of the business challenges in the new media environment is that the continuously changing technology requires constant adaptation by both media organizations and media consumers alike. New developments mean continuously updating, upgrading, and replacing both hardware and software, and it is both expensive and difficult to know when to make a change. If a new product is introduced too soon or at too high a price, marketplace demand may not meet sales or rental requirements to sustain a business decision or investment. For the consumer, buying in too soon may mean spending precious resources on a quickly obsolete technology.

An interesting case in point from the digital age is the evolving state of video game players. In 2005, Microsoft introduced its Xbox 360 with a price tag of about $500. It was reported that Microsoft initially lost money on each console sold, but over a period of roughly a year certain economies of scale helped lower production costs, and by 2006 Microsoft was reported to be making money on each console sold. Competing with the Xbox 360 in the video game marketplace is Sony's PS3, the successor to the PS2. These two devices have vied for dominance in the video game marketplace since the 1990s. Sony has been the leading player in the marketplace, with roughly 60 percent of the market. Microsoft and Nintendo have had about 20 percent each of the market. Sony's PS2 and now PS3 have had the edge in sheer computing power. Microsoft contends that its own edge is in the power of its network, a key consideration for online game players. From the PS2's introduction to the market in 2000 to November 2006, Sony sold 100 million consoles worldwide, with the largest market in North America, primarily the United States, where more than 40 million PS2s were sold.[63] In Asia, sales have totaled 22 million consoles. As of November 2006, Sony planned to ship 500,000 PS3s for sale in the United States, a small fraction of the anticipated demand. With a list price of $500 or $600 depending on the size of the hard drive, some PS3s have sold on eBay for $10,000.[64] It is reported that, as with the early introduction of the Xbox 360, Sony will lose $200–300 per console sold during the first year. GameLife says the components of the PS3 run at least $850.[65] It is anticipated that economies of scale will kick in by the end of the sale of the first 500,000 consoles, driving down manufacturing costs and leading to profitable sales by the end of 2007. At that point, Sony is expected to go into mass production. Confounding the business picture is the reality of game production. Games are so complex that they typically take a year or more to produce. As a consequence, very few games are available during the early introduction of new game player consoles, potentially inhibiting product sales. By the end of November 2006, Sony had sold 197,000 PS3 units in the United States. Microsoft sold 511,000 units of its Xbox 360. Sony sold 6 million PS3 consoles worldwide by the end of March 2007. Nintendo sold 5.3 million units of its new Wii game console and accompanying software in the United States in 2006.[66] Overall, video game retail sales jumped 34 percent in November 2006, with console sales doubling the November 2005 sales. Total video game sales were $1.7 billion for 2006, up from $1.3 billion in 2005. Video game software sales rose 15 percent to $804 million in 2006, up from $702 million in 2005. Microsoft sold 1 million copies of its *Gears of War* title during November 2006.[67]

THE OWNERS OF DIGITAL MEDIA

Just as in the analog age of media, a small number of major companies dominate the digital media landscape. The six biggest players in the digital media age are U.S. companies, and all have interests that cut across most or all media types and in some cases have business interests that extend well beyond the world of media: Rupert Murdoch's News Corporation, General Electric, Disney, Time Warner, Viacom, and CBS Corporation. News Corporation has extensive digital media assets, including satellite television (e.g., DirecTV Group, B-Sky-B), Internet properties (e.g., MySpace, Foxnews.com, NYPost.com), and media properties that are either converting to digital in whole or part or are already largely digital, such as television (e.g., 20th Century Fox Television, Fox Broadcasting), motion pictures (e.g., 20th Century Fox), newspapers (now including the *Wall Street Journal*), magazines, and books. General Electric's media properties are extensive as well, including many digital assets, such as MSNBC.com as well as media enterprises at various stages of digitization, including Universal Pictures, NBC Television, and Telemundo. Disney's media properties range from ABC Television and ABC Radio (73 stations) to Disney.com, Disney Mobile, and Walt Disney Pictures, each of which is either fully digital or heavily digital. Time Warner includes among its extensive media holdings AOL, Time Inc., Warner Bros. Television, and Warner Bros. Pictures, each of which is extensively digital. Viacom includes MTV Networks, BET, Paramount Pictures, iFilm.com, and other media properties, many of which are fully or largely digital. CBS Corporation includes CBS Television, Showtime, CBS Radio (179 stations in forty U.S. markets), Simon & Schuster (books), and the CBS Digital Media Group, which as the name implies leads the parent company's digital strategy. Needless to say, these multimedia giants dominate not just the U.S. media market, but through the Internet and other digital means compete vigorously on a global stage.

Many scholars and other critics are concerned about the growing level of concentration in media ownership, which has shown little sign of slowing in the digital age.[68] In 1983, Ben Bagdikian reported that some fifty corporations dominated the ownership of the mass media in the United States.[69] By 2006, the number of companies dominating the U.S. media landscape had decreased to just the six mentioned here. Philosopher Edgard Morin outlines a Marxist view in which media are understood to be engines of capitalism with little real motivation to serve in the public interest.[70] Profit drives most media, particularly in the digital age, when economic resources are in a heightened state of competition.

The only significant countervailing commercial force has been the emergence of Google, Yahoo, and other Internet companies specializing in media-related business. These companies, many of which are extremely large, have introduced somewhat alternative models to doing business in the digital age. Google, for instance, conducted its initial public-stock offering via an auction approach that opened up its investment possibilities to small as well as large investors.[71]

CONCLUSION

Business models for media in the digital age are in a state of flux. Few media organizations have settled on a viable long-term strategy for making money in a sustainable fashion. There are too many uncertainties, too many unsettled technologies, too many changes happening in the audience or user base for clear answers. At least four business models are vying for position in the media marketplace—advertising, e-commerce or transactional, subscription, and bundled or partnership—although it is not clear which if any will emerge as the solution that so many in the media business are seeking. Success stories exist for each of these models, but few have demonstrated that any model can be applied effectively across a broad spectrum of media properties.

Ownership of digital media is similarly unsettled. Although a half-dozen major players dominate the mainstream media marketplace, relatively new entrants such as Google and Yahoo! threaten to upset the media business applecart.

8 / REGULATION AND LAW OF DIGITAL MEDIA

Since the ratification of the First Amendment to the Constitution on December 15, 1791, the media of public communication in the United States have enjoyed a somewhat privileged legal and regulatory status.[1] The First Amendment guarantees the Congress shall make no law abridging freedom of speech or press.[2] The courts have interpreted and extended this constitutional protection to include generally all forms of public media. Yet certain restrictions and limitations pertain, particularly to newer electronic media, to the circumstances of the communication, and to the type of content and audience. These restrictions are still evolving in the digital age. Among the most significant limitations of the First Amendment revolve around when freedom of speech conflicts with other rights, such as the right to a fair trial, which is protected by the Sixth Amendment. Although the Supreme Court decided in *Near v. Minnesota* in 1931 that there would be no prior restraint (i.e., that government could not block publication), the main possible exception to this principle would be in the case of publication posing a grave and imminent threat to national security.[3] This principle still applies in the digital age. Similarly, when through reckless disregard for the truth inaccurate speech or press inflicts damage on the reputation of a person or organization, the aggrieved party can pursue a civil lawsuit seeking damages for the libelous (in the case of published speech) or slanderous (i.e., in the case of broadcast) speech. This standard is known as "actual malice" and was established by the U.S. Supreme Court in its landmark case *New York Times Co. v. Sullivan* (1964).[4] Actual malice does not refer to acting with malicious intent. Libel laws and the actual malice standard still apply to journalists and media in the digital age. There are other exceptions to the freedom of speech guarantees of the First Amendment as applied in the digital age, including the protection of journalists' sources and the protection of intellectual property rights. I discuss these issues later in this chapter.

From a production point of view, online video is essentially within the same legal and regulatory environment as conventional broadcast television. Issues such as rights, royalties and residuals, potentially libelous speech, and the First Amendment pertain to online video. From a distribution perspective, online video faces relatively fewer regulatory restrictions than conventional television because many of the prevailing federal restrictions on content indecency do not apply. The principle regulatory restrictions come in the forms of limiting underage access to mature video content and other sex-related matters (e.g., eliminating online child pornography) and preventing pirated video distribution. Two relatively comprehensive legal guides to blogging and podcasting, including video, are available for free from the Electronic Frontier Foundation and Creative Commons.[5] Some FCC rule changes may have an indirect impact on online video distribution. CyberJournalist.net reports that the FCC's changes in cross-media ownership rules have the potential to increase the number of converged newsrooms that share resources to create stronger Web presences. Its publisher, Jonathan Dube, observes, "We may see more local sites like tbo.com, the excellent Media General site in Tampa that serves as the online home for both the *Tampa Tribune* and WFLA. If that happens, we'd see more robust local news sites—with better ability to package newspaper and video content—but we might also see fewer local news sites and thus less competition."[6]

One possible regulatory threat to online video is the global nature of the Internet, which makes any online video producer and distributor potentially subject to restrictions from any country, regardless of whether that country is part of the video providers' intended audience. Unless access is blocked by the provider, a local government might interpret some downloadable video files as offensive to local tastes or in violation of local laws and might impose punishments, ranging from fines to imprisonment. Some governments, such as China's, have blocked access to certain Web sites, including some that provide news video from the United States.[7]

DIGITAL MILLENNIUM COPYRIGHT ACT

On October 28, 1998, President Bill Clinton signed the Digital Millennium Copyright Act (DMCA) into law, ending months of spirited debate regarding its provisions.[8] The act implements the treaties signed in December 1996 at the World Intellectual Property Organization conference in Geneva and includes further provisions targeting related concerns.

The DMCA builds on the "No Electronic Theft" Act of 1997 and garnered the support of the software and entertainment industries. It was generally opposed by scientists, librarians, and academics. Largely designed to address the digital age of media, it provides a series of provisions aimed at prohibiting software code cracking. Among its provisions, it criminalizes activities that circumvent antipiracy measures built into most commercial software. It similarly prohibits the manufacture, sale, and distribution of code-cracking devices used to copy software illegally. The DMCA does allow the cracking of copyright protection devices if such activities are conducted as encryption research, to evaluate product interoperability and computer security systems. Nonprofit libraries, archives, and educational institutions are also exempted from the act's restrictions under certain circumstances. Internet service providers are expected to remove material from users' Web sites if that material infringes on another's copyright. It is under this provision that in 2006 the video-sharing network YouTube commenced removing more than 30,000 copyrighted video files. Copyrighted content ranges widely from music videos to segments of feature-length films, such as Eminem's 2002 movie *8 Mile*. Universal Pictures, the NBC Universal subsidiary that distributed *8 Mile,* has three employees searching YouTube daily for studio-owned material.[9] NBC Universal is reported to send more than 1,000 requests a month to YouTube to remove copyrighted material. YouTube complies, but it is easy for another user to upload the clip. The impetus for YouTube's copyright compliance actions was at least in part Google's $1.65 billion acquisition of the site, in addition to legal challenges from both international (e.g., Japanese) and domestic copyright holders (e.g., U.S.–based Comedy Central). The DMCA also mandates that "Webcasters" pay licensing fees to music companies.[10]

Copyright law covers exclusively the form or manner in which ideas have been expressed. It does not cover the actual idea, concepts, facts, or techniques embodied in or represented by the copyrighted work. Copyright law permits satirical or interpretive works or other derivative works, which themselves may be copyrighted. Consider Disney's copyright of the Mickey Mouse cartoon character. Copyright "prohibits unauthorized parties from distributing copies of the cartoon or creating derivative works which copy or mimic Disney's particular anthropomorphic mouse, but does not prohibit the creation of artistic works about anthropomorphic mice in general, so long as they are sufficiently different to not be imitative of the original."[11] The DMCA is designed primarily to protect the rights of copyright holders, but it is also supposed to foster a free and robust media system.[12] The extent to which it achieves these dual objectives depends largely on one's point of view. Under U.S. law, journalists, educators, and others have rights to use intellectual property for educational (nonprofit) activities. This exception to the DMCA is called "fair use" rights. In general, what constitutes fair use is not explicitly stipulated by the act, but is assessed based on four factors, including the purpose and character of the use, the nature of the copyrighted work, the amount and portion of the entire work used, and the likely effect of the use on the market for or commercial value of the copyrighted work.

These rights are restricted, but they generally permit those operating as journalists, educators, artists, critics, and satirists to use excerpts from copyrighted works and in some limited cases the entire works without first obtaining permission from or making payments to the copyright holder. Exactly how fair use applies online is an unsettled matter. Acting as a critic of a talk radio show on KSFO-AM in San Francisco, one blogger posted audio clips from the show to illustrate his criticisms of the show's hosts. Disney's ABC Radio Networks, which owns KSFO, wrote to the blogger's Internet service provider ordering the removal of the audio clips from the host's Internet servers, and the provider complied, although the matter has not been resolved in court.[13] Copyright protections are designed largely to prevent others from exploiting for commercial gain the intellectual properties developed by others or for which the rights are held by another. Copyright is not an indefinite right. In general, "[c]opyright in a work created on or after January 1, 1978, subsists from its creation and, except as provided by the following subsections, endures for a term consisting of the life of the author and 70 years after the author's death."[14] After this term, a copyrighted work enters the public domain, unless a renewal or extension is applied for and granted. In general, copyright provisions apply equally whether a work is in analog or digital form, online or off, and whether in text, audio, or video format, although special provisions may apply.

Copyrighted material falling under corporate authorship (also known as "work for hire") is a special case. The copyright term is 95 years from the date of first publication or 120 years from the creation date, whichever first expires. This definition was challenged in court, but then it was affirmed by the U.S. Supreme Court in *Eldred v. Ashcroft* (2003).[15] The Court held that Congress could extend copyright as long as the extension itself was limited rather than perpetual. The length of U.S. copyright for works created before 1978 is complex, but all works published prior to1923 are in the public domain.

Copyright may be transferred to another person or entity. Copyrighted materials may and generally should be identified as such on all copies distributed domestically or internationally. In the digital age, however, copies may be distributed that do not have a substantial physical form, so the DMCA stipulates that this rule applies to "publicly distributed copies from which the work can be visually perceived, either directly or with the aid of a machine or device." For such visually perceived materials, the symbol © (the letter C in a circle) or the word *copyright* or the abbreviation *copr.* should be used along with the year of first publication and the name of the copyright holder. For audio recordings, the symbol ℗ (the letter P in a circle), the year of first publication of the sound recording, and the name of the owner of copyright in the sound recording should be displayed on the distributed copies of the work. On digital copies distributed online, such information should be encoded into the file metatags (data about or describing a page and used by search engines). To maximize protection and potential for remedies if copyright infringement occurs, authors and artists should apply for copyright registration on a form prescribed by the Register of Copyrights. Copyright for a motion picture is automatically obtained when the movie is created and "fixed" in a copy, whether digital or analog.[16] To register a copyright for a motion picture, it is necessary to complete a copyright registration form and submit to the U.S. Library of Congress a physical copy of the motion picture, whether on film or video, including DVD or other format. Registering copyright is not necessary, but it makes it easier to obtain redress should an infringement occur.

Because of the difficulty of enforcing copyright, "copyright collectives or collecting societies and performing rights organizations . . . have been formed to collect royalties for hundreds (thousands and more) of works at once."[17]

One unsettled area largely unique to the digital, networked media is online file sharing of copyrighted works. Some contend that such file sharing is a form of illegal piracy, whereas others argue that it is legal sharing among private users when done without financial compensation or commercial gain and that it in fact stimulates greater market demand for the product. Research is somewhat equivocal on the matter, with some evidence indicating that file sharing does stimulate demand, and other evidence showing a decline in associated sales. Some artists, such as newer or less-well-known groups, have freely distributed their works online and seen online and offline sales skyrocket. A study by Norbert Michel utilized U.S. Bureau of Labor statistics, which track nearly all household expenses for selected families in order to calculate statistics such as the Consumer Price Index.[18] "According to Michel's methodology," writes Alejandro Zentner, those who owned a computer bought almost 13 percent fewer CDs from 1999 to 2003, with those who bought the most music showing the largest decrease."[19] Michel concludes that file sharing does adversely affect music sales. Other scholars agree, including Zentner, Hong, Liebowitz, Rob, and Waldfogel.[20] Yet the scholarly literature is not unanimous. Oberholzer and Strumpf found no correlation between file sharing and peer-to-peer file sharing, and a paper by a Harvard student found that file sharing benefited relatively obscure artists.[21] A 2004 survey of artists and musicians by the Pew Internet and American Life Project shows that "artists and musicians recognize the advantages of the Internet and have used it to their benefit. Some 66 per cent of musicians surveyed said that the Internet is 'very important' in helping them to create and distribute their music."[22]

In opposition to copyright protection, many academics and others have contended that the DMCA goes too far in protecting copyright and thus inhibits freedom of expression. Critics of copyright as a whole fall into two categories. First are "[t]hose who assert that the very concept of copyright has never been of net benefit to society, and has always served simply to enrich a few at the expense of creativity."[23] People subscribing to this view feel that the robust, free, and unrestricted exchange of ideas offers society the greatest potential benefit. Second are "[t]hose who assert that the existing copyright regime must be reformed to maintain its relevance in the new Information society. The French droit d'auteur ('Rights of the Author'), which influenced the 1886 Berne Convention for the Protection of Literary and Artistic Works must also be noted as a significant alternative to the usual Anglo-Saxon concept of copyright."[24] The DMCA has been offered largely as a response to this second group.

Internationally, many countries have enacted their own legislation to protect copyright. France, Germany, the United Kingdom, Spain, Australia, and other countries have their own copyright laws that generally extend the same principles as those in the United States. Most also subscribe to the Berne Convention for the Protection of Literary and Artistic Works, which directs countries to protect the copyrighted works of other countries. For instance, Germany is required to treat a work that is copyrighted in Spain as if it were copyrighted in Germany, but receiving the protection of Spanish and not German copyright law.

Despite its size and success, Google was found guilty of an international copyright violation by a French court in 2006. The court ordered Google, which provides an automated news-aggregation service culled from thousands of online sources, to remove immediately all links to French- and German-language newspaper reports published in Belgium. Ironically, it was an association of local publishers, normally on the side of freedom of speech and press, that had brought the suit against Google for violating international copyright laws.

One of the key components of the DMCA is the establishment of procedures for what has come to be known as digital rights management (DRM). DRM includes the various technologies that publishers or copyright owners use to control access to and usage of digital data, or content, as well as the hardware and devices that access or play that content. Through DRM, artists and media companies are able to implement payment systems to support the digital and online distribution of digital content, whether audio or music files, video, or other media forms. Some people have criticized DRM as an impediment to use and development of media. For consumers, DRM systems have often made downloading songs or other digital content more difficult, complicated, and slow.

Most file-sharing sites do not use DRM, a factor that is in part motivating major record labels to consider discontinuing their use of DRM for online music sales and distribution.[25] Among those critical of DRM is the Foundation for a Free Information Infrastructure, which sees the technology as a barrier to free trade.[26] Online music distributor iTunes implements a DRM system called FairPlay for its music files, which are compressed using advanced audio coding. FairPlay enables consumers to purchase a song for less than a dollar and transfer it to an unlimited number of iPods. The iTunes DRM system generally blocks consumers from transferring the purchased song to MP3 players other than iPods, though. Consumers are permitted to burn their songs to an unlimited number of CDs.

SETTING INTERNATIONAL STANDARDS

Another arena of international media regulation involves the question of setting standards for the next generation of DVD technology. Although U.S. regulators have taken little action in this regard, European investigators in 2006 began looking into whether DVD manufacturers have exerted pressure on Hollywood movie makers to favor one DVD standard over another. Sony, Panasonic, Samsung, Dell, and several major studios including 20th Century Fox, Buena Vista Home Entertainment, Electronic Arts, MGM Studios, Sony Pictures Entertainment, the Walt Disney Company, and Vivendi Universal Games are backing the Blu-ray high-definition format. Toshiba, Microsoft, Intel, and film studios including New Line Cinema, Paramount Pictures, Universal Studios, and Warner Bros. support the rival standard called HD DVD.[27] Each format promises better pictures and improved audio, but the standards are incompatible, and one player will not play DVDs of both standards. The European Commission is trying to determine whether the DVD manufacturers are smothering competition through exclusive contracts with studios and computer makers. Since 2004, Europe has fined Microsoft hundreds of millions of euros for unfair competitive practices. In Europe, fines for violating antitrust laws can range up to 10 percent of a company's global annual sales, although a settlement is more likely than a fine.

International and domestic communications and regulations sometimes intersect in the digital age, and the results can mean First Amendment restriction. In 2006, U.S. federal prosecutors charged a New York man with giving the political group Hezbollah illegal television access in New York via eight satellite dishes in his backyard. Enacted in 1977, the International Emergency Economic Powers (IEEP) Act is generally used to block international trade of goods and services, but in this case was extended by the PATRIOT Act after September 11, 2001, to target a particular individual or group. A 1988 amendment to the IEEP Act apparently exempts broadcast activities, but it is unclear whether the courts will uphold the PATRIOT Act extension.[28]

Freedom of speech may be constitutionally guaranteed in the United States, but through the Internet speech may be reduced to the lowest international common denominator. Consider the August 28, 2006, case when the *New York Times* blocked access in Great Britain to a Web-published article titled "Details Emerge in British Terror Case." The *Times* provided this explanation for the self-censorship: "This arises from the requirement in British law that prohibits publication of prejudicial information about the defendants prior to trial."[29]

The cat-and-mouse game of censorship online has snared the Internet during the war in Iraq. The Bush administration officially bans the publication of photographs of the coffins of military personnel returning to the United States, and the Pentagon monitors videotapes of combat operations taken by the news media. However, videos of insurgent attacks against U.S. troops in Iraq now circulate online through sites such as YouTube and Google Video, giving Americans unprecedented access to these images. Some are clearly propaganda tapes with accompanying music and Arabic subtitles. Others tell a side of the war story not otherwise told by most U.S. media. One YouTube video titled *Sniper Hit* shows a serviceman being knocked down by gunfire, then standing up again and seeking cover. Soldiers are shown bleeding in some videos.

College campuses have also provided a venue for discourse and debate about the war, but not always with the openness one might expect. In 2006, a video distributed on YouTube revealed an incident at Columbia University in which protesters stormed a stage to prevent a conservative speaker from completing his speech on U.S. immigration policy.

In some international venues, access to the Internet and other digital media has been restricted or censored by foreign governments. The Citizen Lab, a part of the OpenNet Initiative, monitors censorship in forty countries, including China, Iran, and Saudi Arabia.[30] In the case of China, for example, the government blocks many Web sites through the use of software filters because the Communist Party finds the content objectionable or threatening. In other cases, such as North Korea, the Internet is blocked entirely, as are cell phones. Impoverished North Korea hardwires its television and radio sets to receive only government-controlled frequencies. In May 2006, the Committee to Protect Journalists in New York ranked North Korea number one on its list of the "ten most-censored countries." Also on the list are other restrictive regimes such as Burma, Syria, and Uzbekistan. The North Korean Internet domain suffix ".kp" remains unused, although several "official" North Korean sites are available, typically hosted on servers in China and Japan.[31]

A computer program called *psiphon* (pronounced "sy-fon") provides a tool to circumvent such governmental censorship. Developed at the University of Toronto, psiphon was released for general use on December 1, 2006, by an interdisciplinary team of political scientists, software engineers, and hackers.[32] It is downloaded and installed for free and transforms that computer into an Internet access point. It allows users from other countries where Internet or Web access is restricted to log in and use that computer as a proxy device to gain unfettered access to the Internet and Web. Psiphon also permits citizens of censored countries to use the proxy computers to make their own postings to blogs and other Web sites such as Wikipedia.org.

At the same time, some traditional media such as U.S. network television producers have used the Internet to avoid the censorship of government agencies. On December 16, 2006, *Saturday Night Live* on NBC aired a three-minute skit parodying two boy-band singers offering their own male anatomy gift-wrapped in a box and ribbon to their girlfriends. To satisfy FCC language requirements for broadcast television, *Saturday Night Live* edited out a word ("It's my 'dick' in a box") in the chorus sixteen times.[33] But to get around this censorship, it put the uncensored three-minute digital video on its own Web site as well as on YouTube within a week. By the end of the week, the uncensored video had been viewed some 2 million times online, and by January 24, 2007, it had been viewed 11,548,084 times and rated 4.5 of 5 stars on 21,049 user ratings.[34]

One of the venues for potential international regulation of media in the digital age is the United Nations. Through the United Nations' International Telecommunication Union (ITU), various regulations guiding international standards and practices in telephony and other digital communications have been negotiated, such as the allocation of radio frequencies, which can flow across political boundaries. In November 2006, the ITU formally requested that the "I" in Internet be printed in lower case as a matter of official policy, but ultimately decided to leave it upper case. The ITU represents 191 countries and 650 companies, so its decisions can shape online activities around the world. Among the issues on the ITU agenda are cybersecurity, Internet access, the digital divide, and international telecommunications treaties.

In 2004, the Bill and Melinda Gates Foundation and the American Library Association produced a joint report examining the state of the digital divide between those who have access to digital technology and those who don't. The report found that although public libraries had helped narrow the access gap between 1996 and 2004, a substantial divide still exists. In particular, poor communities and their libraries are underserved by technology. Their computers are old, and their access to the Internet is still very limited. Budgets are strained to provide continuing broadband access. The digital divide is not a public-policy priority in Washington, D.C., anymore. Not since Larry Irving and Ron Brown coined the term *digital divide* during the Clinton administration in the 1990s has the federal government made closing that divide a priority.[35] Unless bridging the divide rises on the policy platform in Washington, D.C., the situation is unlikely to improve significantly. It is useful to apply the words of the Reverend Martin Luther King Jr. to this case:

> There can be no gainsaying of the fact that a great revolution is taking place in the world today . . . that is, a technological revolution, with the impact of automation and cybernation. . . . Now, whenever anything new comes into history it brings with it new challenges and new opportunities. . . . [T]he geographical oneness of this age has come into being to a large extent through modern man's scientific ingenuity. Modern man through his scientific genius has been able to dwarf distance and place

time in chains. . . . Through our scientific and technological genius, we have made of this world a neighborhood and yet we have not had the ethical commitment to make of it a brotherhood. But somehow, and in some way, we have got to do this.[36]

TELECOMMUNICATIONS ACT OF 1996

Subsequent to the enactment of the DMCA, Congress passed the Telecommunications Act of 1996.[37] When President Clinton signed the act into law, it provided the first comprehensive update of the Communications Act of 1934.[38] The 1934 act was created at a time of great communications technology innovation, when radio and television were in their infancy, and much change was afoot. It ushered in an era of broadcasting when the so-called invisible hand of government directed broadcasters to act in the public interest, convenience, and necessity in exchange for their free use of the public airwaves. Broadcasters were licensed to transmit their signals over the air, but were regulated by the FCC as established by the act. Broadcasters have received the use of the public airwaves at no cost, but in return they have been subject to regulation by the FCC, an agency of the U.S. Congress. As such, they operate as a public trust and bear certain responsibilities to cover and serve their local communities. In return, they have enjoyed typically enormous profits.

The FCC enforces its various rules and regulations through both financial penalties and the threat of revocation of a station's license, although this threat has only rarely been carried out. FCC order DA-03–3513A1 indicates that a station's license was revoked by the FCC as a penalty for not fulfilling the requirements of its license.[39]

Under the 1996 act, the FCC continues as the federal regulatory agency responsible for broadcasting and other forms of telecommunications (e.g., telephony) utilizing public airwaves or rights-of-way (e.g., telephone wires installed on public lands, or rights-of-way). State and local regulatory agencies as well as local, state, and federal courts act as legal and regulatory bodies shaping communication policies and practices in the digital age. The 1996 act also preserves some of the essential principles of the 1934 act, such as mandating that broadcasters operate in the public interest, convenience, and necessity. Yet this guiding principle is relegated in many ways to a secondary status under the 1996 act. The new guiding ideas are competition and convergence. Competition is the act's strategy to give consumers more alternatives, better service, and potentially better prices and access to media in the digital age. Further, through fostering competition, the FCC hopes to stimulate economic growth in the communications sector, by means of internationally competitive media as well as new communication services. The act acknowledges convergence as it attempts to encourage competition between telephone and cable companies, both of which can deliver the same media services in the digital age, whether through a wireline or a wireless delivery environment. It continues the must-carry rules that require cable television providers to carry local and public television stations within their service area.[40]

The 1996 act largely deregulated telephone, cable, and other media companies. It eliminated or loosened most media ownership regulations. Consequently, many independent stations were acquired by large companies, creating further consolidation in the media industry. Thus, although the act was ostensibly designed to foster competition, it in reality helped reduce the number of major media companies from about eighty in 1986 to five in 2005, as noted in chapter 7.

"In truth, the bill promised the worst of both worlds," writes communications scholar Robert McChesney in *The Problem of the Media* (2004), with "more concentrated ownership over communications with less possibility for regulation in the public interest. Accordingly, both the cable and the telecommunication industries have become significantly more concentrated since 1996 and customer complaints about lousy service have hit all-time highs. Cable industry rates for consumers have also shot up, increasing some 50 percent between 1996 and 2003."[41] A trend toward more private equity-firm ownership of media companies has also emerged in the period since the 1996 act, which raises potential FCC questions about whether equity firms may exert influence over media company operations under rules that limit what is called a *cognizable owner,* or an identifiable owner, and as such fall under the jurisdiction of the FCC. "Cognizable" owners are limited in the number of broadcast stations they may own in a particular market.

Consolidation in the television industry has had other regulatory catalysts, including the FCC's action in the early 1990s that rescinded the Financial Interest and Syndication Rules, which when established in 1970 permitted owners of television and cable TV networks to own the programs they broadcast. The 1996 Telecommunications Act furthered concentration of control by permitting media companies to own more networks and allowing those networks to reach a greater portion of the audience than in the past. Research shows that these actions have led to a reduction in major media companies' use of independent producers as well as to their producing and broadcasting more of their own prime-time programming, thus reducing overall diversity.[42]

The 1996 act also introduced new regulations with implications for diversity. Under the act, telephone companies must share their lines with competitors at regulated rates if "the failure to provide access to such network elements would impair the ability of the telecommunications carrier seeking access to provide the services that it seeks to offer."[43]

Title V of the 1996 act is the Communications Decency Act. It is aimed at regulating Internet indecency and obscenity, but was ruled unconstitutional by the U.S. Supreme Court as a violation of the First Amendment. Portions of Title V remain, however. Among the provisions continuing are the Good Samaritan Act, which "protects ISPs [Internet service providers] from liability for third party content on their services, and legal definitions of the Internet."[44]

One area where indecent, obscene, or at least sexually explicit content is flourishing besides the Internet is satellite radio. Howard Stern, for example, without the restraint of FCC censors bearing down on him or on Sirius Satellite Radio, has been able to expand his sexual antics with various female adult movie stars and models. For those seeking even more graphic displays, video of Stern's act is available on demand via satellite television and some cable systems.[45]

REGULATING THE NEXT GENERATION OF TELEVISION

A key element of the Telecommunications Act of 1996 established guidelines for the introduction of the next generation of terrestrial broadcast television. This next generation is digital. The act outlined a general plan to transition from the long-standing analog transmission of terrestrial television to a digital transmission standard by the end of the twentieth century. This timetable was shifted, however, due to a variety of considerations, including the need to establish an agreed-upon technical standard as well as cost considerations, both to the broadcasters as well as to television set manufacturers and consumers. In the end, the FCC established 2009 as the transition date, when all analog transmissions will cease and a fully digital transmission standard will serve as its replacement. This means that all licensed broadcasters may transmit both analog and digital signals up until 2009, but in 2009 the analog transmissions must end and only digital signals may be sent. All consumers will then need to have in place a DTV set or a set-top box to convert the signal from digital to analog. In the meantime, broadcasters were granted additional spectrum to permit them to broadcast analog and digital signals simultaneously, but upon the 2009 conversion they are required to return the no-longer used analog spectrum to the government for new public uses. The FCC established firm rules to guide broadcasters in their use of the digital spectrum:

The Federal Communications Commission today adopted a standard for digital television (DTV). The standard is a modification of the Advanced Television System Committee's (ATSC) DTV Standard first proposed for adoption earlier this year. The standard adopted today is consistent with a consensus agreement voluntarily developed by a broad cross-section of parties, including the broadcasting, equipment manufacturing and computer industries. The standard allows transmission of one or two High Definition Television programs; four, five or more Standard Definition Television programs at a visual quality better than the current analog signal; many CD-quality audio signals; and the delivery of large amounts of data. The standard does not include requirements with respect to scanning formats, aspect ratios and lines of resolution.[46]

As such, the FCC's DTV rules establish guidelines for multicasting and HDTV broadcasting. They also establish rules for audio transmissions. They leave broadcasters with considerable latitude in terms of rules for whether they transmit using progressive (computer) or interlaced (traditional television) scanning, what aspect ratios—width to height—they use (i.e., either 4:3, which is the same rectangular shape as in traditional television, or 16:9, the more cinematic ratio sometimes referred to as *letterbox*), and how many lines of resolution they use (e.g., enhanced definition or full high definition).

SHIELD LAWS FOR JOURNALISTS IN THE DIGITAL AGE

One of the biggest problems that still plague journalists working in the digital age is the lack of a federal shield law in the United States to protect journalists from federal prosecution. Although all fifty states have some sort of shield law to protect journalists, no such law exists at the federal level. Shield laws are meant primarily to protect journalists from having to reveal the identity of their sources. In some limited cases, journalists agree to protect a source's identity in order to get the source to talk or share a secret document or serve as a whistleblower on government or other wrongdoers; in other words, they promise not to reveal the source to the public or to law enforcement. This agreement may be critical, as it was in the case of *Washington Post* reporters Bob Woodward and Carl Bernstein's famous 1972 Watergate investigation of the Republican National Committee's secret break-in at the Democratic National Party's offices located in the Watergate hotel. Relying on the revelations of so-called Deep Throat (an allusion to a porn starlet of the same era), Woodward and Bernstein were able to obtain information that revealed what actually happened at the Watergate, which ultimately led to the historic and unprecedented resignation of President Richard M. Nixon for his role in and cover-up of the illegal break-in. It was not until 2005 that the true identity of Deep Throat was revealed as then high-ranking FBI official W. Mark Felt.[47] It was necessary to protect his identity at the time of the story because of possible danger to Felt and his career. Journalists and news organizations must be careful when working with anonymous sources because it is a privilege that can be abused, and its overuse can result in a loss of public confidence in the media. Trust can be lost when too many sources are simply identified as "a high-ranking public official." The public has little means to know whether this source and the "facts" have simply been manufactured. The rule established by

Woodward and Bernstein is still relevant in the digital age: facts first revealed by an anonymous source should be confirmed by a second source or somehow authenticated before publication. Yet because of rapid-fire publication by Internet news entities such as Matt Drudge and his online *Drudge Report,* it is increasingly difficult for a news organization to compete while holding out for a second source to confirm the facts.

The lack of a federal shield law led Josh Wolf, a Seattle vlogger, to be jailed by federal prosecutors in August 2006 for not revealing his sources during anti–World Trade Organization protests in April 1999 in Seattle.[48] Whether a federal shield law can be created and passed is a matter of ongoing debate. Some contend that because virtually anyone can be a journalist online, a federal shield law would need to be restrictive in definition or else virtually anyone can invoke it. Perhaps this general exemption would be a good thing for the First Amendment, but a bad thing for law enforcement.

The situation for bloggers may be somewhat brighter in Canada. In November 2006, a judge in Canada ruled that a blogger in Fredericton, New Brunswick, was entitled to the same legal protections as journalists employed by mainstream media. The blogger, Charles LeBlanc, had been using his blog to report on poverty and attention deficit hyperactivity disorder.[49] In June 2006, he traveled to Saint John, New Brunswick, to report on a protest against a chamber of commerce meeting. Mr. LeBlanc was among those arrested when the protesters entered the meeting. Saint John police officers testified that they read LeBlanc's blog to gather intelligence on the protest. After viewing video of the protest shot by the Canadian Broadcasting Corporation, provincial court judge William J. McCarroll found that it contradicted the testimony of the officer who arrested LeBlanc. "Members of the so called mainstream media were taking photographs and filming in the same area without interference from the police," the judge wrote in his decision. "I believe it's fair to say that the defendant was doing nothing wrong at the time he was approached by Sergeant Parks and placed under arrest. He was simply plying his trade, gathering photographs and information for his blog alongside other reporters." The judge added that the police had no right to delete hundreds of photos stored on Mr. LeBlanc's camera.

The U.S. federal government also scrutinizes blogs and other new media content domestically and internationally as a source of potentially valuable information in its efforts to combat terrorism and suspected terrorists. Intelligence agencies such as the Defense Intelligence Agency, the Central Intelligence Agency, and the National Security Agency routinely scan blogs, Web sites, and e-mail to spy on suspected terrorists and terror cells.

PRIVACY

Some problems in the digital age are not only regulatory matters, but issues of concern to the public. Two of the most pressing are threats to privacy and identity theft. Such threats to personal freedom in the information age were foreshadowed by John Wicklein in his 1984 book *Electronic Nightmare*.[50] Although these problems have occurred for decades, they have been raised to an entirely new scale in the age of the Internet. In August 2006, AOL revealed that a staff member had posted online without authorization millions of search words typed in by 658,000 users over a three-month period from March to May. Ostensibly for the use of researchers studying search technologies, the posting revealed personal information about many of the users. Although the data are anonymous—that is, the user's name is not revealed, and a number is used instead—many users could have been offended to see their personal stories told online without their permission. For example, "User 1515830 is apparently an overweight woman with little willpower. She searches for the number of calories in certain foods but later searches for 'baked macaroni and cheese with sour cream.' Tragically troubled, she searches terms having to do with incest, depression, psychotic drugs and 'I hate men.' She also seems to be a teacher ('teaching positions in Denver Colorado'), probably lives in Ohio ('divorce laws in Ohio') and is shopping for curtains."[51]

In some cases, those offended by digital media can find little recourse through legal or regulatory channels. Their only option may be to respond through their own communications. Such may be the case in the 2006 "mockumentary" produced by Comedy Central television. Comedy Central sent a film crew posing as a local television station crew to shoot a documentary about a class taught at Portland State University. In the video report, offered over the air, cable, and online, the crew's producer,

"Tillie Sullivan" (played by Andrea Savage), speaks to a group of students, most of whom are female.[52] "If you need a really big story and you're not getting it, you know, you can always use the 'Nielsen' and the 'ratings,'" she says, holding each of her breasts in turn. "So, is it possible to succeed without flaunting your sexuality, then?" asks a female student. "For a woman, no," Ms. Savage replies. In other words, online media may be the only venue for those unhappy with traditional media.

Government agencies such as those mentioned earlier and the military are developing and testing systems for automatically conducting digital surveillance operations. One system, the Combat Zones That See, uses digital cameras to monitor activity at a military checkpoint—for instance, to scan the faces of those persons seeking passage and use AI software to compare them with terrorist watch lists.[53] Those identified by the software could be subject to interrogation and arrest. Combat Zones That See and similar surveillance technology might be extended beyond military checkpoints to airports and elsewhere, monitoring images or video transmitted via the Internet from personal Web cameras hooked up to social-networking sites.

NET NEUTRALITY

The Internet started as an online environment for open and robust communications that could withstand even a nuclear attack. Developed as a U.S. Defense Department initiative during the Cold War, much of the early growth and use of the Internet was by university researchers and academics. Along the way, the Internet caught the attention of the corporate world and during the 1990s was largely appropriated from the academy by commercial interests. The so-called dot-com bubble grew dramatically in the mid- to late 1990s as investors pored billions of dollars into the Internet and World Wide Web in the hopes of a making even greater fortunes. The bubble burst in 2000, only to be reborn in a more stable, slower-growth model a few years later. Public control over the Internet has been a guiding principle that has made it a hotbed of innovation and experimentation.

Yet as the first decade of the twenty-first century comes to a close, the Internet has been on a trajectory that might end or at least diminish public control. Many of the early shapers of the Internet are fighting to maintain public control over it. They say they are struggling for *network neutrality*. Although there is no consensus on the exact meaning of the term, in this context it means that everyone should have equal access to and potential use of the Internet. Regardless of who someone is, he or she should receive the same bandwidth for the same dollar spent. As Google reports, "Network neutrality is the principle that Internet users should be in control of what content they view and what applications they use on the Internet. The Internet has operated according to this neutrality principle since its earliest days. Indeed, it is this neutrality that has allowed many companies, including Google, to launch, grow, and innovate."[54]

Observes Vinton G. Cerf, Google chief Internet evangelist and code-veloper of the Internet Protocol, "Allowing broadband carriers to control what people see and do online would fundamentally undermine the principles that have made the Internet such a success. . . . A number of justifications have been created to support carrier control over consumer choices online; none stand up to scrutiny." Echoing this sentiment is Tim Berners-Lee, inventor of the World Wide Web: "The neutral communications medium is essential to our society. It is the basis of a fair competitive market economy. It is the basis of democracy, by which a community should decide what to do. It is the basis of science, by which humankind should decide what is true. Let us protect the neutrality of the net."[55]

Advocates of net neutrality have organized an online petition to the U.S. Congress to preserve the open architecture and public control over the Internet.[56] In the Republican-controlled Congress prior to 2007, there was a legislative movement to transfer significant control over the Internet to the major media and communications companies that already had great control over bandwidth, such as the telephone and cable television companies. The U.S. House of Representatives passed a telecommunications bill in 2006 lacking significant network neutrality protections.[57] A 2006 Senate Commerce Committee passed its own bill, similarly lacking network neutrality safeguards.[58] In early 2007, however, legislators in the Democratic-controlled Congress began drafting legislation that would safeguard network neutrality and prohibit broadband Internet firms from charging content providers for priority online access.[59]

CONCLUSION

Whether digital or analog, media operate in a system constrained and governed by law and regulation. Many of the basic laws created during the analog media age continue to operate and govern media in the digital age. Chief among them are the First Amendment to the U.S. Constitution, libel law, and copyright (although copyright law has evolved since the mid-1990s). Yet many of these laws stand on a somewhat shifting landscape in the digital age. Digital technologies, especially those involving the Internet and technological convergence, enable new user capabilities such as file sharing and thus challenge prevailing law. Consequently, new laws and regulations have been enacted in an effort to manage the digital media system. It is not entirely clear who benefits from these new laws and regulations. Some critics contend that the main change is to give for-profit corporate players greater control over their business interests. To a certain extent, this contention is undeniably true. Copyright duration is considerably longer in the digital age. Consolidation of media ownership has continued as ownership rules have been relaxed. Yet at the same time consumers have unprecedented media alternatives in the marketplace. They can go online and access news and entertainment media from around the country and the world. They can buy their television service from cable companies or telephone companies, or they can obtain free TV over the air digitally. Artists can distribute their material digitally and online, build demand for their work, and protect their intellectual property rights. Only through the lens of history will an adequate and complete answer ultimately emerge to this question of the benefits of laws and regulation in the digital media age.

9 / PRODUCTION AND PROTECTION OF DIGITAL MEDIA

Fueling the explosive growth in digital content is the emergence of increasingly affordable, powerful, low-cost, and easy-to-use technologies for producing digital media. High-end digital video cameras have fallen dramatically in price in recent years, making it far more cost effective to shoot quality video rather than film. At the same time, consumer friendly devices such as cell phones and digital cameras capable of shooting near-broadcast-quality video and high-resolution still pictures have flooded the market. Journalists, professional photographers, and consumers alike are now shooting still and motion pictures routinely. Consumers have begun routinely posting their photos and videos online, providing a growing stream of visual media content to complement the content professionally produced by or for major media organizations.

Editing digital video has also become easier and less expensive on any system, whether running Macintosh or Windows or Open Source software. Video postproduction has never been simpler, at least from a technical point of view. A growing number of Web sites offer free online video editing via user-friendly tools. In addition, most video software now makes it relatively easy to embed digital watermarks and other devices to protect copyright and intellectual property for online distribution. Audio is similarly easy to create, edit, and distribute digitally. All this follows on the heals of sophisticated but simple digital tools for word processing and Web site creation, as well as resources for easily creating blogs and podcasts (i.e., creating MP3 format audio or video files for downloading and listening to or watching on a desktop or on portable MP3 players).

TOOLS FOR MEDIA PROFESSIONALS IN THE DIGITAL AGE

Prior to the digital age, media-production tools were largely the province of media professionals. The tools were expensive, complicated to learn, and generally not available to anyone other than media professionals working for commercial or public media organizations. In some cases, serious amateurs could assemble the resources to acquire professional-grade media-production tools, but the challenges were considerable. Writing text could be anyone's province, but getting published still typically required a commercial press or publisher. Creating professional-grade audio or video not only required high-end cameras, microphones, and other acquisition and production tools, but also meant expensive studio time for the editing of the audio and video. Even then, there was little that could be done with the content once it was produced unless a professional media organization took an interest in its distribution.

Then along came digital, computer-based media-production and distribution technologies in the late 1980s and early 1990s, and the world of professional media production rapidly got turned upside down. Seemingly almost overnight, it became possible for even the least-well-funded would-be media developer to create professional-looking content in the form of text, graphics, photographs, audio, video, and other emerging media forms (e.g., immersive media, virtual reality). Although many of the early digital media tools were still somewhat expensive, the prices fell rapidly through the 1990s. Moreover, the software for editing media content not only became less expensive, but also quickly became easier to use. The marketplace for media-production tools exploded, and in the early years of the twenty-first century these tools found their way into the hands of everyone from school children in the midwestern United States to school children in South Africa, from technophiles in Tokyo to technophobes in Tucson. In the summer of 2006, the *New York Times* reported that the hottest item in war-torn Baghdad was the multimedia cell phone capable of talk, picture taking, and video shooting and distributing. Catapulting citizen demand for these tools was the Internet and the World Wide Web, which, simply stated, made it possible for all those would-be media mavens to deliver their newly produced content to a global audience (or a local one, depending on the desired audience or social network in digital media terms).

In only a relatively few years, the miniaturization of motion picture technology has transformed the movie-making business. Consider the case of leading black producer Topper Carew, the founder of the media production firm Urban Neo. With a degree in architecture and a Ph.D. in communications, Carew is unusual on a number of levels.[1] Once based in Los Angeles like most people in the television and movie business, he now runs his operation out of his home in South Portland, Maine. He is perhaps most well known for producing the highly successful *Martin Show* now in syndication and is increasingly recognized for his innovative use of digital technologies for production and distribution. Carew says there is no place anymore for silver nitrate (i.e., chemically based film). It is inefficient and bad for the environment, and it cannot be disposed of safely. Among Carew's new digital productions is a comedian Robin Harris DVD. Carew uses e-mail, the Web, and more to promote this and other productions,[2] which are professional at the highest level, but are made with very compact-quality digital technology. In the days of analog technology, a motion picture used to take five semi trucks of equipment; Carew now does it out of the back of his Volvo.[3]

Media professionals have seen their almost exclusive dominion over the world of media content erode rapidly. In the 1980s, the rise of desktop publishing made it possible for a much-wider range of people and organizations to create documents of a professional quality or at least appearance. But this capability was limited largely to text, graphics, and photographs, and distribution was limited primarily to the print media form. Since the 1990s, a wide swath of the population has produced an explosion of multimedia content, audio and video. Inexpensive but relatively high-quality microphones and cameras, along with easy-to-use and inexpensive or sometimes free editing software (or sometimes bundled in with new computer purchases), have made it possible for nearly anyone to become an audio or video producer, although not necessarily a good one. Talented or even professional audio and video producers who once needed high-priced equipment or many hours in expensive editing studios can now produce audio and video in their own home or office studio at a small fraction of the cost. Postproduction costs have fallen, yet there has been no sacrifice in audio or video quality as the sophistication and capability of these digital tools have increased dramatically.

Online technologies have given rise to wide-scale and inexpensive or free distribution of digital audio and video in the form of podcasting, MP3 file sharing, and the like. Bloggers have emerged as a significant force not just in the entertainment and opinion realms, but also in news reporting. Vloggers have proved important in reporting on major events such as the tsunami that wrecked havoc on much of Indonesia and surrounding areas in 2004. The blogosphere has repeatedly demonstrated its vitality in discerning questionable media, politics, and other activities, such as when in 2006 bloggers identified the manipulated news photo of an Israeli bomb attack in Beirut. Of course, much of the content produced in the blogosphere and elsewhere by amateur media content developers is of dubious or limited quality, and it is sometimes designed specifically to mislead, distort, or propagandize. Yet millions of Internet users spend substantial amounts of time digesting this content, oftentimes giving less time to the consumption of traditional, professionally produced media content, whether journalism or entertainment.

Ten important digital technologies are transforming the production and protection of media content. These technologies are generally mobile and inexpensive, and although a media professional might carry them into or have access to them in the field, most are also widely available to and used by media amateurs.

1. Megapixel Cameras

Among the most important devices are the increasingly high-resolution digital still and motion picture cameras. Reporters, videographers, and vloggers all use these megapixel digital still and digital video cameras to take high-resolution photos and digital movies (MPEG level), which are easily saved and can be instantly posted to the Web. The term *megapixel* refers to the number of pixels, the smallest picture element in a digital image (whether a still or a single frame in a motion picture), in excess of a million, or a *mega*. In many cases, megapixel cameras capture more than 10 million pixels per image. Such high-resolution imagery and video has many advantages. Among the most important is that it allows for zooming in to examine details in the pictures or video or for expanding the size of the image or video frame without significant degradation to the image or video due to pixelation (that is, when the picture becomes fuzzy as individual pixels are enlarged). Further, high-resolution images can be shown on large-screen displays and maintain their crispness. Images and video can be cropped easily, and they can be printed in magazines or other printed media for which image quality is essential. In addition to better resolution, these cameras also capture better color and lighting. A new class of computational cameras developed by Columbia University computer science professor Shree Nayar utilizes some of these enhanced capabilities to enable cameras to capture imagery in difficult-to-light environments. With each pixel illuminated independently, it becomes possible for the camera, using natural lighting, to "see" into a darkened doorway even while the area around the doorway might be brightly lit. With conventional photography and videography, it would be difficult or impossible to capture the entire view inside the doorway without overexposing the area around the doorway. Professor Nayar's computational camera captures the entire scene easily. His computational cameras can also shoot 360-degree views, enabling panoramic photography and videography (see figs. 9.1, 9.2, and 9.3).[4] Many digital cameras can also capture audio, although typically the audio is not of high quality, unless an external microphone is used. One of the potential challenges with the digital camera, as it were, is computer storage. The higher the resolution, the greater the storage requirements. In some cases, only a few very high-resolution images or minutes of high-definition video can meet or exceed the storage capacity of internal or removable memory or storage devices. Increasing storage capacity, miniaturization of storage devices, and falling prices of storage have reduced storage problems, though.

Power can also pose a problem. Megapixel cameras typically place a premium on battery power, and when more features are employed, particularly lighting, battery power is consumed rapidly, and recharging can be a challenge in the field. The highest-quality digital cameras are the single-lens reflex cameras, but they are also the most expensive and difficult to use. They are usually employed by media professionals or highly motivated amateurs. They offer a variety of photographic capabilities, such as interchanging lenses (e.g., using a telephoto lens) or obtaining high-quality images in low-light situations when faster "film"

Figure 9.1 The 360-degree camera, a type of computational camera, developed by Columbia University computer science professor Shree Nayar. Photo used with permission of Shree Nayar.

speeds may be needed. Similarly, high-end, professional-grade digital motion picture cameras are also available, offering a more advanced level of technology, but at a greater cost and steeper learning curve.

2. Personal Digital Appliance (PDA)

Handheld or wearable PDAs and cell phone technology enable mobile telephony and much more, such as shooting video discreetly. These mobile devices' other capabilities include a personal organizer, calendar, address book, high-speed wireless Internet access and Web searching, source finder, e-mail, maps and directions, word processing, and more. Many reporters routinely use portable computers or other mobile devices while in the field to write copy (the text of their stories), crop photos,

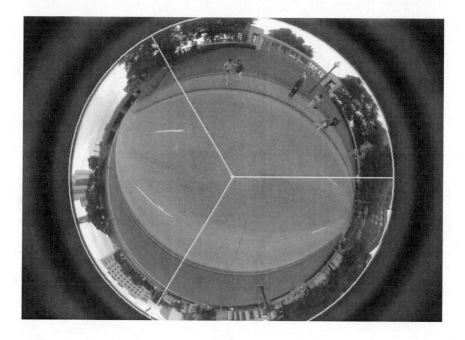

Figure 9.2 A 360-degree photo of Dealey Plaza, site of the Kennedy assassination, Dallas, Texas. Photo used with permission of Shree Nayar.

edit audio and video, and, with wireless Internet connectivity, file their multimedia reports to editors for review and publication. All these capabilities allow the creation of a virtual newsroom or media-production facility. Such mobile production supports both freelance media professionals and low-cost, on-demand media production.

3. Digital Audio Recorders

Digital audio recorders enable reporters and other media professionals to record interviews easily on location. It is a simple matter of transferring the recorded audio files to a laptop computer for voice-to-text translation and thereby easily and quickly create a transcript. A transcript can be helpful in preparing or editing the story or posting a video or audio story with accompanying transcript online for the hearing impaired. Digital audio recorders such as the $250 Olympus DS-50 can record up to 275 hours of audio.[5]

Figure 9.3 Rock musician David Bowie photographed using 360-degree photographic system developed by scientist Vic Nalwa, Fullview.com. Photo used with permission of Dr. Vic Nalwa.

4. Global Positioning System (GPS)

A mobile GPS receiver gives media professionals a simple tool for navigation and location finding. This capability can be valuable whether one is in a remote rural location or in a sprawling metropolitan or urban setting, or when one is in need of transportation from one location to another to interview a source or to capture video of a breaking news event. Moreover, GPS locational information can be stamped directly on photos and video as part of a digital watermark both to protect copyright and to authenticate time and date of a photo or video (for example, in documenting a mass grave or a terrorist camp). Some cell phones feature built-in GPS technology, such as the $700 Pharos G.P.S. Phone 600.[6]

5. Portable Digital Storage Devices

Portable digital storage devices equipped with massive (multigigabyte) capacity are an essential tool for media professionals. They are usually integrated into other devices, but are also often useful for sharing files when returning to the newsroom or working in a virtual newsroom.

Portable USB sticks are a routine part of any photographer's camera case.

6. Production and Distribution Software

A variety of software packages can be routinely installed on a laptop to facilitate media production and distribution. Among the vital software tools are packages to edit video, images/photos, graphics, and audio, as well as word processing; spreadsheet capability; mobile e-mail; high-speed wireless Internet access (requires wireless card as well); a Web browser with various plug-ins such as RealPlayer, Windows Media Player, or Quicktime for video/audio streaming; Web site design; Firewire or USB for high-speed data transfer from peripherals to laptop; and file transfer protocol software for transferring files. Also important is encryption software for creating secure documents and e-mail (e.g., public-key encryption available for free online), which is critically important to protect the security of a document against crackers (people who illegally, unethically, or maliciously modify or circumnavigate computer security systems), competitors, and sources, but also to authenticate the source of a document.[7]

7. Communication Tools

A cartoon says, "Only old guys use e-mail." What do young guys (and gals) use, then? IM software, of course. They use IM to chat in real time online but also to send text, video files, graphics, and images over the Internet between any two locations on Earth. They also use VoIP for real-time, no-cost or low-cost communications (assuming the Internet connection is a flat rate, such as is the case with Skype). This also requires a full-duplex sound card in the laptop (usually standard equipment) and a speaker and microphone, preferably a headset so that a reporter can work hands free. VoIP is ideally done with a high-speed Internet connection. Electronic fax services, such as efax.com, and online hard drives have emerged as essential to the digital journalist's toolbox. They enable a reporter to create his or her own private, virtual newsroom.[8] It becomes a simple matter to store and retrieve documents and files of any type from anywhere and at any time.

8. Satellite Phones

Despite the growing ubiquity of wireless communications, a satellite videophone is still a useful tool for foreign correspondents or even for domestic ones traveling to some rural areas, such as much of the southwestern United States or many American Indian reservations, or even to certain urban areas not yet served by communications companies that are less than fully committed to the age-old notion of universal service once enshrined in U.S. telecommunications policy. A satellite phone can provide communications capability on more than 90 percent of the Earth's surface (primary exceptions are the North and South Poles). Media professionals can use a satellite phone to transmit digital images, audio, and video from remote locations where wireless or landline telephone communications are not available. These devices are still a bit bulky—briefcase size, but fitting discreetly into a backpack—and pricey ($7,500 for the phone, with additional per minute usage charges). Moreover, the quality of audio and video transmitted is less than broadcast quality (twenty versus thirty frames per second), but when covering war or other breaking news in distant locales, a satellite videophone may be the only option for getting images, audio, and video out in a timely fashion.[9] It can be set up or dismantled easily in a few minutes by a single person and comes with its own batteries or can be operated off a car battery via a cigarette lighter adapter. One popular system that many journalists use is Talking Head, from 7E Communications, a British company.[10] Journalists have employed satellite phones for transmitting video for more than a decade, including during the Gulf War in 1991; when a U.S. spy plane was downed on Hainan Island, China, in April 2001; and when the United States launched air attacks on Kabul and elsewhere in Afghanistan in October 2001.

9. Specialized Online Media Resources

A few specialized online resources are worth noting for developments in new media and for their implications in journalism and the media. Former CBS News producer and technologist Dan Dubno's Gizmorama serves as an excellent resource for tracking new media developments, from remote-sensing satellite imagery to GPS to the latest in any kind of gadget, and the CBS News "disasters" site offers a comprehensive set of links for online resources for covering disasters.[11] Assignmenteditor.com offers a comprehensive set of links for the working journalist,[12] and MediaChannel.org's Journalist's Toolkit is also valuable.[13] The *Online Journalism Review* offers many useful insights for reporting in the digital age. Of particular note is the section on new media.[14]

10. Search Engines

Among the most important tools for sorting through the vast mountains of data available on the Internet are powerful search engines. Among the best for journalists are Google and AltaVista.[15]

Two Stanford University graduate students developed Google in 1998 and launched it in 1999. It has been increasingly popular ever since. By 2006, Google had become not only the dominant online search engine, but also a major Internet content distributor, aggregator, and portal. Google searches billions of Web pages, making it one of the largest search engines. It is straightforward and easy to use, with a simple, clear, and intuitive user interface. Its searches are fast and generally reliable. It locates pages based on the number of sites linking to them and how often they are visited, whereas some search engines return pages based on fees paid by the Web sites themselves or by the frequency a particular keyword is found on the page or in the page's metatags.[16] Google also serves as a Web portal with a Web directory, much like Yahoo, another leading search engine and Web portal.[17]

AltaVista is popular among journalists because it has been one of the largest Web search engines since it was developed by the Digital Equipment Corporation in December 1995. It has a variety of powerful features, such as language translation and image search, and is easy to use.

ONLINE AND MOBILE VIDEO

Video for new media is an extremely broad and large subject, ranging from all things digital and video to vlogging. Video for online distribution

Table 9.1 Typology of Content Forms for Digital Media

- Preproduction planning for mobile video
- Brief storytelling in a mobile environment
- Camera and on-screen motion restrictions
- Screen size emphasizing close-ups and location considerations
- Limited text, large fonts
- Quality audio
- Frame rates, resolution, color, and lighting constraints
- Few effects
- Compression to reduce file size

and for mobile devices is a fairly large topic because it encompasses not just desktop displays with Internet connectivity, but cell phones and other mobile platforms (including laptop and notebook computers with wireless Internet access) as well as a variety of production and distribution issues. Yet the topic is relevant and potentially useful to the broader subject of video for new media. The focus here is particularly on mobile devices because this area not only provides a window onto the larger domain of video and media production, but also demonstrates where important changes are occurring and where important implications for media and society are emerging.

There are five main stages of video production for online distribution and for mobile devices. Most of these stages apply more broadly to digital video production and distribution in general. The first stage is preproduction planning (see table 9.1), which encompasses the consideration of the entire process and includes technical, resource, personnel, and location aspects. Of course, if the project is journalistic or documentary, there are also archival research considerations.

The second stage is shooting the video and recording the audio. Animation using Flash is another option, although Flash can be used for live-action video production as well. Shooting includes a variety of considerations, including camera and lens selection, video storage requirements, lighting, and the like. Embedding of digital watermarks is a concern here; it is essential to protecting intellectual property and in authenticating original video shot in the field. Table 9.2 presents the primary considerations for shooting for mobile and online video.

Table 9.2 Considerations in Shooting for Mobile Video and Capturing Quality Sound

- Camera options
- Framing
- Scene selection
- Lighting
- External microphone for quality audio acquisition
- Digital watermarking during image/video acquisition

Table 9.3 Essential Principles and Tools for Editing Mobile and Online Video

- Faster pacing
- More cutting
- Tighter framing
- Careful sequencing (the ordering of shots and images)
- Software tools: Final Cut Pro, Premiere, iMovie
- Online editing tools: Jumpcut, Eyespot, Grouper, VideoEgg

The third stage involves editing. Here, the major considerations are software, from low end such as iMovie to high end such as Final Cut Pro and Adobe Premiere. Online editing is also an option with online video editors such as Jumpcut, Eyespot, Grouper, and VideoEgg. Issues involve not just framing, cutting, and sequencing, but also considering how the end product, the video itself, will be distributed to and displayed by the end user/audience. Table 9.3 presents the essential principles for editing digital video for online or mobile distribution.

The fourth stage is compression and formatting for distribution and display. Among the questions that need to be asked during this stage are: Will the video be produced for multiple platforms and devices such as portable computers or cell phones? Will there be video podcasts on iTunes? Helix Mobile Producer from Real is one option for compression and formatting and provides a flexible tool that can be used by amateurs and professional videographers alike, whether on a limited or a hefty budget.[18] Much of this stage involves technical considerations with significant aesthetic implications: bandwidth, frame rates, video

Table 9.4 Principal Considerations for Compression and Formatting for Distribution and Mobile Display of Digital Video

- Bandwidth: 320 Kbps up to 1.5 Mbps; consideration: length of time required for downloading based on the intersection of file size and user bandwidth
- Frame rate: 30 frames per second
- Video clarity
- Resolution
- Dimensions in pixels
- NTSC video quality with 640 x 480 pixel video
- Codecs (speed and how encoded and compressed)
- Audio quality (higher quality means larger file sizes)
- Output formats: Audio Video Interleave, MPEG, MP3, MP4, QuickTime, Waveform audio
- Producing/converting files for mobile devices
- Hardware: Kinoma for Palm Treo and other devices
- Software: Quicktime for Video iPod

clarity, dimensions in pixels, and codecs (speed and how encoded and compressed).[19] Table 9.4 presents principle considerations for compression and formatting for digital video distribution online and through mobile devices.

Finally, the fifth stage of the process involves the actual distribution of the video, testing its distribution and display, as well as monitoring its distribution, potential viewing, and redistribution (legally or illegally). Rights considerations and piracy concerns, both domestically and internationally, come into play here. Whether the video will be viewed or shared freely (e.g., on social video sites such as YouTube) is a consideration. Providing a syndication service for the video is also a key consideration, as it is for all digital content online. The simplest service is RSS, which uses XML, an advanced version of HTML. It permits authors or content providers to enable a feed that can automatically send content updates to content or Web site subscribers. This capability is especially useful for serialized video and other content, which is a major part of the online video and audio environment, where content is often delivered in short bits and bytes rather than in feature-length programs that consume potentially massive amounts of bandwidth and audience attention span (which is becoming increasingly short in the digital age). Table 9.5

Table 9.5 Considerations in Syndication and Distribution of Digital Video

- RSS (using XML) 425
- Testing distribution and display
- Monitoring of distribution, viewing, and redistribution (legally or illegally)
- Rights/royalty considerations (DRM)
- Digital watermarking
- Devices: require various players, design considerations
- Hardware: Treo 600, 650, 700p (Palm operating system), and 700w (Windows CE) (small screen, 2.5 inches); Video iPod (Apple or Windows operating system; 2.5-inch screen); Siemens PDA (larger screen, 3.5 inches); Sony PS3 (large screen, 4.3 inches, 16:9 aspect ratio, cinematic, high-resolution, game player); T-Mobile Sidekick; Sony DVP-FX701 portable DVD player with a 7-inch screen

presents the key considerations for online and mobile video distribution, syndication, and device display.[20]

PROTECTING INTELLECTUAL PROPERTY

Protecting digital content is one of the great challenges facing content creators and media organizations both large and small. Legal and regulatory considerations were examined in chapter 8. Here the focus is on the technical considerations. Pirating news and video, music downloading, and file sharing are just some of the daily occurrences online. A portion of these activities represent new business opportunities, but others are threats to existing business practices.

One possible method to protect content of all types is encryption. Many DVD producers encrypt their video to prevent unwanted copying of DVDs. Encryption is a form of security for digital data that involves "the process of encoding information in such a way that only the person (or computer) with the key (electronic) can decode it."[21] In early 2007, hackers reportedly broke the antipiracy software protection of the HD DVD format.[22]

A related security technique is the digital watermark. As a form of encryption, a digital watermark is a "pattern of bits inserted into a digital image, audio or video file that identifies the file's copyright information (author, rights, etc.). The name comes from the faintly visible watermarks imprinted on stationery that identify the manufacturer of the stationery. The purpose of digital watermarks is to provide copyright protection for intellectual property that's in digital format."[23] Unlike watermarks on analog print media, digital watermarks are generally designed to be invisible or inaudible.

Among the more interesting opportunities to protect content is emerging software that will enable editors to detect plagiarism and attribution issues quickly and easily, a problem area seen in journalism and elsewhere. One technology now under development and testing is LexisNexis CopyGuard. Although an initial test of the system by the *Baltimore Sun* proved less than reliable in detecting plagiarism, future generations of the technology are promising. CopyGuard uses technology developed by "iParadigms, the Oakland, Calif., software developer of Turnitin, a popular academic plagiarism-detection tool. Using iParadigms' 'pattern-matching' engine, CopyGuard compares each submitted document to more than 6.1 billion documents in LexisNexis and Web databases, and then identifies any matching phrases and their respective sources."[24] This comparison can be done in a matter of minutes or hours, in contrast to a three-week manual examination by one editor at the *Sun* for the alleged plagiarism and attribution problems in six years' worth of columns (six hundred) produced by reporter Michael Olesker. One of the limitations of the LexisNexis software is that it relies exclusively on material published and stored in the LexisNexis database (largely news media). It does not scan the entire World Wide Web and Internet, which may in fact be a resource to which an unscrupulous or lazy reporter might turn.

A content-identification system is planned for implementation at video-sharing network YouTube in 2007. Part of this system deals with royalties, a topic discussed in chapter 7 on finance.

One of the opportunities presented by developments in new media, particularly the increasingly powerful MDAs for accessing and displaying multimedia, is the ability to design video programming uniquely for mobile media. As of 2006, original video programming for MDAs was still in its early stages. Much of it is simply adapted from previous formats. For example, iTunes offers extensive television programming for download, including display on mobile devices such as the video iPod. In 2006, iTunes began offering seventy-five Disney movies, and Sony similarly released five hundred movies for mobile devices, but none of these movies was actually designed for mobile devices.

Yet some program developers and news organizations are developing content designed specifically for mobile devices. Notable examples include four projects produced by the National Black Programming Consortium (NBPC) in 2006. Based in Harlem, New York, the NBPC has as its mission to fund, commission, acquire, and award grants to producers and directors of films and video projects reflecting African Americans and the African Diaspora.[25] NBPC mobile media projects include a series of innovative new media productions. Funded by the NBPC, I serve as a mentor to these projects. Among the projects is *(afro)Galactic Postcards,* a series of five science fiction video podcasts. Audience members play the role of a receiver who "intercepts" a sixty-second transmission from an interstellar traveler making his or her way home or trying to escape, yet maintaining a connection with those he or she has left behind. The messages are delivered via an RSS feed. *Fightin' Words* profiles black American soldiers fighting in Iraq who wrote and produced a hip-hop recording based on their experiences abroad. *Me and My Good Hair* offers a celebration of African American girls and their hair. Told in their own words, the project features photographs, crayon drawings, and animation morphs of girls and their favorite hairstyles. Last is *The Story of Oshun & Ogun,* a short animation telling the West African (Yoruba) fable about little Oshun, who represents love, seduction, and sweet, or fresh, water such as rivers, lakes, and rain. It describes how she returns from hiding the powerful Ogun, a creature of iron, machines, and technology, to help reestablish order in the world.

Also producing video for mobile devices are various other organizations, including news media, such as washingtonpost.com. Its Hurricane Katrina video coverage in New Orleans was produced originally for mobile media. Washingtonpost.com videojournalist Travis Fox used the mobile video platform to document the lives of the people who were still living through the ordeal in New Orleans in the aftermath of the hurricane.[26] Equipped with a portable digital camera and working by himself, Fox produced four character-driven, slice-of-life video reports from New Orleans. The minidocumentaries were distributed on washingtonpost.com and on the *Washington Post*'s video podcast available on iTunes.

In response to the growing amount of new programming developed uniquely for new media, including mobile media, the National Academy of Television Arts and Sciences introduced in 2006 the first Emmy Award

Table 9.6 Design Checklist

- Maintain interactivity
- Maintain linearity of narrative
- Keep shot length short
- Keep story length short
- Serialize stories
- Limit camera movements
- Limit on-screen movement
- Limit on-screen text
- Use large fonts
- Limit special effects
- Utilize computer animation
- Keep framing considerations in mind
- Maximize close-ups
- Keep color considerations in mind

for nontraditional distribution platforms. As the academy notes, "Entries for this award must be original material made-for-broadband or made-for-mobile. These platforms include video blogs; Web site programs including journalistic reporting, event coverage or event analysis; mobisodes (short episodics created for mobile devices); video-on-demand and other video delivered over an [Internet Protocol] network or platform such as wireless, broadband or [video on demand]." The academy notes significantly that entries for this award may not be "material originally produced for television viewing and then repurposed for the new media."[27]

Table 9.6 summarizes the key considerations for digital video and audio design in the online and mobile environment. Table 9.7 similarly summarizes the principal design and distribution constraints and opportunities afforded by digital production and distribution.

CONCLUSION

This chapter has outlined the principal technical and design considerations for producing and distributing digital video and audio in an online, networked environment. Although the focus has been primarily on mobile devices and on Internet-based issues, most of these

Table 9.7 Design and Distribution Constraints/Opportunities in Digital Production and Distribution

Constraints	Opportunities
small screen	audio
mobility	contrast
distractions	resolution
bandwidth	frame rate
device requirements	device requirements
	iTunes option

considerations pertain to digital media production and distribution in general. Developments have dramatically lowered the barriers to creating content for media. Production and distribution technology costs have fallen precipitously, and the tools have become both far easier to use and more portable. Taken as a whole, these changes have made it possible for virtually anyone with an interest in creating and distributing media to do so. It does not mean that everyone has the skills required to produce professional-quality content, nor does it assure that everyone making and distributing content adheres to the accepted standards for the professional practice of journalism and media. In fact, many content creators deliberately exploit these opportunities to create content easily and cheaply to manufacture false or misleading news and other content, sometimes for commercial gain and sometimes for comedic effect.

Next-generation technologies represent a challenging opportunity for new media content innovation. Two broad developments illustrate the potential. The first development involves wearable technologies. As a natural extension of current mobile and gaming technologies, wearable media are already widely present in the market in the form of cellular telephony. These devices are increasingly multimedia enabled, and both virtual- and augmented-reality head-worn displays are on the horizon. Already making inroads with Bluetooth cell phone audio ear wear and in the gaming arena, wearables enable location-based media and other content innovation. Among the opportunities afforded is the potential end of device-size limitations that create image or video-size constraints. The second development is the provision of three-dimensional or immersive media, which creates the potential for more realistic and engaging media experiences. Immersive media can intensify the user's involvement with the content and offer younger audiences a compelling media environment.

Inspiration can be elusive and sometimes comes from the most unexpected places. With the May 2006 passing of Elma Gardner "Pem"
Farnsworth, it is worth recalling the spark that once led her late husband,
Philo T. Farnsworth, to his invention of television. As a thirteen-year-old
boy, Farnsworth plowed the fields on his family's Rigby, Idaho, farm
in the early 1920s, traveling back and forth across the fields behind a
horse-drawn machine, plowing one row at a time.[1] Later, he tried to
solve a problem with a newly emerging machine designed to transmit
pictures through the air. Other inventors had been designing mechanical television devices with whirling discs and mirrors, but struggled
to produce the desired result. Farnsworth's inspiration came when he
realized he could employ electrons to transmit far more rapidly and
to scan an image onto a picture tube in the same fashion as he had
plowed the fields, one row at a time.[2] This inspiration laid the foundation for the development of electronic television, and Pem Farnsworth
worked by her husband's side for decades, helping him advance his
invention.

In some ways, television is in the midst of a new stage of inspiration
and innovation. The convergence of digital technology and the Internet
has led to a radical explosion in the development and distribution of
television, or video, in an online environment.

Unlike most earlier generations of television, the age of online digital
video innovation is a playing field open to virtually anyone. Little technical expertise is needed to experiment. Nor are huge amounts of cash or
other resources required, although access to millions of dollars certainly
does not hurt. Yet when Philo Farnsworth invented electronic television,

the germ of the idea came from his experiences as the thirteen-year-old son of a farmer, with little in the way of resources beyond his own creative mind and initiative. The question today is where can the next generation of pioneers find their inspiration, their field of online video dreams? There is no simple, single answer.

I found inspiration for this book one day in 2006 when I had a few moments to explore the then newly launched Google Video search engine. Browsing under the "television show" heading, and after slogging through dozens of episodes of *Charlie Rose,* I discovered a series I have long enjoyed: *The Twilight Zone.* Scanning through the descriptions of the various episodes available on-demand for a fee (full program in high resolution for $.99 or $1.99 each), I located a favorite: "Perchance to Dream." With a title derived playfully from Shakespeare's *Hamlet* and a screenplay written by Charles Beaumont, the episode tells the story of a sleep-deprived man terrified of the dreams he might encounter if he falls asleep. It begins with a familiar voice inviting the viewer to embark upon "a journey into a wondrous land whose boundaries are that of imagination." As television enters the online age, Rod Serling's invitation might still serve as a guide to those seeking inspiration in the television dimension of imagination. Ironically, as I finished the book, I looked for this same episode on YouTube (now a Google property) on January 25, 2007, and found it as well as many other *Twilight Zone* episodes available on demand—and for *free.*

Media of all types are being reinvented or challenged to reinvent themselves through digital technologies and the Internet. This chapter examines the innovators, inventors, and pioneers who have helped or are helping to lead the reinvention of television and media of all types in the digital age. It is organized by the same areas that have constituted the principle spine of the book. In each area, at least one innovator or inventor is discussed.

THE MEDIUM OF DIGITAL DELIVERY

The Internet has been fertile terrain for innovation. The Internet itself would not exist except for two pioneering computer scientists, Vinton G. Cerf and Robert E. Kahn. Together, they invented in the 1970s the communications protocols on which the Internet runs. Transmission Control Protocol and Internet Protocol are the basis on which most commercial communication networks run. Cerf and Kahn did much of their early pioneering work while collaborating at the U.S. Department of Defense Advanced Research Projects Agency (DARPA). It is that said the phrase *surfing the net* originated from the data that Vint Cerf first sent over the Internet. Since 2005, Cerf has been vice president and chief Internet evangelist for Google, where he continues to explore new ideas for digital communication. Since leaving DARPA, Kahn founded and is the chairman, CEO, and president of the Corporation for National Research Initiatives, a not-for-profit organization devoted to the development of the national information infrastructure.[3]

Building on the pioneering efforts of Cerf and Kahn, computer scientist Tim Berners-Lee invented the online publishing technology known as the World Wide Web. He outlined the initial idea for the Web in 1989 while working at the Conseil Européen pour la Recherche Nucléaire, commonly known as CERN, a high-energy physics laboratory in Geneva, Switzerland, and also the largest Internet node in Europe. He proposed linking Ted Nelson's notion of hypertext (i.e., nonlinear text) with the Internet.[4] He explained his vision in these terms: "I just had to take the hypertext idea and connect it to the [Transfer Control Protocol] and Domain Name System ideas and—ta-da!—the World Wide Web."[5] Berners-Lee developed the first Web browser and editor as well as the first Web server called "httpd" (short for "HyperText Transfer Protocol Daemon"). He launched the first Web site on August 6, 1991.[6] The rest, as they say, is history. But Berners-Lee continues to invent and innovate. In 1994, he founded the World Wide Web Consortium at MIT. In 2004, he accepted a chair in computer science at the School of Electronics and Computer Science, University of Southampton, United Kingdom, where he is developing the next generation of the Web called the Semantic Web, or a World Wide Web consisting of documents with computer-processable meaning. In other words, documents on the Web will be in machine-understandable form, essentially a form of AI, where many new possibilities will emerge. For example, in a media context a computer would automatically search for a particular DVD, find the cheapest price, buy the DVD, and have it delivered to the computer's user.

THE DEVICES FOR ACCESSING, DISPLAYING, AND INTERACTING WITH DIGITAL MEDIA

Among the most apparent success stories for innovation in the domain of digital media devices is the iPod from Apple. Under the leadership of Steve Jobs, Apple has remade not only itself, but much of the music business by developing and marketing a personal digital music device that has captured more than two-thirds of the market. Apple was not the first to produce a portable device for playing MP3 or audio files, but it certainly has been the most successful in the market. The name "iPod" has become synonymous with "MP3 player," just as "Kleenex" is synonymous with "facial tissue" and "Band-Aid" is synonymous with "adhesive bandage." From the iPod has emerged related ideas and terms in the new media sphere as well, including *podcasting*, which basically means producing and distributing audio files (not necessarily music) via the Internet for listening on computers or portable MP3 players. The Apple iTunes Internet store has led the transformation of the music-distribution business in the digital age, demonstrating through the secure iPod device the potential to distribute digital music online to commercial success without rampant music piracy.

Often overlooked in the realm of innovation is the book. Perhaps because it is not typically considered a new medium, the book is rarely examined from the perspective of how it is changing as a medium, particularly from a technical point of view. Yet it is a medium where important and not always so subtle change is occurring. Founded in 1971, Project Gutenberg is the original and largest single collection of no-cost eBooks distributed online via the Internet. Initially distributed only in text form, these eBooks now also include digital audiobooks as well. Michael Hart is the founder of Project Gutenberg, and he continues to inspire the creation of eBooks and other technologies today.[7] Hart's background is in books, literature, and computers. At the University of Illinois, where he obtained a bachelor of arts degree, his formal education involved completing an independent-study program focused on human/machine interfaces. Project Gutenberg is a nonprofit organization that relies on donations and a considerable network of volunteers and partners to create and publish its eBooks. Hart reports that as of August 4, 2006, the original Project Gutenberg site has 20,000 eBooks; the combined catalog of the entire Project Gutenberg consortium offers 75,000. Its partner, the World eBook Fair, as of 2006 offers one-third of a million eBooks and expects to increase that total to one-half million by 2007, to three-quarters of a million by 2008, and to one million by 2009.[8] On February 22, 2006, Project Gutenberg's collection offered its 8,000th eBook, *The Suppression of the African Slave-Trade to the United States of America, 1638–1870,* written by W. E. B. Du Bois and based on his Ph.D. dissertation.[9] Du Bois was the first black American to receive a Ph.D. from Harvard. Most of the books at Project Gutenberg are from the public domain. Most are also in English. But books in more than four-dozen other languages are included as well, with more than 50 eBooks available in Chinese, Dutch, Finnish, French, German, Italian, Portuguese, Spanish, and Tagalog.

Some authors have made their copyright-protected books available in eBook format through Project Gutenberg. Among them is Robert Sheckley, one of science fiction's greatest humorists, who died December 9, 2005 at age seventy-seven in Poughkeepsie, New York. Sheckley's books available at Project Gutenberg include the text and audio version of *Bad Medicine.*[10] Here is a brief excerpt: "Caswell was a choleric little man with fierce red eyes, bulldog jowls and ginger-red hair. He was the sort you would expect to find perched on a detergent box, orating to a crowd of lunching businessmen and amused students, shouting, 'Mars for the Martians, Venus for the Venusians!'" You can hear the book online read by a human.[11] Many of the audio eBooks on Project Gutenberg are read by a computer, and, unfortunately, the computer often fails to provide much emotion to the reading. Among the human-read audio eBook authors available at Project Gutenberg are:

- Hans Christian Andersen (1805–1875) and his book *The Little Match Girl;*
- Lyman Frank Baum (1856–1919) and his book *The Wonderful Land of Oz;*
- Samuel Taylor Coleridge (1772–1834) and his poem *The Rhyme of the Ancient Mariner;*
- Sir Arthur Conan Doyle (1859–1930) and his classic tales of mystery *The Adventures of Sherlock Holmes, The Hound of the Baskervilles,* and *A Study in Scarlet;*

- Benjamin Franklin (1706–1790) and his oft-forgotten classic *Dialogue Between Franklin and the Gout;*
- The Gebrüder Grimm and their children's tales "Briar Rose," "Rapunzel," and "Rumpelstiltskin";
- Edgar Allan Poe (1809–1849) and his sometimes overlooked *Alone;*
- Beatrix Potter (1866–1943) and her children's favorite *The Tale of Peter Rabbit;*
- William Shakespeare (1564–1616), whose many works include "Sonnet 100";
- H. G. Wells (1866–1946) and his timeless science fiction work *The Time Machine;* and
- Walt Whitman (1819–1892), whose available poetry includes selections from *Song of Myself.*

Following up on the low-key success of Project Gutenberg's eBook library, Kara Shallenberg has begun using iPod technology to create her own audio eBook collection of public-domain books and making them freely available as podcasts. The collection is available on LibriVox, a Web site that also relies on a network of volunteers to create its audio eBooks.[12] As of August 25, 2006, its completed audiobook collection had 117 titles, including Jane Austen's *Pride and Prejudice,* Frances Hodgson Burnett's *The Secret Garden* (produced by Schallenberg), and Jules Verne's *A Journey to the Interior of the Earth.* The audiobooks and other extensive audio content in iPod form are available at no cost to anyone with an Internet connection and simple audio software. Other audio content includes short works, poetry, children's literature, nonfiction, and works in languages other than English.

Books in their electronic form offer a variety of advantages over printed books. In electronic text form, eBooks are searchable. This tool is especially valuable for works of nonfiction, where keyword searching for an important phrase, name, or passage is often needed. A reader can also easily annotate an eBook. When the eBook is closed, the eReader software automatically inserts a bookmark. eBooks are downloadable, which makes distribution much easier, less expensive, and quicker, the latter an especially valuable feature for both publishers and readers. They can be placed on portable electronic devices for easy carrying. In fact, with advances in miniature storage technology such as mini–secure disks that come in one GB or greater capacity and can be inserted in most digital cell phones, multiple eBooks can be placed simultaneously on a single device. With the advent of electronic textbooks (e-texts), especially for children in a K–12 environment, this is no small achievement. Many children have routinely lugged around heavy backpacks laden with multiple thick textbooks, to and from class and school every day. With e-texts, schoolchildren's loads can be lightened significantly, both physically and perhaps mentally (i.e., they do not have to worry about losing or damaging an e-text; if lost, the text document can be replaced as easily as another download). Moreover, e-texts are generally much cheaper than paper or hard cover textbooks and offer publishers the advantage of having minimal waste (i.e., there are no excess print runs) and no returns. With eBooks, readers like me who have to rely on reading glasses to read conventional printed texts, are offered the increasing advantage of adjustable font size (i.e., fonts can be adjusted on the fly to almost any size the reader might want for easier reading).

In audio form, eBooks offer the advantages of audiobooks in general, such as the ability to listen to them while one is driving or otherwise engaged. But audio eBooks also have some of the advantages of e-texts in general, such as easy downloading, portability on handheld devices, and searching and fast-forwarding capabilities.

Electronic books have as their main drawback the lack of the tactile experience of holding a printed book in one's hands, and one can also accidentally drop and break an eBook device, with replacement being an expensive proposition. Moreover, the glow of an electronic screen is not always as pleasing an experience for the eye as words printed in black ink on a white page (although the backlit feature can be turned off on most devices). A lightweight eReader device providing its own light source can be useful at times, though.

Among the pioneers developing the possible next generation of tablet displays that can be used for eBooks or e-newspapers is Mark A. Dean, a leading computer scientist and engineer. Dean helped invent the personal computer at IBM and is now developing the flexible tablet personal computer.[13] Frustrated by the bulkiness of newspapers, he developed the idea for a rugged, magazine-size device to download any electronic text. It can also be a DVD player, a radio, and a wireless telephone, and it can provide access to the Internet. Dean's vision is to produce a tablet that can recognize handwriting, take voice command, and talk back.

Dean believes the tablet might be produced cheaply enough so that every student can get one in place of printed books. In terms of a time-table, he says, "We are almost there. The only technology left to conquer is the display, we have the other pieces. We will see it pretty soon—easily within 10 years."[14] Dean has been recognized for his many accomplishments, including helping develop the first gigahertz microprocessor in 1998. In 2004, *Science Spectrum Magazine* named him one of the fifty most important blacks in research science.

THE AUDIENCE OR USERS OF DIGITAL MEDIA

Audiences are transforming into users in the digital media age. For most of the history of the media, the audience was characterized by pas-siveness—in the position of only receiving the reports published and broadcast by centralized news and media organizations. After the rise of the penny press in the mid–nineteenth century, the audience grew increasingly large in size, to the point where media of the twentieth century became known as *mass media.* Audiences were massive, passive, anonymous, and heterogeneous, assembled largely for advertisers to sell their goods and services. Almost as a side benefit, audiences, known collectively as the *public,* learned about matters of public and personal importance, whether candidates for elected office, foreign wars, health concerns, or sports.

Through the advent of digital and networked technologies, the audi-ence has dramatically begun to reinvent itself as an active participant in the public-communication process. Citizens have created their own media and contribute increasing volumes of information, opinion, and entertainment for public consumption. Much of this activity occurs on the Internet, particularly in the form of Web pages, including a particu-lar form of Web site called the *Weblog,* or *blog.* These many millions of blogs are collectively called the *blogosphere,* and it is where much spirited discourse occurs, and pioneers have found a voice.

The blogosphere has proven to be a fertile ground for innovation in the media realm. It is a part of the public sphere where pundits and public alike intersect and interact. Among those achieving success publishing in the blogosphere is Arianna Huffington, a political pundit and author. Huffington reached the national stage as a conservative syndicated columnist, but with the launch of the *Huffington Post* on May 9, 2005, she created a unique voice online.[15] She describes herself as a "former right-winger who has evolved into a compassionate and progressive populist." Through her online report, she features not only her own blog on politics, but dozens of other blogs by a full spectrum of observers. Bloggers on the *Huffington Post* include Gawker, Instapundit, and Romenesko, as well as such diverse newspaper columnists as Molly Ivins, Stanley Crouch, and George Will. Even legendary *CBS Evening News* anchor Walter Cronkite writes a blog for the *Huffington Post.* In a post on March 1, 2006, Cronkite offered these critical observations about the war on drugs in the United States: "As anchorman of the *CBS Evening News,* I signed off my nightly broadcasts for nearly two decades with a simple statement: 'And that's the way it is.' To me, that encapsulates the newsman's highest ideal: to report the facts as he sees them, without regard for the consequences or controversy that may ensue. Sadly, that is not an ethic to which all politicians aspire—least of all in a time of war."[16] One of the useful features of the *Huffington Post* (and of many other online publications) is the bloggers' biographies—for example, readers can examine the former anchorman's background and training in journalism. Such biographies are extremely useful for readers to understand the perspective and credentials that authors, journalists, and others bring to what they write about or cover. At the *Huffington Post,* Dr. Kathleen Reardon writes a blog about health-care issues.[17] As her online bio notes, "Reardon is a Phi Beta Kappa professor of management at the University of Southern California Marshall School of Business. She is the author of numerous articles on communication, persuasion, negotiation and politics, including in the *Harvard Business Review.*" In November 2006, Huffington announced plans to add original reporting to the *Huffington Post.* Among the beats will be the Congress and the 2008 presidential election.

Huffington faces growing competition in the arena of online journalism devoted to the topic of national politics. Launched January 23, 2007, *The Politico* is an online news site with the mission of "covering politics—the lifeblood of the nation's capital—with enterprise, style, and impact."[18] Coverage focuses on three areas: the politics of Capitol

Hill, the politics of the presidential campaign, and the business of Washington lobbying and advocacy. *Politico* staff includes more than thirty writers and editors, such as senior publisher and editor Martin Tolchin, a forty-year veteran of the *New York Times* and founder of *The Hill,* a newspaper covering Congress.

PRODUCERS OF DIGITAL MEDIA

Producing digital media has become a basic fact of life for millions of persons in the United States and around the world. Social-networking site MySpace has more than 100 million members, the majority of whom have created a personal page with at least a modest amount of content, whether text, photos, or multimedia. Not all social-networking sites are for young people or just for entertainment, though; some are for the serious minded. Gather.com, for example, featured "First Chapters" in 2007, a book-writing contest sponsored by publisher Touchstone/Simon & Schuster in which any aspiring unpublished author could upload a manuscript for possible publication and a $5,000 award.[19]

In the context of innovative producers of digital media, there are at least two archetypes. One is the producer who comes from and operates largely in the realm of the professional media organization. Such a producer creates content for an organization designed to generate profit or a public (i.e., audience) and operates within certain organizational constraints that may limit creative options. Among perhaps the more unexpected innovators in new media of this type is singer and songwriter Bob Dylan, known to generations as a brilliant poet and musical innovator. In 2006, Dylan became one of a series of well-known celebrities from music, radio, and other fields to try their hand at being a disc jockey on satellite radio. Dylan's program is called *The Theme Time Radio Hour with Your Host Bob Dylan.* XM invites listeners to "Take a trip back to the golden age of radio. With music hand-selected from his personal collection, Bob Dylan takes you to places only he can. Listen as Bob Dylan weaves his own brand of radio with special themes, listener e-mails and a little help from his friends." Once a week Dylan spins not only his favorite tunes, but his own brand of humor, wisdom, and wit. As he explains, "Songs and music have always inspired me."[20]

Illustrative of the second archetype of producer of digital media is Dr. Steve Mann, a professor at the University of Toronto and an inventor of the wearable computer. At Toronto, Mann directs the Humanistic Computing Laboratory, where he continues the research on wearables that he helped build at the MIT Media Lab.[21] Since at least the 1980s, he has lived as something of a cyborg, a living convergence of digital technology and human. In 1999, he visited my class at Columbia University and there previewed a unique documentary shot entirely through a head-worn camera integrated invisibly into his wearable gear. The documentary examines the state of privacy in today's hyper-security-conscious world. In particular, Mann looks critically at the use of surveillance cameras in public or quasi-public spaces, such as stores, malls, and the like. Rather than examine the topic from the point of view of those who use the cameras, he looks at it from the perspective of the shopper or consumer whose privacy is being eroded by these omnipresent cameras, which today are often connected to the Internet for remote surveillance. Mann's documentary exposes the lengths that store owners and operators go to in order to hide their surveillance cameras and to deny both their existence and their intrusiveness into people's lives, ostensibly for the sake of preventing shoplifting. Mann describes his work in applying wearable media technology to counter institutional surveillance as *sousveillance,* or inverse surveillance. Mann's Columbia visit coincided with the awarding of the Engineering School's Marconi Prize to Vinton Cerf for his coinvention of the Internet (with Robert Kahn). I brought Mann as a guest to a reception honoring Cerf, and when Mann entered the reception area, not only did almost everyone stop talking to look at the living cyborg who had just entered the room (ironically a classically appointed room filled with ancient Chinese artwork from the Ming and other dynasties), but Cerf quickly approached Mann to say, "Steve Mann, you're my hero. I've always wanted to meet you."

Mann once told me that until late 2002 he never disconnected from his wearable computing technology, including head-worn display. While awake, he continuously experienced the world through a digitally mediated lens. In the post-9/11 world, though, he was confronted by airport security while traveling to his Canadian home. They would not permit him to go through the security checkpoint unless he disconnected from his wearable technology. Mann resisted at first, but finally agreed to the terms and removed his wearable devices. Unfortunately, he had been so deeply connected to his media technology that the experience of disconnecting was physically traumatic and caused him to collapse and injure himself at the security area. Much of his $500,000 equipment was damaged as well. Mann has since recovered and resumed his research on wearable technology, and he is now the subject of an entry in *Wikipedia*.[22]

DIGITAL MEDIA CONTENT

Adam Clayton Powell III

Adam Clayton Powell III, son of the great New York Congressman Adam Clayton Powell Jr., is a pioneer of media technology on many levels. He was a top executive at the Satellite News Channel, an early competitor to CNN. He has also been executive producer at Quincy Jones Entertainment, vice president of news and information programming at NPR (1987–90);,and manager of network radio and television news for CBS News (1976–81). Powell is a creative technologist, someone who envisions new applications and uses of technology as well as new technologies that can be developed to do new things or solve existing and emerging problems. He has called technology "the new jazz," and his improvisational view is not surprising. His mother was Hazel Scott, the acclaimed pianist known for improvising on classical themes. She was also the first African American woman with her own television show, *The Hazel Scott Show*. Because Scott was an outspoken critic of McCarthyism and racial segregation, her show was canceled on September 29, 1950, when she was accused of being a Communist sympathizer.

In 2005, Powell III accepted a new post in academia as the director of the IMSC in the University of Southern California Viterbi School of Engineering. He explains the center's work: "IMSC conducts research that will help invent the future of how we work, learn and play. IMSC technologies use audio, video and haptics [tactile data] to augment reality and present the illusion that you are somewhere other than you are—with no goggles or earphones. John Seeley Brown, a member of the center's board, describes IMSC as 'sensing the edge.' It's a nice three- or four-way pun: IMSC is out on the edge, and we work with technologies that intersect with the human senses."[23] Among the media innovations to emerge from IMSC are immersive sound, interactive three-dimensional maps with photorealistic imagery, and three-dimensional audio and video formats and tools to record, produce, and transmit news and information.[24]

Brian Stelter

Capturing the attention of news executives and others interested in the state of television news are the online musings of Brian Stelter, whose popular blog *TVNewser* tracks gossip and developments in the television news business.[25] Stelter founded his blog in January 2004 when he was just eighteen. Originally calling the blog *CableNewser,* Stelter soon changed the name to *TVNewser* when MediaBistro paid him to run the blog. MediaBistro is a Web site that features several widely viewed journalism blogs. It reportedly pays Stelter more than enough to cover his college expenses.[26] A devoted student of television news, Stelter is also a full-time student majoring in mass communication at Towson University in Maryland, where he is editor of the student newspaper, the *Towerlight.*

Among the tidbits reported on *TVNewser* in November 2006 were:

- "Diane Sawyer will take over for Charlie Gibson when he steps down as anchor of *World News Tonight* after the 2008 presidential election, TV insiders agree."
- "NBC launched video podcasts of *NBC Nightly News* and *Meet the Press* last week, and they're already the #1 and #4 podcasts on all of iTunes."
- "CBS will likely use the Super Bowl on Feb. 4 (2007) 'as a re-launch of sorts' for Katie Couric, the NY Post reports."

TVNewser draws an increasingly large audience, with 1.2 million page views in September 2006, a sizeable increase from 150,000 in July 2004, when it moved to MediaBistro.

Red Bank Green

Digital technologies have also presented unique opportunities for the reinvention of local journalism on an online shoestring. *Red Bank Green,* for example, is a very local online news service produced by one man, John Ward, a veteran reporter who in 2006 left the ranks of daily newspaper journalism to pursue his vision of producing quality local journalism delivered online.[27] At the time, he had a full-time job working for the *Asbury Park Press,* one of dozens of newspapers in the Gannett chain. Gannett is the largest daily newspaper chain in the United States and is undergoing its own restructuring for the digital age by replacing its traditional newsroom with an information center and making a variety of other changes to adapt to the digital, networked environment. Ward felt there was an opportunity to reinvent local journalism in the New Jersey community where he lives, Red Bank. His vision is summed up nicely in his estimate of the number of stories out there waiting to be reported: "There are 12,000 people in Red Bank," Ward says. "That's at least 12,000 stories." His wife, Trish, is a Web site developer and graphic artist and is responsible for all the design aspects of *Red Bank Green.* The title is a reference to the very local nature of the reporting and the interactive quality of the medium. It is meant as an online village green or commons where people can meet to learn about and discuss what is going on in the town of Red Bank, New Jersey. Ward practices good old shoe-leather reporting, what many consider the hallmark of great journalism. He walks the town and reports. He stops in stores and chats with business owners and customers. He sees people out around town and talks with them. He asks them what is going on and what is on their minds. He observes and reports. He tells their stories. He has a digital camera with which he takes pictures and shoots video. He has a digital audio recorder that can record up to thirteen hours of audio. He writes and edits on his laptop computer. He has only a few advertisers (with only about $500 in advertising revenue through November 2006), but he hopes to grow the business side of things so it can sustain even more journalism, including investigative reporting. His goal is not to be objective in the sense of traditional mainstream journalism. That is impossible, he says, although it is a worthy pursuit. He writes from his own perspective and with his own style. His goals as a reporter and editor are to be accurate and fair.

Ward is not alone in pursuing a dream of an online newspaper to report local news. Other communities are seeing the delivery of local news reporting online, including communities where local news and local newspapers have never existed. One such community is Mount Hope, New York, a Bronx neighborhood of 130,000 persons that had no local newspaper or other local news provider. For the most part, residents of this struggling Bronx enclave had to rely on the city's major media outlets, weekly newspapers, and regional ethnic news media for occasional local news about the neighborhood, most often only in the form of crime news. But with the rise of the Internet and of cheaper and easier newsgathering, production, and distribution tools, it has become possible to report local news on this more than minute community. The *Mount Hope Monitor* is the new online newspaper covering the Mount Hope community, and it is just one of several new local online newspapers that have banded together as part of the West Bronx News Network.[28] As with *Red Bank Green,* the operation has a low overhead and a streamlined staff that utilizes digital technologies to produce and deliver the news as economically and efficiently as possible. Jordan Moss is the executive editor of the West Bronx News Network, and James Fergusson is the network coordinator and *Mount Hope Monitor* reporter. That's right: one reporter and one editor. Is it the ideal situation? Probably not. But is it better than no local journalism at all? The answer should be clear.

THE DISTRIBUTORS OF MEDIA

In many ways, Google can be seen as an innovator in just about every aspect of digital media. Founders Larry Page and Sergey Brin started Google as a research project in January 1996 while they were Ph.D. students at Stanford University. They predicted that a search engine based on links between Web sites would produce more efficient results than using traditional search techniques largely based on a ranking of how many times a search term appeared on a Web page. The traditional approach could be easily manipulated by overloading anticipated search terms on a page. David Koller reports that the name "Google" came from a misspelling of the term *googol,* which is a reference to 10^{100}, or a 1 followed by 100 zeros.[29] Google has become the proverbial eight-hundred-pound gorilla of the Internet. *Wikipedia* reports that Google had 9,378 full-time employees as of September 30, 2006.[30] Scott Harris reports that the verb *google* has been added to both the *Merriam Webster Collegiate Dictionary* and the *Oxford English Dictionary.*[31] To "google" someone or something means "to use the Google search engine to obtain information on the Internet."

Among Google's innovative efforts are:

- Scholar, which permits users to search for scholarly research on any topic.
- Earth, which provides users free access to imagery and other geographic information on the entire planet; and,
- Book Search, which permits users to search the full-text contents of thousands of books that have been digitally scanned and made available online.

A November 21, 2006, search for books by "Pavlik" yielded several books by me and by others with chapters by me. Among the returns is *Making Journalists: Diverse Models, Global Issues,* edited by Hugo de Burgh (New York: Routledge, 2005, 296 pages), with my contribution appearing on page 245.[32] Google's Print Library Project includes high-profile university and public-library partners, including the University of Michigan, Harvard (Widener Library), Stanford (Green Library), Oxford (Bodleian Library), and the New York Public Library. Google intends to digitize and make available through its Google Book Search service approximately 15 million volumes by 2015.[33]

THE FINANCERS OF DIGITAL MEDIA

Blazing the trail for new media content has been the NBPC: "Since 1979, NBPC has been a leading provider on American public television of quality, intelligent and compelling programming that celebrates the cultural heritage of African Americans and the African Diaspora."[34] While continuing these efforts, the NBPC in the twenty-first century has been funding the development of digital and interactive media also focused on the cultural heritage of African Americans and the African Diaspora. In

August 2006, it launched a program to provide up to fifteen historically black colleges with $75,000 ($5,000 each) to create original media-based projects that examine contemporary issues of civil rights, U.S. history, and local and national leadership. The Web-based, multimedia initiative encourages innovative use of interactive technology at historically black colleges as they work collaboratively with public-television stations. The goal is to enhance understanding of how the civil rights movement is still relevant today. The initiative builds on the award-winning series *Eyes on the Prize: America's Civil Rights Movement, 1954–1985,* which aired nationally on PBS's *American Experience* in October 2006, the first rebroadcast of the series since 1993. Program development at historically black colleges and universities helps foster diversity in media programming and adds to a tradition reflected in the efforts of media leaders such as Oprah Winfrey, Shawn "P. Diddy" Combs, and Spike Lee, each of whom attended historically black colleges.

THE REGULATORS OF MEDIA

Robert W. McChesney is an academic whose research focuses on media regulation. An outspoken critic of big media, he is a research professor in the Institute of Communications Research and the Graduate School of Information and Library Science at the University of Illinois at Urbana-Champaign, where he is also host of the radio show *Media Matters,* broadcast on WILL-AM at the university.[35] Among his most noteworthy endeavors are efforts to reform the media. McChesney contends that the idea of a deregulated media system is a fallacy. The media are, he proposes, a governmentally sanctioned oligopoly. The major commercial media are owned by a few highly profitable corporations who protect their privileged position through policy and legislative influence such as the Newspaper Preservation Act, which permits joint-operating arrangements in U.S. cities where competing daily newspapers once operated independently. McChesney also argues that the mainstream corporate media have controlled news coverage in order to shape public opinion to their benefit. He points to the elimination in the 1980s of the Fairness Doctrine as an example of the problem of big corporate media. The Fairness Doctrine promoted public-interest broadcasting by requiring broadcast licensees to examine controversial issues of public importance and to present these matters in an honest, equal, and balanced manner. Broadcasters challenged the Fairness Doctrine as an unconstitutional infringement of the First Amendment, but in 1969 the U.S. Supreme Court ruled in *Red Lion Broadcasting Co. v. FCC* that it was not unconstitutional.[36] The restrictions of the Fairness Doctrine were nevertheless later eliminated in the 1980s under the banner of "deregulation." To what extent McChesney's general thesis is supported by empirical evidence is unclear. Central to his regulatory reform efforts are greater public involvement in lobbying the FCC to discourage the relaxation of media ownership limits.[37] He encourages citizens to provide public comments to the FCC during its public hearings and policymaking. McChesney hopes that his efforts to reform media by encouraging greater diversity in media ownership will lead to a better, more robust media system.

THE DIGITAL TECHNOLOGIES OF PRODUCTION AND PROTECTION

Among the little-known pioneers, at least outside of the media world itself, is Joseph A. Flaherty Jr., senior vice president of technology at CBS, where he has been employed since 1957. Flaherty advises CBS management on issues and strategies related to broadcast technology and has directed the Engineering and Development Department at CBS since 1967, first as general manager, then as vice president and general manager. He has won many broadcast industry awards, including multiple Emmy awards for technical achievement: the Emmy Award Citation for the CBS Minicam Color Camera in 1969, a Technical Emmy Award for Electronic Newsgathering in 1975, and an Emmy Award for electronic editing systems for programs in 1986. He received in 1994 a Personal Emmy Award for "Lifetime Achievement in Contributions to the Development and Improvement of the Science and Technology of Television." He is the recipient of the David Sarnoff Gold Medal for progress in television engineering. He has also won the National Association of Broadcasters Engineering Award, the Progress Medal of the Society of Motion Picture and Television Engineers, and the International Montreux Achievement Gold Medal. Flaherty is a Fellow of the British Institution of Electrical Engineers and other major broadcasting organizations. In 1985, French president François Mitterand awarded Flaherty the country's highest recognition, the Chevalier de l'Ordre National de la Légion d'Honneur.[38]

Perhaps Flaherty's greatest achievements in the age of digital media are the introduction of HDTV in the United States and the initiative to establish the digital standard for the next generation of television. In 1985, Flaherty observed that "[i]n the U.S., up to 90 percent of all prime time evening programs for all the commercial television networks have for 40 years been produced in high definition 35 mm film. This notwithstanding, we have never delivered a single frame of high definition to the home viewer." The two decades since Flaherty's observation have seen the situation change dramatically, with the advent of HDTV, particularly in digital format, which enables both the production of HDTV and its distribution to the home. Under Flaherty's technical leadership, CBS produced and aired in 1988 the first prime-time program shot entirely using HDTV digital cameras. Now, in 2007, the vast majority of prime-time and other television programming is shot not only in high definition, but on digital cameras rather than on 35 mm film. High-definition programming is extensively delivered to home viewers, although a relatively small portion of the total audience has receivers capable of displaying that HDTV in high-definition quality. Yet the portion is growing. It is expected that by 2010 the majority of homes will be equipped to both receive and view high-definition programming.

Flaherty fought a not insignificant battle to bring HDTV into the United States and to establish the digital standard for HDTV. He is a member of the board of directors of the ATSC, through which he has helped bring HDTV to the United States. He is the former chairman of the Planning Subcommittee of the FCC's Advisory Committee on Advanced Television Service and cochairman of its Technical Subgroup, which developed the ATSC DTV and HDTV standard.[39]

CONCLUSION

Innovation is central to the improvement of media. Digital technology offers many new possibilities for such innovation. This chapter has described people and organizations employing digital technology to provide innovative and inventive approaches to improving media.

Although not always successful, many of these efforts have produced changes in media diversity, public engagement, and enhanced content. One of the fundamental differences between media in the digital age and media in the analog age is that the barriers to entry are much lower in the digital age. As such, the opportunities for innovation are available to a much wider spectrum of the public. Although some of the innovators and inventors discussed in this chapter have been from traditional mainstream media, such as Joseph Flaherty of CBS, others come from a wide range of organizations. Among those described here are the inventors of the Internet and World Wide Web, who come from the world of computer science; a pioneer in eBooks, whose formal training was an undergraduate independent study in the human-machine interface; and a well-known musician-poet who has found a new audience via digital satellite radio. Also described here is the NBPC, which has pioneered the production of new media storytelling in the realm of African American culture and the African Diaspora. It is unlikely that these diverse spirits and views will transform mainstream media into a richer, more eclectic space, yet their commitment to innovation affords an opportunity to reinvent media for the digital age.

11 / ETHICAL CONSIDERATIONS IN THE DIGITAL AGE

In ancient Greek mythology, King Dionysus hosted a banquet for his courtier Damocles to enjoy all the pleasures that wealth could buy. But to teach his courtier a lesson about the perils of wealth and power, he suspended by a single hair a great sword directly over Damocles' head while he attended the banquet. So unnerved was Damocles by the terrifying sword that he foreswore his love and envy of the king's wealth.

Technology represents in many ways an ethical sword of Damocles to journalism and the media. A wealth of new possibilities awaits those who employ the new digital tools for creating and delivering compelling new content, yet these same tools make it ever easier to plagiarize and pirate content. And at the end of the day, though audiences may be more entertained than ever, the media may be no closer to conveying to them the truth or providing quality original content. This chapter examines the ethical challenges facing media in the digital age.

ETHICS CRISIS

We live in a time when ethics—not just in journalism and the media, but in many aspects of modern professional, public, and private life—often take center stage. Whether it is in the state House or the White House, the classroom or the newsroom, questions of ethics abound. A president admits he had an affair with a female intern. A governor admits that he is gay and that he had an extramarital affair with a man. An historian admits she failed to cite properly many of the sources quoted or paraphrased in her book. A journalist admits making up sources and plagiarizing other reporters' copy. Fresh with a rare major book contract, a first-year Ivy League college student admits plagiarizing extensive portions of her new best-selling chick-lit novel. Another writer is forced to admit he simply made up many of the alleged facts in his best-selling nonfiction book, once highly touted on a major television talk show. So who can be surprised when a survey reveals that an increasing number of students do not think ethics is very important and that academic success (i.e., getting good grades and a degree) is their overriding goal?[1]

As a result, Americans face a crisis of ethics, both in society at large and in the media in particular. From my position as chair of a department of journalism and media studies and director of a journalism institute at a major American university, I discuss the topic of ethics in journalism and the media in the digital age and speculate about what might be done to make the practice of journalism and the media more ethical. The goal of practicing ethics in journalism and the media professions is central to the effective functioning of a democratic society.

Veteran journalist and Penn State emeritus journalism professor Gene Goodwin wrote a book titled *Groping for Ethics in Journalism* in 1983.[2] It provided an insightful examination of the challenge that journalists and news organizations face in practicing ethical journalism: to develop a coherent, systematic approach to establishing and maintaining ethical practices in journalism. The discussion here attempts to outline such a systematic framework for practicing journalism and the media professions ethically in a time of heightened economic pressure, technological revolution, and global political uncertainty.

DEFINING ETHICS

Let me begin by defining what is meant by *ethics,* in particular *media ethics.* Theorists define *ethics* in terms of a set of principles of right, or moral, conduct. In journalism and the media, *ethics* usually indicates a set of practices, a code of things that journalists and other media professionals should or should not do. It is a normative concept. These codes are helpful and important, but they are not sufficient, as recent history demonstrates. Consider the notorious 2003 case of *New York Times* reporter Jayson Blair, who despite the *Times*'s ethics code, managed to commit a series of ethical violations that both damaged the paper's credibility and led to his firing.[3] Therefore, I suggest a somewhat different definition of *journalism and media ethics,* one that goes well beyond the standard code established by most news or media organizations and associations. Instead, I offer both a systematic framework for understanding the actions of journalists and other media professionals in an ethics context as well as a prescription for managing an ethical news or media organization.

TWO TYPES OF ETHICS PROBLEMS

In this framework, there are two types of ethics errors: *errors of commission* and *errors of omission.* Errors of commission are things that journalists and media professionals should not do or acts they should not commit, such as accept gifts from sources or do other things that might present a conflict of interest and thereby compromise their integrity or independence; use anonymous sources except under the most limited circumstances; plagiarize others; make up sources or quotes; or write sensationalized headlines.

Errors of omission are things that journalists and other media professionals fail to do, even though they should do them. For example, journalists should ask tough follow-up questions of sources, but sometimes fail to do so, perhaps because they are afraid of losing their access to the desired source. Or a television executive might cast a comedy about a group of friends living in New York City with all-white actors, despite knowing it might serve as a much better role model to young viewers if the cast were to reflect the diversity of life in New York. A movie producer might not object to the gratuitous sex or violence in a new motion picture in the hopes of getting better box office receipts, although she is well aware of what research tells about the harmful effects of such depictions on youthful audiences.

In the context of journalism, these two types of ethical errors result in the potential or real compromise of the truth and its pursuit in a fair and responsible fashion. In the world of media beyond journalism, they diminish the quality or diversity of media content, propagate potentially harmful effects on children, and simply fail to realize the abundant opportunities to create media content with potentially pro-social benefits.

ERRORS OF COMMISSION

Errors of commission are the ethical missteps most commonly seen and debated. The case of Jayson Blair clearly involved errors of commission. He did things he should not have done and thus compromised the truthfulness of the news. There have been other sensational ethics cases involving journalistic errors of commission. Perhaps the most famous case involved the awarding of a Pulitzer Prize to Janet Cooke in 1981 for the *Washington Post* story "Jimmy's World."[4] The story turned out to be a series of imaginary events and fabricated quotations about an invented eight-year-old heroin addict. The *Post* returned the award, but the damage to the paper's credibility, to journalism, and to the truth was already done.

Whether and when to use anonymous sources or to shield the identity of a source are issues that confront journalism whether in analog or digital format. In the networked world, however, where once a name is published it is available worldwide and probably indefinitely because there is no way to remove the name from circulation, the issue of anonymous sources takes on special significance. One area where the issue is especially acute is in the matter of identifying victims of rape or sexual assault, whether male or female. Journalists must often protect sources, or those sources will dry up, or be silenced. Many sources are the victims, the powerless, especially in the case of rape, which is a crime of power, not sex. Most rape victims have little experience with the media, and their identity should never be revealed either before or after trial unless at least two conditions are first met. First, revealing the victim's identity must occur only when the victim gives her or his permission. Second, that consent should be based on a well-informed choice in which all the potential ramifications of revealing her or his identity are made clear to the victim. Revelation of the victim's identity may have many possible significant repercussions. People in the community will know and may react negatively, as has been the case in many rape cases in the United States and the world, where some people blame the victim. The accused may seek out the victim and her or his family for retribution. Moreover, once the victim's identity has been published online, it may never go away and may reach the remotest corners of the Earth. Although in some cases rape victims have stepped willingly and somewhat knowingly into the public spotlight, the results of doing so have not always been positive or expected. In some cases, the victim has been able to reassert some level of control over her or his life and to help other victims step forward. In other cases, however, victims who have stepped forward publicly have suffered severe mental or emotional trauma and posttraumatic stress syndrome, the symptoms not emerging for months or years. Journalists and news organizations must be extremely careful in dealing responsibly with the matter of revealing rape victims' identities, whether online or off. It is not only a matter of naming names. News organizations have sometimes not reported a name, but have given a street name and address, even accompanied by a photograph of the victim's home where the assault occurred, providing more than enough information to identify the victim easily.

Digital technology is in many ways bringing ethical errors of commission to new heights—or lows, as the case may be. Pirating songs via file-sharing sites is as easy as the click of a mouse. Digital effects can make torturing and killing someone on screen in the name of entertainment not only completely seamless, but limited in gore and gratuitousness only by a director's imagination. The advent of the Internet makes it easier than ever for a reporter to steal other reporters' copy, and digital photography is making it a simple and transparent process to change news photographs digitally, resulting in alterations almost invisible to even the most skilled eye. Such manipulations, reenactments, and synthetic images are forbidden (or only frowned upon?) in most news organizations' codes of ethics. Perhaps the most well-known case of a digitally manipulated photo being published as authentic was the notorious November 1994 *Time* magazine cover photo of O. J. Simpson that had been darkened for dramatic effect, making this alleged murderer look sinister and brooding. No one might have realized what had happened except for the fact that the competing weekly news magazine *Newsweek* published the same photo in the same week—the L.A. Police Department mug shot of Simpson—but unaltered.[5] When the two covers were held side by side, it was obvious *Time* had had altered its cover photo.

In November 2000, President Bill Clinton and Cuban dictator Fidel Castro met in New York at the United Nations, but it is unclear whether they actually shook hands, nor did any photographer obtain a photo of them shaking hands. Yet editors at the *New York Daily News* decided that did not matter. They liked the storyline of the two world leaders shaking hands, so they digitally merged two photos of them, each separately about to shake hands and in the merged photo about to shake hands with each other. Of course, such image manipulation is not limited to the digital age. In February 1982, *National Geographic* magazine got into ethical hot water when it published on its cover a photo of the great pyramids of Egypt in which the pyramids had been moved slightly by the editors in a chemical darkroom just to get a better aspect ratio for the cover.

Digital technology has also made it relatively simple for television journalists to create false or misleading imagery. Consider the 2000 New Year's Eve millennium broadcast by *CBS Evening News,* in which digital technology was used to change Times Square. Employing the same technology used to place a virtual yellow first-down marker in National Football League telecasts, CBS deleted an actual NBC television sign in Times Square and replaced it with a virtual CBS logo. Some viewers who knew the real Times Square called the network on its transgression, and *CBS Evening News* anchor Dan Rather subsequently apologized and said it would not happen again. Of course, the technology is used daily on CBS's morning show to implant virtually the CBS logo in various New York scenes. The question of whether viewers are misled or somehow harmed by this digital wizardry has fallen by the wayside.

Moreover, many errors of commission involve not just reporters, but also editors. It is essential, for example, for editors never knowingly to publish synthetic or altered images or video. Such prohibited alterations include the addition or subtraction of material from an original photo, composite images, and the merging of two or more photo elements into a single image. Under very limited conditions, it might be appropriate to publish an image or video that has been modified, but only when that content is clearly labeled as a photo illustration (e.g., perhaps a satire or a visualization showing the potential impact of a new development on a city or rural landscape) and does not mislead the audience.

Ethical problems linked to image and video manipulation have been the focus of much academic research and investigation. Larry Gross, John

Katz, and Jay Ruby raise in *Image Ethics in the Digital Age* (2003) a number of important issues of concern here.[6] Among the key ethical issues for photojournalism in the digital age are maintaining effective professional oversight of photojournalism, avoiding the inappropriate use of pictures of people in pain and distress, and balancing the public's right to know with the potential of digital technology to provide instant transmission. In the rush to deliver dramatic images, there may be little time for reflection on their full meaning and impact. Journalists must balance the public's right to privacy and the media's appetite for spectacle. In the digital age, media in general have pushed even farther the boundaries of what is acceptable in the presentation of images and video. Ethical considerations oftentimes take a distant back seat to commercial interests and the drive for audience ratings. The convergence of digital media and the drive for low-cost reality programming have spawned serious ethical concerns. As Gross and his colleagues write, "Digital technologies and the Internet have combined to satisfy our collective voyeuristic urges in formats less focused on crime or even family feuding. Although it is always artificial to fix a starting point for such things, MTV's 1992 launching of *The Real World*—which itself might be considered an offshoot of *An American Family*, PBS's early-1970s experiment in cinema verité—may qualify for the honor of having initiated the recent flood of 'reality' programming." It is essential to consider the broader ethical ramifications of digital media before blindly pursuing them in the name of greater profits. Bruno Latour and others have observed that it is a misconception that technological innovation by itself can lead to social progress.[7]

One issue sometimes overlooked is how effectively to negotiate control over images originally produced in indigenous media, or media produced by or about native peoples. For these groups, traditionally disenfranchised from mainstream society, it is a fundamental right to maintain control over the copyright of images of themselves. Motion pictures in particular, sometimes in the form of documentary film, have often exploited imagery of traditional or indigenous peoples. In addition, producers of motion pictures and other media need to obtain informed consent for any on-screen depictions of indigenous people or children. This is especially important in the digital age, when images and video can quickly be disseminated worldwide online.

Digital technology also raises new ethical problems for news gathering. For example, omnidirectional imaging, or cameras that shoot 360-degree views, can greatly enhance the field of view for a photojournalist or videojournalist. It can help put news into better context, which can be a good thing, even an ethical improvement. Consider a photo or video of a protest or political rally. A traditional narrow-field-of-view camera might just show the protesters. An omnidirectional image, in contrast, would show not just the protesters, but the entire scene, allowing viewers to see how big the crowd really is or whether there are police nearby, and so on. Conversely, innocent bystanders might not realize they are being photographed by an omnidirectional camera, yet from an ethics perspective they have a right to know they have been photographed.

Hidden cameras, whether digital or analog, raise similar concerns about privacy. Consider also the remote-sensing satellite imagery taken from hundreds of miles above the Earth. These digital sensors can capture imagery less than half a meter or less in size. Do Earth-bound citizens have a right to expect privacy from news cameras potentially photographing them from orbit hundreds of miles overhead? Many nonjournalists might say yes.

Where the picture gets particularly fuzzy from an ethical standpoint is the borderline between the public's right to know and the public's right to privacy. Neither is explicitly protected by the Constitution, but the protection of both is implied in the Bill of Rights (the First Amendment protects freedom of speech and press; the Fourth Amendment protects against unreasonable search and seizure).[8] Therefore, it is a matter of journalistic responsibility to balance these two interests. When the story is important enough or involves public matters or figures, then the right to know will likely prevail. Beyond powerful cameras, there are a variety of increasingly sophisticated electronic tools for tracking people and data. Through the federal Freedom of Information Act or state statutes requests, journalists can obtain a wealth of information about government or public transactions. In many cases, requests allowed by this act are not even necessary. Online databases containing motor vehicle records; electronic toll-collection systems for highways, bridges, and tunnels; and other online records make it possible for investigative reporters to dig into important stories in ways unheard of previously. For example, online federal election campaign-contribution data make it possible for reporters to examine in microscopic detail who is giving what to whom and when in federal elections. Following the money trail is vital to many election stories.

Further complicating the ethical balancing of interests is when and how the media should reveal government secrets. The problem is particularly acute when the secrets may relate to matters of national security. In 2006, this issue moved fully onto the public stage when newspapers such as the *New York Times* revealed the Bush administration's use of extensive warrantless phone taps and monitoring by means of various digital communications technologies.[9]

New Types of Ethics Problems in the Digital Age

New technologies also make possible previously unknown ethical problems. Consider the technology known as *intelligent agents,* a branch of AI wherein computer programs or digital robots can act autonomously on another person's behalf on a stand-alone computer or on a network to fulfill some purpose.[10] Some agents are adaptive and can learn from their environment, changing as they encounter new situations or data and taking in their human masters' actions or preferences.

News organizations are already employing agent technology. Nando.net has employed agent technology to create customized content for readers.[11] Several news organizations have used agent technology to read and sort through Usenet newsgroups (e.g., Agent and Free Agent News & Mail Reader NewsFerret).[12] Other digital media such as Pandora use such systems to monitor users' preferences and to customize their music-listening experience.

Agents can also act as a reporter's online assistant. Imagine an agent whose role is to sort through primary and secondary information collected by traveling about the Internet looking for anomalies or unusual patterns in data. Such "spiders" are already widely used on the Internet to collect Web site information. Agents might also screen or filter out unwanted e-mail (e.g., spam) or other communications. They can be highly valuable in that they act as virtual librarians. But imagine what happens when an adaptive agent encounters a computer cracker's agent, which is optimized to break into secure systems. The reporter's agent learns how to break into secure Web pages and uses this newfound skill to break into the online records of a major financial institution. Once inside, the agent discovers certain financial irregularities and reports them to the journalist, who then uses this information as the basis for an important story on fraud. Do the journalistic ends justify the technological means? If not, who is responsible? Has there been an ethical violation? Have any laws been broken?

Although the typical errors of commission involve reporters and editors, news management can also commit serious infractions of this sort. Consider the 1999 case of the *Los Angeles Times* and the Staples Center. The *Times*'s code of ethics forbids a reporter or the news organization from sharing revenue or having a business relationship with a news subject.[13] Despite that, the paper's management agreed to sponsor the Staples Center, a $400 million sports and entertainment complex opened in 1999 in downtown Los Angeles. When this relationship was publicly revealed, a firestorm of criticism ensued, including from the paper's own editorial staff, which felt it was a serious ethical conflict of interest.

In the online arena, journalists also face other financially driven ethical challenges. Online journalism and online trading make for strange bedfellows. Reporters and columnists reporting online have unprecedented potential to influence stock prices with "day traders" (i.e., online traders). Most online news organizations have guidelines for reporters' investments and prohibit reporters from holding in their portfolio any investments in companies they cover. Other ethical issues involving errors of commission arise with regard to the nexus of editorial and advertising in the online arena.

Media ethics and errors of commission are concerns not only for the media professional. As society moves into a time when media are increasingly characterized by an active audience, when citizens spend much of their time sharing music and video files online and uploading their own content or programming acquired elsewhere, a significant question arises as to the ethical appropriateness of online file sharing and redistribution of content created by someone else. Neither the legal nor the ethical boundaries of online file sharing are clearly and comprehensively defined. In the 1990s, online file sharing emerged as a major activity for millions of Internet users around the world. Uploading and swapping of music, movies, and software grew enormously in popularity with online file-sharing systems such as Napster. After a legal challenge by the music industry, Napster was shut down by the courts, but it eventually reemerged as a legal online music-distribution system. Yet online file sharing continues to be significant and substantial.

Codes of Ethics

Ethical issues have been addressed in the code of online journalism ethics articulated by the American Society of Magazine Editors.[14] The society's online journalism guidelines state that online banner ads should:

- distinguish between editorial and advertising content;
- clearly identify sponsors (e.g., Amazon.com; intel inside);
- clearly display the name and logo of the organization that controls site content;
- label as advertising all special advertising sections, "advertorials";
- never have content created by editors (an *Editor & Publisher* survey from 1999 shows that 84 percent of editors do so);
- not give advertisers or e-commerce partners preferential treatment in search engines;
- respect the privacy of users; and
- have no links in the table of contents.

ERRORS OF OMISSION

Errors of omission may be just as common as errors of commission, but are generally beneath the public radar screen. Omission errors are those things journalists or other media professionals should do, but do not. For example, whenever possible, journalists should interview sources face to face, but on an almost daily basis many reporters sit at a desk and do their interviews by phone or e-mail. Many journalists might not even consider this practice a matter of ethics. They might just call it economical or at most perhaps lazy journalism. But I consider this approach a matter of ethics because it reduces the potential to obtain the truth and undermines the credibility of journalism. Moreover, I argue that ethical journalism is not just about avoiding what is wrong. It is an equal imperative to do what is right. Reporters should pursue with vigor and professionalism an important story, despite the fact that it may be expensive and risky or possibly offensive. To seek the extra source for confirmation of an important (or not so important) fact is essential to ethical journalism. Particularly when an interview is not conducted face to face, reporters should indicate how the interview was conducted (i.e., either by e-mail or phone).

Many other types of ethical errors of omission are often committed. Stories that might be considered of interest to limited audiences are avoided or neglected, and certain sources or perspectives are excluded because they might overly complicate a story. These errors of omission often arise because of the increasing commercial pressures facing American journalism, including print, broadcast, and online media, and because of the space or time limitations of traditional analog media. In the digital age, where time and space take on very different dimensions (e.g., speed is key, but length is much less problematic), reporters can more readily address complex topics, yet newsroom culture and traditions still work against doing so.

Perhaps the most common error of omission involves the lack of or limited usage of corrections. When a newspaper discovers an error in reporting, it typically will publish a correction, but rarely does the correction have the same prominence (location, type size, accompanying photo or illustration) as the original publication. Moreover, when corrections occur online, they are often simply made to the offending copy with no indication of and no link back to the original error. Such an electronic paper trail is important for the public to understand what happened and when and how it was corrected.

ETHICAL CONSIDERATIONS AT THREE STAGES OF JOURNALISM AND MEDIA

In addition to the two broad types of ethics violations threatening the credibility of journalists—including editors, reporters, and media professionals in general (and even lay citizens in an online world)—it is essential to recognize that ethics violations can occur at any of three stages in journalism and media. The ethics issues that arise in journalism and the media typically occur in either of two stages: (1) news gathering and production; and (2) presentation, publication, or broadcast (over the air or online). For instance, Jayson Blair stole copy from journalists at other news organizations, including the *San Antonio Express*. In fact, as the so-called *Siegal Report* indicates, it was a call from editors at the *Express* noting the similarity between Blair's writing and material published in the *Express* that led the *Times* to investigate and eventually to fire Blair.[15] Moreover, Blair fabricated quotes and did not even go to some of the places he claimed he did for his reporting.

Yet there is an important third stage in which ethics is arguably even more important, at least from the point of view of the public trust. Unfortunately, this third stage has often been neglected in considerations of ethics in journalism and the media: it is the postpublication or broadcast/distribution stage and can involve both errors of commission and errors of omission. Prior to the 2003 release of the *Siegal Report* (named for Assistant Managing Editor Allan M. Siegal, who chaired the *New York Times* committee that produced the report), the *New York Times*, for instance, did not have an ombudsperson or public editor, arguing that to have such a position might undermine staff morale and effectiveness. In light of the troublesome Blair case, however, the *Times* in the fall of 2004 instituted two new editorial positions, one of them a public editor who was to perform a role not unlike that of an ombudsperson. At many news organizations that maintain such a position, the ombudsperson often serves as the ethics liaison with the community in the postpublication stage.

This function is essential from an ethics perspective because a responsible news or media organization should respond to community concerns over coverage and initiate impartial responses, including those involving questions of ethics. This is not to say that news organizations should avoid covering certain topics or modify their coverage in order to avoid or minimize particular kinds of effects.

These three stages apply equally to media in general, entertainment as well as journalistic media. For example, ethical perspectives and concerns should guide the preproduction phase of television, radio, and online program development. They should equally prevail during the time programs are aired or content is distributed. How programs impact audiences or how audience members react to racial, sexual, and other depictions should be considered to guide media actions and responses. Finally, even entertainment and other media organizations that are not necessarily involved in news should maintain an ombudsperson. This position can play a particularly important role in the postbroadcast, publication, and distribution phase. Online media and discussion boards, blogs, and other interactive media can play a central role in facilitating discussions among media and their audiences.

In point of fact, some television professionals are beginning to engage their audiences in postair dialogues via blogs and elsewhere. The June 20 episode of the *Rescue Me* series on FX included a violent sex scene between the main character and his estranged wife. After protests from bloggers and other online fans that the scene promoted rape, the executive producer of the series, Peter Tolan, went online June 21 to the discussion board Televisionwithoutpity.com in an attempt to appease fans.[16] "Welcome to writing a television drama. . . . We're trying to do something different," he wrote. "Sometimes we succeed, sometimes we don't."[17]

ETHICS SOLUTIONS

With this ethics framework in place, there are at least three types of actions that media professionals and their organizations can take to prevent or minimize the potential for ethics violations in the future.

Continuing Ethics Education

First, as a foundation, news and other media organizations should mandate continuing ethics education for both their reporters and their editors or other media staff, whether in production or management. Attending periodic ethics workshops should be a requirement for all journalists and other media professionals. Media organizations and professional associations might partner with independent, university-based journalism and media education organizations, such as the Journalism Resources Institute at Rutgers University, to conduct regular workshops on journalism and media ethics. The institute is a logical choice in New Jersey, with its long-standing partnership with the New Jersey Press Association and its successful track record of training workshops for New Jersey journalists. Many universities in other states have similar institutes and centers that might serve as appropriate, independent venues for such continuing media ethics education. In fact, under the guidelines of the national accrediting body for journalism and mass communication, ethics is a cornerstone of accredited journalism and media education programs in higher education in the United States.[18]

Management Strategies

Second, management strategies, practices, and procedures should place a premium on cultivating a culture and environment that fosters ethical journalism. Four vitally important elements are at a minimum required, the first of which is already widely established:

1. A clear set of guidelines for ethical journalism and media practice, including a code of ethical conduct;
2. Open communication between and among reporters and editors, especially for junior reporters, but also for other media professionals;
3. Mentoring programs where junior staff are mentored by more senior staff, with monitoring of all staff made a routine part of the newsroom and media culture; and
4. A complete content archive as a record, which is both essential for media and relatively cost effective and efficient in the digital age.

Management should also periodically conduct systematic evaluations of the entire content domain of the media organization. This evaluation should look not only at quality in general, but at breadth, diversity, and inclusiveness. In the context of news media, coverage should be critically assessed in terms of a range of criteria, including topics and beats; geographic regions; communities defined in terms of race, gender, sexual orientation, ethnicity, religion, and political perspectives; and other factors determined by the editorial staff. Other media organizations should conduct similar systematic assessments to determine how well the public is being served; this assessment should go beyond any legal or regulatory requirements (see chapter 8).

One management strategy that more news and media organizations might easily employ is having greater openness with the public about how newsrooms or media operate. Demystifying the newsroom or media enterprise would help the public better understand the media and also help the media form a better relationship with the public. One step in the process easily facilitated in the digital age is providing online biographies and e-mail contact information for all reporters and editors or other media professionals. Publishing biographies in print or on the air is difficult because of space or time limitations, but these limitations melt away online. Making information about reporting staff publicly available and making it easy for the public to communicate with reporters or management is a good way to reveal to the public the nature, quality, and expertise of editorial staff members. At the same time, this approach addresses an error of omission that many news organizations make—a form of sometimes deliberate public deception or lack of openness.

Many news organizations prohibit their reporting staff from commenting in public on subjects they might cover because of the concern that it will undermine public confidence in press impartiality. This prohibition typically means that reporters may not publicly comment on politics or their views on matters related to politics, such as current or prospective legislation, candidates, and issues of public importance. It is felt that allowing a reporter to reveal his or her views will undermine the public's confidence in the impartiality or objectivity of that reporter in covering the subject at hand. Yet reporters are human; they have opinions, and the public certainly knows and appreciates this fact. It would be more honest for news organizations to acknowledge up front these human qualities, so that the public can put a journalist's reporting into better context and understand when and how personal motivations might potentially influence reporting. The reporter would still do his or her best to be neutral, yet would not be prohibited by newsroom conventions and culture from ever revealing her or his true viewpoints. This matter came to a head in 2006 when a leading reporter for the *New York Times* who covers the Supreme Court for the paper gave a talk at Harvard and revealed her views on a matter soon to be considered by the

Court.[19] The *Times* objected to her making those comments, yet many in the industry applauded her for acknowledging her human qualities and her right as a citizen to hold and express her views. Moreover, many newspapers have traditionally published unsigned editorials, written by editorial staff but published without a byline in order to maintain the illusion that individual journalists do not have opinions or that there is unanimity of opinion among the editorial staff. This is a general misrepresentation that in the digital age can and should be done away with for ethical reasons. Omitting the name of the person who wrote a published editorial is a practice that can in the long run only undermine the public's confidence. With the elimination of space constraints in the online world, editorial writers can now afford to include their names, biographies, additional explanations of what they feel and why, as well as additional documentation to support their views. Such documentation might play the role that footnotes do in academic research papers, although this approach has been studiously avoided in the popular press. Through links, editorial writers and other journalists can provide source material and other documentation to support their positions and reporting, thereby producing both a stronger case and a more ethical, honest form of journalism. Furthermore, just as members of the U.S. Supreme Court can write and publish dissenting opinions, there is no reason why news media cannot similarly permit such dissenting opinions to be written and published online by members of an editorial board.

Employing Cutting-Edge Technologies

Third, news and other media organizations should avail themselves of new techniques and technologies that can facilitate better monitoring of coverage and media content in general. In particular, they should employ two tools in this regard. To begin, all of them should equip their reporters with cell phone cameras. When conducting an interview, reporters should routinely photograph their source and location and file the picture from the field, documenting their presence at the interview venue. These photos might have use in illustrating a story, but, more important, they can constitute evidence that a reporter did not make up a source or an interview. Use of low-cost but highly effective digital audio recorders might be similarly used. Moreover, the use of digital watermarks for authentication, perhaps incorporating GPS stamps, should be considered. Notably, many basic digital cell phones can easily be upgraded with enhanced smart-phone features such as GPS data by installing low-cost or free third-party software or devices.

News or other media organizations should also consider the use of computer-based tools that can automatically detect plagiarism. Such tools have already been developed in education, where plagiarism is a recognized problem among students. Rutgers, for example, is one of a growing number of universities that subscribes to an online service called "turnitin.com" in which student papers can be automatically analyzed for possible plagiarism (see chapter for a fuller discussion on this topic).[20]

The Journalism Resources Institute is seeking news organization partners to develop such a system for journalism, dubbed "News Copy." News Copy would use a branch of computer science called *natural-language processing,* an AI subfield, to compare automatically one news story with similar stories published online anywhere on the Web or in proprietary databases. News Copy is not a far-fetched idea. It would complement the system now being developed collaboratively by the *New York Times* and the firm iParadigms to detect plagiarism based on a comparison with news stories published in LexisNexis, as mentioned in chapter 9.[21]

Editors would develop and use such an AI-based system to compare reporters' copy with text published elsewhere, including in blogs and personal Web pages. The News Copy system would evaluate the copy and provide a measure of similarity, and when a similarity threshold is exceeded (e.g., an editor might set the threshold at a string of four or more words in sequence that match exactly from a second source), an alert would be triggered, notifying the editor of possible plagiarism. The News Copy system might also evaluate copy for paraphrasing, similarity in use of sources, unique news facts introduced into the copy, and other aspects of the reporting that might be of value beyond ethics. Moreover, News Copy might have utility to the reader in evaluating the unique quality of local, regional, and national news providers. Certain aspects of the News Copy system might also be helpful in assessing the degree to which a journalist or news organization is doing original reporting, breaking news, or at least adding new facts to an existing story. At the same time, these tools might help alert editors when it is likely that a source or the reporting in general has been fabricated. In such a system, each article or piece published or broadcast might be tested with something like News Copy, but would not have to be.

Taken as a whole, these emerging digital tools can significantly advance the practice of ethical journalism and media. Journalists and other media professionals must be the front line of defense in the practice of ethical journalism and media practice. But it is essential that media organizations align with journalism and media educators to foster the continuing ethical practice of journalism and media in the digital age, as well as to ensure that journalism and media students will receive an education most effectively steeped in the ethical practices that confront problems of the past, present, and the future.

CASE STUDY: PROPAGANDA DISGUISED AS NEWS

Fake news has a long and inglorious history in the United States and around the world. Since at least the mid-1800s, showmen such as P. T. Barnum have staged for publicity purposes what historian Daniel Boorstin a century later dubbed "pseudo-events."[22] Perhaps the most potentially deceptive form of fake news, the video news release (VNR), emerged in the 1980s as a video version of the traditional news or press release. Having started as oftentimes amateurish promotional video on 1¾-inch tape, mailed, or sent by overnight delivery to selected television stations for possible inclusion in the evening newscast, the VNR has since evolved into a slick public-relations tool and a somewhat disturbing mainstay of much television news, particularly at the local level.[23]

Largely because of their limited production quality, early VNRs were infrequently used in television newscasts. Over the next two decades, however, they became more sophisticated, with producers often linking them to topical events and formatting them to the needs of local newsrooms. The producers also made the sponsor logos less visible and obtrusive and utilized the latest in digital technologies to create high-quality video content.

Consequently, VNRs have become a major tool for profit organizations and not-for-profit organizations alike to get their messages on television news. A 1990 study by Dan Berkowitz and Douglas B. Adams found that 22 percent of VNRs sent to local television stations were used, at least in part.[24] This usage rate is comparable to the use of traditional news or press releases by local newspapers. A 1994 study by John H. Minnis and Cornelius B. Pratt found that 34 percent of print news releases were used at least in part by weekly newspapers.[25]

Under the George W. Bush administration, VNRs have been taken to entirely new heights. This administration has promoted its agenda via VNRs on everything from the Defense Department and war in Iraq to policies at the Census Bureau and the Health and Human Services Department. David Barstow and Robin Stein reported in the *New York Times* in March 2005 that twenty federal agencies have made and distributed hundreds of television news segments since 2002, adding that this barrage of fake news has resulted in the kind of publicity any president would covet.[26] As illustration, consider the script of one Bush administration VNR segment that aired during this period: "Thank you, Bush. Thank you, U.S.A.," an apparently joyous Iraqi American said to a reporter in Kansas City for a piece about the fall of Baghdad. Another report spoke of a "successful" Bush administration "drive to strengthen aviation security"; the "journalist" called it "one of the most remarkable campaigns in aviation history." To viewers, these segments looked no different than any other ninety-second report on the local news. In truth, the federal government produced and distributed both segments. The fall-of-Baghdad report from Kansas City was produced by the State Department, and the aviation report was made by another arm of the Bush administration.[27]

VNRs are an especially appealing tool for public relations or governmental uses because, unlike paid sponsorship or advertising, they exploit the heightened credibility of news. Research by Anne Owen and James Karrh in 1996 demonstrated that viewers see VNRs within newscasts as more credible, or believable, than commercials made by the same firms and shown within the same newscast.[28]

The heightened credibility of VNRs in newscasts is coupled with the popularity of television news for greater impact. More Americans get their news from TV than from any other medium. In fall 2006, already high TV viewership further increased an average of four minutes a day from four hours and thirty-five minutes to four hours and thirty-nine minutes, driven by the appetite for news among thirty-five-year-olds and older Americans, who were tuning in to coverage of major news stories such as the effects of Hurricane Katrina. VNRs selected for use by the roughly 850 TV newsrooms in the United States (630 ABC, CBS, and NBC affiliates; 220 Fox and independent stations, according to Vernon Stone's 2001 update) can easily reach many millions of viewers.[29] One study by Mark D. Harmon and Candace White published in 2001 examined fourteen VNRs distributed in 1998 and 1999; it found that portions of these VNRs were aired 4,245 times by stations across the United States.[30] Further, new technologies have made it increasingly effective to distribute VNRs in digital format via satellite or other broadband technologies. Journalists and news departments can typically view or download the VNRs online before deciding whether to use them. This confluence of factors has helped the VNR emerge as a major part of the television news landscape.

Stations air VNRs for a number of reasons. VNRs are sometimes timely and provide rare or unusual video that might otherwise be hard to get, especially for a local television station on a limited budget. They also sometimes help fill in gaps in stories otherwise lacking good visual material, or they provide interesting video on a slow news day. VNRs are attractive to TV newscasts because they are cheap or free or can even make a station some money (some VNR providers will pay a station to air a VNR) and—this is where things get especially sticky—because they are safe. VNRs typically provide noncontroversial video that feels good to viewers and sponsors. There is usually no risk of criticism from the subject of the story because the subject produced the VNR. In contrast, investigative journalism is expensive, risky, and often controversial, and it can cost the station advertisers.

Measuring VNR Usage

Exactly how widely VNRs are used is somewhat difficult to determine. VNR-production and distribution firms contend that the use is fairly extensive. In contrast, surveys of news directors generally suggest that VNRs are only occasionally or even rarely used, even on local television newscasts. Scott Atkinson, news director at WWNY-TV, the Fox affiliate in

Watertown, New York, said in a telephone interview conducted January 12, 2006, "We never ever use them, except our weekly farm report, which gets them regularly from the U.S. Department of Agriculture. But I'm an absolutist about not using VNRs and even this use is going away."[31]

Surveys indicate that, according to the stations and networks themselves, VNR use at the network news level is even more sparse or nonexistent. One situation in which a network news division might use a VNR in whole or part would be when the VNR itself becomes the subject of a developing news story, and a clip might be incorporated as an illustration. For example, if a group such as Swift boat veterans and POWs for truth had issued a VNR as part of its communications efforts against the presidential campaign of Senator John Kerry, a network news story might have featured a segment to illustrate the group's tactics.

In an e-mail interview January 10, 2006, Jeff Wurtz, senior vice president of sales and marketing at VNR producer News Broadcast Network, said, "NBC, especially the Nightly News, does not use VNRs. Instead they do use third party material such as logos and footage they don't have access to getting. They would never use a third-party VNR with voice-over but may use footage that is unique or exclusive to the vendor for a good story. Additionally, every video package we send has the supplier of the video clearly identified with contact info for the station/network to call on if they have questions on the story, footage or third-party experts quoted in the story."[32]

In 2005, the Radio-Television News Directors Association conducted a survey of one hundred members on their use of VNRs.[33] Based on this survey, the association issued a statement indicating that few TV stations air VNRs, and those that do so usually identify the source. But as association president Barbara Cochran acknowledges, getting good data on VNR use is a challenge. "It's kind of like the Loch Ness Monster. Everyone talks about it, but not many people have actually seen it." A 2006 study by the Wisconsin-based Center for Media and Democracy identified sixty-nine television stations in major markets that apparently aired at least a portion of a VNR during the news in the previous ten months.[34] The center posted on its Web site the VNR segments used by television news operations and reported that none of the stations identified for viewers the sources of any of the VNRs aired during the news.[35] It turns out that the VNRs were produced by communication organizations representing major companies such as General Motors, Pfizer, and Capital One.

The Project for Excellence in Journalism, a nonpartisan media research group, conducted its own survey in 2002 of 103 TV news directors about VNR use. Sixty-six percent reported never using them. Of the 34 percent who admitted using them, 10 percent said they always label VNRs. Yet the remaining 24 percent in this group said they labeled only "occasionally" or "rarely" or "never."[36]

On CBS Newspath (a video news–distribution service), VNRs are transmitted in a separate segregated area and are clearly identified as a VNR feed, explained John Frazee, senior vice president of CBS News Services in a telephone interview January 10, 2006.[37] Moreover, CBS will not accept a VNR unless the company providing the VNR discloses who paid for it. On occasion, CBS will not accept a VNR even when the source is known. Frazee explained that this evaluation is done on a case-by-case basis and typically occurs when the VNR is actually issue advocacy in the guise of news story. Newspath delivers the VNRs via satellite in digital format. Typical of the VNRs was one transmitted on January 1, 2006, with the story slug (a label that identifies the story), "VNR. The title: Wrinkle Reducing Breakthrough. The length: 4:04. The source: VIDICOM. And the 'reporter': Christy Ferrer." CBS clearly labeled this VNR as a VNR, using these terms: "This is a Video News Release. This VNR is not produced by CBS News. The facts and/or claims made in this VNR have not been verified by CBS News. The producers of this VNR have paid CBS Newspath a fee to transmit this VNR and accompanying information to stations, affiliates and clients."[38] Frazee indicated that the fee is in the amount of hundreds of dollars per VNR. As part of the research for this chapter, a January 10, 2006, search of the CBS Newspath archive produced a list of more than one hundred VNRs that had been distributed within the past year via the newswire for possible use by network affiliates.[39]

CNN Newsource has a similar process of formally vetting VNRs before they are accepted for transmission.[40] VNRs must adhere to a variety of formatting requirements, including ensuring that the script approved corresponds with the video.[41] The fee structure for carrying a VNR on CNN Newsource is $2,500 if the VNR is less than five minutes; $5,000 for five to ten minutes, and $7,500 if ten minutes or longer (not to exceed twenty minutes).

CBS also operates a unit that produces and distributes VNRs for hire. A CBS Media Group advertisement in a 2002 issue of *PR Week* encouraged potential clients to hire CBS and "put one of the world's leading media companies to work for you producing video news releases. CBS even guarantees placement on the CBS Newspath VNR feed."[42]

News directors' denial that they use VNRs may be the result of several factors. Sometimes, of course, they may be stating a fact. Other times, though, it may be that they themselves do not make the choice as to whether to use a VNR. The actual decision may be made by a producer, assignment editor, or a specialized health or consumer reporter. Another reason for their denial may be professional embarrassment because using VNRs is generally frowned upon by journalists and educators and is seen as at best lazy reporting and at worst unethical. In addition, just what constitutes a VNR is not universally agreed upon. Some may define a VNR exclusively as that which arrives in a package from a public-relations or VNR-production/distribution firm or labeled as such on a network video feed. A satellite or Internet feed from NASA with footage from the Mars Rover may not be considered a VNR and thus might be used. Local TV news editors may receive VNR material redistributed from a regional or network/national satellite feed (e.g., CNN Newsource, CBS Newspath, ABC NewsOne) or from an international video feed (e.g., the AP or Reuters video feeds), not realizing that the clip comes from a VNR.[43] What constitutes using a VNR is another possible point of confusion. Some in the newsroom may not consider incorporating a five-second clip from a VNR as "using" the VNR. Research shows that the use of short segments of VNRs is not uncommon, though, with more than half (52 percent) of VNR uses being for ten to twenty-nine seconds and one-third (25 percent) being for less than ten seconds.[44]

Few VNRs are used in their entirety. Research shows that just 4 percent of uses are greater than sixty seconds, which would likely be the entire VNR. Instead, reporters or producers tend to select segments to incorporate into a story, with original video shot by a local news crew. A 1996 study by Cameron and Blount examined how newscasts used the VNR "America Responds to AIDS" created on behalf of the Centers for Disease Control. They found that this packaged VNR was heavily edited, with most newscasts using B-roll footage.[45] Most stations did not use the complete VNR. Rather, they incorporated video segments from the VNR into stories featuring video they produced originally about the AIDS issue. In fact, many VNR providers are actually producing and distributing far more B-roll footage than VNRs. Ed Lamoureaux, senior vice president of WestGlen Communications, a leading producer of VNRs, said in a telephone interview that his firm actually produces and distributes B-roll packages at a rate of five to one over VNRs. "Stations have indicated they don't air VNRs in full, so distributing a B-roll package is cheaper and more useful to stations."[46]

VNRs are typically about ninety seconds long, but may be accompanied by additional video, sound bits, and even a proposed script. VNR researchers Harmon and White explain how VNRs are typically used: "A reporter can create a voice-over story in which the video and natural sound are played, while the television audience hears the anchor reading copy, or sound bites and/or visuals from the VNR can be included in a story written by the reporter."[47] A common method of using VNRs is the "voice-over" story, where video is shown as an anchor reads copy on air.

The Harmon and White findings show that stations in any size market use VNRs, but stations in smaller markets are apt to use longer segments. Stations in smaller markets also tend to air VNR segments later in the day or on days subsequent to the initial satellite feed. VNRs dealing with the topics of health, safety, and children are the most likely to be used. Thinly veiled promotional VNRs receive only infrequent usage, although they still sometimes find a home on local newscasts. The Harmon and White study showed that a Priceline.com VNR about "Y2K" travel was used thirty times, for instance. The source of a VNR may also influence a local journalist's decision to use a VNR. In the Harmon and White study, VNRs from the nonprofit American Academy of Pediatrics had 499 station uses; eight VNRs from the federal government, eight from the Consumer Product Safety Commission, and one from the Census Department on census techniques were used 3,585 times. In contrast, three VNRs from private companies (one from Priceline.com and two from a light manufacturing company) were used only 107 times.[48]

The Harmon and White study also showed that stations used a VNR on the same day it is received approximately two-thirds of the time. About one in five VNRs aired the next day after the initial feed. One in ten of the airings occurred within two weeks, with VNRs rarely used beyond that period. The most common time slot for VNR use is the 5:00 to 6:00 P.M. hour, with more than one-quarter of the airings occurring then. About one in five airings occurred during early-morning newscasts between 5:00 and 9:00 A.M. Slightly fewer uses occurred during the 10:00 P.M. to midnight newscast. The rest were distributed throughout the day.

The advent of electronic, digital tracking of VNRs has greatly improved the accuracy of determining how widespread the use of VNRs has become. One leading electronic system is SIGMA by Nielsen Media Research. It covers VNR use in all 210 U.S. television markets. "Because SIGMA places an active code in the Vertical Blanking Interval (invisible to the human eye)," Nielsen Media Research reports that the "technology electronically recognizes and records each airing throughout the entire U.S. with over 95% accuracy."[49] Another system called TeleTrax is a subsidiary of Medialink. An electronically embedded "watermark" in the VNR securely measures its use even when the VNR is digitally altered. The watermark is almost impossible to strip off in editing, so monitoring is highly reliable. A third VNR-monitoring option is provided by VMS,[50] which uses human monitoring in the top-fifty marketing areas. It is an important supplement to automated monitoring because of the slight possibility that even a watermark or a vertical blanking interval code might get stripped away in editing. VMS in 2005 introduced its own automated VNR-monitoring system as well.

A press release from Medialink provides insight into the use and monitoring of its most widely used VNRs:

NEW YORK, March 9, 2004—The European Mars Express space mission and vehicle crash testing of automobiles reached the greatest audiences in the Top 10 Video News Release (VNR) List of 2003 issued by Medialink Worldwide Incorporated (Nasdaq: MDLK), a global leader in providing news and media services for professional communicators. This year's list, the latest in a 15-year annual tradition, also included news about ancient history, popular culture, sports and health.

Topping the list at more than one billion viewers worldwide is the European Space Agency's (ESA) mission to Mars. Shown on newscasts in more than 30 countries including China, France, Russia and Brazil, Medialink's United Kingdom–based production team created a television news story on behalf of ESA about the launch and mission. The video was then distributed by Medialink via satellite to more than 500 television station newsrooms worldwide, many of which incorporated all or part of the video into their news broadcasts.[51]

With its SIGMA electronic tracking system, Nielsen has found VNR use to be ubiquitous. In 1996, a SIGMA survey showed 100 percent of newsrooms using at least a portion of a VNR at least on occasion. Another electronic tracking survey showed a similar level of use in 1999, with more than 90 percent of U.S. television stations reportedly using VNRs.[52] Data on the use of particular VNRs exist, but they are hard to obtain for independent analysis because they tend to be proprietary.

One study indicates that the average newsroom has ten to fifteen VNRs available daily. Making it on air requires high production value and newsworthiness. VNRs typically cost about $10,000 to $25,000 to produce, with higher production values generally requiring greater production costs. Moreover, newsroom editors will edit the VNR content to fit their news needs and adapt it to fit their station's unique format or style.

The largest VNR-production firm is Medialink, which produces and distributes approximately 1,000 VNRs a year, twice the number of its nearest competitor. Medialink sales in 2005 totaled more than $30 million. Such companies are hired by client firms who have a particular story or point of view to tell and hope to do so most effectively or persuasively with the integration of their perspective into an independent newscast.

Based on the interviews conducted for this chapter as well as prior research and an examination of publicly available lists of VNRs carried by major media networks, a conservative estimate of the number of VNRs produced and distributed to TV stations annually in the United States is in the thousands. Taken together with other data on the rate of usage of VNRs in the United States (22 percent of stations use VNRs), it is likely that viewers are exposed to VNR material on a frequent basis, perhaps even almost daily and in all media markets, large and small. Consider this observation from a leader in the VNR industry: "One billion viewers for a single news video (i.e., VNR aired on TV newscasts) is an outstanding benchmark, but not surprising as more and more of the world obtains most of their news from television," said Lucy Hadfield, managing director of Medialink International.[53] It is probably safe to say that, like a disease, the spread of VNRs is rapidly reaching epidemic proportions.

It is also important to recognize that VNRs are rapidly being transformed in the age of digital convergence. Lamoureax of WestGlen Communications said, "VNRs will morph into a form of marketing communication that will be available for viewing on portable devices, such as mobile phones, and other technologies."[54] Perhaps more important, there will be no need to deliver these videos through news channels. They are already available online and are becoming increasingly so. Viewership is easier to measure online, and consumers are able to find VNRs easily through search engines such as Google and Yahoo. The $64,000 question may be, What will happen to television news when consumers—or citizens, depending on one's point of view—can get all their "video news" directly from the source via the Internet or other digital media conduit (e.g., on-demand television via cable or satellite) rather than from a news media gatekeeper?

Ethics of VNR Usage

Another question for television and other video news producers is: What are the ethical implications of using VNRs, and is the truth in any way compromised by their use? Scholarly research on VNR use generally concludes that VNRs constitute audience deception. Viewers of VNRs within newscasts tend to believe that they are seeing the product of a station's news gathering and independent judgment. They do not generally realize they are seeing and hearing the news as told from the perspective of the VNR production company's client. A landmark article about VNRs was published as a cover story in *TV Guide* on February 22, 1992, titled "Fake News." Author David Lieberman argued that newscasters should not "pretend out of pride that what they broadcast is real news, instead of labeling it for what it is." According to Lieberman, "There's a good chance that some of the news they [the public] see will be fake. Not that it's necessarily inaccurate. Just that it was made to plug something else. And it's something the PR community has grown skillful at providing."[55]

Lieberman recommended that newscasts that air even a portion of a VNR should provide a continuous on-air graphic labeling the VNR. Research to date suggests that few stations have implemented this recommendation. Without such labeling, newscasters risk destroying the trust that the public has in their broadcasts. In response, the Public Relations Service Council formed a committee in June 1992 to create standards governing the level of disclosure for VNRs. Debate over VNRs slowed during the remainder of that decade but emerged again in 2004 after the Government Accountability Office launched an investigation into the appropriateness of government-funded VNRs.[56] In June 2005, the U.S. House of Representatives passed an amendment prohibiting the White House and federal agencies from hiring public-relations firms and "journalists" to use fake news to promote government policies for one year. Such legal actions raise serious First Amendment concerns and may represent unconstitutional barriers to freedom of speech and press. Yet the movement to take legislative action against broadcasters reflects the growing sentiment against nondisclosed VNR usage.[57] In April 2005, the FCC published its "Public Notice on VNRs." Current FCC regulations require that broadcasters tell viewers the source of a VNR only when the VNR deals with a political matter or controversial issue or when the station is paid to air the VNR.[58]

Whether the federal government returns to the use of fake news and VNRs to promote its policies, other groups and organizations will no doubt continue to do so. In this context, are there any appropriate uses of VNRs in the news? Ethicists might contend that a VNR should never be used in television news because it is an inherently unethical deception of the audience.

Establishing Guidelines for Using VNRs Appropriately

Yet, realistically, with budget cuts and resource limitations, there is little likelihood that local television stations are going to stop using VNRs or that public-relations firms are going to stop making and distributing them. Under what circumstances or conditions, therefore, should VNR use be acceptable by a local TV station or any other provider of video news (online or off)? There are arguably at least five conditions for using or distributing VNRs in an acceptable manner via the news media.

First, it is important that journalists look closely at the content of the VNR and decide whether its use might in any way result in the deception of the audience. If the answer is no, that no deception would likely occur, then there may be acceptable ways to use the VNR or portions of it. In no circumstances should newsrooms compromise their integrity and independence by airing VNR material produced by a governmental agency promoting its own agenda. The newsroom staff should trace the motivation of the VNR provider and examine whether that motivation is acceptable or is designed to manipulate or persuade the news-viewing public.

Second, just as with traditional press releases, VNRs can contain useful background information, suggest a story idea, or indicate possible sources for a story.

Third, in some rare cases (e.g., the NASA Mars video), VNRs may contain footage that might otherwise be extremely difficult if not impossible to obtain independently. If this is the case, then at least portions of the VNR might be appropriately used. Although network news divisions rarely or never use VNRs as such, they do incorporate video from sources such as NASA when it is the only available source for such footage. And more usage would be generated if the government agency is seen as relatively benign. When the U.S. Defense Department is the only source of war zone video, newsrooms might still use the footage, despite recognizing the biases associated with the source. Lamoureax of WestGlen Communications provides this perspective: "TV news people know what they're doing, and they view what we provide in VNRs (or B-roll footage) as source material."[59] They still have to vet the VNR, though.

Fourth, when a network carries a VNR on its video news feed to affiliates and clients, it should seriously question the appropriateness of accepting payment for carrying that VNR. Accepting payment for transmitting VNRs presents a potential conflict of interest and may erode the news organization's credibility. At least one television network has traditionally not accepted payment for carrying VNRs on its video feed; all media networks should strive for this standard.

Finally, when a VNR is used, it should be clearly labeled as such, and the source of the video should be indicated. Labeling should not be limited to only those circumstances delimited by the FCC, such as whether the station has been paid to air the VNR or its content is political or controversial in nature. Moreover, the station should include on its Web site information about the VNR, its provider, and how, when, and why it was used. Networks that do feed VNR or B-roll material should consider taking things a step farther: they should require those who provide a VNR to incorporate a visible watermark on each frame of video identifying it as a VNR and identifying the source. This practice would automatically ensure that any newscast subsequently airing the video would have no choice but to make clear to the viewer that what is shown is a VNR and not independently produced or obtained by the TV station or network.

By adhering to these VNR-usage protocols, news organizations will keep their audiences informed at the highest levels of journalistic integrity. They will not compromise their commitment to honesty and truth. Ultimately, video news providers thus commit to providing the broadest and deepest possible coverage without jeopardizing the public good with which they have been entrusted.

CONCLUSION

Media organizations have long confronted ethical issues as they strive to build and maintain public trust. Ethical considerations are at least as important in the digital age. Technology has exacerbated certain ethical problems and raised new ones. Journalists and media professionals of all types need to keep an eye on performing their tasks ethically at all times. Without an ethical compass to guide them, the media will lose the confidence of a public that can easily look elsewhere for its entertainment and information. Losing a trusted source of news, however, would undermine the very foundation upon which democracy rests.

This chapter has outlined a two-part framework for understanding the problem and challenge of ethics in the age of digital media. This framework suggests that there are two basic types of ethical problems, errors of commission and errors of omission. Both are equally important, but to date most of the attention in journalism and media codes of ethics and research has focused on errors of commission. Yet fake news is a growing problem in television news, and news decision makers need to exercise caution when considering the use of VNRs or B-roll material received from outside sources and should always label any VNR material as such on air or online.

Media management and professionals at all levels can take several steps to maximize their ability to act ethically. Perhaps foremost is the provision of continuing education for all staff to keep abreast of ethical developments and technological changes that may present new ethical dilemmas. A variety of strategies, including utilizing advances in information technology, should be employed to better monitor coverage and media content for potential plagiarism and other ethical missteps.

Media behaviors begin at a very young age. Even while still in the womb, unborn children are exposed to media content, whether as an accidental by-product of their mother's use of audio media or as intentional exposure to classical music as their parents hope to produce the so-called baby Mozart effect (i.e., that exposure to classical music will stimulate brain development). After birth, babies and children of all ages listen to their parents read them stories. Children see and hear a variety of other media as well. Some parents use television as a pacifier or babysitter for their young children. *Sesame Street* has aired since 1969 as educational television for children, and educational programs designed for children as young as two years of age are now broadcast regularly.[1] Media use by children of all ages is not only substantial but growing with the rise of digital media. As much as children have enjoyed their analog media, they seem to like their digital media—MP3 players and the Internet—even more. They are drawn to interactivity, immediacy, and variety in their media consumption. But they still love their books and other printed media.

Yet many questions abound regarding the impact of media on children and their development. Effects of media use among children can be both good and bad, pro- and antisocial. This chapter examines both the positive and negative effects of media use in the digital age. The discussion is organized into five areas: first, the growing use of computers and the Internet by children, especially teenagers; second, the negative effects of traditional media use that will likely transfer over to the new media of the digital age; third, the pro-social effects of media, especially those emerging in the digital age due in large part to the increased activity level of children using online and interactive media; fourth, the dangers posed uniquely by the new media, especially those involving the Internet and other networked digital media; and, finally, what children, their parents, and their teachers can do to maximize the positive effects and minimize the dangers of media in the digital age.

GOING DIGITAL

Today's youth represent the first generation to prefer a computer to television. Research suggests the average teen spends 44 hours per week immersed in media. This is roughly 6.5 hours of media use daily. The number one activity for teens is going online. Approximately 11 million, or 87 percent, of American teens go online regularly (i.e., nine of ten teens).[2] A 2006 Yahoo-sponsored study found that persons ages thirteen to twenty-four in the United States spend more time online than watching TV or talking on the phone. "Born to Be Wired" shows that this age group spends "an average of 16.7 hours a week online" versus 13.6 hours watching TV, meaning 2–3 hours of Internet use per day. Radio use averages 12 hours a week, and phone conversations 7.7 hours, with books and magazines averaging 6 hours. Some of this media use happens simultaneously via what is known as multitasking. Teens tend to use one or more other media "most of the time," often going online or talking on the phone while watching TV. They sometimes watch television shows online via their computer. Teens are especially drawn to being in "control" of how they surf the Web. They especially like having the ability to personalize their media content, whether online or on their MP3 player or mobile phone or other device. Unlike many of their parents, teens tend not to feel overwhelmed by the abundance of media choices available to them. These U.S. results do not represent an isolated case. A study of teens in Ireland show very similar patterns.[3] Research by the Internet firm Arekibo Communications on behalf of the Ombudsman for Children in Ireland reveals that Irish teenagers are more likely to be found in front of a computer surfing the Internet rather than watching the television. "Our feedback suggests that parents today are far more likely to find their teenage children at home in front of a computer screen than a TV," commented Emily Logan with Ombudsman for Children. "This information shows that teenagers much prefer the Internet to TV because it gives them greater freedom, choice and is more interactive."

One of every two teen Internet users in the United States goes online from home via a broadband connection. They use the Internet for a variety of activities, including doing homework, conducting various information searches, sending and receiving messages, e-mailing, chatting, downloading music and video files, watching feed from someone else's Web camera or performing for their own, and creating digital media of their own by editing video or posting to their own blogs or MySpace accounts. Parents typically support their children's rampant media habits. Nearly two-thirds (65 percent) of American teens have a cell phone. Four in five (80 percent) own or have regular access to a computer. Even more (83 percent) have access to DVD players. More than half (52 percent) have video game consoles. Few teens, especially the younger ones, have the resources to purchase such media technologies, so in many cases a parent or guardian is required to obtain the account or device (e.g., a cell phone).

Children's media expert Dr. Carla Seal-Wanner observes that "[t]hese statistics stand many parents' and educators' hair on end. They worry that the seductive aspects of interactive media and technology distract teens from their studies, may contribute to social isolation, result in overexposure to inappropriate adult content, encourage risk-taking behavior, and condition them to be hyperactive parallel processors who can not settle down long enough to do the focused work demanded in high school to prepare them for entrance to college or the workforce."[4] With master's and doctoral degrees from Harvard University in developmental psychology, Seal-Wanner is a former professor at Columbia University, where she created and directed the Graduate Program in Instructional Technology and Media for a decade. She is also the founder and president of @cess4@ll, a public-interest advocacy organization promoting universal access to quality media for all children.

NEGATIVE MEDIA EFFECTS

Researchers have demonstrated that viewing violence on television or in motion pictures can significantly influence children in a number of ways, depending on both the type and extent of violence viewed as well as the age of the child and other factors. Children who view large amounts of violent programming can become desensitized to the violence and become more aggressive in their own play and other behavior. Extensive playing of violent video games can have the same type of effects. Media use can affect children's development. Young children who view large amounts of television or play long hours of video games or sit for long hours in front of a computer screen can experience negative health effects, including weight gain. Computer and other media use can influence children's neurological development, cognitive development, sexual behavior, attitudes, knowledge, and perceptions of self as well as attitudes toward and behaviors involving the use of substances such as drugs and alcohol.[5]

When I was a teen (more than a quarter-century ago), just about the only window onto pornography or sexually explicit content available to a curious teenager was the magazine rack at a local newsstand or convenience store—that is, until the manager shooed the teen away. A twenty-first-century teen's broadband Internet access dramatically widens that window. Access is not only through a home or cybercafé Internet connection, either. Parents should know that although major wireless phone companies such as Cingular, Verizon, Sprint, and T-Mobile "have voluntarily chosen not to directly offer any adult content for download" to phones, the *San Jose Mercury News* reports that Web-enabled phones provide an easy work-around, especially for motivated, tech savvy teens. "Many mobile phones now have Web browsers, which can make videos, photos or text available for download with a credit card or a charge to a phone account. Sales of explicit videos, adult chats and pornographic images over mobile phones were $500,000 globally in 2004." Juniper Research data forecast that figure to be $2.1 billion by 2009. These figures do not include free sexual video teens may shoot on their own and share among friends or acquaintances. Google has found that pornography accounts for about 20 percent of all searches conducted via cell phones. This is substantially higher than the 8.5percent of searches conducted from the desktop computer, a *San Jose Mercury News* blog notes.[6] Of course, not all of these searches are by teenagers, but the bottom line is that cell phones provide teens a relatively private vehicle into the world of sexually explicit content, including late at night and from under the covers while not quite fast asleep.

On an even broader level, some critics such as Dominique Wolton argue that parents and all others interested in digital developments should pause to reflect on the deep social and other ramifications of the Internet. Wolton states, "[N]ew technologies are being pushed wholesale, without anybody daring to criticize them, or to question whether they are entitled to so much space within the public domain, or to wonder whether they do represent such a massive, unqualified progress."[7] She contends that the Internet is not a medium, but merely a pipe for delivering access to a wide variety of forms of communication. Unlike traditional media, where content is delivered from the supply side, the Internet is a demand-side technology.

NEGATIVE HEALTH EFFECTS

A by-product of the digital age is potential hearing loss. Users of MP3 players are particularly at risk.[8] Many MP3 users listen to their audio via earbuds, or small hearing devices inserted into the ear. The use of these audio devices, especially with the volume on high, can lead to hearing loss. Larry Magid at CBSNEWS.com says that more than half of teenagers surveyed report at least one symptom of hearing loss.[9] Citing findings released by the American Speech-Language-Hearing Association, Magid reports that high school students "are more likely than adults to say they have experienced three of the four symptoms of hearing loss," such as needing to turn up the volume on a television or radio (28 percent of students versus 26 percent of adults), saying "what?" or "huh?" during normal conversation (29 percent students, 21 percent adults), and experiencing tinnitus, or ringing, in the ears (17 percent students, 12 percent adults). Nearly two-thirds of adults (63 percent) say they have experienced none of these symptoms, whereas only just under half (49 percent) of high school students say they have experienced none of the hearing loss symptoms. The study also indicates that most parents are unwilling to put limits on the amount of time their children use earbud devices. Adults tend to use earbuds for longer periods than teens, but teens tend to turn up the volume higher.

One of the health problems that can affect anyone who uses a computer is repetitive strain or stress injury (RSI), one form of which is carpal tunnel syndrome. RSI is particularly common among assembly-line workers, but can also result from overuse of a computer keyboard or mouse. Long periods of typing or mouse manipulation can result in damage to the muscles, nerves, and tendons of the hand or wrist, leaving these body parts in a weakened condition accompanied by a painful tingling sensation and an inability to type or manipulate the mouse or other device. Nonuse can relieve the symptoms, although in severe cases surgery may be necessary. These physiological problems can be especially acute for children because their bodies are still in development.

PRO-SOCIAL MEDIA EFFECTS

At the same time, some use of media, including new digital media, can have beneficial effects. Studies of the popular interactive television program *Blues Clues* have shown that children ages three to five who view the program score better on problem-solving tests than those who do not. Through user-friendly technologies such as the CD and the DVD, children have gained a great level of control over their viewing experiences. Moreover, the falling price of media production and distribution has enabled producers to create multimedia content tailored to children. Australia's popular children's group the Wiggles has generated a worldwide following for its video and musical programming aimed at preschoolers as young as two years of age. First with the VCR and now with even more effective digital devices, children can repeat videos or portions of videos they enjoy and learn from. The Wiggles feature characters wearing distinctive colors (yellow, blue, etc.) and known for their recurring shtick. One character performs magic tricks; another is always hungry and eats. Wiggles songs tend to explore topics familiar to very young children, such as sleep ("Rock-A-Bye Your Bear"), food ("Fruit Salad"), and animals ("The Monkey Dance"). Songs and videos also feature easy-to-repeat actions, such as the "romp bomp a stomp" hand gestures in the song "Dorothy the Dinosaur."

Through the Internet, the Wiggles have built a global following among parents and young children.[10] The Internet also provides children with a window into a vast public archive of news and information of great value in research and learning. Children can be actively engaged in their use of digital media as compared to the largely passive experience of traditional, analog media. More active use of media can stimulate cognitive development and foster creativity. Children can practice self-expression on their own Web site or blog. Writing text messages on a cell phone, or *texting*, can have similar benefits. In some cases, such texting can even be life saving, as was the case in 2006 for a fourteen-year-old girl in South Carolina who was kidnapped in early September and imprisoned in an underground bunker. She managed to get a hold of her captor's cell phone when he was asleep and discreetly sent a text message to her parents. The police located her by determining the origin of the cell signal and rescued her.

Shooting and editing video can be a positive experience for children and is a vital part of new media literacy. Understanding the nature and grammar of digital media can accelerate the potential for children to learn. Active media use, such as video game playing, can improve eye-hand coordination. One study reported in 2006 shows that physicians who spent at least three hours a week playing video games made substantially fewer mistakes (37 percent) in laparoscopic surgery and performed the task significantly faster (27 percent) than surgeons who did not play video games. "I use the same hand-eye coordination to play video games as I use for surgery," said Dr. James C. Rosser Jr., M.D., chief of minimally invasive surgery and director of the Advanced Medical Technology Institute at Beth Israel Medical Center in New York, who demonstrated the results of his study at the center.[11] Laparoscopic surgery involves using a tiny camera and instruments controlled by joysticks outside the body to perform internal surgical operations on patients for a variety of ailments, from appendicitis to colorectal polyps. Although this study did not involve child-age subjects, it is quite likely that youthful game players might see their eye-hand coordination improve as well. Studies have documented similar positive health effects of other video games. One study demonstrated that having cancer patients play a video game in which the patient zaps bad cancer cells helps treatment. In another medical trial, a dance video game was found to help overweight users shed unwanted pounds. The video game *Dance Dance Revolution* has proven so popular an exercise tool among teens that it is expected that some 1,500 schools in the United States will incorporate its use into their physical education curriculum by 2009.[12] Nintendo has sold more than 6 million units of the video game

Brainage, which is designed to facilitate brain development.[13] It is unclear whether playing *Brainage* or other such mentally stimulating video games can foster mental development, but preliminary results suggest a tentative affirmative.[14] Taking a look ahead at the potential positive impact of video games on children is Dr. Rosser's new book *Playin' to Win: A Cybersurgeon, Scientist, and Parent Makes the Case for the Upside of Videogames.*[15] Rosser has conducted other studies of video game use by children and found positive effects on learning and associated behaviors.

The positive potential of reading books is already well established and a vital part of formal and informal education. This potential extends through digital forms. Full-text keyword searching, electronic annotation, and other interactive features can enhance the learning potential of eBooks.

ONLINE DANGERS

One of the most troubling areas of digital media is presented by the online world. Although the Internet is a unique world of knowledge, entertainment, and self-expression, it is also the home of a host of potential and real problems. False and misleading information, deceptive marketing, and the temptation to share copyrighted music and video files illegally are just a few of these problems. The Internet is also a vehicle for the invasion of children's privacy, and the online world can be a distraction from many other positive activities and can suck children into a nearly bottomless pit of mindless drivel.

Worse yet, the Internet contains a realm of child pornography populated by online pedophiles. Since the early years of the Internet, pedophiles have used the Internet extensively to distribute child pornography, oftentimes under the radar screen of law enforcement. Research has shown that for a variety of reasons and in many ways pedophiles have begun to use the Internet not only to distribute child pornography, but to try to form a bridge between the virtual and the real worlds. They have formed active online communities and often communicate with each other about the challenges they face in finding their victims and strategies to overcome these challenges. The biggest problem parents face is how to encourage their children to use the Internet in positive ways without at the same time risking their exposure to pedophiles, who often are highly predatory, well organized, and discreet online when recruiting their childhood victims.

In the book *Beyond Tolerance* (2001), about Internet child pornography, Philip Jenkins, a professor of religious studies at Pennsylvania State University, reports that pedophiles sometimes use the Internet to create alternative realities to justify their behavior.[16] Some pedophiles talk about the true love they feel for and express with children, and they condemn "violent child rapists."

Pedophiles are increasingly using the Internet actively and systematically to organize their activities and to find potential victims. The online community is elaborate and effective. An investigation by the *New York Times* found that there are Internet radio stations run by and for pedophiles.[17] A supposed charity was used to raise money to send eastern European children to a camp where it turns out they were to be visited by pedophiles. An online jewelry company sells pendants revealing the wearer as sexually attracted to children and thereby enables others to recognize them.

Catching pedophiles is also a matter increasingly involving the Internet and the news media. The foundation Perverted Justice utilizes Internet chat rooms and other online forums to track online pedophiles and arrange meetings between them and potential victims.[18] Then, often with the news crew from NBC *Dateline* present to video record the event, Perverted Justice arrests the would-be pedophile when he or she shows up to seduce an intended victim. The Web site states, "In 2006, 220 Internet predators across the country were found, exposed and jailed due to 'To Catch a Predator' sting operations." The Perverted Justice Web site contains considerable information about the operation, resources of potential value to parents, and an interactive map outlining the foundation's sting operations. One potential concern about all the information available on the Web site is its inclusion of full transcripts of online conversations between predator and prey. These transcripts may incite the interest of other predators.

PRIVACY

Teens are drawn to online media in part for the feeling of empowerment these media can provide. Having a vehicle to travel virtually to any location in world or to express one's own spirit, creations, and ideas to friends or a potentially worldwide audience can inspire feelings of achievement. Such new media capabilities can build self-confidence in a socially uncertain teenager. Feeling in control of something as powerful as a computer with broadband Internet access can provide a real rush to a teen struggling with dramatic personal and social change. At the same time, teens are often drawn to the somewhat illusory feeling of privacy that goes with online or other digital media activity. Mom or Dad, teacher or coach, may not be standing over a teen's shoulder as he or she posts to MySpace, texts a friend, or sends an e-mail, so the teen may have the feeling of acting in privacy. The truth is that although Mom or Dad may not know what the teen is doing, in all likelihood someone else, perhaps a stranger, is probably tracking all the teen's online activities.

An illustration comes in the form of firms that market public or quasi-public records online. These records represent something of a double-edged privacy sword. On the one hand, when put online, they can be a bonanza for journalists or investigators (whether law enforcement or private detectives) seeking information about persons or organizations. Moreover, access to such records is protected by the First Amendment. On the other hand, the data made available online for a profit are sometimes not clearly public records, or they lie in a gray area that members of the public may not be aware of. Nor may the courts have ruled on the legal status of some of these data. Consider the case of the data available from Web sites such as whitepages.com.[19] For a fee (about $40), any user can log in and obtain data on just about anyone living in the United States. Data are accessible in a variety of forms, including name, address, phone number, and social security number. Reverse directories are available as well and are especially useful to journalists and other investigators trying to locate a neighbor or potential witness to an event. A reverse address directory permits a reporter to find out who lives at a particular address and what phone number to use to contact the resident. It also permits the reporter to find out the name and address associated with a phone number. The reporter can also click a link to "find neighbors." All this information is available free of charge and to anyone. I conducted a search for information available about my children, both of whom are minors. Because the site requires the person conducting the search to enter an age (at least approximate) for the person sought, I entered my daughter's age and was told no information was available for anyone under eighteen. So, as a test, when I ran the search again and simply said she was eighteen, up popped background information about her. The system is clearly flawed and should not contain information about anyone under the age of eighteen. Containing and providing information about a minor is a privacy violation. Contacting the host organization and requesting them to delete information about a minor is time-consuming at best and unproductive at worst.

PARENTING GUIDE FOR THE DIGITAL AGE

Parents face many daunting challenges *and* exciting opportunities in the digital age. Their children can utilize new media to expand their world, help with their studies and research, as well as spend less time passively watching a television screen. At the same time, going online presents profound new risks for children, and parents are often behind the eight ball when it comes to controlling these online adventures. Although buying a child his or her own computer with Internet access may not be an option for many due to financial reasons, some parents may opt not to provide such luxuries for other reasons. Yet many parents may feel that not giving their children advanced digital technologies in today's high-tech age is both a punishment of and a handicap to their children. "How can children without a computer and Internet access compete with the kids who do have these tools?" concerned parents might ask. Regardless of where one comes down on this issue, one can employ a variety of strategies and techniques to reduce the problems associated with the new digital technology.

Parents should open two-way and continuing conversations with their children about the online world, its dangers and delights, potential and perils. I know parents who rarely discuss these matters with their children. These parents think they are effectively managing the situation by letting the schools, teachers, and administrators set the parameters for students' online behaviors. The problems with this approach are multiple. First, at many schools, the teachers and administrators do not know much more and in fact may know less about new media than the kids do. For many reasons, children take to the new media like fish in water.

They enjoy experimenting with the latest technologies and talk about them with their friends. They share and exchange ideas. Owning the latest technology can be an important status symbol for many kids. Some kids may not have their own computer or Internet access at home, but that does not stop them from creating their own MySpace account and posting racy pictures and raunchy or racist descriptions of themselves or others online (I have seen children's MySpace accounts in which self-allusions to Hitler and the Nazis are included). Children sometimes reveal personal information about themselves or their friends, putting everyone at risk from predators and pedophiles, marketers and scam artists, phishers (people who gain personal data online for criminal purposes), and the like. Here is how a typical scam might work. A child goes to a movie Web site hoping to find a movie playing in her neighborhood. The Web site asks her to enter a home address so the site can indicate where the nearest movie theater is. The child enters the address and finds out where the movie is playing. A new window opens up, and the child enters a new Web address looking for a favorite song. The site helps her find the song and asks if she would like to be updated on future releases by that same artist. The child thinks this is a good idea and says yes. The site asks for an e-mail address and a first name only—for security purposes. Then it uses a hidden software agent, a spider, to collect the information from the previously visited Web site, obtaining the child's address, links it with the name, and automatically enrolls her in a music club. In a week, a CD or a DVD unexpectedly arrives at the child's home with a bill enclosed. Everyone is surprised, but now the family is stuck trying to extricate itself from membership in this club.

A first or early step in this parent-child dialog about the new media should include setting the boundaries for what is appropriate behavior when online. Among the considerations for these boundaries are what Web sites a child is permitted to visit, what information a child might post safely online, how to use a Web cam appropriately, and guidelines for safe e-mail, chatting, IM, and text messaging. Since most e-mail addresses and IM screen names do not reveal much about the identity of the person posting communication, a parent should make it clear to his or her child that communication is permissible only with known persons. The child and parent should write a list of all persons the child wishes to communicate with online and their associated screen names and e-mail addresses. Any other names or addresses should be blocked or first reviewed by the parent or guardian before permitting the child to interact with them. The consequences of inappropriate or unsafe online behaviors should be discussed as well.

In addition to setting boundaries for online behavior, parents should consider establishing boundaries for all the media behaviors their children might engage in, whether at home or elsewhere. Such boundaries include how to use an MP3 player safely by not turning the volume too high when using an earbud; how much time can be spent watching movies or television programs; and what types of video games a child is permitted to play. In some cases, allowing or denying media activity can be used effectively as either a reward for positive behaviors or as a consequence for inappropriate behaviors that a parent wishes to discourage.

In addition to maintaining open and frequent communication channels with a child about new media, another consideration is where and when to give the child home Internet access. Some believe in giving access only in shared, public areas of the home, such as the living room, kitchen, family room, den, or office. This way, when the child is online, parents can easily monitor the online activity. This approach works fairly well in one-child homes. In homes with two or more children, this approach can prove problematic. For many, placing a computer with Internet access in each child's bedroom is a more viable alternative. Children especially like this option, but it needs to be done carefully, and each child should be instructed that the computer is a reward or privilege and can be removed if the rules are not followed.

An important tool for parents to consider employing is software that enables them to monitor their child's online activities. One option is virtual network control (VNC), such as that enabled by RealVNC.[20] This software is available in several forms and generations, some of which are for purchase, but a basic package is available for free download and use. With VNC installed on a child's computer, parents can log on from another computer on the home network and safely and securely monitor their child's Internet use. VNC software uses strong encryption technology to enhance its security. Using VNC software, parents can watch their child's IM activity or other online behaviors. They can see what Web sites their child visits. They can remotely observe virtually anything done on the child's computer. Some might say that doing so is an invasion of the child's privacy. In a sense, this is true. In the online world, however, too much privacy or freedom can put children at great potential risk, through exposure either to pedophiles and phishers or to other problems. Parents can also use such remote monitoring to enhance their child's computer and Internet experience by nurturing and encouraging positive online behaviors when observed. Parents who use such monitoring tools should tell their children that they may be remotely monitored. The RealVNC software permits the parent to "take over" their child's computer and remotely control what it does, including every mouse click. Such technology is somewhat Orwellian in its scope and should be used cautiously and carefully.[21] Employers sometimes use it to administer their office computer networks and to monitor their employees' computer activities.

Other commercial products are also available to help parents monitor their children's online behavior and screen out potentially risky behavior. One product is BeNetSafe, a service that acts as a chaperone for popular social-networking Web sites such as MySpace, Xanga, and Friendster.[22] BeNetSafe is a service that automatically monitors children's online activities at these social-networking sites and sends reports to parents on their kids activities while on MySpace—activities such as giving out their cell phone number, adding someone to their friends list, and posting photos. The reports are e-mailed directly to the parents, with red flags when the children communicate in ways they perhaps should not. Social-networking sites are particularly popular among teenagers. A 2007 Pew study shows that 55 percent of children ages twelve to seventeen in the United States report using social-networking sites such as MySpace and Facebook.[23] Usage is particularly high among older female teenagers, with 70 percent of girls fifteen to seventeen years old using social-networking sites compared to just 54 percent of older male teens.

Parents can also implement time boundaries for when their children are allowed online. One effective technique is to use the Internet router, particularly if the household is equipped with a wireless router through which the children go online. The router can be configured to set the time of day when Internet access is permitted for each user in the household. A parent might permit a child Internet access only from 4:00 to

8:00 P.M. each day, preventing the child from waking late at night or early in the morning and quietly going online without a parent's knowledge or consent.

Another important tool for parents to employ in making the Internet child safe involves the use of settings in popular search tools such as Google. Arguably the most powerful commercial search tool on the Internet, Google provides extraordinary access to a wide cross section of Internet content, including pictures and video. Parents should click on the "preferences" tab on the Google search page.[24] There, they should review the various options available and set the preferences to their own choices. One of the most important settings is the "SafeSearch Filtering" option. Although there is not an option to filter violent imagery, parents can choose one of three levels of filtering for explicit sexual content. They can select "no filter" (unfiltered content, so that all images will appear in a search, regardless of their sexual explicitness), "moderate filtering" (explicit images will be filtered), and "strict filtering" (both explicit text and images will be filtered out). Parents also should be aware that some sites permit the sharing or airing of unfiltered video and other content. Social-networking sites such as stickam.com permit not only the uploading and downloading of video files, the designing of member Web pages, and chat among members, but also unfiltered live transmissions from Web cameras, including from bedrooms, where at least some users are scantily clad.[25] To join the site requires users to be (or at least to say they are) older than thirteen years of age, but nonmembers can tune in to live Web cam transmissions.

Finally, parents need to take seriously the potentially harmful physiological effects of computer and other digital media use, including cell phones. Parents should direct their children not to overuse earbuds when listening to portable audio devices. It is especially important that the volume not be kept too loud. As a rule of thumb, if a person standing near another person listening via an earbud can hear sound from the earbud, then the volume is too loud and can cause hearing loss, either temporary or permanent. Some questions have also arisen as to the potential harmful effects of exposure to radiation emitted by cell phones. Research to date suggests that these concerns are unfounded, and the World Health Organization is expected to issue its cell phone use guidelines by 2008.[26]

As noted, RSI is another physiological problem to treat seriously. Chronic problems can be the result if appropriate steps are not taken. Among the important preventative measures are taking frequent breaks from computer use. Good ergonomics, or posture, is also important. *Wikipedia* explains that "[t]he head and back should form a straight line from the ears to the pelvis. The shoulders and head should not be hunched forward." In other words, do not slouch. It is also important to "[a]void resting the wrists on anything when typing. Hold them straight, rather than bent up, down, or to the side. Use a keyboard rest pad on which the wrists and palms rest to prevent RSI." [27] An interesting 2006 study conducted at Woodend Hospital in Aberdeen, Scotland, demonstrated that proper posture while sitting can also have direct effects on back pain and spinal stress. Unlike conventional wisdom that sitting upright at a 90-degree angle is best, the study demonstrated that the best sitting posture maintains a 135-degree sitting angle. "A 135-degree body-thigh sitting posture was demonstrated to be the best biomechanical sitting position, as opposed to a 90-degree posture, which most people consider normal," said Dr. Waseem Amir Bashir, author and clinical fellow in the Department of Radiology and Diagnostic Imaging at the University of Alberta Hospital, Canada. "Sitting in a sound anatomic position is essential, since the strain put on the spine and its associated ligaments over time can lead to pain, deformity and chronic illness."[28]

PARENTAL CONTROLS FOR DTV

In addition to the controls described earlier for limiting online activities, Web site access, and portable digital device use, parents should also consider using parental controls for limiting the programs their children may watch on television. All TV sets 13 inches or larger manufactured since 2000 come equipped with a federally mandated V-Chip. The V refers to "violence," but the V-Chip also helps parents limit access to programs based on the level of sexual content as well as violence. The V-Chip control is easily enabled from an on-screen menu, and parents can set which level of program rating is acceptable for their children by age or type of content. More details on the use of the V-Chip are available online.[29] In addition to the V-Chip, parents can also use blocking software included with digital cable or satellite TV boxes.

CONCLUSION

Digital media present a wealth of opportunities for children's development. Through the Internet, children gain new opportunities for self-expression, learning, and discovery. DTV offers not only continued access to quality programming, but expanded access to interactive content. MP3 players and other devices allow children to customize their media experience and gain increasing control over their worlds.

Yet all this does not come without a significant cost, both in actual dollars and in dangers to children's health and well-being. Many of these digital media are expensive to acquire and use. Many have high upfront costs to purchase the device needed to access the media and monthly fees for service. Prices can go up based on usage. Teens are often inclined to be heavy users of these devices, resulting in escalating costs for their parents or guardians.

Dangers also lurk in the online shadows of the Internet. Pedophiles, predators, threats to privacy, and pornography are some of the more significant problems posed by the online world. Various new media can also present direct health consequences. For example, earbuds can lead to hearing loss, and RSI can result from overuse of a keyboard or computer mouse or video game. Parents need to take great care to make sure their children do not end up with these problems.

Fortunately, a variety of tools and resources are available to parents and others to ensure the safety of online and other new media. Software and hardware products can enable parents' control over their children's Internet access and DTV watching.

Digital technologies are transforming media in fundamental ways. Some influences of these technologies are potential improvements, whereas others present new problems or expand long-standing ones. This book has examined technology from a series of perspectives, each providing an alternative view on the impact of digital and networking technology on journalism, media, and society, both domestically and internationally.

Yet the assumption underlying this work is that change in the media is not technologically determined. Rather, technology enables certain changes and possibilities. Which of those changes occur and whether they ultimately are improvements or detriments depend largely on policies and the practices of both individuals and organizations in both the media and the public sector. Internet and other digital technologies have given citizens unprecedented capabilities to produce, distribute, and access news, information, and media content of all forms and from all venues.

It may be many years, decades or longer, before the full spectrum of changes stemming from digital developments can be adequately assessed. Suffice it to say here that there are at least four general types of change occurring in the media landscape in the digital age. First, digital and networking technologies are transforming how media professionals do their work and along the way are presenting new possibilities to improve those practices, but are also posing new ethical concerns. Second, the content of media is changing as digital and networking technologies such as the Internet give rise to more interactive, on-demand, and modality-rich storytelling and content forms. Third, structural, cultural, and management changes are occurring in the media system, both at the organization-specific and industrywide levels, presenting regulatory, legal, and business challenges along the way. Finally, relationships between and among media and their many publics are changing. This final impact may be the most significant for media in democratic societies where citizens look not only for entertainment and marketing possibilities in the media, but also for the information and discourse they need to make intelligent decisions about governance. It is in this sense that the future of media rests with the next generation of citizens, the children, who embrace the new technologies but may lack the experience or wisdom to use them safely and effectively. Parents, teachers, media professionals, and policymakers all bear a responsibility to help guide the next generation in wisely utilizing and producing media in the digital age.

INTRODUCTION

1. At http://www.morsehistoricsite.org/.

2. M. Susan Barger and William B. White, *The Daguerreotype: Nineteenth-Century Technology and Modern Science* (Washington, D.C.: Smithsonian Institution Press, 1991).

3. At http://memory.loc.gov/ammem/ndlpedu/collections/dag/langarts.html.

4. *Joseph Avery Stranded on Rocks in the Niagara River*, photographer Platt D. Babbitt, d. 1879, at http://memory.loc.gov/cgi-bin/query/r?ammem/dag:@field(NUMBER%2B@band(cph%2B3j00126; digital ID: cph 3j00126.

5. At http://www.ap.org/pages/about/history/history_first.html.

6. Joseph R. Dominick, *The Dynamics of Mass Communication* (New York: McGraw-Hill, 1990), 92.; Everett M. Rogers, *Communications Technology* (New York: Free Press, 1986), 30.

7. There were other influences: see Marcus Errico, John April, Andrew Asch, Lynnette Khalfani, Miriam A. Smith, and Xochiti R. Ybarra, "The Evolution of the Summary News Lead," *Media History Monographs* 1, no. 1 (1997–98), available at http://www.scripps.ohiou.edu/mediahistory/mhmjour1–1.htm.

8. Robert Picard, "The Economic State of Media Industries," lecture at Fordham University, New York, March 10, 2006.

9. At http://findarticles.com/p/articles/mi_m3617/is_1994_Annual/ai_14698438.

10. At http://www.media.mit.edu/sponsors/sponsors.html.

11. At http://quest.arc.nasa.gov/antarctica/QA/animals/Penguin_Survival.

12. At http://www.stateofthenewsmedia.com/2006/index.asp.

13. At http://www.emarketer.com/Article.aspx?1003872.

14. At http://www1.cs.columbia.edu/graphics/projects/mars/mjwSd.html.

15. See http://www1.cs.columbia.edu/graphics/projects/mars/mjwSd.html.

16. At http://www1.cs.columbia.edu/graphics/people/sinem/papers/Authoring-ISWC2003/S.Guven-ISWC2003.pdf.

17. For example, http://news.bbc.co.uk/2/low/technology/3954659.stm.

18. At http://www.foxnews.com/story/0,2933,230838,00.html.

CHAPTER 1. DIGITAL DELIVERY MEDIA

1. The clip has been posted multiple times on YouTube, and several of the clips have been viewed nearly 50,000 times, including at http://www.youtube.com/watch?v=GsXpRZmbm1Y, http://www.youtube.com/watch?v=yBzhbn8IEPU, and http://moderate.wordpress.com/2006/11/18/cops-taser-ucla-student/.

2. At http://www.fcc.gov/cgb/consumerfacts/highspeedInternet.html.

3. John Hoffman, *GPRS Demystified* (New York: McGraw-Hill Professional, September 4, 2002).

4. L. Nuaymi, *WiMAX: Technology for Broadband Wireless Access* (Hoboken, N.J.: Wiley, 2007).

5. Eli Noam, e-mail received by the author, November 10, 2006.

6. "Net-Neutrality," *New York Times,* May 17, 2006, at http://www.nytimes.com/aponline/technology/AP-Net-Neutrality.html.

7. Peter Grant, "To Ward Off New Competitors, Comcast Builds a Mini Internet," *Wall Street Journal,* October 13, 2005, A1.

8. At http://www.calypsowireless.com/documents/content/news/2005-09-26.pdf.

9. John Carey, "An Ethnographic Study of Interactive Television," paper presented at Rutgers University, October 28, 2002.

10. At http://www.lsi.usp.br/~rbianchi/clarke/ACC.ETRelays.html.

11. The term *communications* with an *s,* in the plural form, refers here to "messages," whereas *communication* without the *s,* in the singular, refers to the overall process or phenomenon of communicating.

12. At http://www.xmradio.com; http://www.sirius.com.

13. At http://www.ses-americom.com/services/broadcast.html.

14. At http://english.aljazeera.net/.

15. See http://www.iridium.com.

16. See http://www.spaceimaging.com.

17. See http://www.gizmorama.com.

18. See http://www.latimes.com/news/custom/showcase/la-endnote_blurb.blurb.

19. See http://www.pdnonline.com/pdn/search/article_display.jsp?vnu_content_id=1000456607.

20. See http://www.apphotomanagers.org/Ethics_in%20_age.html.

21. See http://www.directv.com; http://www.dishtv.com.

22. At http://en.wikipedia.org/wiki/DirecTV.

23. See http://www.newscorp.com.

24. At http://en.wikipedia.org/wiki/Dish_Network.

25. At http://www.engadgethd.com/2006/11/28/directv-to-unveil-sat-go/.

26. Lorne Manly, "Satellite Television in a Portable Box," *New York Times,* January 8, 2007, at http://www.nytimes.com/2007/01/08/technology/08satellite.html?hp&ex=1168318800&en=f60411d41aef0111&ei=5094&partner=homepage.

27. At http://www.dvdinformation.com/News/press/010903.htm.

28. National Cable Television Association, at http://www.ncta.com/ContentView.aspx?contentId=54.

29. Carey, "An Ethnographic Study of Interactive Television."

30. At http://www.answers.com/topic/high-definition-television-in-the-united-states.

31. At http://www.rtnda.org/about/rtndf.shtml.

32. Ed Quinn, telephone interview by the author, October 1, 2002.

33. Jim Topping, telephone interview by the author, September 15, 2002.

34. Richard S. Chernock, John R. Mick, Michael A. Dolan, and Regis Crinon, *Data Broadcasting: Understanding the ATSC Data Broadcast Standard* (New York: McGraw-Hill, 2001).

35. At http://en.wikipedia.org/wiki/Digital_terrestrial_television.

36. At http://en.wikipedia.org/wiki/High-definition_television_in_the_United_States.

37. Topping interview, September 15, 2002.

38. George DeVault, telephone interviewed by the author, September 16, 2002.

39. Quinn interview, October 1, 2002.

40. See http://www.pbs.org.

41. Topping interview, September 15, 2002.

42. Jack Goodman, telephone interview by the author, September 22, 2002.

43. At http://findarticles.com/p/articles/mi_hb3036/is_200210/ai_n7737869

44. John Carey, conversation with the author, November 21, 2006, New York City.

45. At http://www.joost.com/.

46. Jonathan Leess, interviewed by the author, September 5, 2002, New York City.

47. Topping interview, September 15, 2002.

48. Newton Minow, quoted in "'Vast Wasteland' Speech Holds True After All These Years," *Chicago Tribune,* April 24, 2001, 17, at http://janda.org/b20/News%20articles/vastwastland.htm.

CHAPTER 2. DEVICES TO ACCESS DIGITAL MEDIA

1. At http://en.wikipedia.org/wiki/History_of_computing_hardware.

2. John Noble Wilford, "Early Astronomical 'Computer' Found to Be Technically Complex," *New York Times,* November 30, 2007, at http://www.nytimes.com/2006/11/30/science/30compute.html.

3. At http://www.cs.iastate.edu/jva/jva-archive.shtml.

4. At http://pespmc1.vub.ac.be/ASC/ANALOG_COMPU.html.

5. At http://www.columbia.edu/~jp35/lectures/lect_9.html.

6. At http://www.unc.edu/~pmeyer/book/Chapter1.htm.

7. At http://iml.jou.ufl.edu/carlson/1970s.shtml.

8. Geoff Shavey, telephone interview by the author, January 4, 2006; Erica Taub, "TECHNOLOGY; Picture Tubes Are Fading Into the Past," *New York Times,* August 7, 2006, at http://www.nytimes.com/2006/08/07/technology/07tube.html.

9. Markus G. Kuhn, "Electromagnetic Eavesdropping Risks of Flat-Panel Displays," available at http://www.cl.cam.ac.uk/mgk25/.

10. Consumer Electronics Association, "Analog TV Lead Continues to Slip," December 15, 2004, at http://www.ce.org/Press/CEA_Pubs/912.asp; see also http://iml.jou.ufl.edu/carlson/1970s.shtml.

11. "Total HD," *New York Times,* January 4, 2007, at http://www.nytimes.com/2007/01/04/.

12. See http://burningquestions@pcworld.com; http://msn.pcworld.com/news/article/0,aid,126112,00.asp?GT1=8298.

13. At http://www.lge.com/about/press_archive/detail/AB_NARCH%7CMENU_1_20317.jhtml.

14. At http://news.com.com/Blu-ray+a+player+in+PlayStation+pricing/2100-1043_3-6070342.html.

15. Michel Marriott, "HOW IT WORKS; At the Heart of the Wii, Micron-Size Machines," *New York Times,* December 21, 2006, at http://www.nytimes.com/2006/12/21/technology/21howw.html?ref=technology.

16. At http://www.abiresearch.com/abiprdisplay.jsp?pressid=741.

17. John Carey, conversation with the author, November 21, 2006, New York City.

18. At http://www.washingtonpost.com/wp-dyn/articles/A36770–2005Feb18.html.

19. "On-Demand TV 2006: A Nationwide Study on VoD and DVRs," available at http://www.leichtmanresearch.com/.

20. At http://www.mediamark.com/.

21. At http://www.clickz.com/showPage.html?page=3623007.

22. At http://www.imediaconnection.com/content/6516.asp.

23. Eric Pfanner, "TECHNOLOGY; The British Like to Control TV with Their DVRs, Too," *New York Times,* January 8, 2007, at http://www.nytimes.com/2007/01/08/technology/08dvr.html?_r=1&ref=technology&oref=slogin.

24. At http://www.abiresearch.com/abiprdisplay.jsp?pressid=741.

25. David Pogue, "Apple TV Has Landed," *New York Times,* March 22, 2007, at http://www.nytimes.com/2007/03/22/technology/22pogue.html?ex =1332216000&en=87049b8c46d6ae4e&ei=5088&partner=rssnyt&emc=rss.

26. Marty Katz, "A ThinkPad Tablet Tries to Find Its Place in the Sun," *New York Times,*January 4, 2007, at http://www.nytimes.com/2007/01/04/technology/04lenovo.html?_r=1&ref=technology&oref=slogin.

27. At http://dynamism.com/oqo02/main.shtml?gclid=CL6Z45PyOIkCFTBcFQ od_AK9Vg.

28. John Markoff, "A Personal Computer to Carry in a Pocket," *New York Times,* January 8, 2007, at http://www.nytimes.com/2007/01/08/technology/08mobile .html?_r=1&oref=slogin.

29. At http://en.wikipedia.org/wiki/Flash_memory.

30. At http://www.opensource.org/docs/definition.php; http://news.zdnet .com/2100–1040_22–5884683.html.

31. At http://news.com.com/Gates+mocks+MITs+100+laptop+effort/2100 –1044_3–6050276.html.

32. John Markoff, "For $150, Third-World Laptop Stirs Big Debate," *New York Times,* November 30, 2007, at http://www.nytimes.com/2006/11/30/technology/30laptop.html?_r=1&oref=slogin&pagewanted=all.

33. At http://deafandblind.com/phone/demo.htm.

34. At http://en.wikipedia.org/wiki/QWERTY.

35. At http://www.mobileinfo.com/Bluetooth/Bluetooth-vs-WLAN.htm.

36. At http://www.newsu.org/.

37. At http://abcnews.go.com/Technology/ZDM/story?id=2600634.

38. At http://dylanalamode.com/iTunes-and-Sansa-m200.html.

39. At http://www.macrumors.com/pages/2004/12/20041216203103.shtml.

40. John Markoff, "Fever Builds for iPhone (Anxiety Too)," *New York Times,* June 4, 2007, at http://www.nytimes.com/2007/06/04/technology/04iphone .html?ex=1338609600&en=07c94d7d88de0857&ei=5090.

41. At http://www.eink.com/.

42. At http://ebooks.connect.com/.

43. Aaron O. Patrick, "BBC Test May Push Internet TV Closer to Mainstream," *Wall Street Journal,* September 21, 2005, A15.

44. At http://www.slingmedia.com.

45. Richard Siklos, "Can TV's and PC's Live Together Happily Ever After?" *New York Times,* May 14, 2006, at http://www.nytimes.com/2006/05/14/business/yourmoney/14frenzy.html.

46. Intel's cofounder, Gordon E. Moore, made this observation in 1965, and it has served the test of time—hence "Moore's Law." See http://www.intel.com/pressroom/kits/bios/moore.htm.

47. At http://www.mcw.edu/gcrc/cop/cell-phone-health-FAQ/toc.html.

48. Damon Darlin and Barnaby J. Feder, "We Ask So Much of Our Batteries; Need for Power Runs into Basic Hurdles of Science," *New York Times,* August 16, 2006, C1.

CHAPTER 3. AUDIENCES OR USERS OF DIGITAL MEDIA

1. At http://www.census.gov/main/www/popclock.html; http://www.Internet worldstats.com/am/us.htm; http://www.Internetworldstats.com/articles/art110 .htm.

2. At http://www.leichtmanresearch.com/press/081706release.pdf; http://en .wikipedia.org/wiki/Broadband_Internet_access_worldwide. Thanks to Mari Assefa and Jackie Pavlik for designing the figures in this book and to Jon Oliver, School of Communication, Information, and Library Studies, Rutgers University, for his help in printing copies of the original manuscript.

3. At http://www.pewInternet.org/.

4. "Pew Study. Demographics of Internet Users," April 26, 2006, at http://www .pewInternet.org/.

5. At http://www.stateofthenewsmedia.org/2006/narrative_online_audience .asp?cat=3&media=4; Ken Belson, "With a Dish, Broadband Goes Rural," *New York Times,* November 14, 2006, at http://www.nytimes.com/2006/11/14/technology/ 14satellite.html?_r=1&oref=slogin&pagewanted=all; Richard Siklos, "Comcast Is Said to Agree to Carry Fox's Planned Business News Channel," *New York Times,* November 7, 2006, at http://www.nytimes.com/2006/11/07/business/ media/07fox.html; Saul Hansell, "Satellite TV's 3-Headed Rival: Cable Plus Internet Plus Phone, " *New York Times,* September 18, 2006, at http://www.nytimes .com/2006/09/18/business/media/18marketplace.html; Seth Schiesel, "Online Game, Made in U.S., Seizes the Globe," *New York Times,* September 5, 2006, at http://www.nytimes.com/2006/09/05/technology/05wow.html?ref=technology &pagewanted=all; Richard Siklos, "Changing Its Tune," *New York Times,* September 15, 2006, at http://www.nytimes.com/2006/09/15/business/media/ 15radio.html?_r=1&oref=slogin&pagewanted=all; Doreen Carvajal, "Al Jazeera on Television Is Causing Trouble for British Pubs, but It's Not Political," *New York Times,* August 21, 2006, at http://www.nytimes.com/2006/08/21/technology/ 21jazeera.html?_r=1&oref=slogin.

6. *Conference Board Consumer Internet Barometer Study,* October 25, 2006, at http://www.conference-board.org/UTILITIES/press.cfm.

7. At http://www.4rfv.co.uk/industrynews.asp?ID=57193.

8. At http://www.stateofthenewsmedia.org/2006/printable_radio_audience.asp.

9. At http://www.censusscope.org/us/chart_age.html.

10. At http://www.xmradio.com/newsroom/screen/pr_2006_07_06.html.

11. See http://www.sirius.com, December 5, 2006.

12. Shelly Freierman, "The Youngsters Aren't Listening as Much," *New York Times*, October 16, 2006, C5.

13. At http://www.thenewatlantis.com/archive/4/soa/videogames.htm.

14. At http://www.gamespot.com/gamespot/features/video/hov/p3_01.html.

15. At http://www.emarketer.com/Article.aspx?1004176.

16. At http://www.fatal1ty.com/; http://www.cbsnews.com/stories/2006/01/19/60minutes/main1220146.shtml.

17. At http://secondlife.com/.

18. At http://teen.secondlife.com/.

19. At http://secondlife.reuters.com/stories/2006/10/18/virtual-economy-tax-would-be-a-mistake-us-rep/.

20. At http://www.nmc.org/.

21. At http://informationisland.org/.

22. At http://www.thepeoplesplatform.com.

23. At http://Election.thepeopleselection.com.

24. At http://www.metoperafamily.org/metopera/broadcast/on_air.aspx.

25. Neil Postman, *Technopoly: The Surrender of Culture to Technology* (New York: Vintage Books, 1993).

26. Pierre Levy, *Les technologies de l'intelligence: L'avenir de la pensée à l'ère informatique* (Technologies of Intelligence: The Future of Thought in the Computer Age) (Paris: La Découverte, 1990).

27. Jean Baudrillard, The Vital Illusion, Wellek Library Lectures at the University of California at Irvine (New York: Columbia University Press, 2000).

28. At http://www.comscore.com/press/release.asp?press=874.

29. Randy Kennedy, "The Shorter, Faster, Cruder, Tinier TV Show," *New York Times*, May 28, 2006, at http://www.nytimes.com/2006/05/28/magazine/28mtv.html?pagewanted=all; see also http://www.vodreport.com/.

30. ABI Research, at http://www.metrics2.com/blog/industry_insights/movies musictv/; Olga Karif, "The Coming Mobile-Video Deluge," *Business Week*, October 11, 2005, at http://www.businessweek.com/technology/content/oct2005/tc20051011_9768_tc024.htm ; http://www.pewInternet.org/PPF/r/179/report_display.asp.

31. National Public Radio, *All Things Considered*, October 6, 2006.

32. David Folkenflik, "Foley Story Wasn't Reported, Until It Was," October 6, 2006, at http://www.npr.org/templates/story/story.php?storyId=6211216.

33. D. Middleberg and S. S. Ross, *The Middleberg/Ross Media in Cyberspace Survey: Change and Its Impact on Communications,* eighth annual national survey (New York: Middleberg+Associates, 2002), at http://www.middleberg.com.

34. James G. Miller, *Living Systems Theory: Issues for Management Thought and Practice* (New York: McGraw-Hill, 1978).

35. Pablo J. Boczkowski, *Digitizing the News* (Cambridge, Mass.: MIT Press, 2005), 21.

36. Daniel Dubno, interviewed by the author, October 14, 2002, New York City.

37. Bloomberg News, "Google Passes Yahoo in Tally of Visitors," *New York Times,* December 23, 2006, at http://www.nytimes.com/2006/12/23/technology/23 google.html?ref=technology.

38. Jody Raynsford, posted March 25, 2003, at dotJournalism, e-mail: jody raynsford@hotmail.com, available at http://www.journalism.co.uk/features/ story604.html.

39. "Online Newspaper Blog Traffic Grows 210 Percent Over Year," January 17, 2007, at http://www.nielsen-netratings.com/.

40. At http://www.pewInternet.org/PPF/r/184/report_display.asp.

41. At http://www.journalism.co.uk/features/story604.html.

42. At http://www.newmediamusings.com/.

43. At http://www.j-lab.org/schaffer041804.html.

44. At http://www.muckrakingmom.com/frontPage.do.

45. Jürgen Habermas, *The Structural Transformation of the Public Sphere: An Inquiry into a Category of Bourgeois Society,* Studies in Contemporary German Social Thought (Cambridge, Mass.: MIT Press, 1991). "The usage of the words 'public' and 'public sphere' betrays a multiplicity of concurrent meanings" (p. 1).

46. Jürgen Habermas, *Civil Society and the Political Public Sphere* (Cambridge, Mass.: MIT Press, 1989), 37.

CHAPTER 4. PRODUCERS OF DIGITAL MEDIA

1. At http://chasingmills.com/.

2. At http://en.wikipedia.org/wiki/History_of_podcasting.

3. At http://www.byz.org/~rbanks/movableType/webLog/trends/archives/ 2006_12.html.

4. The cell phone video of the execution of Saddam Hussein can be found at http://video.google.com/videoplay?docid=-7532034279766935521.

5. At http://www.nationalledger.com/artman/publish/article_272610720 .shtml.

6. Video and text report at http://nytimes.com, June 18, 2006, Danny Hakim did the text report. See Danny Kakim, "'Star Trek' Fans, Deprived of a Show, Recreate the Franchise on Digital Video," *New York Times*, June 18, 2006, at http://www.nytimes.com/2006/06/18/arts/television/18trek.html?ex=1150776000 &en=7dfc6da8fbcbdd77&ei=5087%0A.

7. At http://feeds.feedburner.com/AICPAMultimedia.

8. At http://www.hillaryclinton.com/.

9. World Editors Forum, *Trends in Newsrooms 2006,* annual report (Paris: World Editors Forum, 2006), 110.

10. At http://www.nydailynews.com/news/regional/story/420936p-355356c .html.

11. At http://link.brightcove.com/services/player/bcpid234479531?bclid =234447498&bctid=234447501.

12. At http://www.emmyonline.org/emmy/docu_new_media_awards.html.

13. Travis Fox, "Fueling Azerbaijan's Future," *Washington Post,* October 4, 2005, at http://www.washingtonpost.com/wp-dyn/content/video/2005/10/04/ VI2005100400654.html.

14. At http://www.dallasnews.com/.

15. David Duitch, telephone interview by the author, May 19, 2006.

16. Jim Landers, "As Neighbors Break Apart, One Faces Economic Disaster," Dallasnews.com, May 12, 2006, at http://www.dallasnews.com/sharedcontent/ dws/news/washington/jlanders/stories/051206dnintdisengage.223e29f6.html.

17. John Granatino, telephone interview by the author, May 19, 2006.

18. Kevin McGeever, telephone interview by the author, May 19, 2006.

19. At http://www.sptimes.com/2006/03/20/Tampabay/Manatee_petting _Just.shtml.

20. At http://hotzone.yahoo.com/.

21. Jesús Martín Barbero, *De los medios a las mediaciones* (Bogotá, Columbia: Convenio Andrés Bello, 1998).

22. Nestor García-Canclini, *La producción simbólica: Teoría y método en sociología del arte, siglo XXI* (Mexico City: Editores, S.A., 1979).

23. Theodor W. Adorno, *Negative Dialectics,* translated by E. B. Ashton (New York: Routledge, 1973), available at http://www.marxists.org/reference/archive/ adorno/1966/negative-dialectics/index.htm; Max Horkheimer, "Enlightenment as Mass Deception," 1944, available at http://www.marxists.org/reference/archive/ adorno/1944/culture-industry.htm.

24. Adapted from John V. Pavlik, "Fake News: One Man's Experience on *The Daily Show with Jon Stewart,*" *Television Quarterly* 36, no. 1 (fall 2005): 44–50.

25. At http://www.pewInternet.org/PPF/r/178/report_display.asp; 2005 Pew Internet and American Life Project, http://www.pewInternet.org/.

26. *Inside Higher Ed* (online publication), at http://www.insidehighered.com/.

27. At http://www.comedycentral.com/shows/the_daily_show/index.jhtml.

28. At http://press.comedycentral.com/tv_shows/ds/videos_corr.jhtml?p=helms.

29. At http://query.nytimes.com/gst/abstract.html?res=FB0910FA395B0C72 8DDDAC0894DB404482; "Correcting the Record: *Times* Reporter Who Resigned Leaves Long Trail of Deception," *New York Times,* May 11, 2003, A1.

30. Carl Bernstein and Bob Woodward, *All the President's Men* (New York: Touchstone, 1974).

31. D. Middleberg and S. S. Ross, *The Middleberg/Ross Media in Cyberspace Survey: Change and Its Impact on Communications,* eighth annual national survey (New York: Middleberg+Associates, 2002), available at http://www.middleberg.com.

32. See http://www.skype.com.

33. Daniel Dubno, interviewed by the author, June 1, 2004, New York City.

34. Dan Dubno, "Eyes in the Sky," CBS News, January 23, 2003, at http://www.cbsnews.com/stories/2003/01/23/tech/digitaldan/main537597.shtml.

35. Herb Jackson, e-mail communication to the author, June 3, 2004.

36. Robert Jensen, *Writing Dissent: Taking Radical Ideas from the Margins to the Mainstream* (New York: Peter Lang, 2001), Robert Jensen, "Embedded Media Give Up Independence," *Boston Globe,* April 7, 2003, 19.

37. See *The New Yorker* at http://www.newyorker.com/archive/previous/?040531frprsp_previous1.

CHAPTER 5. CONTENT IN THE DIGITAL AGE

1. Catherine Foster, "Rights Renewed, 'Eyes on the Prize' Returns," *Boston Globe,* May 26, 2006, at http://www.boston.com/ae/tv/articles/2006/05/26/rights_renewed_eyes_on_the_prize_returns/.

2. Adam Clayton Powell III, "Getting the Picture: Trends in Television News Reporting," in John V. Pavlik and Everette E. Dennis, eds., *Demystifying Media Technology,* 81–86 (Mountain View, Calif.: Mayfield, 1993).

3. At http://www.theopenmind.tv.

4. For example, the Web site for my school, the School of Communication, Information, and Library Studies, at Rutgers is http://www.scils.rutgers.edu.

5. At http://usearch.cc.columbia.edu/cicat/frame.html.

6. John Carey, "An Ethnographic Study of Interactive Television," paper presented at Rutgers University, October 28, 2002; see also http://www.nytimes.com/2006/11/19/arts/television/19manl.html?pagewanted=all.

7. At http://quote.bloomberg.com/apps/news?pid=10000103&sid=abwztjDjVacE&refer=news_index.

8. At http://www.cnn.com/pipeline/?url=http%3A%2F%2Fpremium.cnn.com%2Fpr%2Fpipeline%2Fdownload.html%3Fmode%3Dlive%26stream%3D2.

9. At http://music.yahoo.com/.

10. See http://www.launch.com; http://biz.yahoo.com/bw/031103/35377_1.html.

11. See http://www.hoovers.com/.

12. See http://music.yahoo.com/.

13. See http://www.pandora.com.

14. See http://www.mtr.org/.

15. See http://www.mtvu.com.

16. See http://www.Fox.com.

17. Matt Richtel, "In Raw World of Sex Movies, High Definition Could Be a View Too Real," *New York Times*, January 22, 2007, at http://www.nytimes.com/2007/01/22/business/media/22porn.html?_r=1&oref=slogin&pagewanted=all.

18. At http://www.webopedia.com/TERM/D/digital_watermark.html.

19. At http://www.g4tv.com/.

20. At http://music.columbia.edu/cmc/projects/.

21. David Gonzalez, "A Sliver of a Storefront, A Faith on the Rise," *New York Times,* January 14, 2007, at http://www.nytimes.com/2007/01/14/nyregion/14storefront.html?pagewanted=all.

22. At http://www.technorati.com/.

23. See http://carpetbagger.blogs.nytimes.com.

24. See http://www.rocketboom.com.

25. See http://www.myspace.com; http://www.bsu.edu/security/article/0,1384,37316–5031–40336,00.html.

26. Miao-ju Jian, "New Technologies and New Forms of Music Commodity/Labor: An Economic Analysis of the China's Super Girl," paper presented at the Singapore Communication Workshop, spring 2007.

27. Tom Rosenstiel, "Project for Excellence in Journalism: Election Night 2006. An Evening in the Life of the American Media, November 27, 2006," December 1, 2006, available at http://www.journalism.org/node/3015; see also http://www.nytimes.com/2006/11/27/business/media/27election.html?_r=1&adxnnl=1&oref=slogin&adxnnlx=1164636084-TaZLirCJrYvN567o0Ue0Fw.

28. At http://en.wikipedia.org/wiki/John_Seigenthaler_Sr._Wikipedia_biography_controversy.

29. Bob Tedeschi, "Everyone's an Editor as Wiki Fever Spreads to Shopping Sites," *New York Times,* April 24, 2006, at http://www.nytimes.com/2006/04/24/technology/24ecom.html?ex=1183867200&en=2bccbca49ae700c1&ei=5070.

30. At http://en.wikipedia.org/wiki/John_Seigenthaler_Sr._Wikipedia _biography_controversy.

31. "Wiki's Wild World," *Nature* 438 (December 15, 2005), 890.

32. T. Hollerer, S. Feiner, and J. Pavlik, "Situated Documentaries: Embedding Multimedia Presentations in the Real World," paper presented at the Institute of Electrical and Electronics Engineers International Symposium on Wearable Computers, San Francisco, October 18–19, 1999, available at http://www.cs.columbia.edu/graphics/publications/iswc99.pdf.

33. At http://www1.cs.columbia.edu/graphics/projects/mars/mjwSd.html.

34. At http://news.bbc.co.uk/2/low/technology/3954659.stm.

35. At http://research.nokia.com/research/projects/mara/index.html; http://www.geovector.com/.

36. At http://viterbi.usc.edu/news/news/2006/news_20060201.htm.

37. Laura M. Holson, "Now Playing on a Tiny Screen," *New York Times,* October 17, 2005, B15, at http://www.nytimes.com/2005/10/17/technology/17mobisodes .html?pagewanted=all.

38. Randy Kennedy, "The Shorter, Faster, Cruder, Tinier TV Show," *New York Times,* May 28, 2006, at http://www.nytimes.com/2006/05/28/magazine/28mtv .html?pagewanted=all.

39. At http://www.mobitv.com/.

40. At www.gotvnetworks.com.

41. At http://www.myspace.com/myemmy; John Carey and Lawrence Greenberg, "And the Emmy Goes to . . . a Mobisode? *Television Quarterly* 36, no. 2 (April 2006): 3–8, available at http://www.tvquarterly.net/p3.html.

42. Laura M. Holson, "Nominees Picked for New Emmy for PC and Hand-Held Shows," *New York Times,* April 11, 2006, at http://www.nytimes .com/2006/04/11/business/11emmy.html?_r=1&oref=slogin; Peter O. Price, interviewed by the author, April 10, 2006, New York City.

43. Sharon Waxman, "Computers Join Actors in Hybrids on Screen," *New York Times,* January 9, 2007, at http://www.nytimes.com/2007/01/09/movies/09came.html.

44. At http://www.hollywoodreporter.com/hr/search/article_display.jsp ?vnu_content_id=1002801137.

45. At http://movies.ign.com/articles/717/717128p1.html.

46. At http://en.wikipedia.org/wiki/Motion_capture.

47. At http://www.xmradio.com, www.sirius.com.

48. See http://www.chicagocrime.org.

49. At http://12.17.79.6/; http://www.google.com.

50. At http://www.citypaper.com/news/story.asp?id=11466.

51. At http://outside.in.

52. "36 Hours: City by City," *New York Times*, February 27, 2006, at http://www.nytimes.com/packages/html/travel/20060227_36HOURS_MAP.html.

53. At http://news.google.com/.

54. At http://searchenginewatch.com/searchday/article.php/3579746.

55. At http://www1.cs.columbia.edu/nlp/.

56. At http://www1.cs.columbia.edu/nlp/projects.html.

57. At http://www1.cs.columbia.edu/nlp/projects.html.

58. The articles mashed up came from: news.bbc.co.uk (fifty-seven articles), washingtonpost.com (forty-two articles), baltimoresun.com (thirty-seven articles), foxnews.com (thirty-two articles), timesonline.co.uk, (twenty-eight articles), seattletimes.nwsource.com (twenty-four articles), latimes.com (twenty-one articles), boston.com (twenty-one articles), nytimes.com (seventeen articles), observer.guardian.co.uk (fourteen articles), dallasnews.com (eleven articles), sfgate.com (ten articles), cbsnews.com (ten articles), haaretz.com (six articles), abcnews.go.com (four articles), cnn.com and cbc.ca (two articles). See http://newsblaster.cs.columbia.edu/.

59. At http://www.programmableweb.com.

60. Min Hang, "Venturing for Success: New Business Creation in Media Organizations," paper presented at the Seventh World Media Economics Conference, May 2006, Beijing.

61. Lorenzo Vilches, *La televisión: Los efectos del bien y del ma* (Barcelona, Spain: Ediciones Paidos, January 1993).

62. "Broadcasters as Storytellers," *New York Times*, January 31, 1985, A15.

CHAPTER 6. DISTRIBUTORS OF DIGITAL MEDIA

1. Jarrett Bell, "NFL Tug-of-War Over Revenue," *USA Today*, July 5, 2004, at http://www.usatoday.com/sports/football/nfl/2004-07-05-revenue-cover_x.htm.

2. At http://www.jsonline.com/story/index.aspx?id=544891.

3. Antonio Gramsci, *Selections from the Prison Notebooks* (London: Lawrence and Wishart, 1971).

4. At http://www.zshare.net/audio/papoose-50-shots-MP3.html.

5. See http://www.hoovers.com.

6. See http://www.hoovers.com.

7. At http://www22.verizon.com/content/fiostv/about+fios+tv/about+fios+tv.htm.

8. At http://www.cbsnews.com/sections/i_video/main500251.shtml; http://abcnews.go.com/; www.cnn.com.

9. At http://www.msnbc.msn.com/id/12761265/.

10. At http://video.msn.com.

11. At http://video.google.com/.

12. At http://video.google.com/videoplay?docid=-4973617448770513925.

13. At http://news.google.com/.

14. At http://www.nielsen-netratings.com/pr/pr_060511.pdf.

15. See http://www.youtube.com.

16. At http://video.google.com/videoplay?docid=8191780737516712253&q =genre%3Acomedy&hl=en; http://www.youtube.com/watch?v=GrbKw-TnFdw.

17. See http://www.youtube.com.

18. At http://www.youtube.com/watch?v=9G7gq7GQ71c.

19. Ryan Lizza, "The YouTube Election," *New York Times,* August 20, 2006, at http://www.nytimes.com/2006/08/20/weekinreview/20lizza.html ?pagewanted=all.

20. At http://www.mtv.com/podcasts/#/podcasts/.

21. At http://mefeedia.com/; http://www.podcastvideos.org/; http://vlogdir .com.

22. At http://www.waveofdestruction.org/?s=Phuket.

23. At http://www.wifinetnews.com/archives/002757.html.

24. At http://www.engadget.com/2007/01/04/qflix-promises-to-expedite -download-to-burn-dvd-adoption/.

25. See http://www.nba.com.

26. See http://www.mlb.com.

27. See http://www.real.com.

28. See http://www.hoovers.com.

29. See http://www.cinemanow.com.

30. See http://www.movielink.com.

31. At http://www.bittorrent.com/.

32. See http://www.limewire.com.

33. See http://showsplanet.com/, http://fasttvdownloads.com/; http://www .tvcentral.org.

34. See http://www.itunes.com.

35. Peter Grant, "Online Video Goes Mainstream, Sparking an Industry Land Grab," February 21, 2006, *Wall Street Journal,* at http://www.wizbangblog.com.

36. Joe Flint, "Show Time," *Wall Street Journal,* March 13, 2006, R10.

37. At http://dynamic.abc.go.com/streaming/landing.

38. At http://television.aol.com/in2tv.

39. At http://www.microsoft.com/windowsvista/features/forhome/media center.mspx.

40. At http://www.timewarner.com/corp/management/executives_by_busi- ness/aol/bio/falco_randy.html; Saul Hansell, "NBC and Its Stations Venture

Into Online Video Market," *New York Times,* September 13, 2006, at http://www
.nytimes.com/2006/09/13/technology/13nbc.html; Randy Falco, e-mail interview by the author, January 24, 2007.

41. At http://www.ubergizmo.com/15/archives/2005/04/sony_to_release_1
.html.

42. At http://en.wikibooks.org/wiki/Movie_Making_Manual-Digital
_Cinema_Distribution.

43. At http://www.edwardjayepstein.com/prologue.htm; Edward Jay Epstein,
The Big Picture (New York: Random House, 2005).

44. At http://en.wikipedia.org/wiki/Digital_cinema.

45. At http://www.ereader.com/; http://www.gutenberg.org/wiki/Main
_Page.

46. At http://www.motricity.com/.

47. At http://worldlibrary.net/.

48. At http://www.idpf.org/doc_library/statistics/2005.htm.

49. At http://citesandinsights.info/v6i12b.htm.

CHAPTER 7. FINANCERS AND OWNERS OF DIGITAL MEDIA

1. Katharine Q. Seelye and Richard Siklos, "As Time Inc. Cuts Jobs, One Writer
on Britney May Have to Do," *New York Times,* January 15, 2007, at http://www
.nytimes.com/2007/01/15/business/media/15time.html?pagewanted=all.

2. Katharine Q. Seelye, "Time Inc. Cutting Almost 300 Magazine Jobs to Focus
More on Web Sites," *New York Times,* January 19, 2007, at http://www.nytimes
.com/2007/01/19/business/media/19time.html?_r=1&oref=slogin.

3. Maria Aspan, "MEDIA TALK; Layoffs at Paper Prompt Uproar Over Diversity," *New
York Times,* January 15, 2007, at http://www.nytimes.com/2007/01/15/business/
media/15philly.html.

4. At http://www.johnsonpublishing.com/assembled/home.html.

5. Hani A. Durzy, quoted in Louise Story, "Google Mapping an Offline
Course," *New York Times,* November 21, 2006, at http://www.nytimes.com/
2006/11/21/business/media/21adco.html?ei=5088&en=8ba45cd9081973a7&ex
=1321765200&partner=rssnyt&emc=rss&pagewanted=print.

6. At http://www.freepress.net/news/19211.

7. Montague Kern, lecture on media research, Rutgers University, October 25,
2006.

8. Robert G. Picard, *The Economics and Financing of Media Companies* (New
York: Fordham University Press, 2002), 26.

9. Louisa Ha and Richard Ganahl, "Webcasting as an Emerging Global Medium and a Tripartite Framework to Analyze Emerging Media Business Models,"

in Louisa Ha and Richard Ganahl, eds., *Webcasting Worldwide Business Models of an Emerging Global Medium* (New York: Lawrence Erlbaum Associates, 2007), 9.

10. M. S. Ming and B. P. White, "Profiting from Online News: The Search for Viable Business Models," in B. Kahin and R. H. Varian, eds., *Internet Publishing and Beyond: The Economics of Digital Information and Intellectual Property,* 62–97 (Cambridge, Mass.: MIT Press, 2000).

11. At http://music.yahoo.com/.

12. At http://www.nytimes.com/2006/11/19/nyregion/thecity/19vide.html ?_r=1&oref=slogin&ref=thecity&pagewanted=all.

13. At http://biz.yahoo.com/iw/060501/0125983.html.

14. At http://www.yahoo.com.

15. At http://www.craigslist.org/about/cities.html.

16. Carlot Douglas "Chuck D" Ridenhour, keynote address at Technology Now conference, WGBH-TV, Boston, November 9, 2006.

17. At https://www.google.com/adsense/?sourceid=aso&subid=EN-ET-AS-ADS BY7&medium=link.

18. At http://www.onlinejournalism.org/.

19. Robert J. Coen, telephone interview by the author, January 4, 2007; also see http://www.nytimes.com/2006/11/21/business/media/21adco.html?_r =1&oref=slogin&pagewanted=all.

20. Fitch Ratings forecasting report, 2007, available at http://home.business wire.com/portal/site/google/index.jsp?ndmViewId=news_view&newsId=2006 1130005536&newsLang=en.

21. Stuart Elliott, "Code Promotions, a Madison Ave. Staple, Are Going Online," *New York Times,* August 21, 2006, at http://www.nytimes.com/2006/08/21/technology/ 21adco.html.

22. Louise Story and Eric Pfanner, "The Future of Web Ads Is in Britain," *New York Times,* December 4, 2006, at http://www.nytimes.com/2006/12/04/technology/ 04adcol.html.

23. Miguel Helft, "Internet Giants Vie to Snap Up Web Ad Firms," *New York Times,* May 19, 2007, at http://www.nytimes.com/2007/05/19/technology/ 19soft.html?_r=1&hp&oref=slogin.

24. At http://www.youtube.com.

25. At http://www.flickr.com/.

26. At http://www.youtube.com.

27. Louise Story, "Times Sq. Ads Spread Via Tourists' Cameras," *New York Times,* December 11, 2006, at http://www.nytimes.com/2006/12/11/technology/ 11square.html?_r=1&oref=slogin; http://www.oaaa.org/.

28. Louise Story, "MEDIA: ADVERTISING; Digital Billboard Up Ahead: New-Wave Sign or Hazard?" *New York Times,* January 11, 2007, at http://www.nytimes.com/

2007/01/11/business/media/11outdoor.html?_r=1&adxnnl=1&oref=slogin&adx
nnlx=1168531427-hjIlhLnWmtSpkKyfwOPE+w&pagewanted=all.

29. Barnaby Feder, "Billboards That Know You by Name," *New York Times*,
January 29, 2007, at http://www.nytimes.com/2007/01/29/business/media/
29cooper.html.

30. At http://www.akononline.com/6.asp; Jeff Leeds, "Squeezing Money from
the Music," *New York Times*, December 11, 2006, at http://www.nytimes.com/
2006/12/11/business/media/11music.html?pagewanted=all.

31. At http://www.billboard.com/bbcom/bio/index.jsp?pid=491541; http://
indystar.gns.gannett.com/apps/pbcs.dll/article?AID=/20061207/TECH01/6090
70452/1001/TECH.

32. At http://www.wmg.com/news/article/?id=8a0af8120ee82f39010f3b1f1
db140c0.

33. Leeds, "Squeezing Money from the Music."

34. At http://www.suitcaseofcash.com.

35. Matt Richtel, "ADVERTISING; Verizon to Allow Ads on Its Mobile
Phones," *New York Times*, December 26, 2006, at http://www.nytimes.com/
2006/12/26/business/media/26adco.html?ref=technology&pagewanted=all.

36. At http://www.bmwusa.com/bmwexperience/films.htm.

37. At http://www.wired.com/news/culture/0,1284,44323,00.html.

38. At http://www.bmwusa.com/bmwexperience/films.htm.

39. Louise Story, "Brands Produce Their Own Shows," *New York Times*, November 11, 2006, at http://www.nytimes.com/2006/11/10/business/media/10adco
.html?_r=1&oref=slogin&pagewanted=all.

40. At http://www.jsonline.com/story/index.aspx?id=305598.

41. Dale Buss, "A Product-Placement Hall of Fame," *Business Week*, June 22,
1998, at http://www.businessweek.com/1998/25/b3583062.htm.

42. At http://www.snopes.com/business/market/mandms.asp; Danny Thompson, in the interview "ET and M&Ms," *New York Magazine*, December 1, 1993, 21.

43. At http://www.csmonitor.com/2005/0929/p12s02-wmgn.html.

44. At http://www.baltimoresun.com/business/bal-video0403,0,369978.story
?coll=bal-business-indepth.

45. Frank Ahrens, "NBC Taking Big Step Back from Television," *Washington
Post*, October 19, 2006, at http://www.washingtonpost.com/wp-dyn/content/
article/2006/10/19/AR2006101900205.html.

46. Miguel Helft, "The Shifting Business of Renting Movies, by the Disc or the
Click," *New York Times*, January 16, 2007, at http://www.nytimes.com/2007/01/16/
technology/16netflix.html?_r=1&oref=slogin&pagewanted=all.

47. Brad Stone, "I Want a Movie! Now!" *Newsweek*, September 13, 2006, at
http://www.msnbc.msn.com/id/5915470/site/newsweek.

48. At http://www.yale.edu/opa/v28.n29/story7.html.

49. At http://en.wikipedia.org/wiki/Independent_film; http://en.wikipedia.org/wiki/Digital_cinema; http://history.acusd.edu/gen/filmnotes/costs-movies.html.

50. At http://www.paypal.com.

51. At http://www.thenewtechnopolis.com/ballad.html.

52. Media Metrix, at http://www.comscore.com/press/release.asp?id=361.

53. At http://www.rocketboom.com.

54. At http://www.tuaw.com/2005/11/03/interview-with-andrew-baron-from-rocketboom/.

55. Scripps-Howard Research, *Economic Support of Mass Communication Media: 1929–1957* (New York: Scripps-Howard, 1959); Michel Dupagne, "Testing the Relative Constancy of Mass Media Expenditures in the United Kingdom," *Journal of Media Economics* 17, no. 3 (1994): 1–14 (doi:10.1207/s15327736me0703_1); http://www.leaonline.com/doi/abs/10.1207/s15327736me0703_1;jsessionid=olxCTbDrjd4cTK_KAQ?cookieSet=1&journalCode=me; Min Hang, "Venturing for Success: New Business Creation in Media Organizations," paper presented at the Seventh World Media Economics Conference, May 2006, Beijing; G. Y. Noh, "New Media Departure in the Principle of Relative Constancy: VCRs," paper presented at the annual convention of the Association for Education in Journalism and Mass Communication, August 1994, Atlanta, Georgia, sponsored by the Samsung Economic Institute, available at http://list.msu.edu/cgi-bin/wa?A2=ind9712e&L=aejmc&T=0&P=354; M. E. McCombs, "Mass Media in the Marketplace," *Journalism Monographs* 24 (1972): 1–102, at http://www.yale.edu/opa/v28.n29/story7.html; M. E. McCombs and C. H. Eyal, "Spending on Mass Media," *Journal of Communication* 31, no. 1 (1980): 153–58; M. E. McCombs and J. Son, "Patterns of Economic Support for Mass Media During a Decade of Electronic Innovation," paper presented at the annual convention of the Association for Education in Journalism and Mass Communication, Norman, Oklahoma, August 1986.

56. Michael A. Noll, "The Digital Mystique: A Review of Digital Technology and Its Applications to Television," paper presented at the conference "The Future of Digital TV," November 13, 1997, Davis Auditorium, Columbia University, sponsored by the Columbia Institute for Tele-Information, available at http://www.citi.columbia.edu/digtv.htm.

57. Tom Haymond, VP/GM, NY10-Taxi Entertainment Network, Clear Channel Taxi Media, e-mail interview by author, January 8, 2007; see also http://www.clearchannel.com/Outdoor/PressRelease.aspx?PressReleaseID=1862.

58. Philip Tichenor, George Donohue, and Clarice Olien, "Mass Media and the Knowledge Gap: A Hypothesis Reconsidered," *Communication Research* 2, no. 1

(1975): 3–23; see also http://www.ntia.doc.gov/ntiahome/speeches/urban62698 .htm.

59. At http://www.stateofthenewsmedia.org/2006/printable_radio_audience.asp.

60. At http://www.arbitron.com/national_radio/home.htm.

61. At http://www.foxnews.com/story/0,2933,145455,00.html.

62. Harvey Nagler, lecture on careers in radio, delivered at Rutgers University, October 13, 2006.

63. At http://www.pcworld.com/article/id,123760-page,1/article.html.

64. At http://thelede.blogs.nytimes.com/2006/11/17/gaming-on-the-play station/.

65. At http://blog.wired.com/games/2006/11/isupply_ps3_com.html.

66. At http://www.forbes.com/technology/2007/01/12/gaming.

67. At http://www.businessweek.com/ap/financialnews/D8LSSJKG0.htm.

68. Herbert Howard, "TV Station Ownership Consolidation: 1940–2005," *Journalism Monographs* (June 2006): 1–79.

69. Ben H. Bagdikian, *Media Monopoly,* 6th ed. (Boston: Beacon Press, 2000).

70. Edgard Morin, *Articular los saberes* (Buenos Aires: Universidad de Belgrano, 1999).

71. At http://google-ipo.com/index.html.

CHAPTER 8. REGULATION AND LAW OF DIGITAL MEDIA

1. At http://www.usconstitution.net/xconst_Am1.html.

2. At http://memory.loc.gov/ammem/help/constRedir.html.

3. At http://cryptome.org/decss-1a.htm; http://www.bc.edu/bc_org/avp/cas/ comm/free_speech/near.html.

4. *New York Times Co. v. Sullivan,* 376 U.S. 254 (1964).

5. At http://www.eff.org/bloggers/lg/; http://wiki.creativecommons.org/Pod casting_Legal_Guide.

6. At http://www.cyberjournalist.net/news/000420.php.

7. "China Blocks News not Porn Online," *BBC News,* December 4, 2002, at http://news.bbc.co.uk/2/hi/technology/2540309.stm.

8. At http://www.copyright.gov/legislation/dmca.pdf.

9. Laura M. Holson, "Hollywood Asks YouTube: Friend or Foe?" *New York Times,* January 15, 2007, at http://www.nytimes.com/2007/01/15/technology/15youtube .html?_r=1&oref=slogin&pagewanted=all.

10. At http://thomas.loc.gov/cgi-bin/query/z?c105:H.R.2281.ENR:.

11. At http://en.wikipedia.org/wiki/Copyright.

12. At http://www.copyright.gov/title17/.

13. Noam Cohen, "Bloggers Take on Talk Radio Hosts," *New York Times,* January 15, 2007, at http://www.nytimes.com/2007/01/15/technology/15radio.html; see also http://spockosbrain.com.

14. At http://www.copyright.gov/title17/92chap3.html.

15. *Eldred v. Ashcroft* (01-618) 537 U.S. 186 (2003) 239 F.3d 372, affirmed.

16. At http://www.copyright.gov/circs/circ45.html.

17. At http://en.wikipedia.org/wiki/Copyright.

18. Jacqui Cheng, "Topics in Economic Analysis and Policy," September 26, 2006, at http://arstechnica.com/news.ars/post/20060926–7832.html.

19. Alejandro Zentner, "File Sharing and International Sales of Copyrighted Music: An Empirical Analysis with a Panel of Countries," *B.E. Journal of Economic Analysis and Policy* 5, no. 1 (2005) (Topics), Article 21, available at http://www.bepress.com/bejeap/topics/vol5/iss1/art21.

20. Stan J. Liebowitz, "File Sharing: Creative Destruction or Just Plain Destruction?" *Journal of Law and Economics* 49 (2006): 1–28 (doi: 10.1086/503518); Rob Rafael and Joel Waldfogel, *Piracy on the High C's: Music Downloading, Sales Displacement, and Social Welfare in a Sample of College Students,* National Bureau of Economic Research (NBER) Working Paper no. W10874 (Washington, D.C.: NBER, November 2004); Seung-Hyun Hong, "The Effect of Digital Technology on the Sales of Copyrighted Goods: Evidence from Napster," working paper, 2004.

21. Felix Oberholzer and Koleman Strumpf, "The Effect of File Sharing on Record Sales: An Empirical Analysis," March 2004, University of North Carolina occasional paper, at http://www.unc.edu/~cigar/papers/FileSharing_March2004.pdf#search=%22unc%20harvard%20paper%.

22. A 2004 survey of artists and musicians by the Pew Internet and American Life Project, at http://www.pewinternet.org/PPF/r/142/report_display.asp.

23. At http://en.wikipedia.org/wiki/Copyright.

24. Berne Convention, 1886, available at http://www.law-ref.org/BERN/kw-country.html; http://www.wipo.int/treaties/en/ip/berne/index.html; see also http://en.wikipedia.org/wiki/Copyright.

25. At http://www.iht.com/articles/2007/01/21/yourmoney/music.php.

26. At http://www.ffii.org/.

27. At http://www.Blu-ray.com/; http://www.thelookandsoundofperfect.com/?utm_source=google&utm_medium=cpc.

28. William K. Rashbaum, "Law Put to Unusual Use in Hezbollah TV Case, Some Say," *New York Times,* August 26, 2006, at http://www.nytimes.com/2006/08/26/nyregion/26hezbollah.html?_r=1&oref=slogin.

29. Tom Zeller Jr., "Times Withholds Web Article in Britain," *New York Times,* August 29, 2006, at http://www.nytimes.com/2006/08/29/business/media/29times.html?_r=1&oref=slogin.

30. At http://opennetinitiative.org.

31. At http://www.kcckp.net/en/.

32. At http://psiphon.civisec.org.

33. At http://www.youtube.com/watch?v=1dmVU08zVpA.

34. Jacques Steinberg, "Censored 'SNL' Sketch Jumps Bleepless Onto the Internet," *New York Times,* December 21, 2006, at http://www.nytimes.com/2006/12/21/arts/television/21sket.html?_r=1&oref=slogin.

35. At http://www.ala.org/ala/pr2004/prfeb2004/NewReportFindsLibrari.htm; http://www.ntia.doc.gov/ntiahome/speeches/urban62698.htm.

36. Reverend Martin Luther King Jr., "Sermon. March 31, 1968," in *A Knock at Midnight: Inspiration from the Great Sermons of Reverend Martin Luther King, Jr.: Remaining Awake Through a Great Revolution, Congressional Record* 114 (9 April 1968): 9395–397, also available at http://www.stanford.edu/group/King/publications/sermons/680331.000_Remaining_Awake.html.

37. Telecommunications Act of 1996, Section 251(3)(2)(B), at http://www.fcc.gov/telecom.html.

38. At http://www.fcc.gov/Reports/1934new.pdf.

39. At http://www.fcc.gov/eb/Orders/2003/DA-03–3513A1.html.

40. At http://www.museum.tv/archives/etv/M/htmlM/mustcarryru/mustcarryru.htm.

41. Robert W. McChesney, *The Problem of the Media* (New York: Monthly Review Press, 2004), 53.

42. At http://www.museum.tv/archives/etv/F/htmlF/financialint/financialint.htm.

43. Section 251(3)(2)(B), at http://www.fcc.gov/telecom.html.

44. At http://en.wikipedia.org/wiki/Telecommunications_Act_of_1996.

45. Jacques Steinberg, "Stern Likes His New Censor: Himself," *New York Times,* January 9, 2007, at http://www.nytimes.com/2007/01/09/arts/09ster.html?_r=1&oref=slogin&pagewanted=all.

46. At http://www.fcc.gov/Bureaus/Mass_Media/News_Releases/2000/nrmm0031.html.

47. David Von Drehle, "FBI's No. 2 Was 'Deep Throat': Mark Felt Ends 30-Year Mystery of the Post's Watergate Source," *Washington Post,* June 1, 2005, A1.

48. At http://sf.metblogs.com/archives/2006/08/local_blogger_josh_wolf_jailed.phtml.

49. At http://oldmaison.blogspot.com.

50. John Wicklein, *Electronic Nightmare: The Home Communications Set and Your Freedom* (Boston: Beacon, 1981).

51. Quoted from Kevin Maney, "AOL, Search, and the Twilight Zone," *USA Today,* August 9, 2006, C21.

52. At http://www.comedycentral.com/motherload/index.jhtml?ml_video=72423.

53. Noah Shachtman, "Big Brother Gets a Brain," The Village Voice, July 9, 2003, at http://www.villagevoice.com/news/0328,shachtman,45399,1.html.

54. At http://www.google.com/help/netneutrality.html.

55. At http://dig.csail.mit.edu/breadcrumbs/node/132.

56. At http://action.freepress.net/campaign/savethenet.

57. At http://www.congress.gov/cgi-bin/bdquery/z?d109:HR05252; http://arstechnica.com/news.ars/post/20060328–6474.html.

58. At http://thomas.loc.gov/cgi-bin/bdquery/z?d109:s.02686; http://www.benton.org/index.php?q=node/2173.

59. At http://markey.house.gov/index.php?option=com_content&task=view&id=2536&Itemid=138.

CHAPTER 9. PRODUCTION AND PROTECTION OF DIGITAL MEDIA

1. At http://www.thebollard.com/story_interviews/topper_carew_11.1.05.html.

2. At http://www.urbanneo.com/.

3. Topper Carew, comments made on a panel at the Technology Now conference produced by the National Black Programming Consortium, hosted by WGBH, Boston, November 8, 2006.

4. See Shree Nayar's Web page at http://www.cs.columbia.edu/~nayar.

5. John Biggs, "A Discreet Voice Recorder for Your 275-Hour Podcast," New York Times, January 11, 2007, at http://www.nytimes.com/2007/01/11/technology/11record.html?ref=technology.

6. John Biggs, "Wonder Where You Wander? This Mobile Phone Can Tell You," New York Times, January 11, 2007, at http://www.nytimes.com/2007/01/11/technology/11phone.html?ref=technology.

7. See http://www.pgpi.org.

8. John V. Pavlik, Journalism and New Media (New York: Columbia University Press, 2001), 99–122.

9. At http://www.washingtonpost.com/wp-dyn/articles/A22880–2001Oct7.html.

10. At http://www.7e.com/content/products/thr.html.

11. Dan Dubno, "GPS Devices: Finding Yourself," CBS News, July 20, 2006, at http://cbsnews.com/network/htdocs/digitaldan/; http://cbsnews.com/network/htdocs/digitaldan/disaster/disasters.htm.

12. At http://www.assignmenteditor.com/.

13. At http://www.mediachannel.org/getinvolved/journo/.

14. At http://ojr.usc.edu/content/story.cfm?ID=489.

15. See http://www.google.com; http://www.altavista.com; http://www.hotbot.com.

16. For example, a metatag could be <META name="something" content="something else">; at http://www.philb.com/metatag.htm.

17. At http://directory.google.com/.

18. At http://www.realnetworks.com/resources/howto/mobile/using_helix.html.

19. At http://service.real.com/help/library/guides/realone/ProductionGuide/HTML/realpgd.htm?page=htmfiles/video.htm%23optimize.

20. See http://www.devx.com/xml/Article/10790/1954?pf=true (requires programming) or http://www.bloglines.com/ (easier but less customization possible).

21. At http://computer.howstuffworks.com/encryption.htm.

22. Brad Stone, "A DVD Copy Protection Is Overcome by Hackers," *New York Times,* January 17, 2007, at http://www.nytimes.com/2007/01/17/technology/17movie.html?_r=1&oref=slogin.

23. At http://www.webopedia.com/TERM/D/digital_watermark.html.

24. At http://www.citypaper.com/news/story.asp?id=11466.

25. At http://www.nbpc.tv/.

26. See http://www.washingtonpost.com/wp-adv/ mediacenter/html/Katrina_092606.htm.

27. At http://www.natas.org.

CHAPTER 10. INVENTORS AND INNOVATORS OF DIGITAL MEDIA

1. John V. Pavlik, "Plowing the Online Field of Dreams: Effects of the Online Video Explosion," *Television Quarterly* 37, no. 1 (fall 2006): 15–21.

2. At http://www.farnovision.com/chronicles/tfc-part01.html.

3. At http://www.cnri.reston.va.us/bios/kahn.html.

4. At http://www.livinginternet.com/w/wi_nelson.htm.

5. At http://www.w3.org/People/Berners-Lee/Kids.

6. At http://info.cern.ch/.

7. At http://www.gutenberg.org/wiki/Gutenberg:About.

8. At http://onlinebooks.library.upenn.edu/webbin/bparchive?year=2006&post=2006–05–30,2.

9. W. E. B. Du Bois, *The Suppression of the African Slave-Trade to the United States of America, 1638–1870* (Manchester: Cornerhouse, 1970; originally published in 1896).

10. At http://www.gutenberg.org/browse/authors/s#a2960.

11. At http://www.gutenberg.org/etext/9056.

12. See http://www.librivox.org.

13. At http://www.math.buffalo.edu/mad/computer-science/dean_mark.html.

14. At http://www.math.buffalo.edu/mad/computer-science/dean_mark.html.

15. See http://www.huffingtonpost.com.

16. Walter Cronkite, "Telling the Truth About the War on Drugs," Huffingtonpost.com, March 1, 2006, at http://www.huffingtonpost.com/walter-cronkite/telling-the-truth-about-t_b_16605.html.

17. Kathleen Reardon, "Health Bigots: Another Reason to Vote for Change," Huffingtonpost.com, October 23, 2006, at http://www.huffingtonpost.com/kathleen-reardon/health-bigots-another-r_b_32294.html.

18. At http://thepolitico.com/ourgoal.html.

19. At http://www.gather.com/.

20. At http://www.xmradio.com/programming/index.jsp.

21. At http://www.media.mit.edu/.

22. At http://en.wikipedia.org/wiki/Steve_Mann; http://genesis.eecg.toronto.edu/; http://www.eecg.toronto.edu/~mann/.

23. At http://www.usc.edu/uscnews/stories/12520.html; see also http://www.pbs.org/newshour/bb/media/jan-june07/media_01–01.html.

24. At http://viterbi.usc.edu/news/news/2006/news_20060201.htm.

25. At http://www.mediabistro.com/tvnewser/.

26. Julie Bosman, "The Kid with All the News About the TV News," *New York Times,* November 20, 2006, at http://www.nytimes.com/2006/11/20/business/media/20newser.html?ei=5094&en=c59846000bdadb8b&hp=&ex=1164085200&partner=homepage&pagewanted=all.

27. See http://www.redbankgreen.com.

28. See http://www.thebeehive.org/wbnn.

29. David Koller, "Origin of the Name 'Google,'" lecture at Stanford University, January 2004.

30. Google citing *Wikipedia* at http://googlesystem.blogspot.com/2007/07/googles-evolution-as-seen-on-wikipedia.html.

31. Scott Harris, "Dictionary Adds Verb: To Google," *San Jose Mercury News,* July 7, 2006, at http://www.mercurynews.com/mld/mercurynews/business/14985574.htm; http://www.m-w.com/dictionary/google.

32. At http://books.google.com/books?vid=ISBN0415315026&id=rHh2sMbDBjwC&pg=PA5&lpg=PA5&ots=LKWoCV11bo&dq=john+pavlik&sig=GNWbMOCE6W0TvakdKT-8omn7WOo.

33. Joseph O'Sullivan, "Do You Google?" at http://googleblog.blogspot.com/2004/12/all-booked-up.html; Adam Smith, "All Booked Up," December 14, 2004, Googleblog.

34. See http://www.nbpc.tv.

35. See http://www.mcchesney.com.

36. *Red Lion Broadcasting Co. v. FCC* (1969), available at http://www.epic.org/free_speech/red_lion.html.

37. See http://www.freepress.net/.

38. Dale Cripps, "From the Father of HDTV in U.S.A.—Dr. Joseph Flaherty. CBS—1995," *HDTV Magazine,* June 16, 2005, at http://www.hdtvmagazine.com/history/2005/06/from_the_father.php.

39. At http://www.ascendantimage.com/joseph_a__flaherty,_jr_.htm.

CHAPTER 11. ETHICAL CONSIDERATIONS IN THE DIGITAL AGE

1. Gisele Durham, "Ethics Group Says Too Many Teens Immoral," *Chicago Sun-Times,* January 17, 2000, at http://www.suntimes.com/output/business/cst-fin-ethics12.html.

2. H. Eugene Goodwin, *Groping for Ethics in Journalism* (Ames: Iowa State University Press, 1983).

3. *The Siegal Report* (New York: New York Times Company, 2003), available at http://www.nytco.com/press.html.

4. "The Story," *Washington Post,* April 19, 1981, A12, A15.

5. At http://bztv.typepad.com/instanthistory/2005/07/ojs_arrest.html.

6. Larry Gross, John Stuart Katz, and Jay Ruby, eds., *Image Ethics in the Digital Age* (Minneapolis: University of Minnesota Press 2003), 23.

7. Bruno Latour, *Science in Action: How to Follow Scientists and Engineers Through Society* (Cambridge, Mass.: Harvard University Press, 1987).

8. At http://usinfo.state.gov/usa/infousa/facts/funddocs/billeng.htm.

9. At http://journalism.nyu.edu/pubzone/weblogs/pressthink/2003/10/28/missing_link_p.html.

10. See http://drogo.cselt.it/fipa/.

11. See http://Nando.net.

12. At http://www.forteinc.com/forte/agent/index.html; http://www.ferretsoft.com/netferret/newsferret.htm.

13. Television Digest with Consumer Electronics, "CBS Denies Digital Deception—Use of Digital Technology to Cover NBC Logo in Times Square—Brief Article," Warren Group Publishing, January 17, 2000, at http://www.findarticles.com/p/articles/mi_m3169/is_3_40/ai_59184768.

14. American Business Media, "Editorial Code of Ethics," March 2005, at http://www.americanbusinessmedia.com/images/abm/pdfs/committees/EdEthics.pdf.

15. From *The Siegal Report.*

16. See http://www.Televisionwithoutpity.com.

17. Maria Aspan, "TV Is Now Interactive, Minus Images, on the Web," *New York Times,* July 8, 2006, at http://www.nytimes.com/2006/07/08/arts/television/08fans.html?_r=1&oref=slogin&pagewanted=all.

18. See http://www.acejmc.org.

19. Editorial Desk, "Spies, Lies, and Wiretaps," *New York Times,* January 29, 2006, at http://www.nytimes.com/2006/01/29/opinion/29sun1.html?ex=1296190800&en=4785bb029b806e38&ei=5090.

20. See http://www.turnitin.com.

21. At http://www.ithenticate.com/static/publishing.html.

22. Daniel J. Boorstin, *The Image: A Guide to Pseudo-events in America* (New York: Vintage Books, 1961).

23. John Pavlik, "Disguised as News," *Television Quarterly* 36, no. 3 (2006): 17–25, available at http://www.tvquarterly.net/tvq_36_3/media/articles/36.3 Disguised_as_news.pdf.

24. Dan Berkowitz and Douglas B. Adams, "Information Subsidy and Agenda-Building in Local Television News," *Journalism and Mass Communication Quarterly* 67 (1990): 723–31.

25. John H. Minnis and Cornelius B. Pratt, "Newsroom Socialization and the Press Release: Implications for Media Relations," paper presented at the annual convention of the Association for Education in Journalism and Mass Communication, Atlanta, Georgia, August 1994, sponsored by the Samsung Economic Institute.

26. David Barstow and Robin Stein, "THE MESSAGE MACHINE: How the Government Makes News; Under Bush, a New Age of Prepackaged News," *New York Times,* March 13, 2005, at http://www.nytimes.com/2005/03/13/politics/13covert.html?ei=5090&en=c040ac38c7b344fa&ex=1268370000&pagewanted=all&position =.

27. At http://www.truthout.org/cgi-bin/artman/exec/view.cgi/37/9592.

28. Anne R. Owen and James A. Karrh, "Video News Releases: Effects on Viewer Recall and Attitudes," *Public Relations Review* 22, no. 369 (winter 1996): 369–78.

29. At http://web.missouri.edu/~jourvs/gtvops.html.

30. Mark D. Harmon and Candace White, "How Television News Programs Use Video News Releases," *Public Relations Review* 27, no. 3 (June 22, 2001): 231–22.

31. Scott Atkinson, telephone interview by the author, January 12, 2006.

32. Jeff Wurtz, e-mail interview by the author, January 10, 2006.

33. See http://www.rtnda.com.

34. See http://www.prwatch.org.

35. At http://www.prwatch.org/fakenews/vnr4.

36. At http://medialit.med.sc.edu/news_sources.htm.

37. John Frazee, telephone interview by the author, January 10, 2006.

38. At http://www.newspath.cbs.com/; http://www.newspath.cbs.com/html/nove.html.

39. At http://www.newspath.cbs.com/.

40. At http://newsource.cnn.com/.

41. Michelle Williams Sr., director of contracts, CNN News Services, e-mail interview by the author, January 12, 2006.

42. CBS Newspath VNR Feed, at http://www.newspath.cbs.com/html/nove.html.

43. CNN Newsource, at http://newsource.cnn.com/; CBS Newspath, at http://www.newspath.cbs.com; ABC NewsOne, at http://abcnews.go.com/Reference/story?id=141275&page=2 =.

44. Harmon and White, "How Television News Programs Use Video News Releases."

45. Glen T. Cameron and David Blount, "VNRs and Air Checks: A Content Analysis of the Use of Video News Releases in Television Newscasts," *Journalism and Mass Communication Quarterly* 73, no. 1 (winter 1996): 890–904.

46. Ed Lamoureax, WestGlen Communications, telephone interview by the author, January 22, 2006.

47. Harmon and White, "How Television News Programs Use Video News Releases," 213.

48. See http://www.priceline.com.

49. At http://www.nielsenmedia.com/monitor-plus/SIGMA/index.html.

50. See http://www.vmsinfo.com.

51. At http://www.medialink.com/pressreleases2004/030904.htm.

52. At http://www.nielsenmedia.com/monitor-plus/SIGMA/index.html.

53. At http://www.medialink.com/pressreleases2004/030904.htm.

54. Lamoureax, telephone interview, January 22, 2006.

55. David Lieberman, "Fake News," *TV Guide* (February 22, 1992), 22–28.

56. See http://www.gao.gov.

57. At http://www.sourcewatch.org/index.php?title=Fake_news.

58. At http://www.prwatch.org/node/3790; http://hraunfoss.fcc.gov/edocs_public/attachmatch/FCC-05–84A1.doc.

59. Lamoureax, telephone interview, January 22, 2006.

CHAPTER 12. CHILDREN AND DIGITAL MEDIA

1. At http://www.answers.com/topic/history-of-sesame-street.

2. The Kaiser Family Foundation Media Studies, at http://www.KFF.org; the Pew Internet and American Life Project, at http://www.pewInternet.org; Comscore

Metrics report cited in Steve Rosenbush, "Users Crowd Into MySpace," *Business Week,* November 15, 2005, at http://www.businessweek.com/print/technology/content/nov2005/tc20051115_908925.htm; NowPublic at http://www.nowpublic.com/myspace_stats; Bloomberg/*Los Angeles Times* and Harris polls 2005–2006.

3. At http://www.siliconrepublic.com/news/news.nv?storyid=single5957.

4. Carla Seal-Wanner, "eTEENS: Teens and Technology . . . the *Perfect Storm?*" *Television Quarterly* 37, no. 2 (winter 2006): 5–16.

5. At http://www.nationalchildrensstudy.gov/events/ncs_assembly/2004_January/report012004.cfm.

6. At http://www.netfamilynews.org/nl060317.html.

7. At http://www.nettime.org/Lists-Archives/nettime-l-9908/msg00118.html.

8. At http://www.asha.org/pressevent/zogby.htm.

9. Larry Magid, "Some Hot Recorders for Those Cool Podcasts," *New York Times,* September 21, 2006, at http://www.nytimes.com/2006/09/21/technology/21basics.html?pagewanted=all.

10. At http://www.thewiggles.com.au/.

11. James C. Rosser, telephone interview by the author, January 17, 2007.

12. At http://www.msnbc.msn.com/id/4685909/.

13. Seth Schiesel, "P.E. Classes Turn to Video Game That Works Legs," *New York Times,* April 30, 2007, at http://www.nytimes.com/2007/04/30/health/30exer.html?_r=1&hp&oref=slogin.

14. At http://www.brainage.com.

15. James C. Rosser, *Playin' to Win: A Cybersurgeon, Scientist, and Parent Makes the Case for the Upside of Videogames* (New York: Morgan James, forthcoming).

16. Philip Jenkins, *Beyond Tolerance: Child Pornography on the Internet* (New York: New York University Press, 2001).

17. Kurt Eichenwald, "On the Web, Pedophiles Extend Their Reach," *New York Times,* August 21, 2006, at http://www.nytimes.com/2006/08/21/technology/21pedo.html?ei=5094&en=79822c4e3a3e6773&hp=&ex=1156219200&partner=homepage&pagewanted=all.

18. At http://perverted-justice.com/.

19. At http://www.whitepages.com/9900/.

20. At http://www.realvnc.com.

21. The term *Orwellian* refers to the notions outlined in George Orwell's dystopian novel of the future, set in 1984, when a totalitarian government tightly controls the lives of its citizens. George Orwell, *Nineteen Eighty-Four* (London: Martin Secker and Warburg Ltd., 1949); see http://www.liferesearchuniversal.com/orwell.html.

22. At http://www.benetsafe.com.

23. At http://www.pewinternet.org/press_release.asp?r=134.

24. At http://images.google.com/.

25. At http://www.stickam.com/.

26. At http://en.wikipedia.org/wiki/Mobile_phone_radiation_and_health.

27. Quoted in Emil Pascarelli, *Dr. Pascarelli's Complete Guide to Repetitive Strain Injury: What You Need to Know About RSI and Carpal Tunnel Syndrome* (New York: John Wiley and Sons, 2004).

28. At http://www.rsna.org/rsna/media/pr2006–2/aching_back-2.cfm.

29. At http://www.thetvboss.com.

BIBLIOGRAPHY

Adorno, Theodor W. Negative Dialectics. Translated by E. B. London. New York: Routledge, 1973. Available at http://www.marxists.org/reference/archive/adorno/1966/negative-dialectics/index.htm.

Bagdikian, Ben H. Media Monopoly. 6th ed. Boston: Beacon Press, 2000.

Barbero, Jesús Martín. De los medios a las mediaciones. Bogotá, Columbia: Convenio Andrés Bello, 1998.

Baudrillard, Jean. The Vital Illusion. Wellek Library Lectures at the University of California at Irvine. New York: Columbia University Press, 2000.

Berkowitz, Dan, and Douglas B. Adams. "Information Subsidy and Agenda-Building in Local Television News." Journalism and Mass Communication Quarterly 67 (1990): 723–31.

Bernstein, Carl, and Bob Woodward. All the President's Men. New York: Touchstone, 1974.

Boczkowski, Pablo J. Digitizing the News. Cambridge, Mass.: MIT Press, 2005.

Boorstin, Daniel J. The Image: A Guide to Pseudo-events in America. New York: Vintage Books, 1961.

Cameron, Glen T., and David Blount. "VNRs and Air Checks: A Content Analysis of the Use of Video News Releases in Television Newscasts." Journalism and Mass Communication Quarterly 73, no. 1 (winter 1996): 890–904.

Carey, John. "An Ethnographic Study of Interactive Television." Paper presented at Rutgers University, October 28, 2002.

Carey, John, and Lawrence Greenberg. "And the Emmy Goes to . . . a Mobisode?" Television Quarterly 36, no. 2 (winter 2006): 3–8. Available at http://www.tvquarterly.net/p3.html.

Du Bois, W. E. B. The Suppression of the African Slave-Trade to the United States of America, 1638–1870. Manchester: Cornerhouse, 1970; originally published in 1896.

Dupagne, Michel. Testing the Relative Constancy of Mass Media Expenditures in the United Kingdom. Journal of Media Economics 7, no. 3 (1994): 1–14 (

doi:10.1207/s15327736me0703_1). Available at http://www.leaonline.com/doi/abs/10.1207/s15327736me0703_1;jsessionid=olxCTbDrjd4cTK_KAQ?cookieSet=1&journalCode=me.

Epstein, Edward Jay. The Big Picture. New York: Random House, 2005.

García-Canclini, Nestor. La producción simbólica: Teoría y método en sociología del arte, siglo XXI. Mexico City: Editores, S.A., 1979.

Goodwin, H. Eugene. Groping for Ethics in Journalism. Des Moines: Iowa State University Press, 1983.

Gramsci, Antonio. Selections from the Prison Notebooks. London: Lawrence and Wishart, 1971.

Gross, Larry, John Stuart Katz, and Jay Ruby, eds. Image Ethics in the Digital Age. Minneapolis: University of Minnesota Press, 2003.

Ha, Louisa, and Richard Ganahl, eds. Webcasting Worldwide Business Models of an Emerging Global Medium. Englewood, N.J.: Lawrence Erlbaum Associates, 2007.

Habermas, Jürgen. The Structural Transformation of the Public Sphere: An Inquiry Into a Category of Bourgeois Society. Studies in Contemporary German Social Thought. Reprint. Cambridge, Mass.: MIT Press, 1991.

Hang, Min. "Venturing for Success: New Business Creation in Media Organizations." Paper presented at the Seventh World Media Economics Conference, Beijing, May 2006.

Harmon, Mark D., and Candace White. 2001. "How Television News Programs Use Video News Releases." Public Relations Review 27, no. 3 (June 22): 213–22.

Hong, Seung-Hyun. "The Effect of Digital Technology on the Sales of Copyrighted Goods: Evidence from Napster." Working paper, 2004.

Horkheimer, Max. "Enlightenment as Mass Deception." 1944. Available at http://www.marxists.org/reference/archive/adorno/1944/culture-industry.htm.

Jenkins, Philip. Beyond Tolerance: Child Pornography on the Internet. New York: New York University Press, 2001.

Jensen, Robert. "Embedded Media Give Up Independence." Boston Globe, April 7, 2003, 19.

Jensen, Robert. Writing Dissent: Taking Radical Ideas from the Margins to the Mainstream. New York: Peter Lang, 2001.

Kaiser Family Foundation Media Studies. Web site, 2006, at http://www.KFF.org.

Kern, Montague. Lecture on media research given at Rutgers University, October 25, 2006.

King, Rev. Martin Luther, Jr. A Knock at Midnight: Inspiration from the Great Sermons of Reverend Martin Luther King, Jr.: Remaining Awake Through a Great Revolution. Congressional Record 114 (April 9, 1968): 9395–397. Also available at http://www.stanford.edu/group/King/publications/sermons/680331.000_Remaining_Awake.html.

Latour, Bruno. Science in Action: How to Follow Scientists and Engineers Through Society. Cambridge, Mass.: Harvard University Press, 1987.

Levy, Pierre. Les technologies de l'intelligence: L'avenir de la pensée à l'ère informatique (Technologies of Intelligence. The Future of Thought in the Computer Age). Paris: La Découverte, 1990.

Liebowitz, Stan J. "File Sharing: Creative Destruction or Just Plain Destruction?" Journal of Law and Economics 49 (2006): 1–28 (doi: 10.1086/503518).

McChesney, Robert W. The Problem of the Media. New York: Monthly Review Press, 2004.

McCombs, M. E. "Mass Media in the Marketplace." Journalism Monographs no. 24 (1972): 1–104.

McCombs, M. E., and C. H. Eyal. "Spending on Mass Media." Journal of Communication 31, no. 1 (1980): 153–58.

McCombs, M. E., and J. Son. "Patterns of Economic Support for Mass Media During a Decade of Electronic Innovation." Paper presented at the annual convention of the Association for Education in Journalism and Mass Communication, Norman, Oklahoma, August 1986.

Middleberg, D., and S. S. Ross. The Middleberg/Ross Media in Cyberspace Survey: Change and Its Impact on Communications. Eighth annual national survey. New York: Middleberg and Associates, 2002. Available at http://www.middleberg.com.

Miller, James G. Living Systems Theory: Issues for Management Thought and Practice. New York: McGraw-Hill, 1978.

Ming, M. S., and B. P. White. "Profiting from Online News: The Search for Viable Business Models." In B. Kahin and R. H. Varian, eds., Internet Publishing and Beyond: The Economics of Digital Information and Intellectual Property, 62–97. Cambridge, Mass.: MIT Press, 2000.

Minnis, John H., and Cornelius B. Pratt. "Newsroom Socialization and the Press Release: Implications for Media Relations." Paper presented at the annual convention of the Association for Education in Journalism and Mass Communication, Atlanta, Georgia, August 1994, sponsored by the Samsung Economic Institute.

Morin, Edgard. Articular los saberes. Belgrano, Argentina: Universidad de Belgrano, 1999.

Noh, G. Y. "New Media Departure in the Principle of Relative Constancy: VCRs." Paper presented at the annual convention of the Association for Education in Journalism and Mass Communication, Atlanta, Georgia, August 1994, sponsored by the Samsung Economic Institute. Available at http://list.msu.edu/cgi-bin/wa?A2=ind9712e&L=aejmc&T=0&P=354.

Noll, Michael A. "The Digital Mystique: A Review of Digital Technology and Its Applications to Television." Paper presented at the conference "The Future of

Digital TV," Columbia University, November 1997, sponsored by the Columbia Institute for Tele-Information. Available at http://www.citi.columbia.edu/digtv.htm.

Oberholzer, Felix, and Koleman Strumpf. "The Effect of File Sharing on Record Sales: An Empirical Analysis." University of North Carolina occasional paper. March 2004. Available at http://www.unc.edu/~cigar/papers/FileSharing_March2004.pdf#search=%22unc%20harvard%20paper%.

Owen, Anne R., and James A. Karrh. "Video News Releases: Effects on Viewer Recall and Attitudes." Public Relations Review 22, no. 369 (winter 1996): 369–78.

Pavlik, John. "Disguised as News." Television Quarterly 36, no. 3 (2006): 17–25. Available at http://www.tvquarterly.net/tvq_36_3/media/articles/36.3Disguised_as_news.pdf.

Pavlik, John V. Journalism and New Media. New York: Columbia University Press, 2001.

Pavlik, John V. "Plowing the Online Field of Dreams: Effects of the Online Video Explosion." Television Quarterly 37, no. 1 (fall 2006): 15–21.

Pew Internet and American Life Project. Web site, 2007, available at http://www.pewInternet.org.

Picard, Robert G. The Economics and Financing of Media Companies. New York: Fordham University Press, 2002.

Postman, Neil. Technopoly: The Surrender of Culture to Technology. New York: Vintage Books, 1993.

Rafael, Rob, and Joel Waldfogel. Piracy on the High C's: Music Downloading, Sales Displacement, and Social Welfare in a Sample of College Students. National Bureau of Economic Research (NBER) Working Paper no. W10874. Washington, D.C.: NBER.

Rosenstiel, Tom. "Project for Excellence in Journalism: Election Night 2006. An Evening in the Life of the American Media, November 27, 2006." December 1, 2006. Available at http://www.journalism.org/node/3015.

Scripps-Howard Research. Economic Support of Mass Communication Media: 1929–1957. New York: Scripps-Howard Research, 1959.

Seal-Wanner, Carla. "eTEENS: Teens and Technology . . . the Perfect Storm?" Television Quarterly 37, no. 2 (winter 2006): 5–16.

Siegal Report. New York: New York Times Company, 2003. Available at http://www.nytco.com/press.html.

Tichenor, Philip, George Donohue, and Clarice Olien. "Mass Media and the Knowledge Gap: A Hypothesis Reconsidered." Communication Research 2, no. 1 (1975): 3–23.

Vilches, Lorenzo. La televisión: Los efectos del bien y del mal. Barcelona, Spain: Ediciones Paidos, 1993.

Wicklein, John. Electronic Nightmare: The Home Communications Set and Your Freedom. Boston: Beacon, 1981.

Zentner, Alejandro. "File Sharing and International Sales of Copyrighted Music: An Empirical Analysis with a Panel of Countries." B.E. Journal of Economic Analysis and Policy 5, no. 1 (2005). Available at http://www.bepress.com/bejeap/topics/vol5/iss1/art21.

360-degree images or video: Panoramic, spherical, or omnidirectional images or video shot, recorded, and displayed using any of a number of alternative imaging systems.

3G: Third-generation technologies—in this context, mobile phone standards advanced interactive services such as e-mail, file downloading, and video telephony.

Advanced Access Content System: An international standard for content distribution and digital rights management to limit copying of digital video discs (DVDs).

Advanced Television Systems Committee (ATSC): The standard for the next generation of digital television.

AltaVista: A leading online search engine and Web portal.

artificial intelligence (AI): The computer-based technologies that replicate behaviors associated with human thinking and decision making.

asynchronous orbit: An orbit in which a satellite is not fixed over a single location on Earth and passes overhead at different times of the day.

audience fragmentation: The increasing subdivision of viewers or users of media.

Audio Video Interleave: A video format introduced by Microsoft.

augmented reality: A computer-user interface that adds layers of information onto reality as viewed through a transparent head-worn display.

authentication tools: Digital tools to establish the veracity of content or the identity of the producer or distributor of the content or message.

backpack journalism: Digital news-gathering tools that a journalist can carry in a backpack-size bag.

bandwidth: The capacity of an electronic medium, such as optical fiber, to carry information or data.

bit: An abbreviation for binary digit, the basic unit of data on digital computers.

BitTorrent: A peer-assisted digital content delivery platform enabling individuals to publish and download movies, music, and games.

blog: The abbreviation for Weblog, or online diary, text, and multimedia.

blogosphere: The entire online arena of blogs, numbering more than 50 million as of 2006.

Bluetooth: A wireless broadband local-area networking technology.

Blu-ray DVD: One of two competing high-definition digital video disc platforms.

broadband over power line (BPL): A medium for delivering high-speed Internet access over electrical power lines to the home.

byte: Multiple bits, usually eight.

cable modem: A medium for delivering broadband Internet access to the home via digital cable television.

cathode ray tube (CRT): The standard analog television display device now being replaced by digital displays such as flat-panel and plasma screens.

C-band or Ku-band satellite: Classes of satellite frequently used by media to distribute audio and video.

click fraud: When a person or computer program imitates a legitimate user of a Web site by clicking on an online advertisement in order to inflate audience size artificially.

click through: When a person clicks on an online advertisement.

codec: A program that encodes or decodes digital data, typically audio or video.

Communications Act of 1934: The first federal law governing television in the United States; established the Federal Communications Commission and followed the Radio Act of 1927.

Communications Decency Act: The part of the Telecommunications Act of 1996 aimed at regulating Internet indecency and obscenity, but ruled unconstitutional.

convergence: The coming together of all media in a digital, networked environment.

copyright: The exclusive right to copy, license, and distribute literary, artistic, or musical work regardless of form.

cracker: A person who illegally, unethically, or maliciously modifies or circumnavigates computer security systems.

cybersecurity: The safety issues that pertain online.

datacasting: Distributing data digitally via terrestrial spectrum.

digital: Computer-based forms of content or technology.

digital audio recorder: A device for recording audio content digitally.

digital cable: Cable distribution that has been converted to a computer-based form for expanded capacity and services beyond television, such as voice and on-demand programming.

digital divide: The gap between social and economic classes that exists in access to the Internet and other digital media.

Digital Millennium Copyright Act (DMCA): The U.S. legislation that protects copyright in the digital age.

digital multiplexing: The ability to accommodate multiple channels of television programming through compression.

digital rights management (DRM): The system of technologies for protecting copyright and preventing unwanted copying and distribution of digital content.

digital subscriber line (DSL): A family of broadband Internet delivery services provided by telephone companies.

digital television (DTV): The collection of technologies for producing, delivering, and displaying television in computer-based (digital) format.

digital video disc (DVD): The fixed-format medium for delivering high-resolution, digital motion pictures.

digital video recorder (DVR): A digital device for storing and playing back television, offering other functionality as well, such as skipping commercials.

digital watermark: A technology for protecting copyright of digital content.

digitization: The process of converting analog (noncomputer-format) media content to digital (computer-format) content.

direct broadcast satellite (DBS): Satellite delivery of audio, video, Internet, and other digital data directly to the home.

download: The transfer of data files from a Web site or other online location to the user's location.

earbud: A small audio playback device, or speaker, that is inserted in the user's ear.

eBook: A book converted to digital format.

electronic program guide (EPG): The interactive viewing or channel menu on digital television.

encryption: A computer security procedure referring to the encoding of messages or content in secret form that requires subsequent decoding for interpretation, viewing, or listening; used to prevent unwanted copying or online content distribution.

enhanced-definition television: A format of digital television with higher resolution than traditional television, but not at the high-definition level.

eReader: Software for displaying digital text documents, including books with graphics or other illustrations.

error of commission: An action taken by media practitioners that results in an ethical problem.

error of omission: An action not taken by media practitioners that results in an ethical problem.

extensible markup language (XML): An advanced markup language enabling various applications for the Web.

fair use: A legal exception to copyright restrictions for purposes of education and news.

Federal Communications Commission (FCC): The principal federal regulatory agency governing broadcasting and other electronic media and telecommunications in the United States.

file sharing: User exchange of digital files online.

flash memory: Solid-state computer memory.

flat-panel display: A thin digital display taking a variety of forms, such as liquid crystal and plasma.

frame rate: The number of images shown per second in video, typically thirty for full-motion broadcast quality.

gaze-approximation technology: Technology that enables the user to select an object in a computer display by maintaining the gaze briefly on it, permitting hands-free computing without the need to click on a mouse in a mobile environment and providing improved access for persons with disabilities.

General Packet Radio Service (GPRS): A mobile data service.

geographic information system (GIS): Digital mapping technology.

geostationary/geosynchronous orbit: Orbit in which a satellite maintains position over the same spot on Earth.

global positioning system (GPS): A constellation of satellites permitting Earth-based navigation.

global positioning system (GPS) stamp: A digital watermarking technology based on the imprint of GPS data at the moment of acquisition of an image, a video, or an audio recording.

Google: A leading Internet search engine, Web portal, and provider of extensive online applications.

hacker: A person who develops or modifies digital hardware or software, often in the context of computer security.

haptic media: Digital media that enables touch sensitivity or interaction.

hard drive: A digital storage technology common to many computers and digital devices, utilizing rotating platters and magnetism.

HD DVD: A competing format for high-definition digital video disc.

hegemony, hegemonic culture: The process through which the values of the bourgeoisie become the accepted values of everyone in a society.

high-definition television (HDTV): The next generation of high-resolution digital television with better color rendition, wider aspect ratio, and improved audio.

hot spot: In this context, locations where access to Wi-Fi, wireless broadband, is available.

hyperreality: The idea that media, particularly in the digital age, are for many users replacing reality with an artificial copy world.

hypertext markup language (HTML): The basic markup language for publishing documents on the World Wide Web.

immersive media: Digital media in which the user is surrounded by three-dimensional imagery, motion pictures, and sound.

instant messaging (IM): Real-time online text message sent between or among users.

intellectual property (rights): Those legal protections for the creators or owners of content in any form.

intelligent agent: A software program or robot exhibiting some aspect of artificial intelligence in operating on a human master's behalf.

interactive television/media: Television or other media in which the user can interact in two-way communications with other users or manipulate content.

interlaced scan (*i* label): The method of image presentation on a traditional, analog television screen in which every other line is displayed and a moment later the other lines are added to the image.

Internet: The global network of publicly available computer networks transmitting data by packet switching and Internet protocols.

Internet Protocol television: Television utilizing Internet protocols.

inverted pyramid: A traditional newswriting form in which the most important facts are provided first.

iPod: Apple's device for playing compressed media files such as MP3 audio/music files.

iTunes: Apple's online multimedia store.

laptop computer: A medium-size portable computer.

Limewire: An online application for sharing files.

linear storytelling: A traditional model for presenting narratives from beginning to middle to end.

Linux: An open-source, noncommercial computer operating system.

list-serve: Electronic mailing list.

liquid-crystal display (LCD): A type of flat-panel computer display using liquid-crystal molecules.

local-area network (LAN): A computer network for a limited physical area, either wireless or wired.

mash-up media: Media that offer digital content created by merging two or more data sets.

metatag: Markup data about or describing a Web page and used by search engines.

micropayment: A method of transferring very small amounts of currency, particularly online.

Mobile Journalist Workstation (MJW): A convergent system of digital technologies for news gathering and for producing or presenting mobile augmented reality.

mobile media: In this context, a wide range of portable digital media devices.

mobisode: A video or audio program designed for mobile media.

Motion Picture Experts Group (MPEG): The original compression format for computer video.

Motion Picture Experts Group-2 (MPEG-2): The current standard for broadcast-quality digital video.

MP3: A compression format for digital audio files.

Multichannel Multipoint Distribution Services: A broadband wireless telecommunications technology.

multiplex: In this context, the utilization of compression technologies to deliver multiple channels of programming or data services on the digital bandwidth provided to terrestrial broadcasters.

nanotechnology: In this context, molecular-scale machines or control of matter on a miniature scale.

natural-language processing: A branch of artificial intelligence involving computer speech or text recognition, synthesis, and interpretation.

network neutrality: In this context, meaning that everyone has equal access to and potential use of the Internet, and that those who provide services over the Internet (such as Google, Yahoo, Microsoft) are not forced to pay operators of the telecommunications infrastructure more to ensure that allegedly high-capacity applications receive more reliable transmission.

News Copy: A proposed computer system for identifying plagiarism in journalism and evaluating news-reporting quality.

no prior restraint: A legal principle established in the U.S. Supreme Court case Near v. Minnesota (1931) that the government may not prevent publication.

nonlinear storytelling: Storytelling in which individuals may experience the story in various narratives, not necessarily with the same beginning, middle, or ending.

notebook computer: A small-size portable computer.

online news: News reported online.

open source: A noncommercial effort to create publicly shared and developed computer software.

operating system: The underlying software code that enables a computer to work.

optical fiber: A silicon, or glass, medium of broadband transmission.

PageRank: A patented software tool developed by Google to determine the relative importance of an online document based on an analysis of the documents linked to or from that document.

personal digital assistant/appliance (PDA): A wide range of handheld computer devices.

personal ultrabroadband: A wireless broadband environment for the individual user.

phishing: In a computer context, a criminal technique for gaining personal data online.

pixel: The smallest picture element in a digital display.

pixelation: The degradation of the image in a digital display as the image is enlarged.

plasma display: A type of flat-panel display using neon and xenon gas trapped in many tiny cells between glass panels, where the gas can be electrically charged to emit light.

playlist: A sequence of songs or video, typically selected by the user of a digital media device.

podcast: An audio or video program distributed online.

portable computer: A laptop, notebook, tablet, or pocket-size computer.

portable document format (PDF): A digital document in which a form comparable to ink on paper is preserved.

premium media: Content that is paid for.

product placement: When a product, its name, or some other facsimile is inserted into a television or radio program, a movie, a book, the editorial content of a Web site, or some other media content for a fee or some other economic arrangement and without identifying the promotional item to the audience as a piece of commercially sponsored content.

progressive scan (*p* label): A newer digital technology for how computer displays and many digital TV sets work, including flat-panel displays.

psiphon: A computer program to circumvent governmental censorship of the Internet.

public sphere: A network for communicating information and points of view, gradually transforming into public opinion.

really simple syndication (RSS): Extensible markup language (XML) code for automatically distributing online content updates to subscribers.

relative constancy law: The notion that during most of the twentieth century people in the United States tended to spend a consistent portion of their disposable income on media.

remote-sensing satellite imagery: Images of Earth taken from satellites.

repetitive strain injury (RSI): A type of injury that can occur from frequently repeated motions, such as carpel tunnel syndrome from using a computer mouse.

repurposed content: Content taken from one medium and recycled in another.

resolution: In this context, the sharpness or granularity of an image or video.

ring-tone sales: A new type of audio product sold and downloaded digitally for cell phone use.

satellite phone: A mobile phone that can be used virtually worldwide by connecting to satellite telecommunications.

search engine: A digital tool for finding information on a computer or the Internet.

secure digital (storage or memory) disc: A low-cost, miniature, large-capacity, portable, wafer-shaped digital storage device.

Semantic Web: Next-generation technology in which documents posted on the Web will be encoded with computer-processable meaning.

set-top box: In this context, a digital device that connects a digital medium with an analog device such as a television set.

shield law: In this context, a law that protects journalists at the state level from government efforts to restrict their activities—for example, by protecting the identity of their sources; there is no federal shield law in the United States.

shutter control: In this context, a government action to restrict or block media or public access to satellite imagery of the Earth.

Situated Documentary: A new type of documentary using the technologies of mobile augmented reality.

smart phone: A handheld mobile telephone that encompasses various advanced computer and communications functions, including Web access.

social-networking Web sites: Those sites where users post their own content and interact with others.

speech synthesis: Computer-generated speech.

sponsored digital media: Media content paid for by a commercial sponsor.

streaming: Delivering digital content, such as audio and video, on demand rather than by download; permits movies or audio to play almost immediately and avoids the need to store or copy the content.

synchronize (synchronization): In this context, the mutual updating of a handheld device and a desktop computer device.

tablet portable computer: Essentially a touch-sensitive display with the computer enclosed beneath it.

tactile media: Touch-sensitive computer devices.

Telecommunications Act of 1996: The first comprehensive overhaul of the U.S. Communications Act of 1934.

terrestrial broadcast television: The wireless transmission of television signals over the air via radio waves.

text messaging: The two-way transmission of alphanumeric messages between or among users of mobile phones.

thin film transistor: A type of liquid-crystal display.

Transmission Control Protocol and Internet Protocol: The basic computer protocols for the Internet.

transnational: Media organizations that utilize networking technologies and other forces to operate internationally.

unique visitors: The different individuals who visit a Web site during a set period.

Universal Service Buss (USB): The standard format to interface between digital devices.

Usenet: An Internet discussion system or global online bulletin board system.

V-Chip: A federally legislated microprocessor required in all television sets currently sold in the United States to allow parental controls over the viewing of content based on the sexual or violence contained in the programming and in relation to the viewer's age.

video game: A motion picture gaming environment designed for single or multiple users, either off- or online.

video home system (VHS): The analog-format videotape.

video news release (VNR): Promotional video mailed or more often digitally delivered to selected television stations for possible inclusion in a newscast.

video on demand: Television or other video programming that a viewer may obtain on demand or immediately, often for a fee.

viewership: The audience for a visual medium

virtual network control (VNC): A software tool for administering a computer network and the computers on that network, including monitoring or control of individual computers on that network.

virtual newsroom: A news organization that is created and maintained using wireless technologies to support expanded field reporting.

virtual reality: A set of technologies that permit the user to interact in a completely synthetic computer-simulated environment, involving either wearable devices or a room-based environment, experienced either by oneself or with others, and engaging various senses such as sight, sound, and touch.

vlog: A video Weblog (blog).

voice-over Internet Protocol (VoIP): Voice telephony via the Internet.

Webcast: A multimedia broadcast via the World Wide Web.

Web page: A document encoded in the hypertext mark-up language available via a hypertext protocol transferring data from a Web server to present the page in the user's Web browser.

Web portal: A Web site that gathers information from a variety of online sources for easy, organized access.

Web site: A collection of Web pages, possibly including audio, video, or images, residing on a Web server available via the Internet.

wide-area network (WAN): A geographically distributed computer network.

Wi-Fi (802.11b): Broadband wireless local-area networking telecommunications technology; short for wireless fidelity.

Wikinews: A collaborative free news service that allows anyone to report the news online via the wiki (Hawaiian for "quick") collaborative software.

Wikipedia: A collaborative free online encyclopedia that allows anyone to contribute or edit entries via the wiki (Hawaiian for "quick") collaborative software, although some restrictions have been added to minimize errors.

WiMAX: The Worldwide Interoperability for Microwave Access, a telecommunications technology to link wireless local-area and wide-area networks.

Windows Media Player: Microsoft software for playing multimedia files.

World Intellectual Property Organization: A United Nations agency for protecting intellectual property rights worldwide.

World Wide Web: In this context, the global networked information and publishing environment utilizing hypertext on the Internet.

World Wide Web Consortium: A forum to develop the next generation of the Web.